D1285688

OMAN

OMAN

Sir Donald Hawley

STACEY INTERNATIONAL

Oman
Stacey International
128 Kensington Church Street
London W8 4BH
Tel: +44 (0)20 7221 7166
Fax: +44 (0)20 7792 9288
Email: marketing@stacey-international.co.uk
Website: www.stacey-international.co.uk

First published 1977
Reprinted 1978
Revised 1980
Revised 1987
Revised 1990
Reprinted 1994
Jubilee edition, revised and reconstructed 1995
Revised 2003
Revised 2005
Reprinted 2009

ISBN: 978 1 900988 84 1

Editor
Caroline Singer
Production Manager
Kitty Carruthers
Maps and diagrams
© Stacey International
Cartographers
Draughtsman Ltd (this edition)

CIP Data: a catalogue record for this title is available from the British Library.

Printed and bound in China
by SNP Leefung

For Ruth, Sara, Caroline, Susan and Christopher, who was born in Oman.

Acknowledgements
The text of this new edition is entirely mine and I take full responsibility for it all, but I could not have produced it without the considerable amount of scientific and other research published in the last two decades or so and without the help of a number of people.

I would like to thank all those who in one way or another have enabled me to bring the book up-to-date and to review the progress of Oman since 1970. The material on which I have drawn has been added to the Bibliography. Ralph Daly's assistance in providing references for many of the additions and alterations to the original text and in drawing my attention to published and unpublished material was invaluable. The Ministry of Information kindly facilitated my further researches, for which I am very grateful.

My gratitude is due too to David Insall, who kindly agreed to publication of a reproduction of a picture of old Muscat. I have also received much useful advice and help from the publisher Tom Stacey, assisted by Kitty Carruthers and Caroline Singer, and the staff of Stacey International who are also responsible for the design. To these and many others I am indebted for help and kindnesses.

I remain grateful to all who helped with the original edition, to whom acknowledgement was made in previous editions.

Picture Credits: t=top, b=bottom, l=left, r=right, c=centre

Special gratitude is due to the unfailing help and efficiency of Photocentre of Wadi Kabir, and its processing division, Colorlab, and for the outstanding talents of its photographer Arthur Thévenart, whose photographs appear under the credit of Photocentre.

Saif Al Hinai 16; K Al Moharbi 46(l2); Amouage 223(r2); Alvis Vickers Limited 25(b); Armed Forces Museum 40; BAE Systems 26(t); Bait al Falaj Museum 241(tc); Peter Carmichael 32, 37(r), 46, 62, 63, 70, 100-1, 111(r), 115(2), 116(c), 116-7, 117(t), 140-1(2), 141(b), 158, 166-7, 167(c), 168, 169(3), 171(3), 172-3(10), 174-5(12), 176(tr3), 177(8), 181(t2), 182-3, 184(r), 205(l), 210(2); Robin Clifford 7, 18(t), 24-5, 28(2), 36, 37, 49(5), 54(2), 74, 78-9, 80, 96, 98, 98-9, 114, 118, 120(t), 125, 126, 137, 139(t), 144-5, 146(cr)149, 166(I&b), 167(r), 186(b), 202-3, 219; Joe Cornish 18(b), 129, 132-3, 222(bl), 233(r2); Tor Eigelund 229; Michael Gallagher, 89(4); Sir D. Hawley 61; Hyatt Hotels 221; David Insall 55; Rudi Jackli 28; John Lawrence 131; Caroline Lees 112(3), 113(b); Peter Mason 66; Ministry of Information, Oman 86(b), 120(b), 206-7, 220(lc), 222-3, 225(t), 230-1(6), 238-9; Dr Miranda Morris 181(7), 209(tr), 225(r); Mohamed Mustafa 1, 8-9, 11, 17, 18(l), 27(6), 189, 217, 234; Christopher Mitchell 64, 66-7; NASA 23(c); Oman LNG 218(r); Matthias Oppersdorff 14, 104-5, 106(2), 107, 161(b), 180-1, 184(l), 186(t), 186-7, 187, 188(7), 190(6); Christine Osborne 127, 128, 205(r), 222(lc), 233(bl), 242(2); Peabody Museum, Salem, Mass. 240(t); Petroleum Development (Oman) 87(c), 88(4), 214, 215(3); Photocentre 18(tr), 18(br), 20-21, 22, 34, 42(t), 42, 51(3), 52-3, 68, 70-1, 80-1, 84, 85, 91, 92-3, 97, 102-3, 110, 111(l), 134-5, 138(bl), 141(t), 142(tl&r), 146(tl), 148, 151, 153(2), 159(t), 160(t), 161(t), 162, 163, 164(2), 165, 176(br), 185(t), 190(br), 191(br), 193(br), 203(t2), 209(b), 218(l), 220(t), 232-3, 243, 248; Photographers International 119(t), 122(l); Port of Salalah 212-3, 228; Michael Rice 10, 12; Peter Sanders front cover; Shell International 216; Stuart Sims 75, 76, 94-5, 108-9, 113(t), 116(l), 152(2); Caroline Singer 2-3, 196-7, 197, 206(2), 207(3); Tom Stacey 136(2), 142(c), 144(tl), 146(cl&bl), 147, 200(r), 201(r), 208(c&r), 209(l), 222(t2), 223(t2), 227(2); Sultan Qaboos University 117(b), 121, 122-3, 123(r), 124, 220(b&cr); VT (Vosper Thornycroft) Group 26(c); Roger Wood 13, 23(br), 31(2), 39, 50-1, 143(5), 150, 178(3), 179(3), 192, 193(t3), 224(2).

The publishers would like to thank the following artists for the right to reproduce the following paintings and drawings: Caroline Lees 112(3), 113(t); Stuart Sims 113(t).

The publishers gratefully acknowledge the help of the following:

H.E. Sayyed Hamed bin Salim Al bu Said; H.E. Shaikh Brek bin Hamood al-Ghafiri; H.E. Shaikh Abdulla A-Ghazali; Ali Halal Al Ma'amar; Mohamed Al-Riyami; H.E. Abdul Aziz Al-Rowas; H.R.H. Sayyed Fahad bin Mahmood Al-Said; H.E. Mohamed bin Musa Al-Yousef; Ghazi Al-Zadjali; H.E. Qais Abdul-Munim Al-Zawawi; H.E. Mohammad Al-Zubair; H.E. Shaikh Amor Ali Ameir; Anthony Ashworth; Asprey and Co Ltd; Air Marshal Sir Erik Bennett; Dr. Philip Blair; Kenneth Brazier; Timothy Callan; Mansour El-Amry; Dr. D. Bosch; Richard Carrington; City Colour Ltd; Colonel Malcolm Dennison; Michael Gallagher; Dr. David L. Harrison; Ian Henderson; Derek Henry; Rudi Jackli; Morrison Johnston; Roderick and Gigi Jones; Jeffrey Lamb; Peter Mason, OBE; Mohamed Mustafa; Ministry of Information, Oman; the late W.D. Peyton; Chuck Pringle; Rebecca Ridley; Michael Rice and Co Ltd., Kamal Sultan; David Tatham, CMG; John Townsend; the Wali of Sur; Ann Williams, the late Andrew Williamson.

Stacey International are grateful to the publishers for permission to quote from the following books: Ian Skeet *Muscat and Oman* (Faber and Faber); Wilfrid Thesiger *Arabian Sands* (Longman); Bertram Thomas *Alarms and Excursions in Arabia* (Allen and Unwin) and Alan Villiers *Sons of Sindbad* (Hodder and Stoughton).

CONTENTS

Geographic and tribal names are the responsibility of the publisher.

List of Maps

NB: Maps in this work should not be taken as an authority on international boundaries.

Diagrams

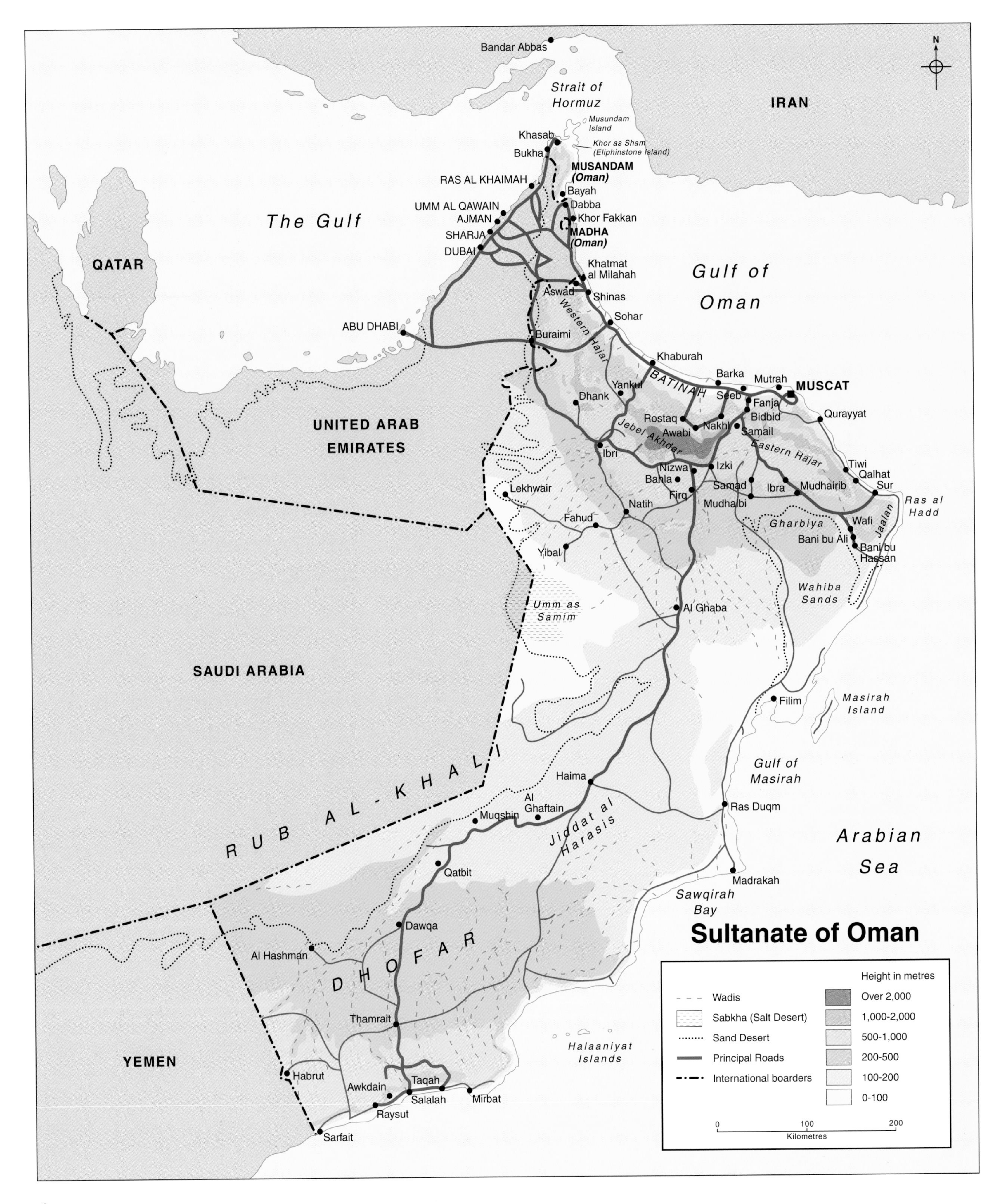
Sultanate of Oman
Bandar Abbas
Strait of Hormuz
IRAN
Musundam Island
Khasab
Khor as Sham (Eliphinstone Island)
Bukha
MUSANDAM (Oman)
RAS AL KHAIMAH
Bayah
Dabba
UMM AL QAWAIN
AJMAN
Khor Fakkan
The Gulf
SHARJA
MADHA (Oman)
DUBAI
QATAR
Khatmat al Milahah
Gulf of Oman
Aswad
Shinas
Western Hajar
ABU DHABI
Sohar
Buraimi
Khaburah
Barka
Mutrah
MUSCAT
BATINAH
Yankul
Seeb
Dhank
Fanja
Bidbid
Quarayyat
UNITED ARAB EMIRATES
Rostaq
Awabi
Nakhl
Samail
Jebel Akhdar
Ibri
Eastern Hajar
Tiwi
Nizwa
Izki
Qalhat
Bahla
Samad
Ibra
Mudhairib
Sur
Lekhwair
Firq
Mudhaibi
Ras al Hadd
Natih
Fahud
Gharbiya
Wafi
Jaalan
Bani bu Ali
Yibal
Bani bu Hassan
Wahiba Sands
Umm as Samim
Al Ghaba
SAUDI ARABIA
Filim
Masirah Island
Gulf of Masirah
Haima
RUB AL-KHALI
Al Ghaftain
Ras Duqm
Muqshin
Jiddat al Harasis
Arabian Sea
Qatbit
Madrakah
Sawqirah Bay
Dawqa
DHOFAR
Al Hashman
Thamrait
Halaaniyat Islands
YEMEN
Habrut
Taqah
Awkdain
Salalah
Mirbat
Raysut
Sarfait
Height in metres
Wadis
Over 2,000
Sabkha (Salt Desert)
1,000-2,000
Sand Desert
500-1,000
Principal Roads
200-500
International boarders
100-200
0-100
0
100
200
Kilometres
N

Introduction

For thousands of years Oman lay along the sea trade routes between East and West. Oman was the link between Arabia and Africa. Oman's sailors were known in the ports of the world; her merchants to the world's seafarers. Patterns changed. Steam supplanted sail; Oman slipped into neglect. Then in the last third of the twentieth century things changed again.

As the mineral resources of the century were husbanded under sound, strong government, the vigour and character of her people were harnessed afresh. The treasures of Oman's heritage were rediscovered and restored. The once famous sites were famous again. Oman's ancient reputation for the grace of its people and for the beauty of its ports and cities began to spread anew.

It has been a wondrous transformation: peace restored where once was conflict; prosperity where there was poverty; hope risen out of disillusion and apathy – Oman's isolation ended. Once more ships queued at her ports. Relations with Arab and other friendly states have been developed. Oman has become synonymous with wise judgement internationally, backed by strength. The ancient Sultanate has moved back into her proper place on the world's stage.

H.M. The Sultan in the gardens of his palace.

1 HM Sultan Qaboos: The New Era

Oman has been revitalised by Sultan Qaboos, who acceded to the throne in 1970. By his pragmatic and enlightened leadership, the Sultan has steered the country through the difficult early years towards an era of unity, peace and prosperity. Oman today is a forward-looking country that has nevertheless managed to retain its sense of tradition and respect for the past.

Seat of government: Muscat's Al Alam Palace which, on its seaward side, bestrides the waterfront.

Sultan Qaboos bin Said: The New Era

Sultan Qaboos bin Said, the twelfth member of the Al bu Said "House" to rule Oman, took control of the Sultanate of Muscat and Oman from his father Sultan Said on 23rd July 1970. The country's name suggested a lack of true unity and the new Sultan promptly and boldly announced his faith in and vision of the future by calling his country "The Sultanate of Oman". It was by no means as certain at the time that his bold declaration would be crowned with success.

The Scene in 1970

In July 1970 the odds were not spectacularly good. The Sultanate of Muscat and Oman under the former Sultan, though never a Protected State like the Gulf States, lay under the shadow of the British, which Britain itself deemed anachronistic. Sultan Said liked things as they were and made no attempt to seek international recognition for his State, even though it was and always had been independent. The delicate balance between the Sultan, exercising power over the coastal regions, and the Imam, the main leader of the interior of Oman, had been upset by the death in 1954 of the Imam Shaikh Mohammad al Khalili.

Shaikh Ghalib bin Ali was then elected Imam and separatist ambitions began to form. Trouble, military and political, was instigated by the Imam's brother, Talib, with Shaikh Sulaiman bin Himyar of the Bani Riyam and Shaikh Salih bin Isa

On the edge of the battlefront in Dhofar in the early '70s, the young Sultan saw for himself the needs of his young subjects.

At Salalah's Hasn Palace the public are drawn by the music of the Royal Guard. All uniformed services have bands.

leader of the Hirth in the Sharqiyah as allies. The aim then was to establish the Imamate, with the probability of oil to be discovered in the area it sought to control, as a separate entity free from the Sultan's jurisdiction. Talib's forces under the banner of the Oman Revolutionary Movement were, however, finally defeated in 1959 when the rebels were dislodged from their retreat in the Jebel Akhdar. Ghalib, Talib, Shaikh Sulaiman, and Shaikh Salih, who became the spokesman of the "Imamate of Oman" in the Cairo of Nasser's period, continued a campaign of propaganda against the Sultanate from abroad.

Imamate offices were established in Cairo, Damascus, Riyadh and Beirut and the "Question of Oman" was taken to the United Nations by supporters of the Imamate. An effort to have it considered at the Security Council in 1957 only just failed. It was placed on the agenda of the General Assembly in 1958 and thereafter referred each year to various committees for deliberation. This was the situation inherited by Qaboos.

Apart from the Omanis associated with the Imamate, there were many other exiles in opposition to Sayyid Said. These included two of the Sultan's uncles: Sayyid Tarik bin Taimur, the eldest and most influential of Sultan Said's brothers, and Sayyid Fahr bin Taimur. Many young men too had despaired of the limited educational possibilities offered in the only three schools in the country and sought education abroad, particularly in Iraq, Egypt and the Soviet Union. Their feelings of antipathy to the situation in their own country were encouraged by the public stance of the host governments. Some of them inevitably became engaged in the People's Front for the Liberation of Oman and the Arabian Gulf (PFLOAG), and the National Democratic Front for the Liberation of Oman and the Arabian Gulf, whose revolutionary intentions were proclaimed in their titles.

Qaboos had yet to acquire new friends abroad. Oman was still considerably dependent on British support, which some saw as something of a stumbling block for the former regime, though with Qaboos's accession this support from Oman's most ancient ally became steadily less objectionable to third party observers in the Arab world. At home, Sultan Qaboos found a country severely affected by the "brain drain" as well as lacking the services and infrastructure of a modern state. When incipient oil revenues had enabled Sultan Said to be bolder than the previous impoverished state of the country had allowed, the developments he undertook were vestigial.

Thus Qaboos was faced with the rebellion in Dhofar, which had precipitated the events leading to his accession and continued to be fanned by the People's Democratic Republic of Yemen (PDRY) with the support of China, the Soviet Union, Iraq and East Germany. A major international problem required solution since the only Omani "diplomatic" representation abroad was provided by the Imamate opposition. There was a shortage of immediate Omani hands to tackle the jobs to be done. As Sultan Qaboos began his reign courage was needed – and it was not lacking.

The First Speech - and the Challenges

On 9th August 1970 Sultan Qaboos made a major speech to his people, the first of an important series of policy speeches subsequently delivered on National Day each year. In it he not only announced the new name of the country and the intention to have a new flag but declared that in future people would no longer distinguish between the coast and the interior and the southern province of Dhofar. He thus stated his unifying aspirations for "The Sultanate of Oman". He also announced the appointment of Sayyid Tarik as Prime Minister in a new government, the lifting of many restrictions which had borne heavily on the people previously, and development plans for the future.

The challenge was to turn Oman into a modern State using the gradually increasing oil revenues; to establish internal peace and security and to avert attacks stimulated from abroad; to attract back talented but disaffected Omanis by convincing them that a new era had started; and to gain the recognition and acceptance of Arab and other countries. These aims were closely interrelated.

Encouraged on his accession by the messages of greeting and goodwill he received from King Faisal of Saudi Arabia, King Hussein of Jordan and the Rulers of the Gulf States, the young Sultan set out to convince Arab countries of the fundamental change of direction and style which he was initiating. Towards the end of 1970, goodwill missions were despatched throughout the Arab world and elsewhere to describe the new vision for Oman and to lobby for admittance to the Arab League.

Shaikh Saud bin Ali al Khalili, who had been appointed the first Minister of Education, led one mission – a significant event, since his family was not only notable but had held the Imamate in the past. Missions visited Egypt, Syria, Lebanon, Iraq, Saudi Arabia, Yemen, Jordan, Kuwait, Libya, Sudan, Morocco, Algeria and Tunisia. Although they were warmly received, not all the governments were immediately won over, especially in those places where there were Imamate offices.

Nevertheless, in 1971 applications to join were lodged with the Arab League and the United Nations and both were successful. Oman thus became the seventeenth member of the Arab League and the Security Council overcame – with surprising ease – the embarrassment of "the Question" of Oman's inscription, and unanimously recommended the admission of Oman to the United Nations. On the 7th October this was endorsed by the General Assembly and only the then People's Democratic Republic of Yemen voted against it, as they had at the Arab League. This was a notable and cheering success, for the Sultanate of Oman had gained international recognition earlier than predicted.

There was nontheless still a long haul ahead for the Sultan and his Government.

The War in Dhofar

The chief challenge to Oman's future still lay in Dhofar. Although the Sultan immediately offered an amnesty to all those who opposed the previous regime and a serious hearts-and-minds cam-paign was waged alongside the war, the

Opposite, *a police helicopter fulfils a policy – shared with all the armed services – of providing civil aid to outlying areas of the southern region, as peace is secured.* Below, *a patrol returns to base after a mission against the Marxist rebels in Dhofar in the war of the early 1970s.*

In this photograph of the early 1970's, the Wali *of Nizwa, the governor of the area and local representative of the central Government, adjudicates upon problems and disputes from the entire region, brought to him for settlement. He is seen seated on the right of the entrance, studying a written appeal. Later he became a government Minister. His sucessor as* Wali *today would be conducting a* barzah (see overleaf).

initial effect on the rebels was minimal. Indeed, for some two years the rebel activities, strongly supported from PDRY and other countries, grew in intensity. Salalah itself was in some danger.

Between 1972 and 1975, however, the military balance began to shift increasingly in the Sultan's favour. This was achieved by expanding the land forces, acquiring helicopters and transport aircraft and strengthening the navy. The tide was turned when the battle of Mirbat was won in 1972 and for the first time the Sultan's Armed Forces (SAF) were able to stay on the Qara Jebel throughout the monsoon. Nonetheless, the Sultan's forces were for some time still unable to dominate the whole of the vast and wild mountain area, even though the country's outer defences had been extended to Sarfait on the Oman-South Yemen border near Hauf. This difficulty was overcome by further expansion of Omani forces; by the welcome arrival of Iranian troops to serve under command; by help from Jordan; and by extension of the continuing help already being provided by British loan service, contract, Army, Navy and Air Force officers, British Army Training Teams and some defensive operational units.

Meanwhile, with growing signs of development and concern for the people's welfare, more and more former rebels were coming over to the Government side. Word spread that the new Sultan's promises were genuine and being realised. The ways of the by now communist-inspired and anti-religious rebel military forces became more distasteful to Dhofaris. Thus, as a result of military and civil measures, the campaign came to a successful end in 1975 and on December 11th the Sultan announced that the war was ended. Non-military support and funds from friendly neighbouring states such as the United Arab Emirates and Saudi Arabia had also contributed to this happy outcome. A handful of rebels found it difficult for a year or two to abandon a way of life to which they had become accustomed. But the strife was over, the territory regained and former rebels converted.

The Government

A sophisticated form of government grew from the simple structure of 1970, in

In the Council room of the restored castle of the administrative centre of Nakhl, the Wali *holds one of his regular weekly* barzahs. *Anyone from the* Wilaya *may bring his or her problem for adjudication or action. The* Wali *coordinates governmental activity and represents the Sultan.*

which Sayyid Ahmed bin Ibrahim, the Minister of the Interior to whom the *Walis* reported, resided in Muscat with a handful of other officials, while Sultan Said bin Taimur took virtually every decision down in Salalah. The Sultanate would never have made the headway it did in international affairs had the whole system of government not been credible in the eyes of the world. On assuming power therefore, Sultan Qaboos showed his intention of ruling through a government of Ministers. Having appointed his uncle, Sayyid Tarik bin Taimur, as Prime Minister, he selected other notables to head the other Ministries. The Sultan himself retained the portfolios of Defence and National Security, Foreign Affairs and Finance, with subordinates assisting him and administering the departments. The Prime Minister and all the ministers were housed in one small building behind the old palace in Muscat. It was easy in those days to call on the whole Government in the course of a morning. The Sultan issued the laws and decrees under his hand, and their validity, like all the treaties, agreements and engagements approved by him, dated from their publication in the *Official Gazette*.

Development

The Government's first priority was to launch development schemes and to lay down the infrastructure of the country. During the first phases, effort was concentrated on the expansion of health and education and on building roads and an airport. The tiny twin ports of Mutrah and Muscat, through which the material for the first stages of the country's development flowed, were replaced by a new port at Mutrah. The need for education was poignantly illustrated by the tented schools which grew up like mushrooms in 1970 and 1971, staffed largely by teachers from Egypt and other Arab countries. A large hospital, the first in the Interior of Oman, was soon opened in Nizwa as a prelude to the build-up of the health service. In the south a small port was constructed at Raysut near Salalah and tarmac roads began to appear. As the Sultan gained control of the Jebel area above Salalah, mosques, clinics, schools and water supplies were installed in the villages.

The quality of life soon began to improve. A new international airport at Seeb opened Oman to the world, replacing the earlier airstrip at Ruwi, where the approaches lay so alarmingly close to the mountains that the Chief Pilot of Gulf Aviation remarked that its closure removed the 'most interesting aspect of flying in the area'. The first of the highways later to cover Oman was constructed between Muscat and Seeb. The telephone system and Posts and Telegraphs became more sophisticated. Water and electricity supplies to the towns, and later the villages of the coast and interior, were gradually provided.

From this small but determined beginning, and within the guidelines of a series of Five Year Plans – refined in 1995 by plans based on a '2020' concept – Oman grew into its present state, a country with the most modern facilities yet managing to retain the character of its past. Vast sums from Oman's oil revenues were spent, but the manifestly high standard of the infrastructure indicated that the Omanis have got value for money and that the expenditure represented a wise long-term investment. There will never again be such an explosion of building and welfare activity, and in future much of the development will lie in the hands of the private sector.

The Growth of the Government

Early in Qaboos's reign, many Omanis from Dhofar as well as from the North took advantage of the amnesty which he offered in 1970, notwithstanding the continuation of fighting in Dhofar. As a result of this courageous and open-hearted policy, talented Omanis with aspirations for their country were appointed to posts in the new government. This undoubtedly helped Qaboos to bring the Omani people together. Considerable numbers of well educated and well qualified Zanzibaris of Omani origin were welcomed back into Oman by the Sultan and their own families at this time. Many were experienced in holding governmental posts in Zanzibar and were well suited to office in Oman, although at first they tended to be more fluent in Swahili than Arabic.

Representation

Having created the structure of a good and diverse government of ministers, the Sultan decided that it was time for the people's voice to be heard through an officially-constituted body. The first stage in popular representation came in 1981 with the establishment of a State Consultative Council with 55 members. It was a modern adaptation of the traditional accessibility of earlier Sultans and of the *Walis*, put in a modern context. In 1991 the *Majlis Ash' Shura* was formed. It had no government representatives, but instead consisted of 59 members selected from those nominated by the people of each *Wilaya* (Governorate). From then on the movement towards more democratic representative institutions quickened, and in the larger *Wilayas* where the population exceeded 30,000, the number of members was increased to 80.

The elections in each *Wilaya* were arranged by a committee under the chairmanship of the *Wali*. By 2001, the total number of male and female voters had risen to 175,000 – about a quarter of the Omani population over the age of 21. Although women could stand for election and 21 did so in the 2000 election, only two women gained seats.

Since 1991, the Majlis Ash' Shura *has advised the Sultan. The Council contains members chosen by the people of each* Wilaya, *and the Sultan presides.*

The Constitution of 1996

In 1996 there was a further, and very significant, constitutional change with the promulgation on 6 November (24th Jamada al Akhira 1417 AH) of the Basic Statute of the State – a comprehensive document, drafted predominantly by the Sultan himself. It stated the philosophy of government, the policy towards security, the economy, education and social development and guaranteed the rights and freedoms of the individual. It became Oman's written constitution and the whole framework of government was formally set within it.

The Sultan is Head of State, its highest and final authority and the Supreme Commander of the Armed Forces. He is the symbol of national unity and his person is inviolate. His functions are set out in Article 42 and include: maintaining the country's independence and territorial integrity; protecting internal and external security; safeguarding citizens' rights and freedoms and upholding the rule of law. He also presides over the Cabinet of Ministers and appoints ministers and judges.

The Statute sets out the powers and responsibilities of the Council of Ministers and of Ministers personally; it also provides for the appointment by law of other specialised councils to assist the Sultan in 'formulating and implementing the general policy of the State'. Such Councils include the Ruling Family Council and the Defence Council. Most significantly, the Statute also provides for the establishment of The Oman Council, consisting of two 'houses' – the *Majlis Ash' Shura* (Consultative Council) and the *Majlis Al Dawla* (State Council), like a Parliament – or at least a *Parlement* in the French sense. The jurisdiction, constitution and procedure of the councils is prescribed by law and the Sultan addresses a joint session of the two chambers from time to time. The already existing *Majlis Ash' Shura* was thus given further formal recognition and its continuance assured.

The *Majlis Al Dawla*, set up in 1999, was appointed by the Sultan to support the *Majlis Ash' Shura* with its accumulated knowledge and expertise. Its members consisted of former ministers, ambassadors, senior judges and officers and it may thus be compared to an upper house – an assembly of the 'great and the good' – though without specific revising powers. Its members, who are ineligible for election in the lower house, are appointed for a renewable term of three years. Their number must not exceed those of the *Majlis Ash' Shura*. In 2003, four of its 53 members were women, reflecting Qaboos's commitment to promote women to senior positions.

The Statute also prescribed for the first time the means of determining future succession, confining the possibilities to male descendants of Sayyid Turki bin Said bin Sultan (Sultan from 1870-1888), born of Omani Muslim parents. The Ruling Family Council is required, within three days of the throne falling vacant, to determine the successor to the throne. If, however, the Ruling Family Council does not agree on the choice of successor, the Defence Council 'shall confirm the appointment of the person designated by the Sultan in his letter to the Ruling Family Council.'

Under the Basic Statute, Oman is defined as 'an Arab, Islamic, Independent State', with Islam as the State's religion and Islamic Sharia the basis for legislation. The official language is Arabic. Citizens' rights are guaranteed with provisions upholding freedom of speech and forbidding arbitrary arrest and torture. An accused person is presumed innocent until proven guilty and the supremacy of the law is the basis of governance. The judiciary, comprising a Supreme Court, Appeal Courts and Lower Courts, is independent. The Supreme Judicial Council is headed by the Sultan and is responsible for drawing up general judicial policy, safeguarding the judiciary's independence and supervising the proper functioning of the courts so that the sovereignty of the law is upheld.

From the very start of his reign, the young Sultan placed a high priority on the education of girls, and to the opening up of new professions for women, such as banking and the police force.

The Cabinet is entrusted with the implementation of state policy and the day-to-day running of the government in all its aspects. The performance of Cabinet ministers is, however, subject to some monitoring and control by the *Majlis Ash' Shura*, as public service Ministers are required to attend televised plenary sessions and face searching questions from the members.

Regional and Local Government

In 1970, government outside Muscat was in the hand of the *Walis* – governors of the region and representatives of the Sultan and the central government. They were usually members of the ruling family or others with a long tradition of service and holding office. Their resources were very limited and some did not have so much as a Land Rover to facilitate administration. But they carried on the ancient system of government by sitting in majlis – *barza* – every day, hearing the people's causes, except the judicial ones which were the province of the *Qadhis*, and generally exercising authority in their *wilayas*. Within a year or two of Qaboos's accession, the *Walis* were given modern office accommodation and housing, abandoning the great crumbling forts from which they had administered their areas, to the conservators and archaeologists, who have restored them for posterity.

Central Government departments also had their own representatives in the important regional capitals. Typically there would be a director for education, a director of health and a variety of other experts. In Dhofar, where the *Wali* is also a Cabinet Minister, nearly every central government ministry was replicated with a large offshoot in Salalah.

Municipalities outside the capital were also given responsibilities for the general environment, public hygiene, healthy water and food and pest control – overseen by the Ministry of Regional Municipalities, Environment and Water Resources. But the *Wali*, as the representative of the Sultan, became the coordinator and was specifically charged with holding a weekly *barza*. Thus as the state developed, the skein of government grew appropriately to meet the challenge in the regions as well as at the centre.

Women's Opportunities

In 1994 women were for the first time entitled not only to participate in the elections in the *wilayas* for the *Majlis Ash' Shura* but also to stand as contestants – and the first women were inducted into the assembly. In many parts of Oman, women played a more overt role in communal life than elsewhere in the Arab world. Acting upon his belief that women should play an increasing role in public life, Qaboos developed this tradition and, from the earliest days of his reign, women served in the Royal Oman Police. Subsequently, women also attained high rank in the

This sculpture in the Capital Area celebrates the importance of the horse in Oman's history.

The public gardens at Qurm reflect the beauty of the country's landscape.

Army and the other Armed Forces as well as in more obvious governmental spheres such as education and health. By 2002, a number had already reached the rank of Under-Secretary, there was a woman ambassador at The Hague, and a young female engineer had been in charge of the works on the central part of the Sultan Qaboos Grand Mosque.

Qaboos's Personal Influence

Qaboos's liberal approach and open-mindedness showed from the start of his reign. A visionary and a perfectionist, he put his personal stamp on all development and his early intervention to prevent architectural desecration and bad taste resulted in the harmonious nature of both public and private buildings. He also gave particular attention to the conservation of the country's notable monuments as well as gardens, fountains, tree planting and general beautification.

In 1971, at a time when it was necessary for Oman to make its mark abroad, Qaboos was acutely aware that there was no accommodation suitable for the reception of other Heads of State. The old palace on the seafront in Muscat was knocked down and replaced by the imposing Alam Palace and a small yet elegant palace in the Sultan's garden at Seeb. In the old town of Muscat, the Diwan of the Royal Court was built, designed in the style of the adjacent Bait Graiza – a wonderful example of traditional Omani building. This fine Islamic architectural style has influenced many subsequent buildings throughout the country.

Qaboos later developed another splendid palace on the sea near Barka which became his principal residence. He named it Bait al Baraka – 'the house of blessings' – and its pavilions, round reception building, observatory, and concert hall were set in extensive and beautifully tended grounds. He also built another residence in homage to Oman's traditional architecture of the Interior, in the style of a fort at Ezz near Nizwa, one of the ancient capitals of Oman. In the south, the old palace at Salalah was beautified and extended. Thus Qaboos established his presence in the main centres of historical Omani government. He also maintained contact with his people through annual tours to different parts of the country, accompanied by senior ministers. The staging of National Day celebrations at different locations each year gives an

Oman's military music (above) *has set new standards internationally. The Royal Oman Symphony Orchestra* (below), *drawn from young Omani men and women, has introduced a repertoire of Western and Oriental music to an ever-growing audience.* (Overleaf) *Young Omanis have preserved the riding skills of their forefathers.*

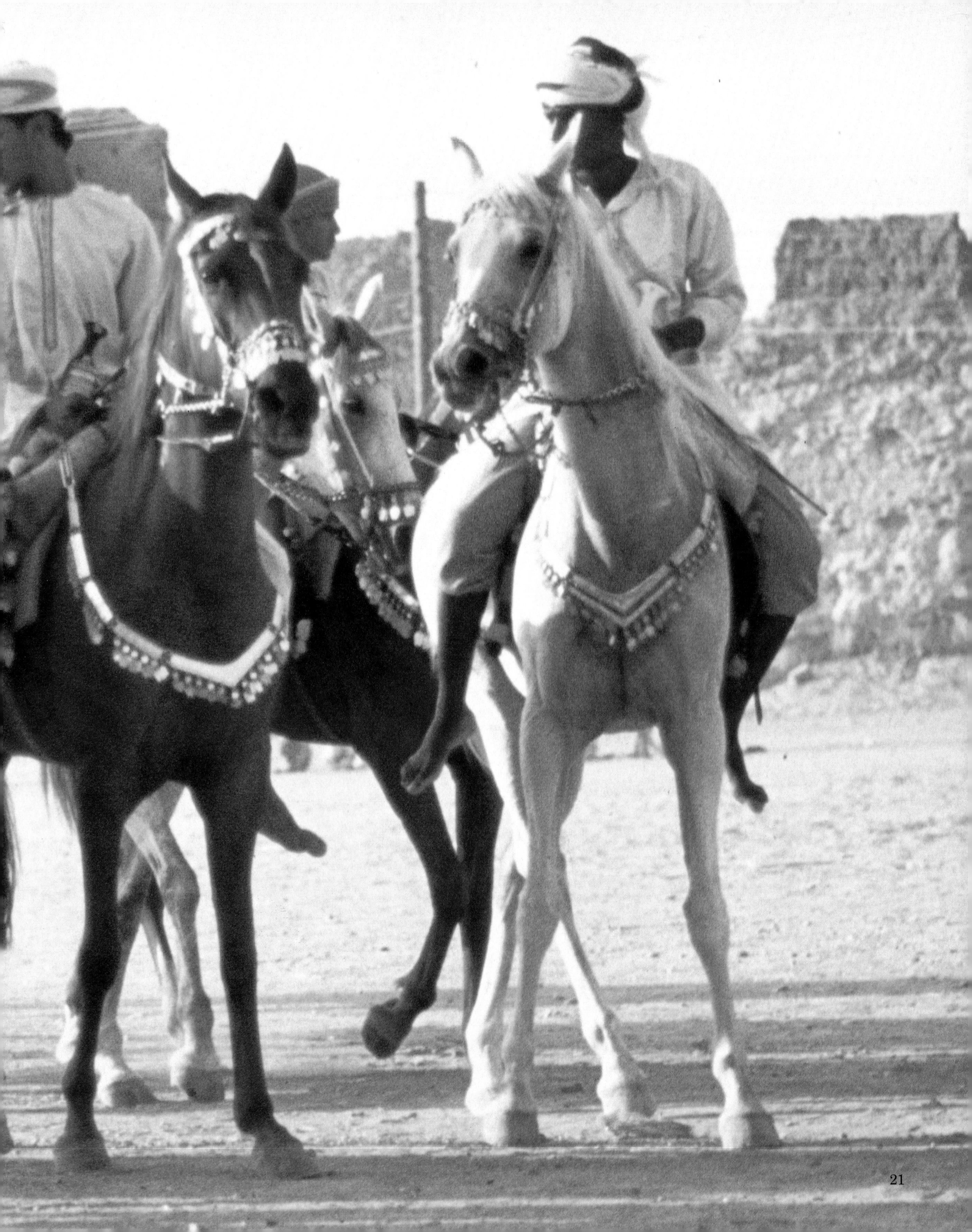

extra fillip to development in regions outside the capital.

During his education in England, Qaboos developed a love of music, particularly military music and the organ, and in 1972 he set out to create a first-class military band fit to play at the Edinburgh Tattoo. His dream was realised in 1984, when the Omani military band stole the show at Edinburgh with its brass, bagpipes, fife and drum, and its perfectly executed manoeuvres. His delight in music also inspired Qaboos to found the Royal Oman

Sohar's monument to the ibex reflects Oman's commitment to wildlife conservation.

Symphony Orchestra, composed entirely of young Omani men and women. After a few years they were playing with well-known guest artists from all over the world. Most Arab countries have military bands in the Western tradition but Oman's Armed Forces and Police also have many excellent bands and both they and the symphony orchestra have acquired varied repertoires of oriental and occidental music, some of which has been specially composed for them.

Another example of Qaboos's quest for excellence came in 1980 with the foundation of the Sultan Qaboos University, which he envisaged as a sort of 'Oxford in Oman'. He encouraged scientific research, and invited archaeologists and distinguished scientists to build up a considerable corpus of learning, including Oman's unique geology, ecology, wildlife, plant and marine life. A notable example was the detailed survey of the Wahiba Sands carried out by Britain's Royal Geographical Society, which was supported by the Omani Government.

Foreign Policy and Relations

From the early days of his reign Qaboos undertook state visits abroad to explain his vision of the new Oman and to give his country a higher profile. He attended the Shah of Iran's elaborate celebrations of the 2500th anniversary of the Persian monarchy at Persepolis in October 1971 and followed this in December with a state visit to Saudi Arabia. There, Qaboos was welcomed as 'His Majesty the Sultan of Oman'. The greatest significance of this visit was that it put an end to any concept of an 'Imamate of Oman', independent of the Sultan.

Oman's long-standing connections with India and Pakistan were reinforced and relations with Jordan and Egypt in particular grew closer as these countries gave strong support to Qaboos's Oman from the outset. Over the years diplomatic relations with other countries were established and an increasing number sent resident missions at ambassadorial level. Until 1972 only Britain and India had resident missions

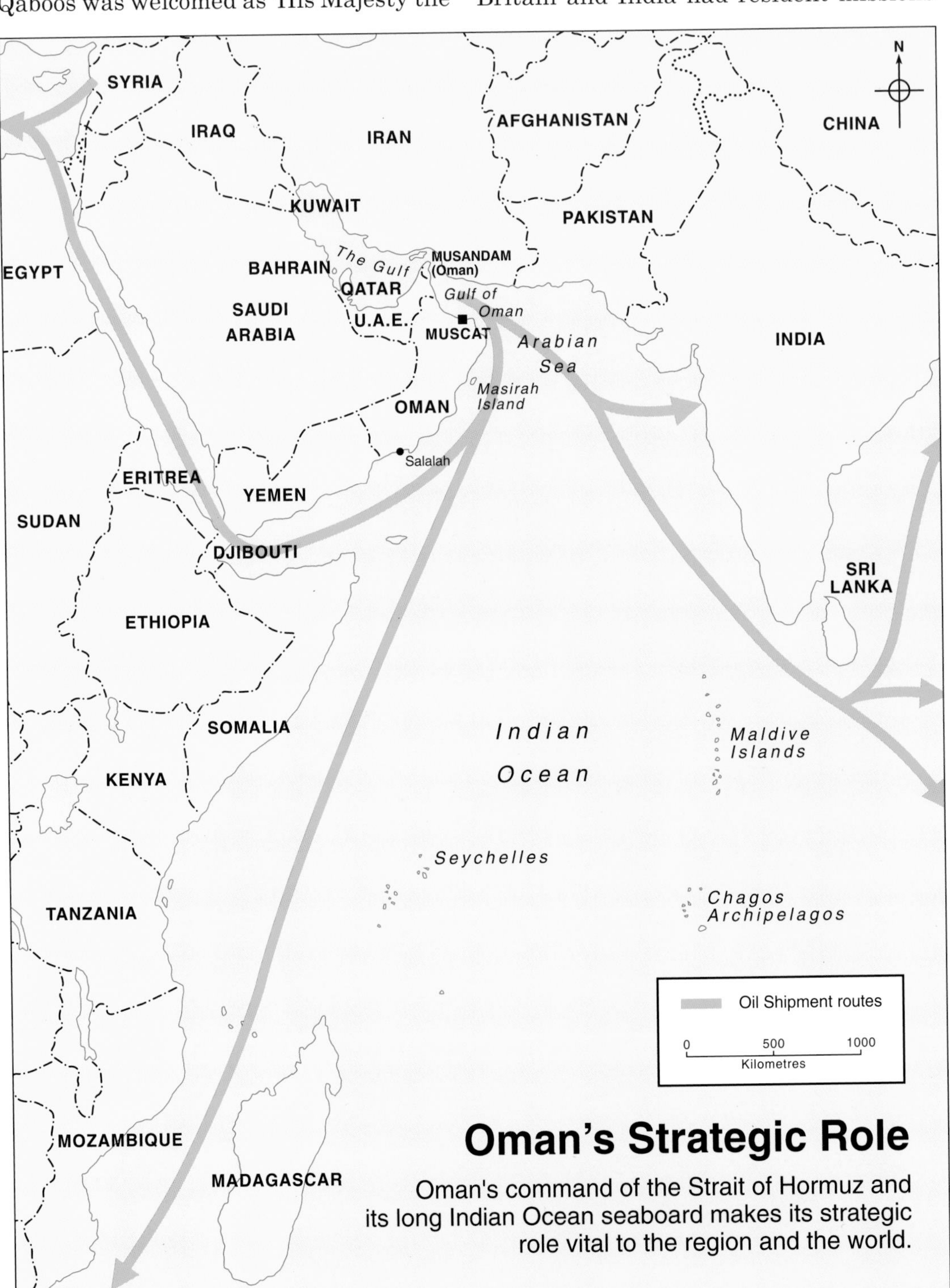

in Muscat, but by 2003 Oman had diplomatic relations with 136 countries and belonged to every significant United Nations, Gulf, Arab, Islamic and Afro-Asian organisation. In 2000, Oman acceded to the World Trade Organisation (WTO) which placed the country in a stronger position to meet regional and international political, economic and developmental challenges.

The principles underlying Oman's foreign policy are based on the charters of the United Nations and the Arab League, in particular respect for the sovereignty of other nations and belief in peace, full justice and mutual respect. In practice this has meant good neighbourliness, non-alignment and the encouragement of cooperation between the Gulf states and particularly those of the Arab Gulf Cooperation Council (AGCC), consisting of the United Arab Emirates (UAE), Bahrain, Qatar, Kuwait and Saudi Arabia as well as Oman.

Oman's policies in the past often appeared to run counter to the political wisdom of the day, but subsequently came to be applauded as far-sighted. The Omani agreement with the US in 1982, for example, giving the US access to Omani air and naval bases in certain circumstances, was criticised at the time but praised when these bases had to be used in response to Iraq's invasion of Kuwait in 1991 and again during operations against Iraq in 2003. At the time of the Iran-Iraq war of 1980-1988, Oman was determined to keep a dialogue going with Iran when Gulf states generally took sides by supporting Iraq. This 'bridge' to Iran proved valuable not only to Oman but also the countries of the West. Oman was one of only three Arab countries that did not break diplomatic relations with Egypt when in 1979 President Sadat made peace with Israel, and also maintained its long friendship with Britain through the Anglo-Omani Joint Commission.

Oman continued to urge amicable settlement of the dispute between Iran and the UAE over the Tunb Islands and Abu Musa, and in 1990 acted as broker for the resumption of diplomatic relations between Iran and Saudi Arabia after a three year break. The situation in Yemen has always been sensitive for Oman, not only because of the long period of active hostility by the Peoples' Democratic Republic of Yemen (PDRY) from the late 1960s to the 1980s but also on account of its proximity and long historical ties. The state visit Qaboos paid to Yemen in 1994 was, therefore, important not only in symbolising the end of the conflict between Yemen and Oman but also in providing him with the opportunity to reconcile President Ali Abdullah Saleh and Vice-President Ali Salem Al Beedh.

Oman was an early supporter of the Middle East peace process launched at Madrid in 1991, and recognised that it would lead to direct contacts between the Arabs and Israël. Oman regards the achievement of a comprehensive and lasting peace in the region as of the highest priority and, before Israeli military actions against the Palestinians and the Intifada began in 2000, an incipient Israeli mission was installed in Muscat. After the deterioration in the situation after 2000, Oman continued to support the Palestinian struggle and to seek a solution to problems in the Golan Heights and southern Lebanon. In 2002, Oman signed up to the Organisation of the Islamic Conference to combat terrorism.

After the Gulf War of 1991, Oman became concerned about the welfare of the Iraqi people and, at the Arab League Summit in Beirut in March 2002, helped to secure rapprochement between Iraq and Saudi Arabia, and Kuwait. Oman also formalised its own bilateral relationship with Iraq and ratified an agreement to set up a free trade zone to promote closer cooperation.

Oman's ancient connection with East Africa has been revived in recent years. At the beginning of Qaboos's reign, many skilled Zanzibaris and Kenyans of Omani origin were given welcome and employed in the service of the Sultanate. In 1987 an Omani Consulate-General was opened in Zanzibar and a number of local aid projects in Tanzania were undertaken, including assistance in building a new airport and preserving the Zanzibari archives – the repository of many important documents on the history of Oman and East Africa. Modern contacts between Oman and Tanzania, Kenya and South Africa are encouraged, and Oman joins others in sending aid to African countries struck by natural disasters.

In 1996 the Sultanate began consciously to look in other directions, and actively participated with India and Mauritius in laying down the foundation of an economic bloc of Indian Ocean countries. Oman later became one of the 14 founding members of the Indian Ocean Rim Association for Regional Cooperation (IORARC). In October 1999, the Association held its first seminars and an exhibition in Muscat and subsequently hosted meetings aimed at improving trade links and inward investment between members including Australia, Malaysia, Indonesia, Sri Lanka, Yemen, Tanzania, Mozambique and Madagascar. This initiative, together with the establishment of Port Salalah, a large container port in Dhofar, revived in modern form the pattern of Oman's ancient trading links with Africa and South-East Asia.

At the time of the Sultan's accession many of Oman's borders were not fixed or agreed with neighbouring countries and the very limits of the country's jurisdiction

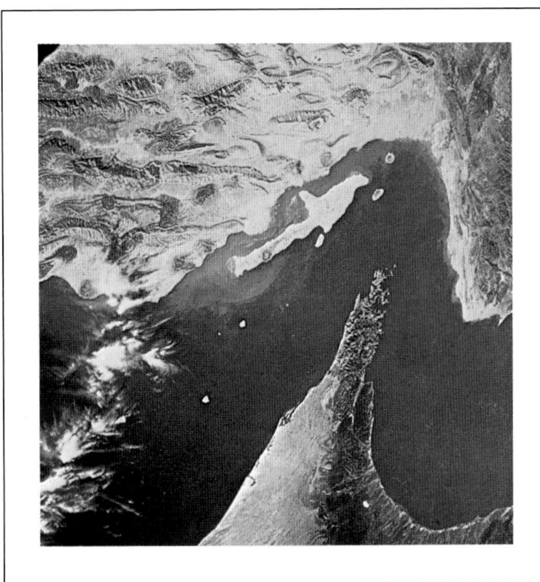

Oman's strategic significance is vividly shown in this satellite picture of the Musandam Peninsula and the Strait of Hormuz, patrolled by the Navy.

On National Day (November 18), Oman's armed services turn out on parade and perform aerobatic fly-pasts. Meanwhile, police marine patrols watch over tankers off Mina al Fahal (left), *and a Piranha armoured personel carrier is put through its paces* (right).

were in doubt. The boundary with Yemen, which lay in the war zone of Dhofar, had not been settled and was in dispute. The long boundary with Saudi Arabia, though broadly agreed, contained disputed parts and the complicated borders with the UAE were not clearly established. By 1995 all the boundaries had been agreed and, in many places, demarcated. The establishment of Oman as a strong state within secure borders is one of the most notable achievements of Qaboos's reign.

Oman was elected to the United Nations Security Council in 1994 and over the years has played an increasingly

Regiment and the Mountain Regiment – had a long history from the 1960s and 1970s and formed the core of the fighting force in the Dhofar campaign of the late 1960s and 1970s. Other regiments were added later: the South Oman Regiment, which was also involved in Dhofar; the Oman Coastal Regiment; the Western Frontier Regiment and the Parachute Regiment. The Armoured Brigade consists of three Armoured Regiments equipped with Challenger Two Main Battle Tanks and Scorpion Light Reconnaissance vehicles. There are also the Special Forces and the Firqat Forces, originally formed as irregulars in Dhofar, with responsibility for reconnaissance and rural security.

The Royal Guard of Oman, concentrating on the advanced technical education of boys, has become an élite corps consisting of some of the fittest and best trained men in the army and is also responsible for performing ceremonial duties. Army officers are trained at the Sultan Qaboos Military Academy, while senior army officers, together with those from the other services, attend the Staff College. The army has its own health service.

The officers and men of the Royal Air Force of Oman (RAFO), have reached a remarkable standard in handling very advanced weapons. RAFO is equipped with Hawk (100 and 200 series), upgraded Jaguar fighters and F-16s. They also have Super Lynx 2000

important role in world affairs. Oman's standing has changed dramatically from the early 1970s when ambassadors were despatched abroad with little beyond their own personalities, their distinctive Omani dress and the Omani flag to establish the first embassies.

Defence

After the promulgation of the Basic Statute of the State in 1996, defence was placed formally within the ambit of the Defence Council, chaired by the Sultan and including the head of the three Armed Services and the Inspector-General of Police and Customs.

The Royal Army of Oman consists of three arms – infantry, armour and artillery, with a collected strength of 20,000 troops. The infantry has two brigades, each of four battalions. Four regiments – the Muscat Regiment, the Northern Frontier Regiment, the Desert

Above: *The Hawk Mk103 forms an important part of the Royal Air Force of Oman's fighting capacity.* Below: *One of the Royal Navy of Oman's corvettes.*

helicopters. As trainers they have Pilatus PC-9s, while transport aircraft includes C-130s. The Rapier missile system, with facilities for early warning and control over Oman's air space, provides air defence. Communications and command systems have been recently updated, and a training school for military and civilian air traffic controllers has also been established.

The Royal Navy of Oman, based at the Said bin Sultan Naval Base at Wudam, is equipped with technical, administrative, training and fleet support facilities to defend the country's thousand-mile coastline. It consists of, *inter alia*, two corvettes, eight fast patrol boats, and fast attack craft armed with Exocet missiles. Its role also includes hydrographic surveys in Oman's territorial waters. It holds annual naval exercises codenamed *Asad al Bahr* or 'Lion of the Sea' after a famed Omani sailor, reflecting Oman's long history as a maritime state.

Oman's military academies provide for the training of officers and men. They include Sultan Qaboos Staff and Command College, the Sultan Qaboos Military College, the Sultan Qaboos Air Academy, the Air Force Technical College, the Royal Guard Technical College, the Air Forces Command and Control College, the Royal Navy Training Centre and the Officer Training School. A new joint training college is also being developed.

All three Services hold annual exercises with AGCC countries, and in 2001/2 a major exercise codenamed *Saif Sareea*, or 'Swift Sword', was successfully held in Oman, involving both British and Omani forces.

The Royal Oman Police (ROP) has grown from 75 constables and one officer in 1970 into an impressive, smart and well trained national corps today. ROP headquarters are based in Al Qurm and there are eight regional headquarters. The police force is divided into directorates with special responsibilities for branches such as operations, investigation, immigration, passports and visas, traffic, customs and civil defence. The ROP also has responsibility for airport security and for the Police Coastguard Unit at Port Sultan Qaboos, which is equipped with fast patrol boats and helicopters. Remoter regions are policed by the sections mounted on horse or camel, while police dogs are used for guard, inspection and

tracking purposes. Oman was the first country in the Middle East to have women police officers and women have come to play a significant role in the force.

The Sultan Qaboos Academy for Police Sciences in Nizwa is the main training centre, and awards BA degrees in law and police sciences. The band of the ROP, started in the 1970s under Qaboos's inspiration, is an excellent brass and pipe military band, popular with the public at civilian functions and at National Day parades and tattoos.

Conclusion

Oman has been forged under Sultan Qaboos into a modern, respected country which plays a role in regional and international affairs greater than its size might suggest. The country's modern architecture and planned development complements its natural stark beauty. The Omani people have retained their traditional dignity, innate sophistication and charm as they move into the modern world.

The Omanis of the present era are a fortunate and privileged generation. Circumstances for earlier generations were often hard, and in the 1950s and 1960s, many Omanis had to seek work in the oilfields of Kuwait, Iraq, Bahrain and Qatar. In the first years of the twenty-first century, their prosperity, health, educational opportunities and amenities exceed anything their forefathers could have imagined. Yet the people who live though the coming decades cannot expect the dramatic advances and expansion of wealth experienced by the present generation particularly as, with an average of more than six children per family, the population is bound to increase.

Historians of the future may well pick over the details of Qaboos's reign and conclude that some things might have been done differently. But Sultan Qaboos's achievement in forming Oman into a respected modern state will be testified by the records and memories of the extraordinary flowering of the period and by the many beautiful buildings constructed during his reign. The Sultan is a great supporter of architecture, and during his reign many spectacular buildings including palaces, ministries, Sultan Qaboos university and thousands of mosques have been erected, including the Sultan Qaboos Grand Mosque which opened in 2001.

Sir Christopher Wren wrote on St Paul's Cathedral: *Si monumentum requires, circumspice* – 'If you wish for a monument, look around'. A similar tribute is due to Sultan Qaboos not only for the buildings he has inspired, but also for the state he has moulded.

The Listening Sultan

Qaboos's practice of meeting his people in tours of the country has varied from the general gathering, (as above), *to the more intimate discussion,* (below).

2 History

Influences from south and north Arabia and Yemen, from Mesopotamia and Iran, and from the Indian subcontinent and Africa, came together in the ancient past to mould the Omani nation. But it is perhaps above all the sea which has given Oman's history its special consistency and drama. As merchants, sailors, explorers and missionaries of Islam, the Omani people have, since the very earliest days, headed out onto the seas to shape the future of their nation.

In a photograph from the early 1970s, the Wali and his Askars stand beneath the Great Round Tower at the fort of Nizwa. The fort was built over a thirty year period starting in the 1650s, making use of the remains of earlier forts on the site dating back to the twelfth century. The uniquely large tower was filled with earth to a height of fourteen metres to provide a raised lookout platform above the level of the surrounding oasis. At times, Nizwa has been Oman's capital, and has always been an important administrative centre. This fort has since been wholly renovated.

As befits an Arab people much concerned with genealogy, Omanis have a long pedigree. But it is not yet possible to trace the provenance of Oman's inhabitants beyond about 12,000 BC. Then, at the end of the Ice Age, Oman was much wetter and greener than now – and more populous. The people made their camps on the terraces in the *wadis* and hunted gazelle, oryx, wild goat, ostrich and the other wild animals which then abounded. Their diet was supplemented by berries and wild fruits but they had not yet learnt to harvest crops. Their stone tools and weapons – arrow heads, knives, scrapers and borers – were of high quality. Shisur in Dhofar was an important centre for flint production and stone age tools have also been found in the Wadi Bahla, Ibri, Izki, along the coast of northern Oman and elsewhere.

The vigorous rock art - like this ferocious bull - has been a feature of northern Oman since prehistory. The image is achieved by pecking out the surface with a sharp tool.

There follows a long gap in our present knowledge until the end of the fourth millennium BC, when light begins to dawn. Rays are cast both by archaeological discoveries which have revealed the existence of a distinctive culture at that period, and by references in Sumerian tablets. A tower structure at Hili near Buraimi dates from between 3300 and 3000 BC. Distinctive biconical jars and other pottery deposited in some of the numerous stone tumuli near Jebel Hafit and in burials near Ibri closely resemble finds of the Jemdet Nasr period (2800-2600 BC) in Mesopotamia and at Shahr-i-Sokhta and Tepe Yahya in eastern Iran. Many cairn graves of this period exist on hills and ridges all over Oman.

The Umm al Nar culture, so-called because it was first identified on Umm al Nar island near Abu Dhabi, was clearly widespread in Oman in the third millennium BC. At Umm al Nar itself pottery, beads, copper daggers and a pot with a hump-backed bull suggest links with the Indus valley and Baluchistan. The large number of buildings at Bat, dating from the Umm al Nar period 2700-2000 BC, comprise the most impressive monument of this period – recognised by their inclusion in UNESCO's list of notable world monuments. Many buildings are circular with masonry of very high quality dressed with ashlar stone. There are many tombs, some of which are of beehive design and also round towers, one of which – an early predecessor of Nizwa's great round tower – is 65 feet in diameter. Similar ancient buildings of this period have been found, for instance, in Hili and Amlah, as well as Bisya, Salut and Wadi Aghda in the Sharqiyah.

This was clearly a vigorous civilisation and Bat must have been an important centre with its prosperity based on the substantial and lucrative copper trade from the mountains of Oman, and on agriculture. The picture emerging is of stable and prosperous village communities living for the most part along the banks of the *wadis* and relying on flood irrigation for the cultivation of their wheat. Their tombs were intended in some instances for multiple burials but greater men had large graves of their own. Their pottery was wheel-made and often painted with simple but effective designs. They had beautifully fashioned bowls of stone and alabaster, they spun cloth and wore jewellery.

There was considerable freedom of movement by donkey and probably camel, which was already domesticated – as we know from an Umm al Nar tomb. The location of the settlements suggests that the people then used the land routes through the Buraimi and Ibri areas to the Oman coast through the Wadis Jizzi, Hawasina and Samail and across the desert to the northern coast.

Their houses might have been built of stone or less substantial materials like the *barastis* of more modern times. But their public buildings often had massive stone-walled enclosures and fortified watch towers. Perhaps some of the settlements in Oman at this period may have resembled Bahla with its great fort and seven mile encircling mud wall enclosing dwellings and cultivation. In the Legend of Gilgamish "Uruk of the Walls" is thus described: "The world of Gilgamish was hemmed in by the mighty mountains ..... Uruk was a city of many-coloured temples, of brick houses, market-places and open groves of trees."

The smelting of copper was widespread in Oman in the Umm al Nar period. At Maysar near Samad, for instance, the stone housing, wells and stairway of a copper mining and smelting community of the third millennium have been found.

A feature of particular interest was the discovery in a number of burials of exotic funerary vessels which had close counterparts from sites in south-eastern Iran. Other objects, possibly of foreign manufacture, were carved stone bowls and small rectangular boxes deposited with the dead. Similar boxes are known from burials of the Kulli culture of southern Baluchistan at a time when that culture was strongly influenced by the Indus civilisation. A seal from Harapa also establishes a direct link between Magan and the Indus valley. At many later periods of history Oman and the north shore of the Gulf were subjected to the same influences and there was considerable mercantile activity in the area at this period.

Mesopotamian inscriptions of the era refer specifically to the countries and commodities involved in trade with southern Iraq. Three names are repeatedly mentioned: Dilmun, Magan and Maluhha, and all three were actively engaged in trade during the third millennium. Dilmun has now been convincingly identified with Bahrain and Maluhha was probably situated on the west coast of the Indian sub-continent in the area controlled by the Indus valley cities. Lately, Magan has been convincingly identified as copper-bearing Oman. Magan's geographical location could thus be exploited for trading both up the Gulf and outwards towards India and Africa, as indeed occurred until recent times.

In Sumerian, Magan denotes a seafaring people. Its shipwrights were specifically mentioned in Sumerian inscriptions of 2050 BC. Recent finds at Ras al Hadd include boats of the third millennium. Throughout recorded history Omanis have been seafarers and Oman's periods of prosperity have stemmed from intelligent exploitation of geographical position, seamanship and trading acumen. The Arab geographer Mas'udi in the tenth century AD wrote of the shipwrights of Oman, and shipbuilding has continued in Sur up to the present time, using teak and other woods imported from India as well as indigenous Omani woods. Omanis were for many centuries ubiquitous on the seas.

The great King Sargon of Agade (2371-2316 BC), whose empire stretched from Syria and the Mediterranean to the Taurus mountains in the east and the Gulf in the south, boasted that ships from Magan as well as Dilmun lay alongside his wharves. A century or two later Ur-Nammu (2113-2096 BC), famous as a reformer and prolific builder, claimed to have "brought back the ships of Magan" – perhaps by making trade with Ur more attractive or by reopening silted canals. Magan and the Sumerian cities must, therefore, have had a mutual interest in close trading relations. Even when Naram-Sin of Agade (2291-2255 BC) conquered Magan, Magan's King Manium was honoured by having the Sumerian city of Manium-Ki named after him.

The various commodities which came from Magan were eagerly sought after in the luxurious cities of Mesopotamia. Gudea, Patasi (or Prince) of Lagash in Sumer, claimed in about 2200 BC that Magan, Dilmun and Maluhha all brought tribute or gifts and that the building material imported for the god Nin-Gir-Su included diorite and wood. Fine stone for building and diorite for carving was present in Oman in the 3rd millennium and timber for boat construction, export and fuel was also then available from the forests around the Jebel Akhdar, which lasted until well into the Islamic era. Other imports mentioned are onions and dates.

Lu-Enlilla, an agent of the temple of Nanna during the reign of Ibbi-Sin, the last king of the third dynasty of Ur (2029-2006 BC), had well developed trading links with Magan and exported barley, garments and "merchandise for buying copper" from there, importing – besides copper – ivory, red ochre, bamboo and precious stones. "Fishes eyes", (pearls) as well as copper were in great demand in the Sumerian cities, where the coppersmiths had reached a high degree of skill; copper is frequently recorded as among the cargoes carried by ships to these cities. Copper ore mined and smelted in Oman in the Jebel Ma'adan near Sohar in the third millennium showed a nickel content similar to copper used in Sumer.

Magan, like Oman later, was also famous for its goats. The goddess of the

Beehive tombs - dating from the third millenium BC - were constructed for important people.

Oman – legendary Magan – exported copper during the second millenium BC to the Sumerians and Ur in Mesopotamia. This natural archway stands above today's Lasail mine, richest copper-ore deposit in the country. Remains of spoil heaps, tunnels and furnaces evidence its long history. Today's Oman Mining Company *has made the arch its symbol.*

country was Nindulla or "the Queen of the Flocks" – most probably goats. Moreover the word Magan bears some etymological resemblance to Maazun, as the Persians called Oman, and to Jebel Ma'adan near Sohar where there are ancient copper mines. On the western shoreline of Abu Dhabi there is an area known as Mijan, which local tradition – surprisingly in view of the present stark and bare nature of the terrain – associates with an ancient sea-going people. These names are all sufficiently similar to suggest a possible common origin, given how longstanding many place names are in this part of Arabia. Slight differences in pronunciation, the lapse of time and the intonation of different tongues are known to result in such variations.

Although no written record has been found specifically identifying Magan with Oman, all this points very strongly to such an identification. Magan also seems to have embraced the present UAE as well as parts of southern Iran, with ports for its *entrepôt* trade on the Gulf of Oman – probably near Sohar – and along the northern coast as at Umm al Nar and perhaps elsewhere.

The "Dark Ages"

After the flowering of civilisation in the third millennium, there is another of those curious gaps which recur from time to time in any nation's history. So far there are few leads as to what happened in the second millennium BC, although long narrow tombs discovered at Qattara in the Buraimi area and Al Qasais near Dubai have yielded rich hordes of artifacts including beautiful gold dress ornaments, bronze bowls, jewellery, daggers and pottery dating from this period. However, direct trade between the Mesopotamian cities and Magan and Maluhha came to a sudden end about 2000 BC. Thereafter merchandise from these places was landed for onward transit at Dilmun, the citizens of which grew temporarily rich on trade with Magan and Maluhha. Dilmun itself suffered a temporary decline about 1800 BC at roughly the same time as the Indus valley civilisation was wiped out by the Aryan invasion, but in the intervening period of two hundred years copper and diorite were no doubt the main commodities traded between Magan and Dilmun.

After about 1800 BC Dilmun ceased to be an international emporium for over a thousand years and its exports appear to have been confined to agricultural products such as dates. No doubt much the same occurred in Oman, for little is heard for a considerable time about any maritime activity in the Gulf and nothing about Oman in particular. Nonetheless certain finds at Buraimi indicate a connection in the fourteenth and thirteenth centuries BC with Luristan, and Oman may at this stage have come under some degree of Persian influence. It could possibly be that this decline of local civilisation caused the migration of the Phoenicians – who may have originated in this area – to the Levant.

Archaeological sites dating from the first millennium BC have been identified in Oman and a measure of prosperity returned to the area with the rise of the Assyrian Empire. By 700 BC an Aryan prince in India had built up a civilisation once more and trade with India was re-established. The seafarers of Oman probably shared in this trade and also traded with Africa, carrying spices, perfumes and rare woods to Dilmun, as well as copper from Magan itself.

The Assyrian King Sennacherib (705-681 BC) attempted by destroying Tyre to resurrect the prosperity of the Gulf trade route. This had suffered when the Phoenicians developed the Red Sea route for bringing oriental merchandise to the Levant and Mediterranean countries. However, it was not until the Persian Achaemenid dynasty united western Asia, when Cambyses (550-521 BC) conquered Egypt and his successor Darius I vanquished parts of India, that there was a revival of interest in sea routes and Darius commissioned a Greek seaman, Scylax of Caryinda, to explore the sea route between India and Egypt. Even this, however, did nothing to revive the Gulf route.

When Alexander the Great's admiral,

Nearchos, sailed with a fleet of 1,500 vessels in 326 BC from India he referred in his journal to a Cape of Arabia called Maketa (which was probably Ras Musandam), "whence cinnamon and other products were exported to the Assyrians". This suggests that trade was continuing between Oman and Teredon in the Shatt al Arab at the head of the Gulf, which Nearchos described as "the emporium for the sea-borne trade in frankincense and all the other fragrant products of Arabia". Before his death Alexander despatched expeditions to explore the south and west side of the Gulf. Archias reached Bahrain, Androsthenes went somewhat further east and Hieron of Soli seems to have reached the Musandam peninsula without actually doubling it. These explorations, however, came to a sudden end with the death of Alexander himself.

During the Hellenistic period there was a port at Ad Dur in Umm al Qawain, the importance of which is indicated by remains stretching over two kilometres. Its prosperity was apparently based on its favourable position on trading routes, as the discovery there of Persian, Roman and Nabatean potsherds also testifies. A contemporary site at Mleiha on the caravan route along the western edge of the Hajar range has been excavated and confirms the strength of trading links during this epoch. The frankincense trade from Dhofar was at its height in the Hellenistic period; it was then exported from the port of Samhuram near Salalah and also across the deserts to the north. A fortified trading post has recently been discovered at Shisur, believed by some to be Ubar, a city mentioned on the map of Claudius Ptolemy in 150 AD but subsequently "lost", its fame surviving only in *Bedu* tradition.

Early in the third century BC there seems to have been sea-borne trade between the Gulf area and Ceylon, then called Taprobane, from which merchants in the Gulf also brought back cargoes such as gold from the Far East; and the Roman Author Pliny (23-79 AD) in his *Natural History* later gives a detailed description of the Arabian shore of the Gulf, mentioning Omana, Batrasave and Dabenegoris Regio as cities of Oman. Though these places have not been identified with certainty, Omana was probably in the region of Sohar, Batrasave was Ras al Khaimah and Dabenegoris Regio, Dabba. At this time Pliny remarks that the planks of Arab ships were sewn together, as many of the small boats in Oman still are, and they made use of the north-east monsoon for trading with India. However, the seas were so infested by pirates that ships running to India from the Red Sea carried cohorts of archers. It may well be that the mariners of Oman were among those who had been driven to piracy by a decline of legitimate trade.

Between the second and third centuries AD the Gulf was not subject to any single influence. Piracy flourished periodically, but Trajan's expedition in 116 AD through Iraq to suppress the pirates did not reach as far as Oman. However, when the Sassanid King Shapur II (310-330 AD) mounted retaliatory raids on the Arab shore for acts of piracy committed during his reign, he seems to have sent a force at least as far as the Musandam peninsula.

The Earliest Arabs

Legends persist about the period between the prehistory which the spade has so far revealed and recorded history. Arab genealogists name Al-Arib as the earliest inhabitants of the Arabian Peninsula and the Arabs, like most other peoples, have stories about ancient heroes of gigantic stature. Circles of great stones in several parts of Oman may date from these legendary days. The most famous heroes were Ad, who reputedly inhabited the sand-dunes between Oman and the Hadhramaut, and Thamud, both of whom gave their name to early Arab tribes. The Thamud tribe survived until classical times and were specifically referred to by such authors as Strabo. Two heroic sisters, Tasm and Jadis, also gave their names to tribes, suggesting that Omani society at one stage was matrilineal, and their descendants settled in the Buraimi area. Other ancient tribes which have influ-

Samhuram ("The Great Scheme") on the Dhofar coast was the rich port, 2000 years ago, which sent incense to Rome. King Il'ad Yalut, its founder, so this tablet runs, sent forth armed settlers.

enced place names in Oman are the Sohar, who reputedly inhabited the Batinah, the Obal or Wobal who are commemorated in two places, one in the Wadi Bani Ruwaha and the other near Rostaq, the Bahila, who gave their name to the town of Bahla, and the Akk, who gave their name to the Wadi Akk. Another tradition holds that Sam ibn Nuh – Shem the son of Noah – ruled the country from Hejaz as far as Oman and that the town of Sohar was founded by his grandson, Suhail. The tomb of Nabi Ayyoub (the Old Testament Job) is reverenced on the Qara mountain overlooking Salalah. Early connections between Oman and the Himyarite Kingdoms of south Arabia and Yemen are also the subject of tribal tradition, which includes the story that the Queen of Saba in south Arabia – the Queen of Sheba – ruled the area.

There may have been a big invasion of Oman from south Arabia early in the eighth century BC. Ya'rub, a descendant of the Joktan – Qahtan as the Arabs call him – extended the rule of the Ya'ruba tribe (which gave a dynasty to Oman in the seventeenth and eighteenth centuries AD) all over south Arabia and Oman, Hejaz and Hadharamaut respectively. Ya'rub's successor Yashjab was weak and lost Oman but his son Abdul Shams, to whom is attributed the wonderfully constructed sluice dam at Marib in Yemen, regained Oman. Abdul Shams ruled the whole of south Arabia and founded two dynasties, the latter of which, the Himyarites – the Omeritae – ruled Yemen from 115 BC until nearly the time of the Prophet Muhammad. Himyar himself, so called because of the red robe he wore, was the son of Abdul Shams and his name is still used in Oman. Himyaritic rule may not, however, have lasted for long, as the Persian Cyrus the Great, the founder of the Achaemenid dynasty, conquered Oman in about 563 BC.

The Coming of the Azd

Persian control of Oman probably persisted during the era of the Achaemenid dynasty founded by Cyrus – who reigned 550-530 BC – and it was during this time that many of the finest underground water channels, the *falajes*, were laboriously constructed. Perhaps this explains the name of the great *falaj* Daris (Darius) at Nizwa. The course of events in Oman between the Achaemenid dynasty and the Sassanid (226-640 AD) is obscure, but at least part of the country probably remained Persian, as the author of the *Periplus of the Erythrean Sea*, writing in the second century AD, noted that Oman belonged to the Persians.

Omani cavalry vanquished the elephant-borne Persian troops.

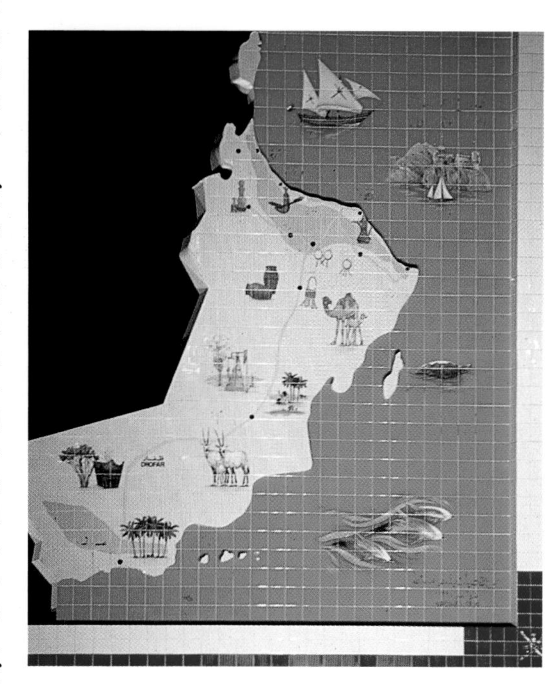

Oman's ancient activities, and sources of wealth and trade, are celebrated in this floodlit plaque in the capital area.

During the Sassanid period, however, Ardashir I (226-241 AD), the first of the dynasty, seems to have regained firm control over Oman and he sent a group of Azd tribesmen from Sohar to become sailors in Shihr in south Arabia. His involvement with the peoples of the Arabian littoral was probably aimed at controlling and expanding maritime commerce at a time when it was becoming possible for ships to sail out more boldly on the high seas using the prevailing winds and monsoons. However, his action in transplanting Azd sailors may well have been the beginning of the great traditions of Mukalla and the people of Hadhramaut.

The Azd are the main tribal grouping in Oman. Arab sources clearly show that at the time of the first wave of Azd migrations to Oman led by Malik ibn Fahm – whether he was a historical personality or, as some people think, a legendary hero associated with the first of the migrations to be documented by Arab historians – the Persians were well established in the fertile agricultural areas. This wave probably came at the turn of the second and third centuries AD and Arab tradition generally associated it with the bursting of the great dam at Marib, though social disruption in the irrigated area of Yemen may rather have been the cause of this exodus.

Sirhan ibn Said, the eighteenth-century Omani author, may well have been giving a heroic account of the early history of the Azd tribe, but he tells the tale of Malik ibn Fahm in some detail. Malik assembled a force of 6,000 men and placed his son, Honat – who may have given his name to the Bani Hina tribe and hence the great Hinawi faction of Oman – in charge of the vanguard. When Malik arrived in Oman he found the Persians holding the country for a Persian monarch called Dara – presumably not Darius the Great, as this would be a very clear anachronism. The Persian king's representative, the *Marzuban*, had his capital at Dastarjird near Sohar, in the area the Persians called Mazun. Malik sent a messenger to the *Marzuban* requesting land for his people to settle, but the Persians decided that they "did not want this Arab to settle among us." The two sides, therefore, prepared to do battle on the plain near Nizwa. Malik, mounted on a piebald charger, wore a red robe over his armour, with an iron helmet and yellow turban on his head. The Azd, led by Malik, relied heavily on their cavalry while the Persians used elephants. The issue was decided only on the third day when Malik slew the *Marzuban* in a single combat. Thereupon the Persians sued for a truce.

There has evidently been some telescoping of history here as the tribes associated with the Malik ibn Fahm incursions came in waves over several centuries. The main area of Arab settlement in the first instance was around Qalhat and in the Jaalan, but the Arabs later made much deeper inroads and a formal treaty between the Arabs and Persians was concluded during the reign of the Sassanid King Khusrau (Chosroes)

Anurshirwan (531-578 AD). The terms provided that the Persians should withdraw their forces to Sohar and leave the western part of Oman within a year. As Awtabi put it, "The Azd were kings in the mountains, deserts and other parts of Oman." Under this treaty the Arabs were given a degree of autonomy and their ruler, known by the Sassanids as Julanda – which later became a proper name used by the family of Azdi rulers of Oman – was officially confirmed by the Sassanids. According to some accounts the Persians were still in part of Oman at the dawn of Islam, for the Prophet Muhammad sent a letter to the local Persian ruler in Dastajird, calling on him to become a Muslim. The Persians' refusal to comply with the request eventually led to their being driven from Oman by the Azd.

Islam and the Early Imamate

THE call of the Prophet Muhammad in Mecca rapidly affected the immediate course of events and indeed the whole future of Oman. In about 630 AD (9 AH) Amr ibn al As arrived in Oman bearing a letter from the Prophet to Abd and Jaifar, the two sons of al Julanda ibn Mustansir who were then joint rulers of the Arab part of Oman. The Omanis did not take long to decide to embrace the new religion, despite an attempt at apostasy by a rival to the Julanda princes, Dhu' Taj Lakit, on the death of the Prophet in 632 AD (11 AH). His claim to be a prophet himself met with swift retribution and he and his followers were decisively beaten in a great battle at Dabba by the Caliph Abu Bakr's General, Hudhaifa ibn Muhsin and Abd and Jaifar's contingent, some time between 632 and 634 AD (11-13 AH). Hudhaifa remained for a while in Oman as governor. Then in 636 AD (15 AH) the second Caliph Omar ibn al Khattab (634-644 AD: 13-24 AH) appointed Othman ibn Abil Asi, who launched a great expedition against Sind from Omani ports, as governor of Oman. A governor appointed by the Caliph may have remained in Oman until the contest between Mu'awiya, the Umayyad Caliph, and Ali, the last orthodox Caliph (656-661 AD : 36-41 AH).

Mediaeval Arab Cartography

Arab trade by sea increased rapidly after the establishment of Islam and, during the ninth century, Arab geographers under the Abbasid Caliphs in Baghdad began to take a keen interest in travel and sea routes. Ibn Khurdadhba described the route to China in about 850AD and an Omani merchant made the voyage to Canton at about this time. Mas'udi in about 947 AD described personal experiences on voyages to India, Oman and east Africa. Such voyages, particularly in Sohar's heyday in the tenth century as the major seaport of Islam, gave rise to stories like *Sindbad the Sailor* and *Kitab Aja'ib al Hind (The Wonders of India). See also Section 8.*

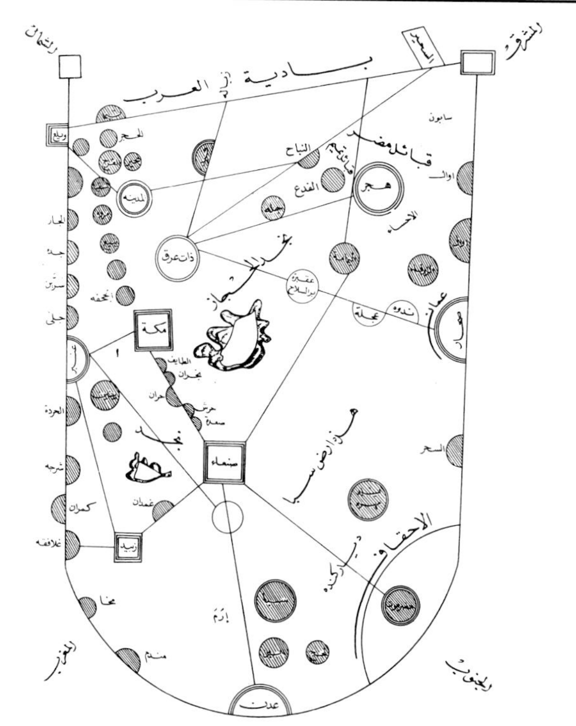

The earliest Arab maps showed Baghdad and Basra at the centre of things, but cartography became increasingly sophisticated as the centuries went by.

Oman and Sohar were marked on early maps in the ninth and tenth centuries. Omani seamen, such as Ahmad ibn Majid in the fifteenth century, made important contributions to navigation techniques and exploration.

Parts of the great castle and walled city of Bahla date from pre-Islamic times. The city was for a long time the capital of the Nabhani dynasty which controlled Oman before the Ya'ruba. Now extensively restored, Bahla castle has been named by UNESCO as one of the world's sites of special archaeological significance.

Omar showed some concern, after the defeat of the Persian army at the battle of Qadisiya in 636 AD (15 AH), that the Persian King Yezdjird might ask for the help of the "King of Oman", which suggests that Islam had not yet been completely established in Oman at that time. However, the Persian population of Oman rejected the idea of conversion and this led the newly-converted Azd to attack them in their capital Dastajird, where they capitulated after the death of their leader, Maskan.

The Omanis played an important part in the early spread of Islam when Basra in southern Iraq became a dynamic centre for the Arab conquests of the vastly rich Persian Empire. The Azd and other tribes from Oman and Bahrain first started to move towards Basra to participate in the campaign against the Persian Province of Fars in about 637 AD (16 AH). The Caliph Omar appointed Kaab ibn Sur al-Laqiti of the Bani Hirth, a former Christian, *Qadhi* in Basra in 18 AH. The Azd were the largest single tribal grouping at the Battle of the Camel near Basra in 656 AD (36 AH) between Ali ibn Abu Talib, the fourth Caliph and husband of the Prophet's daughter Fatima, and a coalition of opposition elements of which the Azd formed part, led by Aisha, the Prophet's widow. Aisha's party was defeated, though she was given a residence at Medina, with all the honour due to her rank.

There were three clans of the Azd: Daws, Shanu'a and 'Imran, from which a distinctive "Azd Oman" grouping emerged. This group attained great prosperity in Basra between 665 and 683 AD (45 and 64 AH) on account of the favour they found in the eyes of Ziyad ibn Abihi, the Governor appointed by Mu'awiya, who was famous for reorganising the town in *akhmas*, "Fifths", and of his son Ubaidalla. The reorganisation had the effect of enhancing Omani standing by giving them leadership of a number of tribal groups and attracting, around 678 AD (59 AH), another wave of Omanis who left their homeland, rather as the Omanis were drawn to Iraq and the oil-producing Gulf states in the 1950s and 1960s.

Some sixty years after they had heard the call of Islam, the Azd reached the apogee of their power. Their leader, al Muhallab ibn Abi Sufra, gained control of Basra so effectively that it became known as Basra al Muhallab. The Omani contingent in his army was by far the largest, numbering some 3,000, and they fought against Khawarij fanatics as well as in the conquest of Khorasan and Kerman, thereby gaining enormous wealth. Thus for a while the Azd became the most powerful group in the Eastern Caliphate.

After the death of al Muhallab in 702 AD (82 AH), however, their fortunes changed for the worse. Al Hujjaj ibn Yusif who was sent as Governor of Iraq by the Caliph Abdul Malik ibn Marwan (685-705 AD : 66-86 AH), had a profound distrust of the Azd, remarking sardonically during his early days as Governor, "O people of Iraq, you are slaves of al Muhallab." When his growing strength gave him opportunity, he set out to break this powerful clan and arrested Yazid ibn al Muhallab, who had succeeded his father as Commander and Governor in Khorasan.

This was part of a carefully laid plan to break all opposition to Umayyad rule. Al Hujjaj then attempted to deal with Oman, which was becoming an increasingly important refuge for dissidents as the Azd returned home. He made several unsuccessful attempts and then conscripted an army of 40,000 from the Azd's tribal enemies and placed them under one of al Muhallab's former gener-

The seven-mile long walls surrounding Bahla castle conjure up Sumerian cities such as Uruk, city of Gilgamesh (in today's Iraq), as a large cultivated area lies within. The wall has defensive towers and gates, and the fort dominates the plain beneath (left).

als, al Khayar ibn Sabra ibn Dhuwaib al-Mujashi, and attacked the country, which was then ruled by Sulaiman ibn Abbad and his brother Said, grandsons of Abd al Julanda. One prong of the attack was on the Batinah coast and the other through Julfar. Al Mujashi's land force was defeated by Sulaiman's army at Boshar but the sea force defeated Said at Barka, forty miles west of Muscat. Said fled to the Jebel Akhdar but Sulaiman swooped on Mujashi's fleet of 300 ships at Muscat and burnt it. Sulaiman then defeated Muhashi's land force at Samail causing it to fall back to Julffar. Mujashi therefore requested reinforcements from al Hujjaj, who sent a fresh force. This was too much for Sulaiman and Said. When they heard from an Azdi well-wisher who had deserted from the Caliphate forces that reinforcements were on their way, they realised that further resistance was useless and departed to "one of the districts of Zanj" in east Africa, thus illustrating Oman's age-old connection with this area.

Yazid ibn al Muhallab in Basra meantime found favour with later Caliphs but on Omar II's death in 720 AD (102 AH) declared war against the new Caliph, Yazid II ibn Abdul Malik, and occupied Basra. His revolt was short-lived and he was defeated, dying with many of his Azd troops heroically in battle. The

Azdis then returned home to Oman which had been handed back to its own people on Omar II's death. Their victorious enemies sang "The fires of al Mazun (Oman) and its peoples are extinguished. They sought to kindle a revolt but you have left no standard for them to follow nor any soldier to al Muhallab's people." Thus ended an epoch of notable Omani achievement abroad.

The Early Imamate

The early Imamate in Oman arose out of a vision to create the true and ideal Muslim state; events, and doctrinal differences in Iraq affecting the Azd, gave the necessary spur.

The first Imam was Julanda ibn Mas'ud, who – a strong proponent of the fundamentalist Ibadhi doctrine – was elected first of the "rightful Imams" in 751 AD (135 AH). His Imamate was, however, short-lived and he was slain in battle by an army sent by the first Caliph of the Abbasid dynasty, Abu'l Abbas as-Saffah. There followed a period of tyranny and confusion but in 801 AD (185 AH) Warith ibn Kaab was elected Imam and thereafter the Imamate was continuous for three hundred years or more.

The Imam exercised spiritual, political and military functions in different portions according to the state of the country. As the name implies, the Imam was always spiritual leader, bound to lead the people in the Friday prayers, and the final judge of appeal on all religious matters. To the extent that he could impose his will, he also administered the secular government and imposed taxation. When necessity arose he acted, if he had the personality, as military governor as well. But his power was always limited in fact by the complicated tribal structure and this, combined with the general Ibadhi philosophy, ensured that temporal authority was seldom absolute. The isolation of the Omanis of the Interior in times past has centred round Ibadhism and to some extent this explains the dichotomy, so often apparent in Oman's history, between the Ibadhi Interior and the outward-looking coastal areas where the people are mainly Sunni and Shia.

The election of the Imam, Rashid ibn Walid, in Nizwa, was described by the Omani historian Salil ibn Razik in the tenth century and illustrates the generally approved method. Four eminent men of virtue and probity met under the presidency of Shaikh Abu Muhammad Abdulla in the house of the Imam-to-be. There the principles by which the country should be governed were agreed, and those assembled gave their allegiance to Rashid. A great crowd of people, representing many of the towns in Oman, were assembled on the plain of Nizwa. Shaikh Abu Muhammad addressed them, proclaiming Rashid as Imam, and called them to give him their allegiance, which they did by coming up to him singly or in pairs. The new Imam appointed governors over all the towns and districts, and collectors of *sadaqat* – voluntary alms for religious purposes – and led the next Friday prayers in Nizwa.

Between the beginning of the ninth century and 887 AD (274 AH) attacks by Caliphate troops were repelled and Indian pirates, the *Bawarij*, were successfully warded off by a fleet specially constructed in the time of the Imam Ghassan ibn Abdulla (807-824 AD : 192-209 AH). However, severe disturbances followed the deposition of the Imam as Salt ibn Malik which increased politicisation between the Nizar (northern or

Sohar in the 4th-10th centuries AD

Brickmaking from local clay, copper smelting and the making of glassware were the main industries of Sohar during this period.

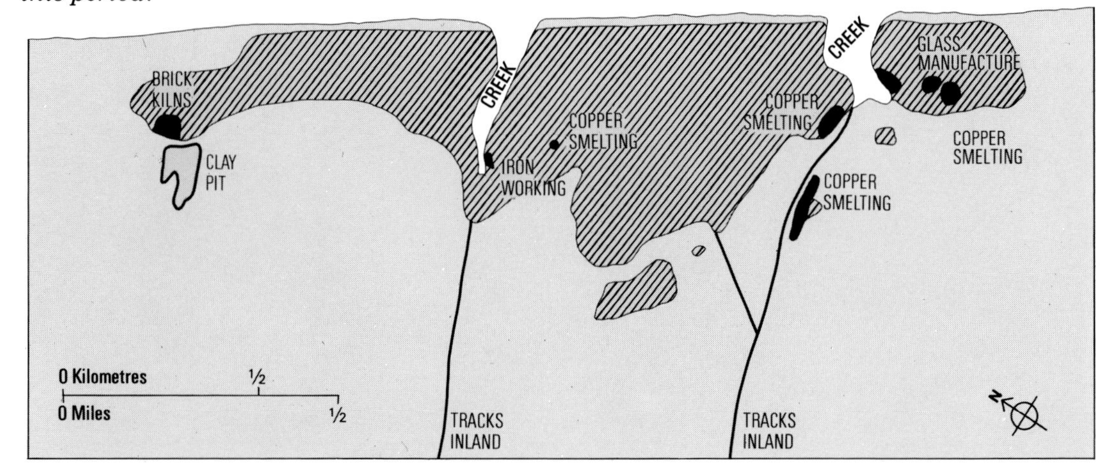

Sohar Fort 1500 AD

The fort at Sohar guarded a major port and, because of its strategic position, helped to command the Straits of Hormuz, a vital seaway.

GATEWAY

CENTRAL TOWER

The map below, indicating historic sites, carries no modern frontiers.

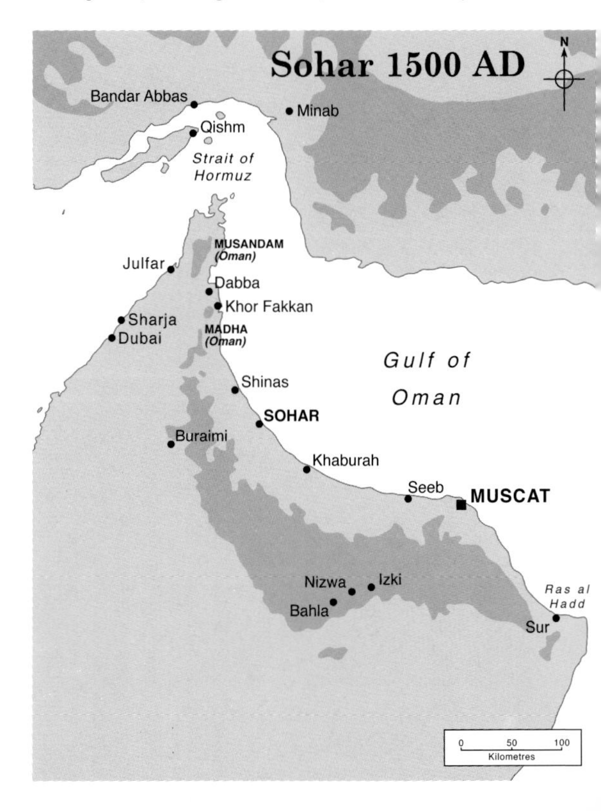

Adnan) and the Yemeni (southern or *Qahtan*) tribes. The Nizaris appealed to the Caliph al Mu'tadid (892-902 AD : 279-290 AH) and Muhammad ibn Nur, the Caliph's governor in Bahrain, collected a force of about 25,000 Nizaris clad in chain mail to march on Oman. In 893 AD (280 AH) the country was overrun. These were black days; as the Omani historian Sirhan ibn Said commented: "Thus Oman passed out of the hands of its inhabitants. It was not that God changed His grace which was in them, but they themselves changed the disposition of their souls by sin." The "bloody assize" of Muhammad ibn Nur – a reign of terror, during which the invaders cut off the hands, feet and ears of their victims and put their eyes out – has never been forgotten. It was a period of desecration during which the invaders blocked the *falajes* and burned the religious Ibadhi books. After Muhammad ibn Nur's invasion, eight Imams were elected in quick succession. It is not clear how firmly the Caliph's writ then ran, though coins were minted in Oman between 892 and 930 AD (279-318 AH) in the name of the Saffarids, who briefly controlled southern Iran. Ahmad ibn Hillal, who was left to govern Oman after Muhammad ibn Nur withdrew, identified himself with Omani interests, encouraging trade particularly after he left his capital at Bahla for Sohar, and defending Sohar's interests against the covetous Caliph al Muqtadir (908-932 AD : 296-320 AH).

The opportunity for Oman to prosper arose with the weakening of the Caliphate's central authority during the ninth and tenth centuries AD (third and fourth centuries AH) when North Africa, Egypt and Syria broke away; local dynasties seized power in Khorasan, the lands beyond the Oxus and Sistan; Persia was partitioned; and eastern Arabia fell under the influence of the strong Carmathian movement, which stood for social reform and justice based on equality. Circumstances became favourable for the development of Sohar as the major *entrepôt* of the area when the Carmathians conquered Oman shortly after they had sacked Mecca in 929 AD (317 AH). The Ibadhis found them moderate overlords and for some thirty-five years Oman remained under the control of the Wajihid family, independent of the Caliphate but paying tribute to the Carmathians. During this period the already great level of Omani maritime activity was expanded, Sohar became the greatest sea port in Islam, and Omani fleets traded with Africa and Madagascar. Twice Omani naval forces sailed to Basra, which had become the great commercial centre of southern Iraq, from which ships sailed even to the Far East. The Julanda family may have lost their control of Oman, but they were still firmly entrenched at Huzu on the southern Persian coast, where they exacted dues from all the ships entering and leaving the Gulf and between the years 950 and 960 AD (338-349 AH) Julandi coins were minted in the name of Radwan ibn Jaafar, "the Lord of the waters, ruler of the fortress of Huzu". The precise relationship between the Omanis and their cousins at Huzu may now be obscure but there is little doubt that in the tenth century AD (fourth century AH) it was the Omanis who ruled the waves in the Gulf and Indian Ocean.

A Daylamite family, the Buyids, seized power in Baghdad making the Caliph virtually their prisoner, and by 980 AD (369 AH) they had brought Persia and most of the Gulf as well as Iraq back under the central authority of Baghdad. Sohar's naval power and mercantile customs revenues in Iraq and southern Persia – as well as its prosperity – attracted natural envy. Mu'Izz ad Dawla sent a fleet to Oman in 965 AD (354 AH) under Abu al Faraj Muhammad ibn Abbas. The expedition landed at Julfar, the present-day Ras al Khaima, and marched on Sohar, where they systematically destroyed property, including seventy-nine ships, and massacred many people. Not long afterwards, the Julandid fortress of Huzu on the other side of the Gulf also fell to the Buyids. Sohar's glory was, however, not extinguished until 971 AD (360 AH) when the city which had been "the emporium of the whole world" was devastatingly sacked by the Buyids and most of its inhabitants killed.

Buyid domination of Oman was short, for their hegemony of the Gulf area lasted for less than a hundred years, their empire collapsing before the wave of Seljuk Turks from the steppes of central Asia in 1055 (447 AH). The first Seljuk Governor of Kerman, Qawurd Qara Arslan Beg, collected a fleet of transports at Hormuz and in 1064 (457 AH) invaded and occupied Oman, thus putting the finishing touches to an expansion southwestward from Transoxania which had been going on since the tenth century.

There followed almost three hundred years of disorder in the Gulf. The coast of Oman was held by the Seljuks only for some eighty years and then successively by the people of Basra and the Turkoman Ghuzz. The coastal towns were also raided by the Muzaffarid dynasty of Fars and people from the island of Qais as well as Omanis from the Interior, and Abul Fida, writing in the early fourteenth century, described Sohar as merely a village in ruins. Oman lacked unity and the Interior was ruled by Maliks of the Nabhan tribal dynasty. The Arab chronicler, Sirhan ibn Said,

The saintly Bibi Maryam was commemorated by a mosque, which still stands among the ruins of the once prosperous city of Qalhat.

noted that he had not been able to find any record of Imams for over two hundred years, between 1153 (548 AH) when the Imam Musa ibn Abu Jabir died, and the reign of Imam Habis ibn Muhammad, who died in 1406 (809 AH).

Dhofar was, however, relatively prosperous at this time and Marco Polo in the thirteenth century refers to its important export of horses. Ibn Batuta visited in 1331 (731 AH), when it was ruled – from his large palace with the cathedral mosque alongside it – by Sultan al-Malik al-Mughith, son of al-Malik al-Fa'iz, who was closely related to the King of Yemen. The country was then prosperous, depending largely on its seaborne trade; but it was more remote from northern Oman, to which Ibn Batuta reckoned that it was a twenty day land journey. There were many mosques and those attending followed the custom of shaking hands with each other formally after the morning and afternoon prayers. The Sultan's custom was to have drums, trumpets, bugles and fifes sounded at his gate every day after the afternoon prayer and on Mondays and Thursdays there was a parade of troops outside his audience hall for an hour.

After the fall of Sohar, Siraf was the first of three city states which successfully grew rich on the Far Eastern and African trade. Siraf declined after the fall of the Buyids and its place was taken by Qais, which later vied with Hormuz for supremacy of the Gulf until the Hormuzis eventually came out on top. The fame of Hormuz spread to Europe. In *Paradise Lost* Milton wrote of Satan:

> High on a throne of royal state, which far
> Outshone the wealth of Ormuz and of Ind
> Or where the gorgeous East with richest hand
> Showers on her Kings barbaric pearl and gold.

The Amir of Hormuz, Mahmud ibn Ahmad al Kusi, established his authority by landing at Qalhat in the thirteenth century AD (seventh century AH) and summoning two of the Bani Nabhan Maliks ruling in Oman, after which he subdued part of the country. The Hormuzis were well established on the seaboard from the early fourteenth century (eighth century AH) and Qalhat served as the twin capital with Hormuz itself. Muscat was the other principal centre of Hormuzi power in Oman, though Sohar was also important to them. It is doubtful, however, if the Hormuzi writ ran far inland, for when the Portuguese Albuquerque arrived in 1507 he remarked that every house in Muscat had a secret cupboard where valuables could be stored in the event of a raid from the Interior.

During this time the Bani Nabhan ruled central Oman mainly from Muqniyat on the Dhahirah side of the Jebel Akhdar. Though tradition may be unfair to them, they have not generally left a good name. There are, however, exceptions and Al Fallah ibn al Mushin, the most famous of the Nabhan "Maliks", showed integrity, liberality and statesmanship. It was he who built the fine fort at Muqniyat – al Aswad – and he was also a patron of poets and a noted agriculturalist who introduced the mango tree into Oman. He was succeeded by his son, Arar, whose reputation was as good as his father's, and other Maliks won some renown for success in war and peace, though this era is very sketchily chronicled.

Nonetheless, the final verdict on the dynasty, at least by the Omani historians of the Imamate, is that their misrule caused widespread evils. On the death of Malik ibn al Hawari in 1435 (839 AH) the chief citizens assembled to appoint Abu al Hassan Abdulla ibn Khamis al Azdi as Imam, thus restoring the Imamate.

To dominate the Red Sea and the Gulf, Afonso Albuquerque declared total war in the name of the King of Portugal on all who opposed him.

There is some confusion about where power lay during the next period, as the story of Sulaiman ibn Muzaffar al Nabhani and the Imam Muhammad ibn Ismail shows (1500-1529 : 906-936 AH). Sulaiman, alone in his room in the fort at Bahla, heard a voice say "Enjoy yourself, son of al Nabhan, a few more days. Your rule will soon be over. So prepare for death." It was shortly after this supernatural manifestation that, regarding the voice as a delusion of the devil, he set off with his companions by camel to Nizwa, where next morning he saw a woman going to bathe in the *falaj*. He attempted to molest her but she ran away and appealed to Muhammad ibn Ismail who came out of his house to protect her. Muhammad plunged his dagger into Sulaiman's heart and killed him on the spot, whereupon the people of the neighbourhood were so delighted that they elected him Imam. Thus, despite the renewed election of Imams, there were apparently also Nabhani Sultans, such as Sultan ibn Muhsin ibn Sulaiman al Nabhani, up to the time of Nasir ibn Murshid, the great Ya'rubi Imam whose reign began in 1624 (1034 AH).

European Powers Enter the Scene

The Portuguese

Since the beginning of Islam the Arabs, despite internal quarrels and feuding and the rise of dynasties in rivalry with the Caliphate, had controlled the lucrative trade from the East. Arab seamen and merchants had a virtual monopoly of the spices which were increasingly sought after in Europe, and the Omanis, however severe their internal dissensions, had continued to profit. The prosperity of their coastal towns attested by the Portuguese at the beginning of the sixteenth century showed this very clearly. The Portuguese decisively broke this monopoly.

A combination of circumstances inspired the discovery of the route round the southern tip of Africa, the Cape of Good Hope, by Vasco da Gama in 1498 (904 AH). First, the Portuguese had been growing increasingly skilful as seamen and explorers since the time of Henry the Navigator in the early part of the fifteenth century. Second, they had become accustomed to oriental luxuries during the earlier Moorish occupation and hoped to capture a share in the spice trade. Third, Portuguese national consciousness had been moulded in their numerous battles against the Muslims and their ventures in the Indian Ocean were a continuation of Christendom's anti-Muslim thrust. This may explain, if not justify, the cruelty of Portuguese methods. Fourth, the Portuguese were determined to discover the mysterious land of Prester John, which at the time aroused great interest in Europe.

Vasco da Gama's voyage revolutionised the trade of Europe. The Portuguese increased their naval and military strength in the Indian Ocean, and Portuguese ambitions in the area were proclaimed in King Manoel I's title "Lord of the Conquest, Navigation and Commerce of India, Ethiopia, Arabia and Persia". By one of the ironies of history, a famous Omani seaman, Ahmad ibn Majid, piloted Vasco da Gama from Malindi in east Africa across the Indian Ocean to Calicut thus unwittingly helping to bring about the downfall of Arab primacy on the seas.

It was perhaps King Manoel's predecessor, Joao II (1481-1495 AD), who first resolved to overthrow Arab commercial supremacy and in 1506 Afonso de Albuquerque set out for the East with a royal letter of appointment from King Manoel as Governor of India to supersede the Viceroy Francesco de Almeida. Clearly there had been some jockeying for position at King Manoel's court. Albuquerque arrived in the Indian Ocean in command of a fleet of five ships with instructions to blockade the Red Sea to the Eastern trade on which Egyptian and Venetian prosperity was based. The Venetians indeed were alive to this new menace to their trading position, and through the Consul which the Serenissima maintained in Alexandria, instigated the Mameluke Sultan of Egypt to petition the Pope to forbid all Christians to trade in the Arabian Sea and the Indian Ocean; the Venetians only came in on the act, of course, when the merchandise reached Egypt safely! Venetian diplomacy failed in this instance and the Portuguese pursued their conquests unmolested.

Albuquerque had personal ambitions as well as official instructions, and he hoped to establish a great empire in the East. After seizing Socotra as a base for the blockade of the Rèd Sea, he aimed to capture Hormuz which then controlled the lion's share of the Gulf trade. Albuquerque's objective was simple and strategically sound. He sought to dominate the two main channels through which trade of the East had flowed for countless generations: the Red Sea and the Persian Gulf. It was natural, however, that he should first deal with the ports of Oman, which were not only sub-

Cannonarchy

The arrival of cannon and gunpowder in the Indian Ocean in the late fifteenth century, – in Portuguese ships – was to change the history of Oman. Portugal's ruthless empire builder, Afonso de Albuqerque, sacked Muscat in 1507. Local vessels naturally had little chance of defending themselves against the heavy weaponry of the Portuguese. Albuquerque's aim was to protect the Portuguese eastern empire and control the trade routes by his well armed fleet and heavily defended coastal forts. From his time onward the cannon became an essential weapon of war, both for Oman's defence from outside assault, and in settlement of its internal quarrels

Above: *An inscription on a Portuguese gun at al Hazm*

The coat of arms on the cannon (above) *indicates that it was captured by the Omanis when the Portuguese were driven from Muscat in the mid-seventeenth century.*

The muzzle-loading cannon (left) in the *castle at Hazm is Portuguese.* Centre left : *A cannon bears Spanish arms.*

*The Portuguese forts of Mirani (*above*) and Jalali (*opposite*), were completed in 1587 and 1588, when King Philip of Spain (*below*) was also King Filipe of Portugal.*

ject to Hormuzi supremacy, but also important in their own right as harbours from which Omani fleets launched their operations all over the Indian Ocean.

Albuquerque, like Vasco da Gama before him, relied on Omani pilots but this did not predispose him in favour of the Omanis of the coastal towns, which he found in a flourishing state, supported by thriving agriculture in the interior. Even though he had come on a long sea voyage and Oman was by no means the first country he had visited – he had called in at ports in east Africa *en route* – Omani agriculture left a deep impression on him. Of Qalhat, his first port of call, he wrote: "All their supplies of corn, barley, millet and dates come from the interior, for there is plenty of these products there. This port is a great *entrepôt* of shipping, which comes thither to take horses and dates to India." Muscat, he noted, was the principal *entrepôt* of the Kingdom of Hormuz, and he remarked "Muscat is a large and very populous city ... There are orchards, gardens, and palm, groves, with pools for watering them by means of wooden engines. The harbour is small, shaped like a horseshoe and sheltered from every wind ... It is of old a market for carriage of horses and dates. It is a very elegant town with very fine houses and supplied from the interior with much wheat, millet, barley and dates for loading as many vessels as come for them." Sohar too he regarded as very beautiful with the fine houses and he noted that the extensive land behind Sohar was all cultivated with wheat, maize and barley and that as the country was thickly wooded many cattle and horses were bred. He observed that the five hundred odd cavalrymen which the town boasted wore "steel armour covered with plates of iron, arranged after the manner of roof tiles with slates and strong enough to resist a shot from a crossbow", that ultimate weapon of the Middle Ages. The forequarters of their horses were similarly defended.

Khor Fakkan was equally prosperous. "In the interior are many estates with good houses, many orange trees, lemon trees, zamboa trees (*Pomum Adami*), fig trees, palms and all sorts of vegetables and many water pools, which they use for irrigation; in the fields is much straw stubble, as in Portugal, and there are many millet fields ... In the town there are large stables for horses and many straw lofts for their straw, for this port

Muscat's Fort Jalali, once a Portuguese bastion, fell to Sultan ibn Saif in 1649 – and is today a museum.

exports many horses to India."

On his way to Qalhat in 1507 (913 AH), Albuquerque destroyed every Arab vessel he came across, thus declaring total war on all those who opposed the Portuguese at sea. He left Qalhat, which accepted his overlordship, unharmed but later, suspecting "disloyalty", pillaged it. Qurayyat and Muscat were not so accommodating and were sacked and burned; the old men were not put to death, having instead their ears and noses cut off. Albuquerque again dealt out death and destruction at Khor Fakkan on his way to Hormuz where he quickly defeated the huge Hormuzi fleet. Albuquerque made the youthful Shaikh Saif al Din a vassal of Portugal and immediately built a fine fort, Nossa Senhora da Victoria, the first of a great chain of Portuguese forts on the Indian Ocean and in the Gulf.

Then followed an era of sea battles, with fighting between the Portuguese and the local people and later between other European powers as well, but the Portuguese never completely disturbed the pattern of Gulf life and trade. They attempted to control and profit from the traditional patterns though, locked up in their great forts, they remained remote and unsympathetic towards the local people. Relations between Oman and the Portuguese officials were never easy. The Portuguese attempted to secure the customs revenues of Hormuz and Portuguese officials were put in charge. This led in 1521 (927 AH) to a general uprising in Hormuz and its dependencies on the coast of Oman – Muscat, Qurayyat and Sohar – as well as Bahrain. Nevertheless they held supreme, though not unchallenged, control of the Gulf and Indian Ocean for about a hundred years, preventing local vessels from trading without Portuguese passes.

The Ottoman Turks who took possession of Egypt from the Mameluke Sultan in 1517 (923 AH) reacted to the continued Portuguese blockade of the Red Sea by sending a huge fleet under Sulaiman Pasha, the Governor of Egypt, against the Portuguese in the Indian Ocean in 1538 (945 AH). In 1550 (957 AH) Piri Rais, the Captain-General or Admiral of the Turkish fleet, made a further attempt to curb the activities of the Portuguese and with a large naval force swept the Gulf and parts of the Indian Ocean, capturing Muscat and temporarily deporting the Portuguese garrison there. For some reason not entirely plain, the Governor of Basra reported that the expedition had been a failure and Piri Rais was executed in Cairo on orders from Constantinople in 1551 (958 AH). In 1581 (989 AH) the Turks under the command of Ali Beg seized Muscat for the third time, and the Portuguese, who were caught unprepared, fled to the Interior until the Turks withdrew.

It was this disgrace to Portuguese arms which caused the government in Portugal to order increased fortification in Muscat and the construction of the powerful forts of Mirani and Jalali. But the Portuguese did not merely bequeath military architecture. They brought missionary zeal, expressed in bricks and mortar in three churches: a cathedral attached to an Augustinian priory, another church somewhere near where the British Embassy later stood at the foot of the rock overlooked by fort Jalali, and the small chapel of Mirani which is the only one of the three still surviving.

The Dutch followed the Portuguese in search of the riches of the East and their first expedition round the Cape of Good Hope to Indonesia was sent out in 1594 (1003 AH). From here they were able to export valuable spices, including cloves and benzoin. They quickly realised that the Indian Ocean and the Gulf too were areas of crucial strategic and commercial interest and soon made their appearance there, trading with south India for peppers and Ceylon for cinnamon. The English and French had similar aspirations, and both were eventually to have closer contacts with Oman than the Dutch. John Newberrie of London arrived in Hormuz in 1580 (988 AH) and with another Londoner, Ralph Fitch, blazed the trail for British interests. When the Dutch shortly afterwards raised the price of pepper from three shillings a pound to eight shillings, the merchants of London, who had already been stirred by reading of the Londoner's travels, published in 1598 in Hakluyt's *Voyages*, founded the English East India Company in 1600 (1009 AH).

The activities of two other Englishmen, the Sherley brothers, gave the British the edge in acquiring influence at the court of Shah Abbas I, "the Great", who came to the throne in 1587 (985 AH) and, reigning until 1629 (1038 AH), restored the fortunes of Persia. Shah Abbas had for some years aimed to drive the Portuguese, whose general position had been weakened by their expulsion from Bahrain in 1602 (1011 AH) at his hands, from Hormuz itself, their main stronghold. For a while his interests coincided with those of the English traders, whose ships joined in a successful attack on the famous *entrepôt* in 1622 (1032 AH). Shah Abbas was quick to follow up his success at Hormuz and temporarily drove the Portuguese from Sohar, which they had occupied in strength in 1616 (1025 AH) and Khor Fakkan.

Persian success was, however, short-lived and Ruy Freire de Andrade, commander of the forts at Muscat, whose name was dreaded throughout the area, recovered both places. The Portuguese held Sohar until 1643 (1053 AH), when the Imam Nasir ibn Murshid finally drove them out, but Portuguese hold on the Arabian shore was weakening all the while as the century wore on, despite such measures as the strengthening in 1649 (1059 AH) of the Fort at "Cassapo" – Khasab at the tip of the Musandam peninsula.

The Imam Nasir had succeeded in weakening the grip of the Portuguese in Oman but they still retained Muscat, and it was left to his cousin and successor, Sultan ibn Saif, who followed him as Imam in 1649 (1059 AH), to administer the *coup de grâce*. It is generally agreed that Muscat's nearly impregnable defences fell as a result of a "stratagem" which deprived the Portuguese of supplies and enabled the Omanis to attack the forts successfully. When the Portuguese commander of the Mutrah fort subsequently surrendered to the Imam, Portuguese influence in Oman came to an end, but naval warfare between Omanis and Portuguese continued to the end of the seventeenth century even as far away as the coast of east Africa.

The British

The long association between Oman and the British commenced in the middle of the seventeenth century when in 1645 (1055 AH) the Imam Nasir wrote to the English East India Company offering them trading facilities at Sohar. The company responded quickly and in 1646 (1056 AH) their representative Philip Wylde arrived to negotiate a treaty, which was duly signed in February. It granted the English a trading monopoly, the freedom to practise their own religion and extraterritorial jurisdiction. How long it in fact remained in force is not clear, but it was the forerunner of numerous treaties of friendship with Britain over the following three centuries.

The English had been giving the Imam discreet help against the Portuguese, and when the *Fellowship* called at Muscat in 1650 (1061 AH) the captain was offered "the best house in the town", if the company would establish a trading factory there. So well disposed was the Imam in fact that in 1659 (1070 AH) he negotiated a treaty with Colonel Rainsford of the East India Company, providing that the English should have one of the forts, be given part of the town for residence, provide a garrison of one hundred soldiers and share the customs with the Omanis. However, the death of Colonel Rainsford caused the Imam to have second thoughts, possibly at the insistance of the Dutch, who were becoming strong and successful rivals for the trade of the area. Nonetheless, the English were again invited to trade in Muscat and open a factory and, though this was never established, the East India Company's ships from then on visited Muscat regularly.

The Dutch

The Dutch East India Company established a factory at Bandar Abbas shortly after a joint action with the British against the Portuguese commander Ruy de Andrade off Bandar Abbas in 1625 (1035 AH) which enabled them to gain their initial foothold in the Gulf. This led Ruy de Andrade to retire with some of his vessels to Khor Kuwai on the opposite shore on the Arabian coast where he established a temporary base.

Although relations between Dutch and English were initially cordial, the Dutch, who were able to trade spices from the Far East to which the English had not yet obtained access, were for a while the more successful. The English silk monopoly granted by Shah Abbas lapsed on his death in 1629 (1039 AH) and the Dutch company received substantial help from their home government, while the English had to fend for themselves. The Dutch held political and commercial supremacy for the greater part of the century. In 1670 the Dutch East India Company leased an office in Muscat mainly to facilitate their mail service and a commercial mission arrived there in 1672 (1083 AH). By 1680 (1091 AH) they were firmly established both at Basra and Bandar Abbas but with the decline of metropolitan Holland in the eighteen century, Dutch influence was gradually eclipsed by the British and French. In 1759 (1173 AH) they had to abandon Bandar Abbas and in 1765 (1179 AH), when they abandoned their last settlements at Kharg Island, Dutch influence in the area virtually ceased and the field was left open to the ever sharpening rivalry between British and French.

The French

The French as well as the English and the Dutch were eager to supplant the Portuguese. The French East India Company was founded in 1664 (1075 AH) and as early as 1667 Muscat featured in their strategic thinking, de Lalain, the French Ambassador to Persia, advocating that it should be seized and turned into a French naval base. Between 1699 (1111 AH) and 1719 (1132 AH) French representatives in Persia pored over their maps. Several paper schemes, all of which envisaged French troops in forts Jalali and Mirani, were hatched with the intention of extending their influence to Muscat in collaboration with the Persians. It was not, however, until 1749 (1163 AH), when French privateers attacked British vessels in Muscat harbour, that there was any direct contact with Muscat.

The French Company, like the English and the Dutch, established a trading factory at Bandar Abbas, though it was closed comparatively early in the eighteenth century. In 1759, during the Seven Years' War, a French naval squadron under Count d'Estaing captured and nearly destroyed the English East India Company's property at Bandar Abbas. With the Dutch virtually removed from the scene, Anglo-French rivalry grew in the area generally over the next few decades. This was naturally not without its effect on Oman, particularly when Napoleon's star rose towards the end of the century and he revived French ambitions for a great Empire in the East.

Sultan Nasir was "a man of perfect integrity and... justice personified", according to the Omani historian Salil ibn Razik.

The Ya'ruba Dynasty

THE first two Imams of the Ya'ruba dynasty, as we have seen, managed to dislodge the Portuguese from their strongholds in Oman. From then until now Oman has never been occupied by any foreign power except between 1737 and 1747 (1150 AND 1160 AH), when the Persians, who became involved in the great Omani civil war between Ghafiris and Hinawis, remained for a while on part of the coast. Instead Oman's relations with the larger powers has been regulated by treaties of friendship and commerce and specific understandings. Even when the British Empire was at its zenith Oman, though within the British zone of influence, retained its independence notwithstanding Lord Curzon's remark in 1903 (1321 AH) "I have little doubt that the time will come ... when the Union Jack will be seen flying from the castles of Muscat." This Ya'rubi action was, therefore, an early success for Omani nationalism.

When Nasir ibn Murshid rose to power, Rostaq (above) *was his base.*

The reputation of the Ya'ruba dynasty did not depend on this alone, and the best of their rule is still associated, historically as well as in the popular mind, with a period of renaissance. The unification of the country under strong rulers led to a revival of naval and military prowess, to commercial prosperity, to the encouragement and flowering of learning and the erection of buildings of strength, beauty and elegance. According to Omani chronicles, the first Imam of the dynasty, Nasir ibn Murshid, made the "sun of salvation" shine on the long-afflicted people of Oman.

Nasir lived near Rostaq at this time of contention and strife. Tiring of this, seventy of the *Ulema* met together in the year 1624 (1034 AH) and urged him to accept supreme power as Imam. This after some demur he did and, starting from his base at Rostaq and Nakhl, Nasir began the task of uniting the country. The people of Nizwa early sent word inviting him to take over. Samail and Izki quickly followed suit and, with the possession of these key towns in the heartland of Oman, he moved against the Dhahirah, taking the towns of Dhank, Ibri, Ghabbi, Muqniyat and Bat in quick succession. Despite backsliding, treachery and setbacks, Nasir was able to move on and obtain control of Tuam – the old name for the Buraimi al Ain oasis complex in the area then known as al Jauf. With these successes behind him, Nasir turned his attention to the coastal area. The Portuguese in Muscat and Mutrah sued for peace, and an agreement was reached that they would surrender their possessions at Sohar, pay an annual tribute to the Imam and allow Muslim Omanis to visit Muscat without let or hindrance.

However, when Nasir later sent messengers, the Portuguese in Muscat treated them harshly and refused to pay the tribute agreed. One of Nasir's chief supporters – a successful general, Qadhi Khamis ibn Said al Shaksy – was sent to Muscat and a further agreement reached by which the Portuguese agreed to pay the tribute due, to restore the fortified posts at Mutrah recently seized, to permit Omanis to trade freely and to abstain from acts of war. This agreement was enough to make Nasir suspend further hostilities against the Portuguese, but not to prevent him later recapturing Sur and Qurayyat which the Portuguese still held. After this he turned his attention to the Sharqiya thus concluding the process of internal unification.

The rest of his reign was not entirely free from attempts at rebellion. However, he was clearly an outstanding personality both as ruler and military commander and the Omani historian, Salil ibn Razik, epitomises the regard in which he was held: "He was a man of perfect integrity and an eminent example of justice personified." This, judging by Omani written and oral tradition, was not merely a eulogist's phrase, for a number of exceptional powers were attributed to him and he was even credited with miracles.

On Nasir's death in 1649 (1059 AH) his cousin Sultan ibn Saif, who had already acquitted himself well in war at the cap- acquitted himself well in war at the capture of Sur and Qurayyat from the act was to oust the Portuguese from Muscat, thus greatly enhancing his prestige, and he then ordered a *jihad* – or holy war – against the Portuguese, sending ships to attack their stronghold on the coast of Gujerat.

The mighty round tower of Nizwa broods over and protects the city and plain alike.

The great fort at Nizwa, below, *before its restoration, took Sultan ibn Saif twelve years to complete.* Right, *one of Nizwa's defensible gateways.*

It was Sultan who built the great round fort at Nizwa, which took some twelve years to complete, and he renewed the aqueduct between Izki and Nizwa. He also fostered trade, attaching particular importance to the export of horses, for which Oman was then noted, and furthered Oman's external relations by sending emissaries to India, Persia, San'a in Yemen, Basra and Iraq. The historian Salil ibn Razik sums up his accomplishments:

> Oman revived during his government and prospered and the people rested from their troubles. Prices were low, roads were safe, merchants made large profits and crops were abundant. The Imam himself was humble towards the one Almighty God and compassionate towards his subjects, condoning their offences when such condonation was lawful and never keeping himself aloof from them. He went about without an escort and would sit and talk familiarly with the people, saluting great and small, freeman and slave.

Sultan's son Bil'arub, who succeeded him in 1668 (1079 AH) began his reign well, following the good example of his immediate predecessors. He built the great fort of Jabrin and renewed the water supply, after which he moved the capital there from Nizwa. The college he established there, for which he paid masters' salaries and pupils' expenses, produced many learned theologians and famous scholars. His reign was, however, later marred by serious differences between him and his brother Saif ibn Sultan and constant family feuds. These led even the learned and devout shaikhs of Oman to follow "the counsel of the demented" and in their divisions they brought great disaster on the country. It was, of course, the ordinary people who suffered most, and willing "a plague on both your houses", nicknamed Bil'arub "the calamity of the Arabs" and his brother Saif "the scourge".

Above: *Buraimi*

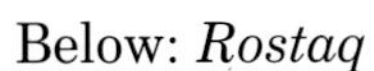

Below: *Rostaq*

Above: *Shinaz* Below: *Barka*

Above: *Sohar* Below: *Khadra*

Above: *Suwaiq*

Below: *Qurayyat* Bottom: *Ras al Hadd*

The map below sites only some of the many forts which scatter the land.

Shinaz
Sohar
Khaburah
Suwaiq
Barka
Mutrah
Mirani
MUSCAT
Jalali
Qurayyat
al Hazm
Rostaq
Nakhl
Dariz
Nizwa
Birkat al Moz
Bahla
Jabrin
Sur

Forts

Principal Forts

0 50 100
Kilometres

Above: *Nizwa* Below: *Bahla*

Below: *Sur*

Below: *Bait al Falaj*

Built in the 17th century, Jabrin is among the finest of Oman's castles. It was once a seat of learning. Rising amid an oasis of palm trees (above) *and with a comanding view across the surrounding plain* (right), *Jabrin has been devotedly restored.*

Jabrin: interior aspect

The Ya'ruba dynasty, which ruled from 1624 until 1748, gave strong central government to Oman. Jabrin was built at the apogee of the Ya'ruba period, in approximately 1670, by the Imam Bil'arub, whose father had expelled the Portuguese. Designed as an elegant country home, it became for a while the Imam's capital. An important school was also founded there by the Imam. Bil'arub himself was eventually supplanted by his brother Saif and buried in a tomb beneath the fort.

Jabrin: ceiling decoration

The lovingly restored central courtyard (seen in part *left)* is overlooked by verandas and elegant arched doorways *(right)* in the Moghul style.

The painting of ceilings is a feature of central Oman – even relatively modest houses have ceilings gaily painted in Islamic designs, incorporating geometric patterns, flowers and occasionally verses from the Qur'an. The Imam's room at Jabrin contains some of the finest examples.

Birkat al Moz restored

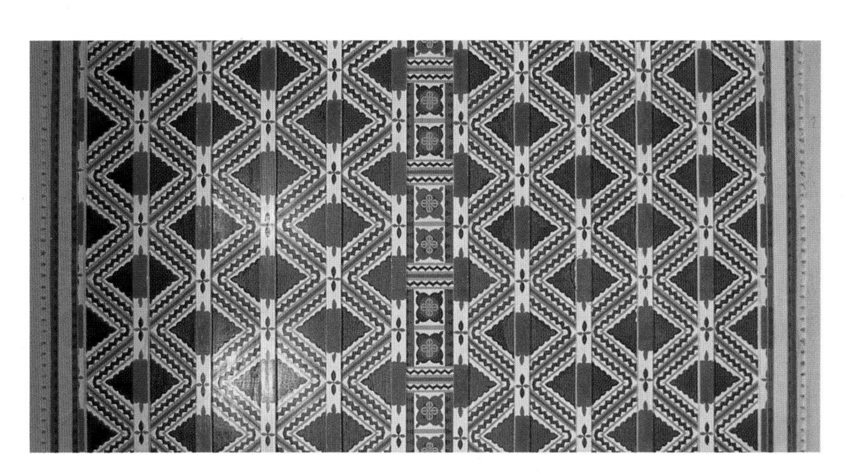

The gaunt facade of Birkat al Moz (seen left *in 1970) would have been lost to posterity but for modern Oman's fierce loyalty to heritage. The restored fort stands proud, its interior glories re-created (*above *and* right*).*

It was Saif who proved the stronger and obtained control of all the major forts. This gave him sufficient power to procure his own election as Imam, even during his brother's lifetime. Some people maintained that Bil'arub was still the rightful Imam, whilst others reckoned that Saif's election was justified. But eventually the hapless Bil'arub was besieged at Jabrin by Saif and a large army. Losing all hope Bil'arub prayed for death and, as the chronicles relate, "God granted his petition." He was buried in his own splendid and beautiful fort at Jabrin.

Saif's motives and methods may not

The restored fort of coastal Barka rises in cubist splendour.

have been unexceptionable, but after the death of his brother no one contested his earlier election as Imam. He proved a strong ruler, carrying the war against the Portuguese even to their settlements in east Africa and India. Saif's strength impressed the Arabs in east Africa, and in 1698 (1110 AH) the Omanis of Mombasa, which had been in Portuguese hands since 1503 (909 AH), sent a delegation requesting his assistance in ousting the Portuguese from all their settlements north of Mozambique.

Earlier, in about 1694 (1106 AH) the Omanis attacked the Portuguese position in Salsette Island near Bombay, plundering and burning it. At this time they also turned to privateering on the high seas and to naval warfare. In this they had no monopoly, for Europeans such as the "Feringhis" and the "Muggs" engaged in it in the Gulf and Indian Ocean so wholeheartedly that the British and other Europeans were blackballed at the Court of the Great Mogul.

To combat lawlessness at sea, the principal European nations agreed in 1698 that the British should police the southern waters, the Dutch the Red Sea and the French the Gulf, which was theoretically a splendid early example of European cooperation but unfortunately still-born.

The Imam Saif benefited from Omani naval expeditions, acquiring great wealth and owning seven hundred male slaves. This enabled him to promote agriculture by building new *falajes* and repairing others, for example at Rostaq, al Hazm and al Bazili in the Dhahirah. He planted so many trees that he was reputed to own a third of all the date palms in the country, and in Barka alone he planted 30,000 young date trees and 6,000 coconuts.

He was, according to some accounts, also the Onassis of his time, owning twenty-eight ships, of which one, *al Falak*, was armed with eight large guns. According to European accounts the Omani fleet in 1715 consisted of one ship of 74 guns, two of 60 guns, one of 50 guns, eighteen of between 12 and 32 guns and a large number of *trankis* or rowing vessels, each carrying from 4 to 8 guns. On his death in 1711 he was buried at Rostaq, and his son who succeeded him as Imam, Sultan ibn Saif II, built a fine dome over the tomb which was, however, destroyed in the nineteenth century by the Wahhabis.

Sultan ibn Saif II also continued the warfare against the Portuguese. He moved his capital from Rostaq to al Hazm where he built the fine fort, spending all he had inherited from his father as well as borrowing from the religious endowments – *awqaf.* His reputation for power and justice was formidable and on one occasion when he was masquerading as an ordinary Arab carrying a water skin – a habit which several Omani rulers have shared with the famous Caliph Haroun ar Rashid – an Arab menaced him with a sword and demanded water.

"And what if I refuse?" said the disguised Imam.

"Why", came the response, "I would smite you with this sword, if it were not for Sultan ibn Saif!"

Bait al Falaj

For long the army headquarters, Bait al Falaj dominates the Ruwi plain in the capital area. One of its glories is its finely carved and painted ceilings.

The Civil War

This oil painting of European trading galleons moored in Muscat's natural harbour – with Fort Jalali in the background – is attributed to the Dutch painter Jan Peeters (1642-1680). There was evidently a jetty built out from a bluff beyond fort Mirani.

ON the death of the Imam Sultan ibn Saif II 1718 (1131 AH) at al Hazm, where he was buried, the unity which Oman had known for the greater part of a century came to an end and a period of civil war, comparable with the Wars of the Roses in England, followed. The trouble began over who should succeed Sultan as Imam. After so long and successful a period of dynastic rule the rival leaders and ordinary people thought that Saif, the young son of Sultan, was the natural successor, even though he had not yet reached puberty. The *Ulema*, the learned men, favoured Muhanna ibn Sultan, whom they thought had all the necessary attributes for the office. The legal argument they deployed against Saif's appointment was that as a minor he was not entitled to possession of his own property and *a fortiori* he could not, as required of the Imam, take charge of property belonging to the State or to orphans.

However, the *Ulema* knew that popular sentiment ran in favour of Saif and did not dare to press Muhanna's case openly. They therefore resorted to a political ruse and, producing the young Saif before the assembled people., made an announcement capable of *double entendre* in Arabic: either "Your Imam is Saif ibn Sultan," or "It is Saif ibn Sultan who is standing before you." He was nonetheless proclaimed Imam and the guns were fired as an act of traditional recognition. In May 1719 (1132 AH), however, after the original tumult over the succession had died down, the *Ulema* felt strong enough to come out into the open. They therefore smuggled Muhanna into the fort at Rostaq and proclaimed him Imam from there. Muhanna took effective control and started his reign well, abolishing the customs at Muscat and thus enabling large trading profits to be made. Prices were low and the harvest good, but despite these promising auguries, his reign was in the event to be very short and under him the country enjoyed tranquillity for the last time in many years.

Even the people of Rostaq itself remained hostile to him and Ya'rub ibn Bil'arub, the son of the Imam Bil'arub, added his influential weight to the opposition by besieging him in Rostaq fort and demanding his surrender. Muhanna was tricked by a promise of safe conduct to come down from the fort, but Ya'rub broke his word and ordered Muhanna and his supporters to be bound and flogged, after which Muhanna was imprisoned and murdered. Ya'rub's intervention had perhaps not been entirely selfless and he was himself elected Imam after expressing pious contrition for the death of Muhanna. He then moved to Nizwa taking the boy Saif with him but, in doing so, incensed the tribes who thought that the Imamate should be preserved for Saif when he came of age. Another rebellion broke out, this time led by Bil'arub ibn Nasir al Ya'rubi with the support of the Bani Hina tribe who captured Rostaq, thus dominating the trade routes from the Interior to the coast. The revolt spread like wildfire, Ya'rub was compelled to stand down, and the boy Saif was elected Imam for the second time.

This might have led to a period of stability, but in fact the reverse was the case. A long civil war was sparked off by an incident at Rostaq, where the tribesmen had gathered to swear their allegiance to Saif. Bil'arub, who had played so large a part in Saif's restoration, was not unnaturally appointed regent to the boy, but for some unknown reason he used on the occasion of this gathering threats of such severity against the Bani Ghafir tribe and their leader, Muhammad ibn Nasir al Ghafiri, that they were provoked into immediate opposition.

Muhammad may have felt that the second formal election of Saif had been something of a sham and that Bil'arub would in fact wield power in a manner favourable to the Bani Hina and detrimental to the Bani Ghafir. At all events he wrote to the former Imam, Ya'rub, and urged him to raise his standard again, turning at the same time to the tribes of the Shamal, the present United Arab Emirates, for support. This was in fact forthcoming from the Bani Yas, the Bani Qitab and the Naim of the Buraimi area. The force which Muhammad mustered marched to Nizwa, and having consolidated there attacked Bil'arub's army at Firq. Bil'arub surrendered and Saif, who had by now reached puberty, was proclaimed Imam yet again, this time under the auspices of Muhammad ibn Nasir and the Bani Ghafir. Ya'rub died shortly afterwards, on 21st March 1723 (1136 AH) and thus one of the rivals for the Imamate was removed from the scene.

Fighting over the succession had led to increasing tribal enmity and the whole of Oman then became engulfed in desultory warfare between two factions – the Hinawi, based on the Bani Hina tribe and the Ghafiri, based on the Bani Ghafir. After the death of the former Imam, Ya'rub, the Hinawis rallied to a new leader – Khalf ibn Mubarak al Hina'i, nicknamed "Tiny". Endowed with skill and determination he responded to Muhammad ibn Nasir's "capture of the King" by seizing the coastal towns of Muscat and Barka.

Muhammad meanwhile appointed *Walis* in the boy Imam's name over the different districts of Oman and assembled a force of some 15,000 men who included the Bani Riyam and a considerable force from the North led by Rahma ibn Mattar al Hawali, the Amir of Julfar – Ras al Khaimah – with which he attacked the Hinawis at Barka. The result was inconclusive, but Khalf and the Hinawis turned the tables by instigating countermoves in the Dhahirah and by capturing Rostaq and Sohar. Khalf then had the advantage of holding the important passes and the richest ports, but Muhammad had the advantage of larger forces. However Muhammad's reliance on tribesmen from the Shamal may have accentuated animosities as the Hinawis could not forgive him for introducing Sunnis into an internal Ibadhi quarrel about the succession to the Imamate.

Muhammad then obtained control of the Sharqiyah, where the Hinawi faction were won over by force of arms. This success enabled him to attack the Hinawis in their area of strength on the Batinah coast. But in 1724 he took an unexpected step. Summoning the tribal chiefs and *Ulema* to Nizwa, he expressed a wish to give up responsibility for waging wars and administering Ibadhi affairs and suggested that another regent for young Saif should be appointed. His motive is obscure. Possibly he had had enough, or his health was under strain. Perhaps he was sufficiently patriotic to ask himself where the civil wars were leading Oman, for he had all along positively identified himself with the Ya'ruba dynasty and he was perhaps at heart more sympathetic to them than to Bani Ghafir factionalism. It could, however, be that his purpose was more Machiavellian and that he was angling for the Imamate. However this may be, the shaikhs and *Ulema* would not accept his resignation but instead proclaimed him Imam. Unfortunately for Oman his appointment did not end the civil war, which continued for another four years. He built up his control over much of the country in the next year or two and then attempted to attack Khalf's forces at Sohar. This move brought the end which, like the final act of a Shakespearean tragedy, resulted in the death of both leaders in the fighting under the walls of the great fort.

Before this, however, Muhammad sent a message warning the Hinawi garrison of Sohar not to resist. The messenger treacherously changed sides and remained with the Hinawis, who though prepared for Muhammad's army nonetheless lost the battle. The townspeople of Sohar then submitted to the Imam Muhammad. Khalf was meanwhile in Muscat where he gathered a force to march against Sohar. But realising that the odds were against him, unless he could detach from Muhammad's forces the contingent from the Shamal, he resorted to a stratagem, inducing the owner of a field of standing millet to destroy it and to complain to the Imam Muhammad that the damage had been done by Arabs of the north. Muhammad, having heard the case, gave judgement that damages should be paid to the plaintiff. But the latter, acting at Khalf's instigation, refused the damages and demanded that the "offenders" should be punished. Muhammad then ordered that the "offenders" should be bastinadoed, even though their own chiefs asserted their innocence. This so incensed the northern tribesmen that they quit their camp and returned home. Khalf's ruse had worked and seizing his opportunity he attacked at once but only to face defeat and death. Fate was, however, to deal impartially with the two great protagonists and Muhammad was struck by a bullet fired from the fort when in hot pursuit of the Hinawis.

Saif saddled the Shah's wild steed, galloping through Wadi al Kabir, leaping to the top of the wall on which he landed on his feet.

The Hinawis thereupon surrendered to Saif ibn Sultan who was once again proclaimed Imam in Nizwa in March 1728 (1140 AH). At last, one might have thought, peace must return to Oman, but internal divisions and dissensions remained so severe that in 1733 (1146 AH) yet another Ya'rubi contender for the Imamate, Bil'arub ibn Himyar, was elected and Oman again had a split Imamate. The situation had gone from bad to worse; but blacker days were still to come. When Muhammad and Khalf died the Ghafiris held Nizwa, most of central Oman, the Dhahirah and the Sharqiyah. The Hinawis held Rostaq, the Batinah area and Jabrin. Saif then took over these Hinawi territories including Muscat and Bil'arub the area held by the Ghafiris.

Saif, however, judged that he was not strong enough on his own and brought in Baluch mercenaries from Makran, the first recorded instance of Baluchis coming to Oman for military service. Later, when defeated even with their help, he wrote to Nadir Shah of Persia requesting assistance. Tradition relates that the Shah in reply sent a very powerful and restive horse with the message that, if Saif could maintain his seat on it, the Shah would send as many soldiers as he desired. Saif had it saddled and managed to master it, riding furiously through the Wadi al Kabir in Muscat, with stones flying up behind in every direction. On reaching the Bab al Mitha'ib the horse leaped the wall on the top of which Saif landed safely on his feet. This display of horsemanship sufficiently impressed the Shah's messenger, but unfortunately the horse broke its legs and was killed. It is a tribute to Saif's character that he "greatly regretted the death of the horse."

The Safavid dynasty had virtually come to an end with the abdication of Shah Hussain after the Afghans had invaded Persia in 1722 (1135 AH) and the country remained unsettled until a leader of genius, Nadir Quli, who came to the throne as Nadir Shah in 1736 (1148 AH), expelled them. He ruled for only eleven years, but in this short time managed not only to restore order but also to pursue an expansionist policy. In response to Saif's appeal he sent 500 men and 1,580 horses, with the help of Dutch transports – the British were unwilling to become involved – to Julfar and Khor Fakkan. The local Arabs submitted and Saif's forces, joining those of Latif Khan, the Persian "Admiral of the Gulf", advanced to engage and defeat Bil'arub's army at Falaj Sumaini near Buraimi in 1736 (1149 AH). But Bil'arub recovered and in the following year (1150 AH), a fresh Persian force of some 6,000 arrived in

Julfar. Saif by now regretted his invitation to the Persians, realising that their ambitions extended beyond merely helping him. It was, however, too late and the Persians reduced the Dhahira area to submission and started to levy taxes. In view of the heavy fighting between Omanis and Persians, Saif went to the Wadi Bani Ghafir to meet Bil'arub and the Bani Ghafir agreed that, in order to heal Omani divisions and enable both factions to join against the Persians, Bil'arub should stand down from the Imamate in favour of Saif. All went well for a time and Saif relieved the people of tax imposed by the Persians. However things again turned sour for him in 1741 (1154 AH) when the *Ulema* and tribal chiefs, who were dissatisfied with him – the reason is not clear, unless it was divinely ordained, as Salil ibn Razik the Oman historian suggests, that "the people of Oman had to undergo the consequences of their fickleness and love of change" – conferred the Imamate on Sultan ibn Murshid al Ya'rubi.

War broke out between rival Imams, whose fortunes ebbed and flowed until Saif lost Muscat to Sultan and, despite earlier disenchantment, again turned to the Persians , who still maintained a garrison at Julfar, for help. Saif offered to give the Persians the fort at Sohar – the centre of their influence in Sassanid times – in perpetuity. They replied somewhat loftily that Saif was a sincere friend and ally and they did not need such a gift as they had everything in abundance!

Nadir Shah assembled another fleet, which sailed for Julfar in June 1742 (1155 AH) and Saif and Taqi Khan, the Persian commander, who was also *Beglarbegi* of the province of Fars, met there to sign a treaty. By it the Persians agreed to restore the Imamate to Saif in return, despite their earlier reticence, for recognition of Persian suzerainty over Oman. Persian troops then marched down the Batinah and attacked Sohar, where the fort was held by Ahmad ibn Said who later became the first Imam of the Al bu Said dynasty. He successfully withstood their siege, but the Persians took Muscat and Mutrah. They then redoubled their efforts to take Sohar, but Ahmad, even though his own supplies were very short, sallied forth every day to attack them.

In 1743 (1156 AH) one of the complications of the Omani scene was removed with the death of the Imam Sultan. The unfortunate Saif again became disillusioned with the Persians when they refused to hand over the forts of Muscat and Mutrah to him and he slipped away from their camp, as they were encircling Sohar, to the fort of al Hazm. There he died of a broken heart shortly after hearing of the defeat and death of the rival Imam Sultan in a cavalry engagement near Sohar with the Persians. What a strange mixture of feelings must have assailed him towards the end of his tragic life! He said to one of his officers just before his death: "This is my castle and my grave. I am become an eyesore to everyone, and the quiet of death will be preferable to any happiness which dominion has afforded me."

With the death of Saif and Sultan no other member of the Ya'ruba came forward, but Ahmad ibn Said continued to fight against the Persians single-handed. The Persians maintained the siege of Sohar for nine months in all, but after Saif's death agreed with Ahmad to withdraw from there whilst retaining Muscat. Ahmad was not slow to find a means of exerting further pressure on them and he established a thriving market at Barka, which diverted imports and trade from the Interior away from Muscat.

Ahmad then made up his mind to get rid of the Persians once and for all. He invited them to a vast gathering at Barka, for which the preparations were so lavish that the local people began to complain. Great dishes of meat were sent to the tents which the Persians had pitched on the plain. Their fifty officers were invited to a banquet by Ahmad. His undisclosed object was similar to the ruse by which Muhammad Ali Pasha later ended the influence of the Mamelukes in Egypt in 1811 (1226 AH). When all the guests were at dinner, the drum of the fort was sounded and the crier proclaimed "Anyone who has a grudge against the Persians may now take his revenge." This was the signal for a wholesale massacre which only 200 odd Persians survived.

Thus in 1747 (1160 AH) their adventure in Oman was ended – although a garrison remained in Julfar until 1748 (1161 AH) – and Ahmad ibn Said who became a popular hero was elected Imam.

The Al bu Said Dynasty

AHMAD ibn Said was a man of outstanding courage, vigour, enterprise, generosity and personality, and all these qualities were as much needed after he became Imam as before. The factionalism of the civil war did not disappear overnight and it was not long after he was elected Imam that the Ya'ruba started intriguing with the support of the Ghafiri faction. Bil'arub ibn Himyar, the former Imam – Saif ibn Sultan's rival – was induced to show his hand by a report that the Imam Ahmad ibn Said was dead. Ahmad had in fact only gone into hiding in Yankul and, hearing of Bil'arub's action, he emerged and raised the Hinawi tribes. Setting off through the Wadi Samail, and gathering increasing strength, he defeated Bil'arub's army at Firq near Nizwa. Bil'arub himself was killed and Ahmad punished those who had joined Bil'arub against him, though he later showed his magnanimity by pardoning them.

Thereafter Ahmad's difficulties lay nearer home for his two sons, Saif and Sultan, led him something of a dance and at one time seized the two forts in Muscat. Ibn Rahma al Hawali, the Amir of Julfar, grasped the opportunity provided by their family dissension to besiege Rostaq with some 30,000 men, but this only caused family solidarity and patriotism to reassert itself. Father and sons were immediately reconciled and ibn Rahma, who had previously fought an inconclusive battle with Ahmad's forces at Bithna in the early 1750s (1160s AH), withdrew.

Another threat in the early days of Ahmad's reign came from Nasir ibn Muhammad ibn Nasir, who led a faction of the Ghafiris in opposition until he and Ahmad were reconciled by a marriage which made them brothers-in-law.

Though Ahmad had his early difficulties in securing internal peace after the civil war, Oman in his day was an important power to be reckoned with externally. By 1775 (1189 AH) his fleet consisted of thirty-four warships – four of 44 guns, five frigates mounting from 18 to 24 guns and the rest ketches or galiots mounting from 8 to 14 guns. The British were

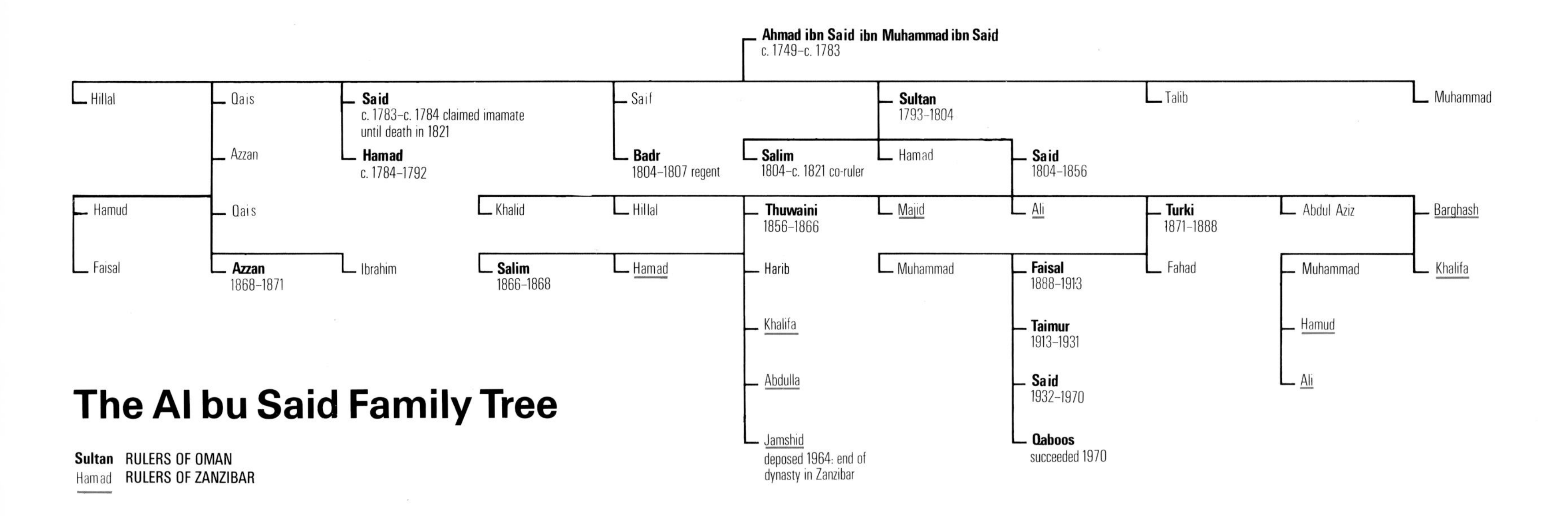

The Al bu Said Family Tree

involved militarily with Oman even at this stage, and in 1758 (1172 AH) the captain of an English ketch hired her to the Imam for a naval expedition against the people of Ras al Khaima. Sea power enabled Ahmad to assert Omani influence abroad and to carry the war against the Persians further afield. In 1756 (1170 AH) the Persians besieged Basra and, when the inhabitants wrote to Ahmad seeking help, he himself led an expedition of ten large ships, a number of smaller ones and a force of 10,000 men. He drove the Persians out after his ship, *Ah-Rahmany,* had managed to break the iron chain which the Persians had stretched across the river. So delighted was the Ottoman Sultan, within whose jurisdiction Basra fell, that he ordered the Governor of Basra to pay the Imam *kharaj*, or a subsidy, which continued until the reign of Said ibn Sultan ibn al Imam Ahmad 1804-1856 (1219-1273 AH).

The Mogul Emperor, Shah Alam, was grateful also for the cooperation of Ahmad's fleet against pirates on the west coast of India. He therefore sent an envoy to Oman to make a treaty agreeing to aid Ahmad with money and men against his enemies and to establish a resident mission in Muscat in what came to be known as "the Nabob's house".

At home Ahmad proved a good administrator of a generally strong central government and gained a reputation for liberality. On his way from Rostaq to Muscat he used to distribute sweets to the children of the poor. Though he was always accessible to his people, he kept some state and had a personal bodyguard, which included a thousand free men, a thousand Zanzibaris and a hundred Nubian slaves. When on the march, his retinue carried four banners, attached to staffs, two with gold at the head and two with silver. He also included in his retinue *Qadhis*, scholars, notables and even executioners – described by Salil ibn Razik, the Omani historian, as a "brave set of fellows"! He was assiduous in attention to administrative detail and visited Muscat, which yielded a very good income from customs; revenue from this source alone ranged from at least one *lakh* of rupees to perhaps as high as three or five *lakh*s. These visits from Rostaq were usually of twelve days' duration and on the eleventh day, when he inspected fort Mirani, all dues on goods then deposited in customs were remitted. Curiously, Ahmad never succeeded in obtaining the Ya'ruba fort at al Hazm and this remained in the hands of the Ya'ruba family until 1861 (1278 AH).

Ahmad died in Rostaq in 1783 (1198 AH) and his son Said was elected Imam, despite a general desire that the older and most intelligent son, Hillal, should succeed. Hillal, who suffered from a cataract, had gone to Sind for a cure and never returned to Oman. On such slender threads do the succession of kings and the fate of nations depend. For Said was not a popular ruler. As *Wali* of Nizwa he had earlier antagonised the local population by establishing a personal monopoly of indigo dyeing, and this as well as other measures alienated him from the people. Efforts were consequently made to appoint first his brother Qais and later his son Hamad as Imam in his place. Hamad in fact later became *de facto* ruler of Oman, residing in Muscat whilst his father remained at Rostaq, thus beginning the dichotomy between Sultanate and Imamate which so bedevilled internal politics later.

Hamad, who was perhaps the first of the family to be formally designated Sayyid, surrounded himself with men of learning and piety and gained a reputation for justice. His reputation for bravery was only equalled by that of his uncle Sultan, who later assumed the rule. Hamad added a tower to Fort Mirani in Muscat, facing the Mukalla cove, which he armed with great guns. A man of determination, he built forts in Ruwi and Barka, and had a ship called *Ar-Rahmany* built for him at Zanzibar. He acquired Lamu in east Africa and had designs on Mombasa and even Bombay.

During Hamad's administration there was a severe drought, but after he had led the people in prayer in the Wadi al Kabir at Muscat, rain, accompanied by thunder and lighting, came in abundance. The valleys ran with water and a period of prosperity followed. After mustering a large army – whether to reduce al Hazm, to attack his uncle Qais at Sohar, to make war on his father or to attack Mombasa, is still a matter of speculation – Hamad died suddenly in 1792 (1206 AH). He was buried in Muscat and his father the Imam Said held a funeral feast in Fort Jalali after which he returned to Rostaq and thereafter neglected the administration of his subjects utterly. As a result of his indolence the reins of government were taken up by his brother Sultan, another son of the Imam Ahmad ibn Said, and it was not long before Sultan had effective control of Muscat and the greater part of the country.

Sultan was tall in stature, of noble countenance, and brave; and his reputation in Oman was second to none. In taking Muscat from the representative whom the Imam Said had put in to succeed Hamad there, Sultan and his men sang, as they came down the *wadi* with drawn swords, "The right has overcome and has overthrown the wrong!" But he was practical as well as idealistic, and realising the importance of stability to Muscat's trade he hastened to assure the merchants and notables of immunity for themselves and their property.

During the latter half of the eighteenth century, goods were carried between the Gulf and India by both European and Arab vessels and the merchants of Muscat had a lion's share of this trade. Sayyid Sultan had fifteen ships of between 400 and 700 tons and three brigs based on Muscat alone, whilst at Sur there was a fleet of 100 or so sea going vessels of various sizes. Import duties at Muscat amounted to 6 or 6.5 per cent *ad valorem* on merchandise of all kinds and about five-eights of the whle Persian Gulf trade passed through this port from which ships sailed to Malabar, Malaya, Zanzibar and Abyssinia.

Sayyid Sultan claimed the exclusive right to protect navigation in the Gulf and indeed at this time Oman controlled both sides of the Gulf, as parts of southern Persia had been leased from the Persians. He tried – though without ultimate success – to make a preliminary visit to Muscat obligatory on all vessels proceeding up the Gulf, a stratagem which had made earlier *entrepôts* in the Gulf area prosperous in their own heydays.

Sultan's grip on Oman itself was so firm that the European powers – particularly the British and French, whose interests began to conflict in the East as well as in Europe – dealt with him as the effective ruler and both powers formally addressed him as if he were the elected Imam. The dim existence of the Imam himself in Rostaq was of little political consequence.

The French base in Mauritius, the Ile de France, became a flourishing colonial possession, whose Governor maintained contact with the rulers of Oman, and well chosen gifts were from time to time exchanged. Even earlier the French Consul in Basra had struck up a personal friendship with Ahmad ibn Said and in 1785 (1200 AH) the French sent a mission under the Comte de Rosilly to Muscat seeking permission to set up a factory and a consulate, though this in fact came to nothing.

Rivalry between the British and the French grew in intensity with the rise of Napoleon's star. His ambitions for a vast eastern empire alarmed the British, who had been consolidating their power in India since the Seven Years War and were very sensitive about their communications with home. Napoleon's arrival in Egypt heralded a diplomatic struggle between the two powers for influence in Oman. Despite an earlier incident when they had seized an Omani frigate, the *Saleh*, off Sohar, the French were well thought of in Muscat and in 1799 (1214 AH) Napoleon addressed a letter to Sultan which read:

> A l'Imam de Muscat – Je vous écris cette lettre pour vous faire connaître ce que vous avez déjà appris sans doute, l'arriveé de l'armeé française en Egypte. Comme vous avez été de tout temps notre ami, vous devez être convaincu du désir que j'ai de protéger tous les bâtiments de votre nation et que vous engagiez à venir à Suez, où ils trouveront protection pour le commerce. Je vous prie aussi de faire parvenir cette lettre à Tippoo-Saib par la première occasion qui se trouvera pour les Indes.

The British had got off the mark even earlier and had decided to forestall the French. Their suspicions had already been aroused by the activities of two eminent French naturalists, Messieurs Bruguière and Olivier, who made journeys to the Gulf area, and thus Napoleon's letter was intercepted by a British agent. The reference to Tippoo Sahib who was in rebellion against them in India particularly alarmed the British authorities.In 1798 (1213 AH) Sir Harford Jones, who later led a mission to Persia, was appointed Resident at Basra to forestall French influence with the Pasha of Baghdad. In the same year the British Government in Bombay sent Mirza Mahdi Ali Khan, one of the Persian gentlemen of good family who were employed in the British service at the time, to Sayyid Sultan of Muscat. A treaty in the form of a *Qaulnameh* was signed, by which the Sultan bound himself to take the British part in international matters; to deny the French or their allies the Dutch "a place to fix or seat themselves" whilst warfare between them and the British continued; to dismiss from his service a Frenchman who was commanding one of his vessels; to exclude French vessels from the inner cove of Muscat; and to permit the British to garrison Bandar Abbas which the Sultan then claimed – an offer which was not in fact taken up. The Governor-General in India and his brother, Sir Arthur Wellesley, who later became the Duke of Wellington, feared that the French might attempt to invade India through Persia and doubted the strength of Sultan's commitment. They therefore sent an impressive mission in 1800 (1215 AH) under Captain John Malcolm – one of the East India Company's most able young officers, who later became General Sir John Malcolm, Governor of Bombay – to conclude political and commercial treaties with Fath Ali Khan, the Shah of Persia. "Boy" Malcolm – his nickname through life – also called at Muscat on the way to negotiate a more formal treaty with the Sultan. This reaffirmed the earlier treaty and provided that "an English gentleman of respectability should always reside in the port of Muscat" and that the friendship of the two countries should "endure till the end of time or the sun and moon cease in their revolving careers." Sayyid Sultan found no difficulty in agreeing the terms. He was however somewhat upset at having to dismiss his French surgeon and for this reason the first British representative appointed to reside in Muscat was a doctor, Assistant Surgeon A. H. Bogle.

The British recognised the Omanis as the predominant power in the area and calculated that an alliance with them would help contain the growing power of the Qawasim of Ras al Khaimah who were beginning to harass British as well as local shipping. Anxieties had been aroused by an incident in 1797 (1212 AH) when the *Viper*, a 14-gun cruiser of the Bombay Marine was lying off Bushire.

Shaikh Salih, one of the Qasimi shaikhs, who was also there planning to intercept Omani ships sailing from Basra to Sur, called on the British Resident with professions of friendship and requested that the British should neither give protection to Omani ships nor despatch any goods in them – an interesting request, suggesting that the British were already doing this. His plea for ball and powder was met by the captain of the *Viper*, but the Shaikh nevertheless suddenly attacked the British ship, perhaps having received no firm assurance about the British attitude over Omani ships.

During the latter part of the eighteenth century there was constant warfare between the Omanis and the Qawasim, who sought a greater share of the Gulf, Indian and African trade enjoyed by the Omanis. These wars also had roots in tribal and factional considerations, arising from the direct involvement of the tribes of Shamal in the Omani civil war. Ahmad ibn Said had tried in 1758 (1172 AH) to reduce the tribes of Sir – the Ras al Khaimah area – and in 1762 (1176 AH) obtained recognition of his authority from all the tribes but not from the historical port of Julfar, whose Amir, Shaikh Saqr, invaded Oman in 1763 (1177 AH) and even threatened Rostaq. Niebuhr, however, who visited the Ras al Khaimah area in the 1760s, commented that though these tribes recognised the overlordship of the Imam they were in fact independent and often at war with their former masters.

Meantime a new element had appeared on the already complicated scene. A boy born in Uyaina in Saudi Arabia in 1703 (1115 AH) was to have a great influence on the fortunes of south-east Arabia. As a child Muhammad ibn Abdul Wahhab showed unusual religious fervour and as a man became a formidable fundamentalist reformer, preaching the oneness of God and a return to God's word as revealed in the Qur'an. The Al Saud shaikhs of Dira'iya and Najd were won over, and by the last quarter of the eighteenth century the tribes of Njad were welded together under the leaderships of the Shaikh of the Al Saud who, after the death of its founder, became Imam of the new movement. This by then had become a religio-military confederacy of desert people and common cause was maintained by keeping fanaticism at white heat. The fuel required was constant expansion and this had important consequences for Oman in the nineteenth and twentieth centuries. In 1800 (1215 AH) the Wahhabis arrived in Buraimi, which had been indisputably part of Oman throughout countless generations, and the alliance which developed between Wahhabis and Qawasim involved Oman in warfare on land and sea for several decades.

Meantime, however, the French made further attempts to win influence in Oman despite the treaties made with Britain. Talleyrand advised Napoleon in 1803 (1218 AH):

> Mascate est une place importante. L'Imam qui y'gouverne, et dont la domination s'étend fort avant dans l'interior des terres et même sur quelques districts de la côte de Mozambique, est un prince indépendent sous tous rapports.

This led Napoleon to appoint M. Cavaignac as Consul. He arrived in Muscat on the 3rd October 1803 (1218 AH) with his baggage, clearly expecting to set up house. Sultan, however, honoured his treaties with Britain by firmly refusing to accept Cavaignac. No doubt the "English gentleman of respectability " had been earning his keep, though he maintained no grand style locally and lived in a "miserable house". Sultan no doubt realised that the British were the only power who could and might help him against the Wahhabis and he did not want to antagonise them for the sake of the French. It was no doubt sour grapes which made Cavaignac comment: "Ce pays et ses inhabitants sont tout à fait misérables" and that all that Muscat needed in the way of representation was "un agent commercial de la dernière classe".

Sultan was at the time involved in hostilities against the Wahhabis, who had reached Barka on the Batinah coast, and the Qawasim. A man of courage and decision, he swept the whole Gulf in 1804 (1219 AH) with fourteen warships and visited Basra to seek aid from his Turkish friends. On the return voyage he transferred to a smaller vessel near Lingeh to cross to Oman, but when the rest of the Omani fleet was not sufficiently close to give protection his ship was attacked by the Qawasim; Sultan was shot through the head and buried at Lingeh.

The Qawasim attack on two British brigs in 1805 (1220 AH) and renewed fears of French involvement in Muscat aroused fresh concern in Bombay and consequently Captain David Seton, who had been Political Agent in Muscat for a short time in 1801 (1216 AH), was sent back to the Gulf to report. He recommended that the East India Company's cruisers should be sent to assist the fleet of Badr ibn Saif – who had succeeded Sultan in Oman – against the Qawasim. The Council at Bombay approved his recommendation, though with considerable apprehension, for it involved taking sides and abandoning the traditional policy of standing aloof from Arab wars. Seton was, therefore, sent fresh instructions, while still in the Gulf, and told to act "with the greatest of moderation, to aim at pacification by means of negotiation, and to avoid hostilities, at all events with any classes of armed boats belonging to either side of the Gulph ... which may have respected the British flag." At the same time cruisers of the Bombay marine were strictly forbidden to fire on Arab ships unless fired on themselves.

The internal Omani scene again became complicated on Sultan's death. The family was divided about the successor and, though the British dealt with Badr, presumably because he was *de facto* ruler on the coast, Omani historians reckon that the rule passed jointly to Sultan's two sons, Salim and Said until Said died of paralysis in Muscat in April 1821 (1236 AH). But Qais, the ablest surviving son of the Imam Ahmad who still held Sohar, also had aspirations, supported by the shadowy Imam Said in Rostaq. Badr, who had initially supported the cause of Said and Salim, was killed by Said in somewhat strange circumstances when they were playing with arms in the fort at Nakhl.

The Reign of Sayyid Said ibn Sultan

The nineteenth was a century of long reigns and Sayyid Said who was born in Samail in 1791 (1206 AH) reigned for fifty-two years, from 1804 to 1856 (1219-1273 AH) – an era during which Britain's paramountcy in the area was being consolidated. Said came to be preferred over Salim with the latter's consent, principally because of the influence of his aunt, Moza, the daughter of the first Imam Ahmad. Said concluded a treaty of Amity and Commerce in 1807 (1222 AH) with de Caen, the French "Captain General of the East", but it was short-lived as he and the French were driven out of the Ile de France, Mauritius, by the British, with whom Said maintained close relations for the rest of his reign. Their direct involvement against the Qawasim and indirect support against the Wahhabis stood him in good stead, though initially, as we have seen, there were doubts amongst some British officials.

Qasimi attacks on British ships led the Governor-General of India, Lord Minto, to write that the independence of Oman was an important interest which involved British cooperation "against the Joasmee pirates". Joint operations with Said were undertaken but Said's final triumph did not come until 1820 (1236 AH), when Qasimi power was finally destroyed and treaties were signed with the shaikhdoms which later came to be called the Trucial States.

Wahhabi influence on the Bani bu Ali and this tribe's piracies prompted Said to prevail on Captain T. Perronet Thompson, who was left as Political Agent in Ras al Khaimah after the 1820 treaties, to launch a British expedition against them. It was a unsuccessful and ill-fated venture which resulted in Captain Thompson's court martial, though he survived it to become a full general in the British Army. A second and successful expedition was sent in 1821 (1237 AH) under the command of General Sir Lionel Smith.

Sayyid Said was a great ruler who had stamped his personality on affairs long before the death of the pathetic Imam Said in about 1821 (1237 AH). His biographer Salil wrote of him "Praise be to God through whom Said, the happiest of rulers, attained quiet prosperity and perennial glory, decreeing to him sublime eminence in the sphere of happiness and renown, insomuch that by the Divine aid vouchsafed to him he subdued the sovereigns of his time, acquired dignity by the battles which he fought with his enemies, conquered with the sword hitherto unknown countries and made a straight road over the dissevered necks of the rebellious."

Said, however, did not rule a universally tranquil country even after acquiring ascendancy over his rivals. The scene was perhaps somewhat comparable with England in Henry II's time when those who held the great castles were often in rebellion. The Wahhabis too ate into Said's territory to a greater or lesser extent throughout his reign. Nonetheless there was never, after the first few years, any real doubt about his authority. The character of the "Imam" – as he was inaccurately called by Europeans, for he was never formally elected – impressed many travellers who described his liberality, charm, and ease with his people. For instance, Lieutenant J. R. Wellsted wrote in 1835 (1251 AH): "He possesses a tall and commanding figure; a mild, yet striking countenance; and an address and manner courtly, affable, and dignified ... It is noticed by the Arabs, an instance of the warmth of his affections, that he daily visits his mother ... and pays in all matters implicit obedience to her wishes. In his intercourse with Europeans he has ever displayed the warmest attention and kindness ..."

Muscat has perennially captured the imagination of travelling artists. This particular watercolour was done by Major C.F. Hinchcliffe in 1857 – still in the age of sail when it was a major entrepôt.

Abroad Said had considerable pretensions, ranging from the Gulf region, southern Persia and Baluchistan to the east coast of Arabia and Madagascar. He claimed Bahrain, but was never able to subdue or hold it for long. But he retained the hold on southern Persia, which his father Sultan had acquired with the capture of the Hormuz , Qishm, and Henjam Islands from the Bani Ma'in tribe in 1794 (1209 AH) and also the lease of Bandar Abbas and other fortified posts on the southern coast of Kerman, which his father had obtained from the Shah for an annual sum of 60,000 *Tumans*. He also retained Gwadur, which remained a part of Oman until 1958, and Chahbar which his father Sultan had added to Oman's possessions. Said's motive, like his father's, was to strengthen Oman's control of trade passing through the Straits of Hormuz, and Persian expulsion of his *Wali* and other officials from the coast of Kerman in 1854 was a great personal blow to him – indeed may have hastened his end. For, although the treaty with the Persians negotiated in 1856 (1273 AH) provided that Oman could appoint representatives there for a further twenty years in return for an annual rental of 16,000 *Tumans*, the Persians thereby terminated Oman's pretension to these areas as of right. The blow may have been the greater, as Said had earlier taken one of the daughters of the Prince Governor of Shiraz as his bride. (There were no children of this marriage.)

Sayyid Said made his greatest impression on Africa where, from 1829 (1245 AH), his heart and main interest lay. He secured Mombasa from the Mazari, who had established a local Omani dynasty, and made Zanzibar his second capital. He aimed to extend his influence by a dynastic marriage with Queen Ranavolana of Madagascar in 1833 (1249 AH) but, when she refused and suggested a young princess, Said did not take the offer up. Five years later he offered another Queen in Madagascar, Seneekoo Nossi-be, his protection. This offer was accepted and a treaty between them provided that she should pay Said 30,000 dollars a year in return. This arrangement, however, lapsed when the Queen accepted French protection in 1840 (1256 AH).

Said was very much the "Sailor Sayyid" and travelled great distances at sea. He had about twenty ships of his own for private trade and gave his personal attention to Oman's considerable naval forces. It gave him great pleasure to command his own flagship, the *Shah Alam*, in person and it was perhaps, therefore, fitting that he should have presented the English "Sailor King" William IV with a fine ship of war, which was subsequently called the *Liverpool*. He received in return a handsome yacht, called the *Prince Regent*. He also presented a grey mare to King William IV on his coronation in 1830 and an Arab stallion to Queen Victoria on hers. But not all presents exchanged with the British crown were so practical and acceptable. Queen Victoria sent a state carriage and harness in 1842 (1258 AH) – despite the fact that there were no suitable roads for such carriages in Zanzibar – and in 1844 (1260 AH) a silver gilt tea service. Said made the Kuria Muria Islands – as today's Halaaniyaat Islands were then known – over to the Queen Victoria as a gift in perpetuity on 14th July 1854 (1270 AH), a gesture which prompted an embarrassed gift of a snuff box from her Foreign Secretary, Lord Clarendon. The islands were returned to Oman in 1967.

Sayyid Said had thirty-six sons and daughters. One daughter, Sayyida Salma, obviously a woman of great character and charm, married a young German from Hamburg, Herr Ruete, and took the European name Emily. She recorded the story of her life and included many fascinating details about the Royal Family and local customs in a book published in English and French, called *Memoirs of an Arab Princess*. Her son, Rudolf Said-Ruete, wrote a biography of his maternal grandfather, Sayyid Said, which was published in England in 1929.

Zanzibar

Sayyid Said Sultan gave fresh life to the age-old Omani interest in east Africa, particularly by introducing cloves as a cash crop in Zanzibar and establishing rice plantations, thus creating increasing prosperity. Many of the great European travellers in Africa have left accounts of him and his successors there: and Burton, Speke, Livingstone, Grant and Stanley all had good reason to thank the Al bu Saidi rulers of Zanzibar for assistance in their African explorations. The Arabs of Oman had penetrated Africa as far as the Congo – albeit in connection with slaves as well as more legitimate forms of trade – and their knowledge and hospitality greatly assisted the European newcomers.

Omani connections with Zanzibar and the east coast of Africa probably go back into remote antiquity. The first recorded mention, however, of Omanis going to east Africa is the flight of Sulaiman and Said to the "land of the Zanj", when the Caliph's troops forced them out of Oman at the end of the seventh century AD. The first Portuguese travellers found large colonies of Omanis settled there in flourishing cities, on which ibn Batuta also commented in the fourteenth century.

However the modern dynastic connection can perhaps be dated to the Imam Sultan ibn Saif, the second Imam of the Ya'ruba dynasty. The Arabs of Mombasa appealed to him for aid after he had expelled the Portuguese from Muscat, and in 1652 (1063 AH) he attacked Zanzibar, killing a large number of Portuguese, including an Augustinian priest. Eight years later, having created a more formidable navy, Sultan ibn Saif besieged Mombasa and defeated the Portuguese there, though it was left to his son, the Imam Saif ibn Sultan, to capture Mombasa, Pemba and Kilwa and to drive the Portuguese from all their coastal possessions north of Mozambique. The Imam Saif appointed Omani *Wali*s in several places – a Mazrui at Mombasa, a Nabhani at Pate and a Hirth at Zanzibar – and he established military garrisons at Zanzibar and Pemba.

In 1739 (1152 AH) the Mazrui *Wali* of Mombasa threw off his allegiance to the Imamate, which by then had become much weakened by the civil war, and Pate and other states followed suit. However the Imam Ahmad ibn Said was made of sterner stuff and made very sure that Zanzibar was well garrisoned, particularly as the Mazruis of Mombasa continued not only to assert their independence but also to attack Zanzibar itself. Zanzibar thus remained subject to the ruler of Oman from the middle of the seventeenth century until the middle of the nineteenth century, though it was not until the reign of Sayyid Said ibn Sultan that very serious attention was given to developing this part of the Omani dominions.

The Sultanate Divided

When Said died in 1856 at the age of sixty-two on the sea voyage from Muscat, his body was taken and buried in the garden of his residence at Zanzibar. Two of his sons, Majid and Barghash, had been with him there, and Majid, who immediately assumed authority in Zanzibar, confirmed all the appointments of the officials made by his father in his African dominions. Said's son Thuwaini was *Wali* of Muscat and his son Turki *Wali* of Sohar at the time of his death.

Thuwaini, with the support of the majority of the people of Oman itself,

The British Connection

In 1646 the Ya'rubi Imam Nasir ibn Murshid made a treaty with the East India Company giving "the English" the exclusive trading rights at Sohar. Not until 1800 was there any permanent British representative in Muscat, after the treaty made in that year providing that "an English gentleman of respectability" should always reside in the port of Muscat, and that the friendship between the two countries should "endure till the end of time or the sun and moon cease in their revolving careers".

claimed the succession to the whole Sultanate, though his brother Turki asserted the same independence as many of *Wali*s of Sohar had done at various times in the past. Recognition, however, by the people of Zanzibar and the African possessions left Majid in a strong *de facto* position and he made an amicable arrangement with Thuwaini to pay him 40,000 crowns annually. Dispute subsequently arose as to whether this sum was tribute or subsidy and, when in 1860 (1277 AH) Majid refused to pay, Thuwaini resorted to arms and assembled an imposing force. Part of this had actually sailed for Zanzibar when the British Government intervened to prevent bloodshed and both parties agreed to submit their dispute to the Viceroy and Governor-General in India, Lord Canning.

Brigadier, later Sir William, Coghlan was appointed to inquire into the merits of the opposing cases and Canning's award in 1862 (1279 AH) was cordially accepted by the rival brothers. Majid was declared ruler of Zanzibar and of the African dominions, but required to pay to the ruler of Muscat 40,000 crowns annually and the two years' arrears. This arrangement compensated the ruler of Muscat for relinquishing his claims to Zanzibar and adjusted the inequality between the two inheritances, for by this time Zanzibar was by far the richer part. With this rather odd, but empirically wise, settlement the two Sultanates went their own ways. It was at this stage that permanent British representation in Muscat, suspended since 1810, was resumed at Thuwaini which was thought to have been at a disadvantage in the arbitration compared with Majid, who had been advised throughout the award proceedings by Captain Hamerton, the British Resident in Zanzibar. International recognition to the creation of the two Sultanates was formally given by a joint declaration made at Paris in 1862 (1279 AH) by which the British and the French undertook reciprocally to respect the independence of the two sovereign Sultans.

In the middle of the nineteenth century Oman was still described as "a first rate Asiatic maritime power". However, a very rapid decline set in after the death of Sayyid Said as a result of economic causes, the splitting of the Sultanate and instability in Oman itself. The loss of its considerable navy, which was happened to be anchored at Zanzibar when Said died, added to Oman's difficulties and the introduction in 1862 of the steamer service run by the British India Steam Navigation Company between India and the Gulf put the Omanis at great disadvantage as their ships ceased to be competitive in the carrying trade. In a very few years their maritime power dwindled to virtually nothing. The gradual elimination of the slave trade, on which much of Oman's shipping was engaged, was another element in Oman's decline, particularly as the agriculture of the Interior depended heavily on slave labour.

Thuwaini's reign was not free from internal strife. In 1861 his brother Turki rose against him in Sohar and the Yal Saad of the Batinah and the Bani Jabir also rebelled at the instigation of Qais ibn Azzan of Rostaq, who also allied himself at this stage with the Wahhabis. There were renewed incursions by the Wahhabis in 1864 (1281 AH), and they made insistent demands for financial contributions. With the aid of the Janaba and Bani bu Ali tribes, they raided Sur, but the British interceded to give the Omanis respite. Thuwaini's end came in 1866 (1283 AH) when he was shot with a double-barrelled pistol by his son Salim in the fort at Sohar whilst enjoying his siesta. Salim's motive is not entirely clear, though Thuwaini was popular neither with his people nor the Al bu Said family.

Salim immediately proclaimed himself as his father's successor but such was the horror of patricide that recognition only came slowly. For a while uncertainty prevailed, trade came to a halt and Turki, basing himself at Yankul in the Dhahirah, again went into opposition. The Zanzibar subsidy was temporarily withheld – the first exercise of a political tool, which was to be used on several later occasions. Omani influence at Bandar Abbas which they had held for so long was weakened. For the Persians took the opportunity on Salim's accession to terminate the lease as they were entitled to do but renewed it at an increased rent of 30,000 *Tumans* for eight years. Opposition to Salim built up rapidly and in 1868 (1285 AH) Azzan ibn Qais captured Barka, Muscat and Mutrah in quick succession, forcing Salim to leave by ship. Thus ended a short, unpopular and unhappy reign.

Azzan demonstrated ability and force of character such as Oman had not seen for a while, and, with the assistance of the influential Khalili family and Salih ibn Ali, the leading Shaikh of the Hirth of the Sharqiyah, gained control of the whole country. He expelled the Wahhabis from Buraimi, which they had held intermittently since 1800 (1216 AH) and paid a subsidy to his ally the Shaikh of Abu Dhabi for protecting the Buraimi frontier of Oman. Salim's attempts to raise support against Azzan only met failure, but Turki, who also aspired to the Sultanate, was more successful. Obtaining funds from the Sultan of Zanzibar, he allied himself with the Shaikhs of Dubai,

Below, left, is seen the entrance to the Consulate, built in 1890. It later became the Embassy, until 1994. The (British) Royal Coat of Arms is seen above the lintel. The first modern Christian missionary to Oman was Thomas Valpy French (1825-1891), formerly Bishop of Lahore, whose grave (*below*) lies in a cove just east of Muscat proper.

The great-grandfather (Sultan Faisal) (far left) *and grandfather (Sultan Taimur)* (left) *of the present Sultan.*

Above: *Oman's coronation gift to King Edward VII of England.*

Ajman and Ras al Khaimah and, landing at Khor Fakkan, went to Buraimi, winning over the Naim and Bani Qitab tribes on the way. On 5th October 1870 (1287 AH), Azzan's and Turki's forces met in battle in the Wadi Dhank and, rather surprisingly, Turki's side won.

Azzan and his brother Ibrahim, who had meantime wrested the fortress of al Hazm, which this branch of the family still possesses, from the descendants of the Ya'ruba dynasty, retired to Sohar. Turki, supported by Saif ibn Sulaiman of the Bani Riyam, won part of the Sharqiyah over and advanced on the capital. Azzan and Saif ibn Sulaiman were killed in battle at Mutrah.

Turki assumed the rule but had no easy passage, for Salim, Ibrahim ibn Qais, Salih ibn Ali of the Hirth, and Abdul Aziz ibn Said, Turki's younger brother, were all in opposition, though fortunately for Turki, not united. Turki was recognised as Sultan by the British in November 1871 (1288 AH), an advantage which Azzan ibn Qais had never had, though recognition of him was about to be forthcoming just before Turki supplanted him. It was not until 1875 (1292 AH) that Ibrahim ibn Qais made submission to the Sultan and thus began paving the way, as it were, for the very long service which his son Ahmad was to give the Sultan Said ibn Taimur, up to 1970 (1390 AH), as his Minister of the Interior. However, troubles between Hinawis and Ghafiris persisted, and in 1874 (1291 AH) Salih ibn Ali sacked Mutrah and attempted to take Muscat. This humiliation, together with ill health and the influence of an unscrupulous adviser named Numaish who quickly amassed a dubious fortune, prevented Turki from fulfilling early promise. In 1875 (1292 AH) he retired to Gwadur and his brother Abdul Aziz, with whom he had become reconciled, assumed the regency of Oman. In 1873 (1290 AH) Salim again attempted to return to Oman but was captured by HMS *Daphne* and sent to Hyderabad in Sind, an area with which Oman has had much contact through the ages. There he died disappointed in 1874 (1291 AH).

In 1875 (1292 AH) with health and spirits restored, Turki staged a surprising come-back, landing at Mutrah unannounced whilst his brother Abdul Aziz was away in the Wadi Samail, and resumed the rule. In 1877 (1294 AH) Salih ibn Ali and the *Mutawwain* accused Turki of "irreligiousness and laxity of morals" and launched another attack on the capital. The British responded to the Sultan's request for assistance, and HMS *Teazer* shelled the rebels in the *wadi* behind the town. This was enough to give Turki strength to carry on, but in 1883 (1301 AH) Salih ibn Ali decided to make a further supreme effort to depose Turki, in alliance with Abdul Aziz ibn Said.

They informed Colonel Miles, the British Political Agent, that an attack on Muscat was impending and requested that British subjects should be removed out of harm's way. Abdul Aziz himself led a bold night attack on the walls of Muscat, the attackers clothed in black to give them extra protection, and Turki went to the ramparts to rally the defence. The attack was repulsed and Abdul Aziz's forces fell back on Sidab on the out skirts. Turki then appealed to the British Political Agent, and after British subjects had taken to boats, HMS *Philomel* shelled the rebel positions. This, combined with the timely arrival of friendly shaikhs of the Hirth and Masakira, enabled Turki to win the day. His second son, Faisal, pursued the rebel and brought the tribes back to allegiance. In the latter part of this reign, Turki reverted to dependence on the Ghafiri tribes, who had won the battles of Dhank and Muscat for him, rather than the Hinawi tribes on whom he depended in his middle period. Turki used his own relations and other prominent and able men in his administration, including Said ibn Muhammad and a strong character of slave stock, Sulaiman ibn Suwailim. He had a reputation for sound judgement and was a good ruler, enjoying the friendship and regard of the British authorities in India, who presented him with two batteries of 12-pounder guns for the Muscat forts. He made a treaty in 1873 (1290 AH) with Sir Bartle Frere for the suppression of the slave trade and henceforth made sincere efforts to enforce it.

In 1879 (1297 AH) Dhofar was re-occupied by troops from northern Oman after an interval of fifty years. At the beginning of the nineteenth century Dhofar +had been ruled by Muhammad ibn Aqil Ajaibi, a former buccaneer and slave trader who governed it in a strangely enlightened manner for about twenty-five years. He was, however, assassinated in 1829 (1245 AH) and thereupon Said ibn Sultan sent a force to occupy Dhofar though, as the troops were required for service in east Africa, it did not stay long. Dhofar may earlier have been subject to the Ya'ruba Imams, but it is not clear how firmly their writ ran. At a much earlier period in History, the Hadhramaut as well as Dhofar had formed part of the Omani Ibadhi state. Although a separate Hadhrami Ibadhi state had persisted for a while, the Ibadhis had disappeared from south Arabia by the thirteenth century AD.

After Muhammad ibn Aqil's death, an American, Abdullah Lorleyd, who had been captured as a boy of ten at sea in one of Muhammad ibn Aqil's piracies and turned Muslim, established some degree of personal autonomy by organising daring expeditions against the Qara tribes. Nonetheless, after 1829 (1245 AH), the shaikhs of Dhofar seem always to have paid homage on the succession of a new Sultan in Muscat. Despite this, there was a strange interlude between 1875 (1292 AH) and 1879 (1297 AH) when Dhofar fell into the hands of Fadhl ibn Alawi, a Mopla priest expelled from India for his part in the Mopla rising of 1852 (1269 AH). The Dhofari shaikhs had apparently met him during a pilgrimage to Mecca, been impressed with his reputation for sanctity, and invited him to Dhofar, He quickly managed to gain temporal control and with remarkable effrontery sent a letter to the Sultan, Sayyid Turki, describing himself as the governor of Dhofar on behalf of the

Formal salutes were fired from ancient muzzle-loading cannon battery on the battlements of fort Mirani until 1973.

Ottoman Porte. However, his rule lasted only a brief period and in 1879 (1297 AH) a general revolution started by the Qara tribes forced him to leave the country.

Dhofar was regained for the Sultan by a sea expedition under Sulaiman ibn Suwailim, the ex-slave. Sulaiman ibn Suwailim's rule, exercised personally and through his son Ali, was heavy handed and the Al Khatir and Qara tribes made several attempts at rebellion. Meantime, Fadhl ibn Alawi continued to intrigue with the Ottoman *Wali* of Basra – who at one time sent a Turkish flag and a commission to Salalah – and with the Khedive in Egypt to stage a come-back.

A further rebellion lasted from 1895 (1313 AH) until 1897 (1315 AH) and the British Resident in the Persian Gulf accompanied the Sultan's forces in HMS *Cossack* to recover control. Thereafter, Omani administration improved markedly, but Fadhl again tried, unsuccessfully, to persuade the British Government to recognise him as the ruler of Dhofar with "a national flag, green with pentagonal ventre".

In 1888 (1306 AH) Turki died, succeeded by his son Faisal, then twenty-three, and even Salih ibn Ali, who had caused so much trouble to Turki, responded loyally. Faisal had married in 1881 his cousin Aliya, the daughter of Thuwaini, and this, along with continuance of the Zanzibar subsidy, helped to consolidate his position. It was not long, however, before opposition arose. Faisal's uncle, Abdul Aziz, attempted to take Muscat, and the notorious Hamad ibn Jahafi also joined him. Dissensions between the Hinawis and Ghafiris grew in intensity and tribal fighting broke out. In 1895 (1313 AH), a serious attempt at rebellion had the support of the new Sultan of Zanzibar. Until then, relations between the two Sultanates had been cordial, but in 1893 (1311 AH) Hamad ibn Thuwaini who had spent his earlier years in Oman, where he had many friends, succeeded Ali ibn Said in Zanzibar. A stream of Omanis made their way to Zanzibar in 1894 (1249312 AH) and they encouraged Hamad to take over the Sultanate in Oman.

The rebels took Muscat and held it for a while until an accommodation was reached with British help. The rebellion, however, had alarmed Faisal who strengthened the defences of Muscat and Mutrah, but his difficulties were increased by shortage of money and the treachery of his *Wazir*, who was secretly involved with Shaikh Salih ibn Ali. Nonetheless he gradually expanded his influence again.

It was not long before Oman became a bone of contention between Britain and France, after the French and Russians had determined on concerted effort to weaken British influence around the Indian Ocean. The main Franco-British disagreements were over use of the French flag to protect Omani vessels – a practice to which Faisal as well as the British objected for it enabled slave-trading to be resumed, although this was not the French intention –, the French desire to open a coaling station at Muscat, and the arms trade.

At the end of the century a kind of diplomatic duel for influence was fought out between the British Consul, Major (later Sir Percy) Cox and the French Consul, M. Ottavi. The British prevailed and Sultan Faisal revoked his gift to the French of a coaling station at Bandar Jissuh, near Muscat. A compromise solution, however, provided for two coaling stations, one French and one British, of equal area and identical design in Muscat Bay, and the buildings erected by each country were only knocked down in 1972 when the new Oman naval base was built on the site. Further differences between Britain and France were only cleared up as the *entente cordiale* developed and after reference to the Hague

Tribunal of the flag dispute.

In 1901 Muscat was brought into telegraphic communication with the world by the connection of a cable from Muscat to Jask, which linked in with the Indo-European telegraph system. Although Oman remained independent, Britain's influence grew with the visit in 1903 of Lord Curzon, then Viceroy of India, and, following an outbreak of bubonic plague, with the British Agency taking charge of health and quarantine in Muscat.

Faisal's administration ran into considerable debt and his financial difficulties were multiplied by closure of the Indian mint, which caused him to mint *pice* in Muscat when the scarcity of Indian *pice* caused hardship to the poorer people. However, Faisal had no serious rival to the throne and his administration improved as he grew older.

In 1913 (1332 AH) Faisal, whose reign had latterly been relatively uneventful, died and was succeeded by Sayyid Taimur, the offspring of his union with Sayyida Aliya. In the same year the tribes of the Interior, uniting again under an elected Imam, Salim ibn Rashid al Kharusi, rebelled. Taimur, who had been groomed to succeed his father was thus immediately faced with a serious situation, particularly as Hinawis and Ghafiris were united in their opposition to him.

In 1915 (1333 AH) the tribes of the Interior, led by the Imam, attacked the capital with the aid of Isa ibn Salih of the Hirth in the Sharqiya, but were repulsed by 700 British Indian troops at Bait al Falaj. A conference at Seeb between Taimur and the Imam in the same year was abortive as the latter refused to hand back the forts in the Wadi Samail which, captured in 1913 (1332 AH), were essential to Muscat's prosperity. The Sultan's subsequent demonstration of his ability to tax produce from the Interior led to a compromise in what has erroneously been termed " The Treaty of Seeb" on 25th September 1920 (1339 AH). Under this the Sultan agreed not to interfere in "internal affairs" in central Oman; not to impose taxation in excess of 5 per cent on goods brought from the Interior; and to allow the tribes to enter Muscat and the coastal towns in freedom and safety. The tribes on the other had agreed to remain in a state of peace and amity with the Sultan's Government. This administrative *modus vivendi* worked satisfactorily during the Imamate of

Sultan Said bin Taimur, father of Sultan Qaboos, reigned from 1932 to 1970 – a period of which the first decades were lean times of the Sultanate.

Muhammad ibn Abdulla al Khalili, who succeeded Salim al Kharusi as Imam when the latter was murdered in 1920 (1339 AH), but things went badly wrong on his death in 1954 (1374 AH). Sayyid Taimur's reign, like his father's, was characterised by financial difficulties accentuated by the trade depression of 1923 (1342 AH) and 1924. He appointed Mr Bertram Thomas, the well known author and Arabist, first as Financial Adviser, and later as *Wazir*, to help him overcome these difficulties. However, Taimur, who never had much stomach for the throne, abdicated in 1932 (1351 AH) in favour of his son, Sayyid Said ibn Taimur and lived in retirement in Bombay until his death in 1965 (1385 AH).Sayyid Said took over a country still in debt and by his own sustained and patient efforts largely restored the situation. However, his careful stewardship, which enabled him to hand over the state's finances in a flourishing condition on the succession of Sultan Qaboos in 1970 (1390 AH), eventually alienated him from the people of Oman. The first part of Said's reign was relatively uneventful, but the death of the Imam in 1954 (1374 AH), combined with the need for oil exploration in the Interior, led to an internal crisis which was heightened by Saudi

A view of Mutrah before Sultan Qaboos's accession. The picture shows the walls of the old city, whose gates were opened at dawn and shut at sunset even after the wall had been breached to make a motor road. The gate collapsed in 1973.

aspirations in the area. The new Imam Ghalib ibn Ali attempted to establish central Oman as a separate principality independent of the Sultan and no doubt his dream of the possibility of oil wealth was a factor. In December 1955 (1375 AH) the Sultan's forces responded by entering the main inhabited areas of the Interior without resistance and the Imam was permitted to retire to his own village.

However, his brother Talib, perhaps the more forceful of the two, escaped to Saudi Arabia and thence to Cairo. In 1957 (1377 AH) he returned and gained a considerable following, including Shaikh Sulaiman ibn Himyar, the paramount Shaikh of the Bani Riyam. Although they were defeated at a battle at Firq in August this year, following British intervention, their leaders maintained themselves for a considerable time in the mountain fastnesses and it was not until January 1959 (1379 AH) that they were driven out with the help of the British Special Air Service Regiment. Even then the "Question of Oman" remained a live issue in Arab and international politics, and was inscribed yearly on the agenda of the United Nations, to which Said steadfastly refused to send any representation.The matter was finally resolved in 1971 (1391 AH) when the Sultanate of Oman under Qaboos, after other countries had ceased to back the separatist movement, was admitted to the Arab League and to the United Nations. Earlier, the need to define boundaries for the purposes of oil concessions had involved Oman in dispute with Saudi Arabia, and this to some extent conditioned Saudi Arabia's attitude towards the dissident Imam. The Wahhabi incursions into Oman in the nineteenth century had never left them with any substantial control, and they had been turned out of the Buraimi area in 1870 (1287 AH) never to return until 1950 (1370 AH). In that year a Saudi force under Turki ibn Ataishan occupied the village of Hamasa, one of the villages in the Buraimi complex of oases, of which six fell within Abu Dhabi and three in the Sultanate. Sultan Said was minded to throw them out and mustered the tribes at Sohar with the intention of marching on Buraimi in force.

He was, however, restrained by the British Government and the case was put to arbitration – a process which dragged on unsatisfactorily until October 1955 (1375 AH), when Sultanate troops and the Trucial Oman Scouts ejected the Saudis.

It was perhaps Said's tragedy that after oil revenues had begun to accrue to Oman on an increasingly generous scale in 1967 (1387 AH), he was unable to abandon the habit of economy and careful husbandry which had been imposed on him at an earlier stage by hard necessity. He did initiate some plans for development but they were too small-scale to satisfy the widespread aspirations of his people for education and for medical and other services and amenities.

This, combined with the isolation he had imposed on himself by remaining in Salalah and never visiting northern Oman after 1958 (1328 AH), and the rebellion which started in Dhofar in 1965 (1384 AH), made the events of 1970 (1390 AH) and the takeover by Sultan Qaboos inevitable. Said died in exile in London in 1972 (1392 AH).

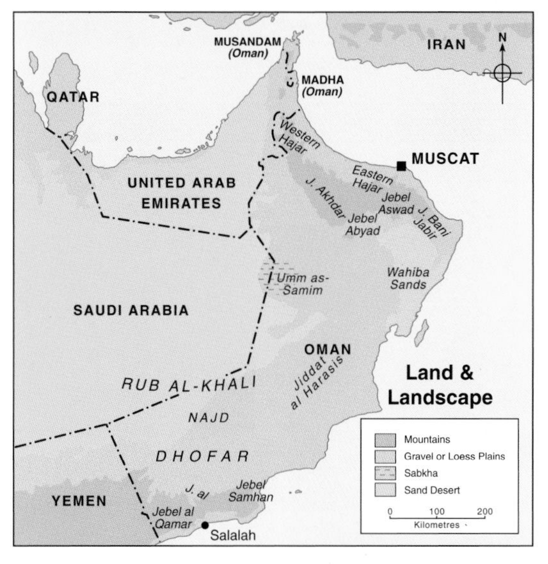

3
The Land and the Landscape

Oman's terrain is rich and varied. Its contrasts are remarkable. Take the majestic heights of the Hajar mountains; the great emptiness of the Rub' al-Khali's dunes; Dhofar's hills which turn lush and green in the monsoon rains, and its southern steppes; the towering cliffs of the southerly littoral; trim villages set in the clefts of wadis *and girded by palm-groves; and a thousand miles of coastline varying from miles of sandy beach to the rock-girt coves of Musandam and Muscat itself.*

Still water in the shelter of a rockface (far left)*, at Wadi Shab, is a sudden gift that occurs repeatedly in northern Oman. Besides its magnificent mountains and cultivated areas, Oman's terrain includes sand deserts* (top left)*, vast plains where camels graze* (above left)*, and a rugged coastline* (left)*. The map shows the distribution of the types of terrain.*

Geography, Climate & Geology

OMAN is a land of stark beauty and contrasts. Magnificent mountains of many shades of red, grey and green stand out jagged against the clear blue sky. Flat plains stretch as far as the eye can see. Neat villages girded by extensive green palm groves are serenely set in barren *wadis* and along the ocean shore – formerly cut off from each other but now linked by a fine network of roads. Deserts roll away in the Rub' al Khali – the Empty Quarter – that great sand sea with mighty waves of dunes rising to six hundred feet or more in height. The coastline changes character from hundreds of miles of flat beach to the rocky inlets around Muscat and the dramatic, unique mountainous Musandam peninsula – Ruus al Jibal – with its bare fjord-like scenery. The hills of Dhofar, catching the south-west monsoon from May to September, turn green like no other part of Arabia; and the cliffs rise majestic along Dhofar's coast.

A land of 309,500 sq. kms, Oman's 1700-km coastline sweeps in a great crescent south-westwards from Jazirat as Salamah in the extreme north – where Oman is separated by only 55 kms from mainland Iran across the Straits of Hormuz – to its southern border with the Republic of Yemen. It stretches through 26° of latitude from below 17° N. to above 16° N. broken only by a curious band of territory 90 kms wide belonging for historical reasons to the United Arab Emirates. Oman is thus an important part of the bridge between the great landmasses of Africa and Asia. The 1993 national census put the population at just over 2 million people, increasing at a rate of 3.5 per cent per annum, with the average number of children in a family being 7.4. The country is rather sparsely populated with a great concentration in the capital area, which stretches from Seeb in the north to Quriyat in the south. Here lie the centres of government, commerce and industry in a huge area of impressive buildings and beautiful plantings of trees, shrubs and flowers blending with the natural environment. The capital area's population was measured at over 622,000 with another 539,000 Omanis living along Al Batinah coast.

Below*: seamen of the Musandam peninsula have traditionally traded up the Gulf and across the Straits of Hormuz.*

Geographical Divisions

Traditionally there were five *wilayat*, or Governorates, in northern Oman which reflected geographical areas. These were Batinah, based on Sohar; Sharqiyah, based on Samad; Dhahirah, based on Ghabbi near Ibri; Sir, based on Nizwa; and al Jauf, based on al Buraymi (Buraimi). However, topography and cli-

Oman's most northerly point, Khasab, the administrative centre of Musandam, is also the Arabian peninsula's Land's End – set in a natural harbour ringed by mountains. The Wali *presides from his fort,* above, *over a population largely of Shihuh tribesmen and mariners.*

mate divide Oman somewhat differently – indeed into seven zones which affect the distribution of wildlife.

Firstly, the **Northern Mountains** which stretch for 500 kms in a mighty sweeping curve running roughly north-west to south-east from Cape Musandam nearly to Ras al Hadd. In Musandam – its name means "anvil", on which the waves constantly strike their hammer blows – the mountains fall precipitously into the loch-like inlets. Further south the Hajar range is divided into two – the western (Al Hajar al Gharbi) and the eastern (Al Hajar ash Sharqi) which, dominated by the limestone massif of the Jebel Akhdar, rises to 2980 m, the highest point in eastern Arabia. The Arabs liken the Jebel Akhdar to a backbone, calling the area which lies on the Gulf of Oman Al Batinah, or "stomach", and the area to the west Adh Dhahirah, or "back". A number of great *wadi* passes run broadly east-west through the Hajar range from the sea to the desert. The Wadi al Ham is in the UAE sector, and among the most significant to the south are the Wadi al Qor, the Wadi al Hawasinah, the Wadi al Jizi and Wadi Samail. The Wadi Samail is the largest and most striking and is regarded as the major "divide" between Al Hajar al Gharbi and Al Hajar ash Sharqi. Important towns and villages include Nizwa on the west and Rostaq on the east. Both are former capitals of Oman. They lie in the hills below the central massif surrounded by enormous date plantations, watered by the ancient and sophisticated *falaj* – water channel – system which also feeds the settlements lying much further from the hills. To the west of Al Hajar ash Sharqi and south of Al Hajar al Gharbi lies the Sharqiya area with its many settlements, such as Ibra, Al Mintirib and Al Mudaybi, lying on the plain at various distances from the mountains.

The second area comprises the **Coastal Plains**, which are arid where the mountains are somewhat distant. However, the well cultivated Batinah coastal plain, built up over centuries by the outwash from the many *wadis* descending from the mountains, stretches for 270 kms from the north-west to Muscat and varies in width from three to thirty kilometres. This was traditionally the major agricultural and date-growing area and the palm gardens were watered by wells drawing from the subterranean run-off from the hills. Heavy pumping in recent years by mechanical pumps has given rise to a salinity problem in this area. The natural vegetation here consists of thorny acacias – particularly *Acacia tortilis* and *Acacia ehrenbergiana*.

Further south the Jaalan lies on the sea-coast between Al Hajar ash Sharqi and the Wahibah sands (Ramlat al Wahaybah). The ancient seaport of Sur lies in the north of this area and to the west on the edge of the sands are the important settlements of Bilad Bani bu Hassan and Bilad Bani bu Ali.

In the Dhofar Governorate the cultivated Salalah plain extends 50 kms from Taqah in the east to Raysut in the west. The population of Dhofar was put at near 175,000 by the 1993 census with some 80,000 concentrated around Salalah itself.

The Hajar range, stretching in a mighty sweeping curve from Musandam to Ras al Hadd, dominates the geography of northern Oman, peaks rising to 10,000 feet. By tenacity and ingenuity, Omanis have built for themselves a life against the flanks of the mountains. The vertebrae of the range are divided by deep wadis*, like Wadi Bani Khalid (*below*).*

Thirdly, an **Alluvial Outwash Gravel Plain** lies inland between Al Hajar al Gharbi and the sand desert trailing away to the west. It stretches from Al Buraimi to meet the central gravel desert to the south. It contains many towns and settlements, most of them close to the mountains, such as Ibri and Dank in the north and those in the Sharqiya, which depend on extended *falaj* systems. To the west of the *wadis* and south of Yibal, one of Oman's producing oilfields, lies an area of quicksands, Umm as Samim, near the border with Saudi Arabia – a vast salt-lake when flooded, and treacherous mud flat (*sabkha*) at other times. Wilfred Thesiger, the first European known to have seen them, described them thus: "The ground, of white gypsum powder, was covered with a sand-sprinkled crust of salt, through which protruded occasional dead twigs of *arad* salt bush. These scattered bushes marked the firm land; farther out only a slight darkening of the surface indicated a bog below. I took a few steps forwards and Staiyun (a guide from the Duru tribe) put his hand on my arm saying 'Don't go any nearer – it is dangerous.' I wondered how dangerous it really was, but when I questioned him he assured me that several people, including an Awamir raiding party, had perished in these sands, and he told me once again he had himself watched a flock of goats disappear beneath the surface." The extent of this phenomenon was formerly said by the desert Arabs to be a two days' march in every direction and only a few Duru were aware of the safe routes. Nowadays people in four-wheeled vehicles drive across it in a matter of hours.

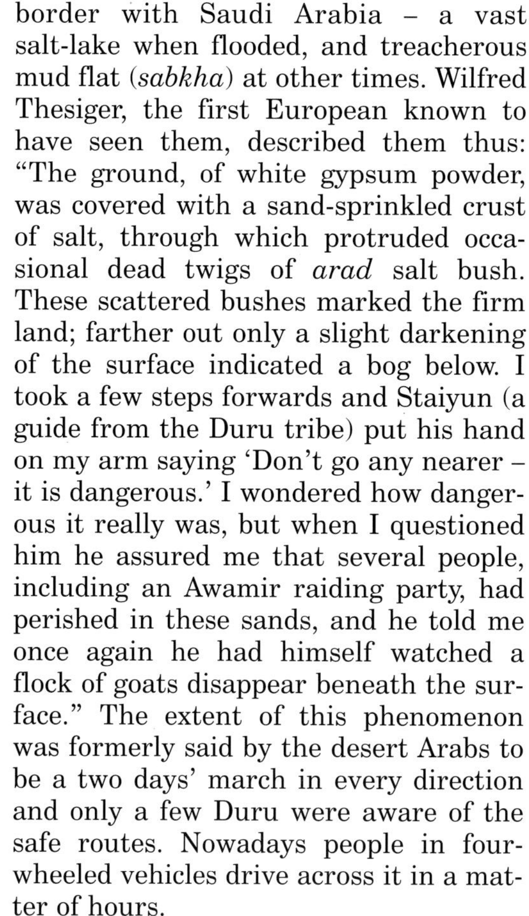

Fourthly, the **Central Gravel Desert**, in which there are small hills in places, is an arid steppe with an elevation of 100-200 m which sweeps south-west across the Najd north of the mountains of Dhofar to the Yemen border. It is the largest and driest zone and experiences extremes of hot and cold. Jiddat al Harasis, a limestone plateau where the Harasis *Bedu* live, lies in this region and there are scattered oases watered from artesian wells, some of which may be 36 fathoms deep. According to Bertram Thomas, local lore holds that such water holes called *khasfa* were made by "a falling star and not the sons of Adam". Thesiger in 1956 described the wildlife he saw in the Jiddat al Harasis: "Gazelle grazed among the flat topped acacia bushes and once we saw a distant herd of oryx looking very white against the dark gravel of the plain. There were lizards about eighteen inches in length, which scuttled across the ground. They had disc-shaped tails, and in consequence the Arabs called them 'The Father of the Dollar' (Abu Qirsh)." Sadly the oryx were wiped out and the gazelle decimated by unauthorised hunting parties, though happily an Oryx Project described later and conservation measures have now restored the situation.

Despite the erratic rains (except in Dhofar) Oman's northern mountains guard a few precious pools of permanent water, such as at Bilad Sayt (above). *The management of the alluvial* wadis (left), *sometimes in violent flood, for permanent agriculture, is one of the northern villagers' outstanding skills.*

Fifthly, the **Sand Deserts.** The great sand desert, the Rub' al Khali, reaches into Oman from Saudi Arabia. Further to the east adjacent to the coast lie the Wahiba Sands, an area of some 9400 sq.kms. The Wahiba Sands stretch on the seaward side from near Ras al Hadd and from Mudhayrib in the Sharqiya to a little south of Nuqdah on the coast in the Gulf of Masirah with dunes rising to some two hundred feet – rusty red at the base and honey-coloured higher up. Under the sands lies the largest area of aeolianite rock deposit in the world. The area was the subject of a very detailed scientific survey carried out between 1985 and 1987 by the Royal Geographical Society in London with the active support of the Oman Government.

Sixthly, the **Dhofar Highlands** stretch westwards from Hasik on the Halaaniyaat (formerly Kuria Muria) bay for 290 kms to the Yemen border. The chain comprises Jebel Samhan, which reaches 1812 m, Jebel Qara, which reaches 960 m, and Jebel al Qamar, which rises to 1400 m. The northern edge of these mountains slopes gently towards the Najd desert area and the steeper southern slopes, at the base of which there are springs, fall away into the sea.

Dhofar has a number of unique aspects. Between May and September the area is affected by the south-west monsoon, *khareef*, which blankets the south-facing escarpments in moisture laden clouds. This produces an atypical area of woodland some 240 kms long but only some 3 to 30 kms wide, which turns the south-facing slopes bright green for a short season making the area look like rolling downland, though the north-facing slopes remain relatively bald. The vegetation of Dhofar varies greatly between the coast and the dry steppe of the Najd.

Salalah, the capital, is nearly a thousand kilometres by road from Muscat. This road runs through terrain which until recently was the haunt only of the *Bedu* and oil exploration parties. Now, however, it is tarmacadamed all the way both to Muscat and the UAE. It has replaced the sea as the principal means of communication for passengers and commercial goods, though air communications are now open to internal and international flights.

Seventhly, there are the **Coasts**. The coastline is emergent, except for the coastal cliffs, and often has a shelf reef exposed at low tide. This is backed by small dunes bound by grasses and other halophytes, which can live off brackish water. Intertidal flats are extensive in such areas as the Barr al Hikman peninsula and Ad Duqm, and the creek mouths of many *wadis*. Some are lined with reeds (*Phragmites*), mangrove (*Avicennia*) and

bulrushes (*Typha*). Masirah is Oman's largest offshore island and the Juzor al Halaaniyaat lie off shore in the south of the Arabian Sea. Another group is Juzor ad Daymaniyat in the north of the Gulf of Oman. There are also many other smaller islands, notably off the Musandam peninsula.

Towns

The *raison d'être* of the towns on the coast and of the towns of the Interior differ markedly. The coastal towns have for countless generations provided a livelihood for fishermen, sailors and merchants involved in the import and export trade and pearling. On the other hand, the main towns of the Interior are dependent on important agricultural areas and form centres for the despatch of produce to the coast and the receipt of goods for distribution in the Interior. Some towns too, such as Nizwa, Rostaq and Muscat, in the past acquired special significance because of their military strength – there were massive forts at all three of these places – and because they were all capitals of Oman at various periods.

One small coastal town which epitomises Oman is Tiwi. Ibn Batuta, who visited Oman in the fourteenth century AD, described Tiwi, which lies between Qalhat and Sur, as "one of the loveliest of villages and most striking in beauty, with flowing streams and abundant orchards". The Wadi Tiwi, whose outlet to the ocean the

To the east and south of the northern uplands, the terrain gives way to arid steppes, and then the great sand desert of the Rub' al Khali encroaches. Yet no part of Oman's territory is unpeopled.

settlement straddles, is one of the most remarkable in Oman and gives an indication of how extensively some of the other *wadi*s may have been cultivated in the past. It is a *wadi* with constantly flowing water and both sides are thick with palms for miles inland. The unique feature, however, is that the cultivated areas are on numerous small terraces which in the early 1970s climbed to a greater height above the *wadi* bed than in any other valley in the country.

Climate

Oman is situated at the margin of two moisture-bearing air masses, one coming from the Mediterranean and the other from the Indian Ocean, and in consequence rainfall is irregular. The Mediterranean currents sometimes fade out, which results in lower precipitation than usual, whilst the summer rain brought by the Indian Ocean air currents may not materialise if their track in any particular year does not quite reach the Oman peninsula. Sometimes, however, cyclonic storms occur. Although December and January tend to be the months with the heaviest rainfall, the pattern of precipitation is erratic. For

Southern Dhofar, in contrast to the rest of the Sultanate, alone rejoices in an annual monsoon, which turns parts of its coastal jebel *into territory which a casual glance could mistake for New Guinea (as* below*). Most productively – though the green will later wither – it produces rolling pasture land for cattle and sheep.*

instance, in 1972 total rainfall was 108 mm, of which 92.95 mm fell in February. In Muscat itself the average rainfall is 90.3 mm, though in some years this amount is greatly exceeded. In the Jebel Akhdar, the rainfall may reach 250 mm or even 400-500 mm in an exceptional year. In Salalah, the highest rainfalls ever recorded have in fact been in May and November.

Sometimes several inches fall within a few hours, turning the dry beds into rushing torrents which sweep everything before them – trees, boulders, goats and other animals, and sometimes people and cars. The roiling water may subside after a few hours but leaves a wake of desolation, although of course any rain benefits

the country by recharging the water tables. A particularly tragic example of flash flooding occurred in June 1890 when a cyclonic storm hit Oman, and between midnight on the 4th and midnight on the 5th, 11.25 inches (28.3 mm) of rain fell. The waters rose with such violence that seven hundred people were drowned. The Imam himself, al Warith ibn Kaab, was drowned in 807 AD (192 AH) near Nizwa with seventy of his people; all were washed away as they tried to cross the Wadi Kalbuh.

Climatically, Oman has enjoyed a less savoury reputation than it deserves. The Arab geographer Abdul Razak wrote of Muscat in the fourteenth century with some hyperbole: "The heat...was so intense that it burned the marrow in the bones, the sword in its scabbard melted into wax and the gems which adorned the handle of the dagger were reduced to coal. In the plains the chase became a matter of perfect ease for the desert was strewn with roasted gazelles."

Both Alexander Hamilton and John Ovington, who visited Oman in the early

As the wadis *approach the sea, they spread their bounty and make (as at* Wadi Tiwi *above, north of Sur) for famously beautiful sites.*

eighteenth century, referred to people cooking fish in the heat of summer on the dark rocks surrounding Muscat. Grattan Geary, the editor of the *Times of India*, who visited Muscat in 1878, remarked that when the *Shamal*, the hot wind from the desert, blows, sleepers were watered during the night like plants with a watering pot. Other devices were also used to keep people cool before air-conditioning was introduced, and it was the custom of the people of Muscat to sleep on the roof in a damp sheet. Mrs Cox, the wife of the British Political Agent at the turn of the nineteenth century, gave herself pneumonia by an *excès de zèle* in substituting a blanket for a sheet!

These literary passages and similar ones referring to Muscat as the hottest place on earth indicate how people felt in the past about Oman's climate. The facts are that there were two distinct periods – the hot summer months from May to September and the cool winter months from November to March. The daily average maximum temperature in Muscat may reach 41°C in the height of the summer, in late June and July, whereas by contrast the highest daily average temperatures recorded in Salalah in Dhofar reach only just under 30°C in the hottest month, May. The minimum average temperature for Muscat is 16.3°C and for Salalah, 18.5°C. The relative humidity in Muscat ranges between 94 per cent in July and 20 per cent in May, whilst in Salalah it varies between 96 per cent in August and 54 per cent in December.

Geology

Formation of the Land

Over 800 million years ago tectonic plates squeezed very old oceanic sediment and rock together to create the continental crust now lying beneath Oman and Arabia. Oman now comprises part of the south-east of the Arabian plate not far from where the Eurasian and Indian plates meet; but it is not at present affected by that clashing and separation of plates, which give rise to earthquakes and tremors in neighbouring countries. For the last 20 million years the land has been essentially dormant.

Oman's dramatic landscape, however, does take its present shape from the squeezings, bucklings and foldings of the crust at different times in the past. Crusts were folded into mountains, some of which eroded to become flat again, and past sequences of plate movements changed Oman's position on the surface of the globe, swinging it from the equator to sub-polar latitudes. With general changes in the earth's climate this has meant that Oman has at some times experienced the glaciers of Ice Ages and at others steamy tropical heat. Oman's last great pluvial period was before and after the Pleistocene Ice Ages, that is, between two million and 10,000 years ago. Global sea level has varied at different times by some 150 m above or below the present level. Only 20,000 years ago, at the end of the most recent Ice Age, the world sea level was 130 m lower than now. Thus at times much of Oman would have been submerged whilst at other times the land area was greater. The

Behind Sohar's long foreshore lay Oman's great mediaeval trading city.

shelves now round Oman's coasts have traces of ancient river channels to demonstrate this and the edge of the marine shelf slopes to the deep ocean floor 3,000 m below.

As recently as about 9,000 years ago the gulf now separating Arabia and Iran lay above sea level, as it had for several millennia – lowland with lakes and rivers. The post-Ice Age invasion of the sea was the last major episode in the complex geological history of the area. There have at times been environments supporting a multitude of living things and others which were virtually lifeless. Some of the granite and metamorphic rocks in and around Muscat and to the west of Salalah, including Juzor al Halaaniyaat, are survivors of the very oldest Basement period dating from 650-800 million years ago, though Jebel Ja'alan, dating from between 850 and 1,000 million years ago is probably Oman's oldest rock.

Many of Oman's rocks were formed by molten magma surging from deep below the earth's surface when the land's situation at plate margins gave rise to great upheavals. This phenomenon produced the massive crystalline bodies of rock with uneven surfaces, which feature largely in Oman's landscape. The Samail Ophiolite in the Al Hajar range comprises the largest surface of crystalline rocks. Sedimentary rocks, frequently upturned, reversed, buckled and laid on their sides, also abound. They were produced by rock erosion or by chemical and biological processes which create limestones, dolomites and gypsum. Each stratum could be laid down over widely differing periods and thus one layer might have been laid down by a single tide or a whole Ice Age. Such sedimental structures contain many fossils of animals and plants living at the time; these are found even on the top of the Jebel Akhdar.

Mighty upfoldings in the earth's crust resulting in massive surface changes created the mountains in the north and south 30 to 40 million years ago in the Oligocene period – the most recent phase of stress caused by plate movements affecting Oman. The jagged shape of all Oman's mountains demonstrates the different processes of erosion which have attacked them since their creation.

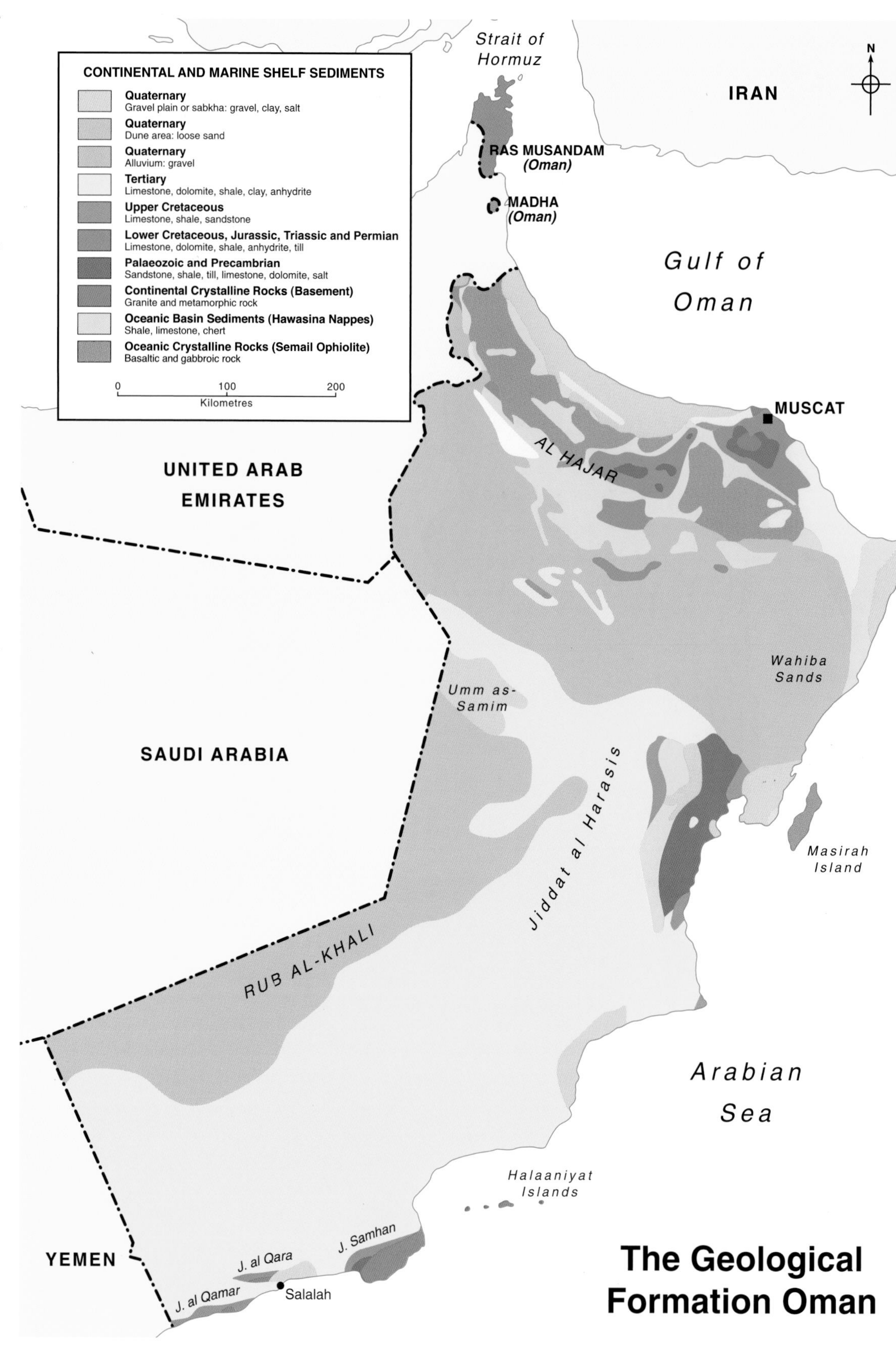

The Geological Formation Oman

Torrential water was a phenomenon of one past epoch and the great boulders now lying in the wadis could only have been brought there by massive flows of water. Sun and wind have also been major causes of erosion.

Mountains, Intermediate Zone and Plains

The magnificent al Hajar range consists of very hard, resistant sedimentary rocks, formerly deeply buried, and softer sedimentary rocks and crystalline igneous rocks, of which serpentine is the most conspicuous. The Jebel Akhdar, where the highest peaks are, is composed of very dense limestone in thick beds, for the softer sedimentary rocks disintegrated more quickly and now constitute the lower ground. The crystalline rocks tend to form jagged but lower peaks. The Jebel Akhdar was essentially created by one large upfolding, out of which the great amphitheatres of the Ghubra and the Wadi Sahtan bowls and the Wadi Mistal have been carved by erosion. The crest of this range is formed by a great plateau, which gradually falls away south-westward. The summit is thus as easy of access from this side as it is difficult from the north-east. In the mountains of the Musandam peninsula with their spectacular fjords, which have no counterpart in Arabia or Iran, "Musandam limestone" of the Jurassic or Lower Cretaceous age, much folded and 5,000 feet thick, predominates.

The Dhofar range consists of one large, gently tilted slab of Tertiary limestones, which slopes northwards. The southern edge falls to the coast sharply in a series of crustal blocks, and erosion has laid open many other sedimentary rocks down to the basement rock. This face of the slab now forms the 100-metre escarpment of the Jebel Qara range, which catches the south-west monsoon and turns these south-facing slopes into gentle green rolling country for a few months each year. The northern part drains away in wadis into the Rub' al- Khali. It is not surprising that these great ranges contain considerable mineral deposits: copper, asbestos, magnesite, potash, phosphate, coal, chromite and manganese.

Between the mountains and the plain, eroded rock debris spreads out in great fans of alluvial deposits, consisting of large sedimentary material which become gradually smaller as the fans spread out away from the mountains. The configuration of the rocks demonstrates former water channels and attests to Oman's more rainy past. High terraces remain from former times and cross-sections reveal how gravels have become cemented in rock: lime-rich waters slowly evaporating after each *wadi* flood turn into a lime cement which welds boulders and pebbles together.

The plains which form large parts of central Oman are formed from horizontal mid-Tertiary limestones of the Oligocene and Miocene periods, the surface representing sea-bed levels of the time when the limestones were laid down in the form of calcareous marine sands and muds.

Many of the harder limestone pebbles which lie on the surface have been formed into beautiful shapes – ventifacts – by dustladen wind.

In some areas the surface has been disturbed by salt plugs – diapirs – which are pillars of salt coming up from six or more kilometres below the surface in the ancient Huqf group of sedimentary rocks. Salt pans or *sabkha* are also formed when temporary lakes caused by spasmodic heavy rainfall dry out. The most notorious of these is Umm as Samim, "the mother of poisons", called this because the salt crust of this enormous *sabkha* is so treacherous to cross. Sand covers many areas of the plains, in particular the eastern sand sea known as the Wahibah Sands. This, studied in depth by scientists working under the aegis of the Royal Geographical Society in London, illustrates the complex geological past. The western sand sea is the fringe of the Rub' al-Khali.

Curiosities

Oman has a number of geological curiosities which merit mention. The most spectacular is the great limestone cave – believed to be the largest in the world and created by rain water dissolving the rock – at Hayl Salma in the Al Hajar Ash Sharqi. The seven holes by which it can be entered are known by local people as Khoshilat. It has now become known as Majlis al-Jinn. There are a number of large craters such as Lehob (Habhab) in the Jiddat al Harasis and Tawi Atair in Dhofar. Scattered fragments of meteorites and fulgurites have been identified. There are also geodes, the largest and best formed of which occur west of Thamrait in Dhofar. These are small hollow rocks lined with crystals, hard balls lying loose in stony desert.

Flora

Rainfall changes the aspect of Oman. Many of the desert plants are shortlived annuals, the seeds of which are resistant to drought. But after heavy rains, which literally make the desert bloom, small plants and flowers appear in profusion including northern type flowers such as tiny wild pansy and cowslip. As the Arabian peninsula was separated by the Red Sea from the African continent only in recent geological times, many of northern Oman's plants are African in character and origin. The dominant *Acacia* for instance, with long roots like those of other large trees of the area reaching subterranean water even in summer, spread into Arabia before this separation.

There are two strange plants of this zone. First the 2-5 m tree called locally *Shakhr,* or *'Usher* in other parts of Arabia. This is *Calatropis procera* which grows in very poor soils and when it bleeds, produces a copious white liquid like latex. The other is *Cistanche phelypaea* of the Broomrape family (*Orobranchaceae*) which is leafless. It emerges after heavy rain, drawing its sustenance from a stem attaching to the roots of other plants. It produces a fragrant spike of yellow flowers and grows up to a metre in height.

The mountain *wadis* at heights of between 350 and 1,050 metres form a distinct zone from the lower levels and desert, though *Acacia*, *Ziziphus spina-christi* (which produces edible fruits called *nabag*) and *Prosopis* extend into this zone. Where water is close to the surface, oleander (*Nerium mascatense*) abounds in the *wadis* together with grasses, bulrushes and sedge. The *falajes* of cultivated areas contain maidenhair and *Pteris* ferns and in early spring peach, apricot and almond blossom may be seen together with blue and red pimpernel (*Anagallis arvensis – Primulaceae*), dandelion and other *Compositae*. There are *Tecomella* with their golden flowers and *Acridocarpus* to be seen at this level.

Above the *wadis* through the mountains, the vegetation on the steep slopes changes. Acacias are more stunted and the leafless fleshy *Euphorbia larica* begins to appear – green with white sap. Species of *Convolvulus* and *Lavandula subnuda* with its violet flowers are widespread. Higher still, between 1,200 and 1,300 m on the northern face of the Jebel Akhdar, *Reptonia mascatense* (*But*) and *Olea africana* (wild olive; *'utm*), which abound at higher levels still, begin to appear. Juniper (*Juniperus macropoda*) grows from 1,500 m and is widely dominant around the summits. In the intermediate levels there are *Sageretia spiciflora* (*nimt*) with its edible fruit; *Euryops*, a bright yellow member of the *Compositae* family, *Ebenus* with its yellow flowers and *Dodonaea* with the dwarf fern *Cheilanthes* growing in the shade of boulders. Other plants here are *Viola cinerea* and *Dionysia mira*, bright yellow and primula-like, which is associat-

The mountains, above, *tiered behind Ibra as the sun descends. Acacias grow strongly in the plain. The Wadi Mistal is both watered and protected by the steep crags that enclose it – the site of palm groves and maize (*above right*).*

ed with Oman's unique animal, the *tahr*. Consequently local people call it *shajarat al wa'l*.

Junipers grow to 10 m in height above 2300 m with tussock grasses and low shrubs in between. Several of the plants at higher levels have an Asiatic rather than an African origin, tending to prove the existence of a land bridge until relatively recent times. Henna is produced from the safflower, *Carthamus tinctorius*, (known locally as *Shawran)* which grows wild, originally having been cultivated in and around villages. Similarly aromatic myrtle, *Myrtus communis*, is found in and close to mountain villages.

On the Jebel there are also cotton plants, wild potatoes and several species related to alpine plants, which are apparently survivals from the last Ice Age. There are also northern and Indian plant species including primula, violet, and honeysuckle.

The vegetation of Dhofar varies greatly between the coast and the dry steppe of the Najd. There are six broad bands. Firstly, the **coastal plain,** which is rather bare except where farmed. In the past it was widely cultivated, producing a great variety of crops and vegetables, of which considerable quantities were for instance grown for British troops in Iraq in the 1914-1918 war. Whereas the date palm is distinctive of northern Oman, the coconut palm reigns supreme over the Salalah plain. After rain which – unlike the monsoon mist – is spasmodic, the whole plain turns green with herbs and grasses, notably *Dichatium micrathum*. In cracks between the rocks *Euphorbia hadramautica* is plentiful.

Secondly, near the **mountains** there are scattered groups of *Acacia tortilis* and in the foothills the scenery is dominated by an umbrella-shaped evergreen, *Boscia arabica*.

Thirdly, the woodland vegetation on the **escarpment** consists chiefly of many-stemmed bushes such as *Acacia senegal* and *Commiphora*, including *Maytenus dhofariensis*. In the heavily wooded *wadis* there are, *inter alia*, succulent stemmed *Cissus quadranularis* and *Cyphostemma ternatum* and various sorts of *Ipomaea*. The valleys contain dense areas of *Ficus sycamorus, vasta* and *lutea* and, where they debouch on to the plain, *Ziziphus spina-christi* and *Acacia nilotica* abound. A rich herb community also flourishes there including *Withania qaraitica,* which is endemic. At higher levels the woodland is semi-evergreen with *Olea europaea*, *Euclea schimperi*, *Commiphora*, *Dodonaea angustifolia* and *Rhus somaliensis* among the plants. The *Ficus vasta* is the largest tree on the rolling grassland summits and the commonest grasses there are *Apluda mutica*, *Themeda quadrivalvis* and *Brachiaria*. On part of Jebel Samham, *Pappea capensis*, a tree widespread in Africa, grows – its only habitat in Arabia.

Fourthly, as the effect of the mists become less pronounced further from the sea, the **dry plateau** produces *Euphorbia balsamifera* and stunted *Commiphora*. Fifthly, in the **north draining *wadis***

where the vegetation becomes sparser, the commonest varieties appear to be *Acacia etbaica* and the rosette tree *Dracaena serrulata*. Sixthly, in the **desert and pre-desert** areas the *Boswellia sacra* of the *Burseraceae* – the incense tree – grows. In shallow depressions the ground palm *Nanorrhops ritchieana* and more or less leafless shrubs like *Euphorbia schimperi* also grow. Further into the desert the succulent *Zygophyllum qatarense* is often the only plant to be seen, but in other places the *Prosopis cineraria* is widespread, with roots of sixty feet or more reaching down to the water level.

The best incense, for which Dhofar has been famous throughout history, comes from the Najd beyond the area directly affected by the monsoon, growing on a tree up to 5 m in height, usually with several trunks and highly resinous in all parts – *Boswellia sacra* of the *Burseraceae* family. After tapping, it produces resinous globules later harvested in the form of gum. Although some of this was exported by sea, much was carried by camel caravan over long desert routes to the north. The *Bedu* of the area hold a long tradition that a lost city, Ubar, lay in the sand to the north of Najd, which belonged to the ancient Arabian tribe of Ad, who deserted it when it lost its water supply, though some believe that its Ad inhabitants suffered some severe heavenly punishment on account of their sins. The discovery at Shisur in 1991 of a strong fort with a large collapsed cistern, which clearly lay on the incense route, has led to identification of this with the Ubar of legend.

In the creek mouths of *wadis* reaching the sea, there are reeds, mangrove, and bulrushes.

Wildlife

Mammals

"A mythical and heraldic animal" is the description of the unicorn, but the legend of this fabulous beast may originate from the Arabian White Oryx (*Oryx leucoryx*), whose two horns look like a single one when this timid creature is viewed from the side. The last original herd of oryx in the wild was on the Jiddat al-Harasis and, like other herds, it was wiped out by a motorised hunting party from outside Oman in October 1972. However, Sultan Qaboos, who has taken a deep personal interest in conservation of his country's wildlife, decided exactly two years later that the dream of re-establishing these beautiful animals in the wild should be brought to reality.

This was the beginning of the White Oryx Project at Yalooni, where they were last seen. The aim was to follow up the good but unsuccessful work done since 1962 by the World Wildlife Fund and the Fauna Preservation Society in London with the encouragement of far-sighted rulers in Arabia. Fortunately nine oryx captured earlier had been sent to the Phoenix Zoo in Arizona – one from the London Zoo originally given by Sultan Said bin Taimur, three captured several years earlier in Hadhramaut, one female from Shaikh Jaber bin Abdulla Al Sabah of Kuwait and four from King Saud of

Oman is profoundly committed to the protection and conservation of its varied wildlife, which includes several species unique to the country. Perhaps the most symbolic is the Arabian Oryx which, by 1972, had been hunted to the point of extinction in the wild. Operation Oryx was launched by Sultan Qaboos in 1975 to restore the oryx to its natural habitat in the remote Jiddat al Harasis in central Oman. The World Wildlife Fund contributed to the feasibility studies, and in 1982 the first breeding pairs of oryx arrived by air from Arizona's Phoenix Zoo, plus a specimen from the London Zoo and others from neighbouring rulers. Today, the Arabian Oryx Sanctuary (above) *covers approximately 27,500 square kilometres of central Oman.*

the Kingdom of Saudi Arabia.

The Sultan's Adviser for Conservation of the Environment, Ralph Daly, coordinated planning with the World Wildlife Fund, the International Union for Conservation of Nature and Natural Resources and the Fauna Preservation Society. The trustees of the world Herd of Arabian Oryx in the USA donated animals, with others coming from the Shaumari Wildlife Reserve in Jordan. Animals were bred for these sources at the Sultan's Omani Mammal Breeding Centre near Muscat and then sent to Yalooni, where they were reared before being introduced into their own natural habitat. In January 1982 the first ten creatures were successfully released into the wild. By December 1994 there were approximately 228 oryx living free in herds of from two up to 35 animals in an area of some 16,000 sq. kms. The population consisted of about 94 males, 107 females and 27 calves.

The aim was to secure a wild population of at least 300 with a captive breeding pool of seven or eight animals at Bait al Baraka, through which new genetic material would be introduced to the wild population from time to time to give security against premature deaths caused by drought or bovine tuberculosis.

Oryx in their natural habitat are found in herds of up to around 25 with a dominant male, or herd bull, and a dominant female. They can cover great distances and have a unique ability to respond to windborn indications of rain. This enables them to survive in the desert, continually seeking out fresh grazing. After release the oryx are constantly monitored by a team of Harasis Bedu rangers, who take a great pride in their job and whose tracking skills are such that they can follow the faintest traces over very stony ground for many miles. Unfortunately the whole careful and complex scheme has been put into the greatest danger by the resumption of hunting by groups from outside Oman, travelling in fast four-wheel drive cars.

The Omani *tahr* (*Hemitragus jayakari*) is named after Lt Col A.S.G. Jayakar of the Indian Medical Service, the British Agency Surgeon in Muscat in the second half of the last century. He secured its identification as a unique species, related to the chamois and musk ox. The name means 'half goat'. The male has short curved horns and a well marked blackish spinal crest with a coat which becomes shaggy in winter, and legs with ruffs. The females have smaller horns and less well-defined markings. It is about 60 cm at shoulder and 90 cm in total length. Before the last Ice Age between 100,000 and a million years ago, the oak forests of Europe were inhabited by a larger version of the *tahr*; but the *tahr* were not as successful as their relatives – the ibex and true goats – and now the Arabian tahr with a total population of about 2,000 is only found in the mountains of northern Oman. As such it is one of the rarest animals in the world.

The Sultan, with his personal love of wildlife, decreed their preservation and introduced conservation measures in 1976, since when their numbers have gradually increased. This has involved persuading some of the mountain tribes to keep domestic stock out of special conservation areas, as the *tahr* needs free water and a diverse flora on which to feed and caves for shelter in extreme weather. Their preferred habitat is between 1,000 and 1,800 metres altitude and they are preserved in the Wadi Sarin Nature Reserve.

Nubian ibex (*Capra nubiana*) are also found in Oman and confusingly they and

Determined action has saved Oman's tahr *from extinction, and has turned former hunters into their protectors.*

*Arabian oryx (*above*) shelter contentedly from the heat.*

Right*: Blandford's Fox was recently rediscovered in the Dhofar mountains, while Ruppell's Sand Fox is encountered on the outcrops of the Jiddat.*

the *tahr* are both known by local people as *wa'l.* They face competition, however, from the feral donkey – descendants of domesticated animals which have escaped into the wild. There is some slender evidence that the Asiatic mouflon (*Ovis Ammon*) might formerly have existed in Oman and field research is proposed to establish whether or not it still exists.

Gazelle were at one period threatened with near extinction but conservation measures were also taken for them. Now there are some 200 on the Jiddat al Harasis and large numbers in the mountains and coastal areas south of Quriyat. The main types of gazelle are the Mountain gazelle (*Gazella gazella*) and the rhim (*Gazella subguttorosa marica*). Red foxes (*Vulpes vulpes arabica*) abound and Ruppell's sand fox (*Vulpes ruppelli sabaea*) is found in desert areas. Wild cat and the Arabian leopard (*Panthera pardus nimr*) still survive. The Arabian wolf (*Canis lupus arabs*) howls in the mountains of the Jebel Akhdar and Dhofar, where the striped hyaena (*Hyaena sultana*) is also found. There are also hyrax (*Procavia capensis jayakar*) – the coney of the Bible, the Arabian hare (*Lepus capensis omanensis*) and the black hedgehog (*Parraechinus hypomelas niger*), a relict species. The Ethiopian hedgehog (*Paraechinus aethiopicus dorsalis*) is more widely distributed. There are

*Although a danger to domestic goats and sheep, the Arabian Wolf (*below*) has held its own in the wild on the Huqf escarpment.*

several gerbils including Cheesman's gerbil (*Gerbillus cheesmani arduus*), Gallagher's gerbil (*Gerbillus dasyurus gallagheri*) and jerboa (*Jaculus jaculus vocator*). Other rodents of particular interest include the spiny mouse (*Acomys dimidiatus*), the golden spiny mouse (*Acomys russatus*), White's spiny mouse (*Acomys whitei*) identified as a species new to science and the black rat (*Rattus rattus*). There are several varieties of bat, including the Egyptian Fruit Bat (*Rousettus aegyptiacus arabicus*), the Oman mouse-tailed bat (*Rhinopoma muscatellum*) and the minute Bodenheimer's Pipistrelle.

Reptiles and *falaj* fish

Lizards, some of which are aggressive, are found all over Oman; they include Agamids like *Phrynocephalus arabicus*, Skinks like *Mabuya tessallata*, Lacertids and Monitors. Geckoes are numerous and ubiquitous, and two new species have been identified in Oman: the *Pristurus celerrimus minimus* and *Teratoscincus scincus*.

Among the less attractive creatures there are the horned viper (*Cerastes cornutus*) found in many parts of Oman, puff adders, and other vipers including a relict species with horns (*Pseudocerastes persicus*) found in the Jebel Akhdar. A diminutive boa (*Eryx jayakari*) is found in the sands and harmless Colubrid snakes are widespread. Camel spiders which are three or four inches in length, with long hairy legs, pendulous bodies and a nasty bite are also common, as are centipedes, scorpions, beetles, hornets, wasps, many varieties of fly, mosquitoes near pools, biting ants and termites, which make conical mounds on the Salalah plain similar to

*The caracal lynx (*left*) has been adopted as the emblem of Oman's Natural History Museum. It is well camouflaged, and a fearless hunter. So also is the Arabian leopard (*second picture*) which though of great rarity is still reported at various points between Musandam and Dhofar. The striped hyena (*third picture*) makes its lair in caves. It has a characteristic cackling cry. Sand gazelles (*bottom*) are larger and paler than the more common Arabian gazelle, of the Jiddat area.*

those in Africa. Small fish (*Aphanius dispar*), which have teeth enabling them to eat debris and nibble the toes of bathers, help to keep *falajes* clean and free of mosquito larvae, and are also found in *wadi* pools.

In the past the arrival of a swarm of locusts was welcomed by the *Bedu,* who caught and ate them. When they came in vast numbers they were to be seen for sale in town market places.

Butterflies

There are more than seventy butterfly species in Oman, which lies at the junction between the Ethiopian (*Afro-tropical*), the Oriental (tropical Asia) and the Palaearctic (temperate regions of the Middle East and Europe) zones. There are examples typical of all these zones in Oman, as well as certain endemic species specially adapted to subdesert zones. Only the most hardy species can survive the aridity of the climate, but there are many very beautiful examples flitting round the gardens and cultivations, and they are specially plentiful around the Jebel Akhdar and the Qara mountains in Dhofar. *Papilio demoleus* – largely black-and-white – is an Oriental butterfly which has penetrated Oman. *Papilio demodocus*, which is also black-and-white, is an Ethiopian butterfly which has reached Dhofar but not other parts of Oman. Other examples in Oman of Ethiopian varieties, the distribution of which can be very intricate, are the brown and yellow *Spialia colotes* and *Colotis phisadia*, *Charaxes hansali* – one of the largest and most handsome butterflies of Oman with distinctive markings and cream borders – and *Spialia mangana*. Examples of the eremic butterflies are *Elphinstonia charlonia*, *Pontia glauconome* – the Desert White which is ubiquitous in Oman – two Apharitis species and *Tarucus rosaceus*, the Mediterranean Pierrot with its distinctive lavender blue colour and a continuous black line just beyond the border. Representatives of the *Palaearctic* species include the spotted orange *Melitaea abyssinica*, the white and mottled *Artogeia krueperi* and *Hipparchia parisatis*, brown with white borders – and in the Musandam area the bright blue *Pseudophilotes vicrama*.

The species of butterflies indigenous to Oman come from the *Papilionidae*: *Pieridae* (subgroups *Pierinae* and *Coliadinae*), including the bright Grass Yellow *Eurema hecabe*; *Danaidae,* of which the only example is *Danaus chrysippus* of warm red, brown and yellow with black and white edges; *Nymphalidae* (subgroups *Charaxinae* and *Nymphalinae*); *Satyridae*; *Lycaenidae* (subgroups *Theclinae*, *Aphnaeinae*, *Polyommatinae*); and *Hesperidae* (subgroups *Coelidinae*, *Pyrginae*, *Hesperinae*).

Birds

Oman is rich in the variety of its birds, both resident and migratory. Of the 372 or so species known, most are of Palaearctic origin but species found include Indian, African, Antarctic and endemic birds. Though some breed in Oman, most are visitors for summer or winter or birds of passage. For the true bird lover the magnificent *The Birds of Oman* by Michael Gallagher and Martin W. Woodcock is indispensable and a short summary can do no justice to the richness of the subject. The largest bird in Oman, however, was the ostrich but this became extinct in the 1930s or earlier.

The great birds of prey still found include various *Accipitridae* such as honey buzzards, kites, vultures, harriers, hawks, buzzards and eagles, including Verreaux's Eagle (*Aquila verreauxii*). The eagle-like Osprey (*Pandion haliaetus*) is seen plunging for fish in the seas. There are ten species of the *Falconidae* of which the Sooty Falcon (*Falco Concolor*) and the Barbary Falcon (*Falco pelegrinoides*) are local breeders. Nine species of owls of the *Tytonidae* and *Strigidae* occur, of which six breed in Oman. As for the many sea birds, Oman has four species of Petrels and Shearwaters (*Procellariidae*); three to five species of Storm-Petrels (*Hydrobatidae*); four species of Skuas (*Stercorariidae*); eight species of gulls (*Laridae*); seventeen species of Terns (*Sternidae*); one species of Tropicbirds

(*Phaetontidae*) – a robust white sea bird with two extraordinary central tail-feathers; the Brown and the Masked Booby of the *Sulidae* family and the Socotra and Great Cormorants from the *Phalacrocoracidae*. There are fourteen species of Bitterns and Herons, of which two or three may breed in Oman: the Common and Demoiselle Cranes; three species of Ibis and Spoonbill; the White and Black Stork and the Greater Flamingo.

Oman has eighteen species of swans, geese and ducks; swans are scarce, geese are occasional winter visitors and fourteen species of ducks are often to be found as migrants near the coast. There are three species of grebe of which the Little

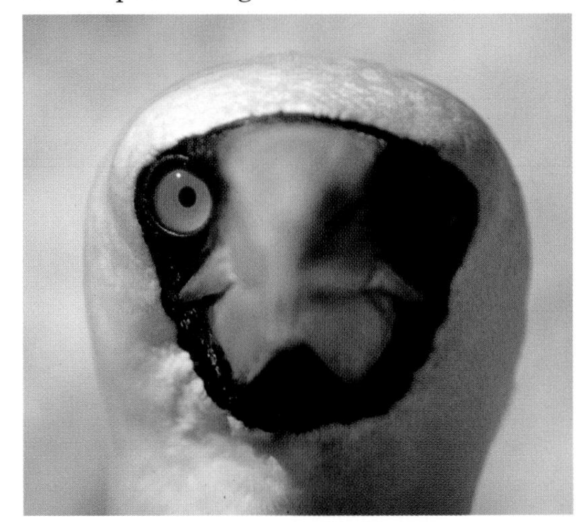

Grebe (*Tachybaptus ruficollis*) breeds in Dhofar. There are eight species of rails, crakes, moorhens and Coots of which the moorhen breeds in Salalah. There are jacanas, stilts including the Black Winged Stilt (*Himantopus himantopus*), and avocets, oystercatchers and stone curlews; but the Crab Plover (*Dromas Ardeola*) of which there is only one species worldwide is specially significant because it

breeds in Oman. There are several other plovers and lapwings; and coursers, sandpipers, snipe, godwits, curlews, woodcock, stints, redshanks and greenshanks. Five species of the *Phasianidae* are found including the Arabian Red-legged Partridge (*Alectoris melanocephala*) which breeds fairly commonly in the Jebel Akhdar and Dhofar.

The Little Bustard and the *Houbara* (McQueen's Bustard) – *Chlamydotis undulata* – live in the semi-desert and grassland and are now protected species in Oman. There are four species of sandgrouse, all of which breed in Oman. The distinctive Hoopoe (*Upupa epops*) too breeds in Oman and of the three species of kingfisher found two breed in Oman – the Grey-headed Kingfisher (*Halcyon leucocephala*) and the White-collared Kingfisher (*Halcyon chloris*). There are three species of bee-eaters which breed in Oman and the Blue-cheeked Bee-eater (*Merops Superciliosus*) with its flashing colours is common on the Batinah. There are also pigeons and doves, cuckoos, nightjars, swifts and wrynecks. The large number of *Passeriformes* include larks, swallows and martins, wagtails, bulbuls, robins, redstarts, chats, wheatears, thrushes, warblers, flycatchers, babblers, tits, sunbirds, orioles – the bright yellow Golden Oriole (*Oriolus oriolus*) – shrikes, crows and ravens, starlings, sparrows, weavers, chaffinches and buntings.

Oman's wildlife is so rich and varied that it takes time and skill to discover.

*Oman has its wildlife reserves on some of its rocky islands, where the Red-billed Tropic Bird (*above*) is a resident.*

Far left: *the striking masked booby has established on Oman territory the only known breeding station for its species in the Arabian Sea area. Beneath it, in flight, is seen Verreaux's Eagle.*

Left: *in the deep woods and caves of the Dhofar mountains, is seen the Spotted Eagle Owl.*

Domestic Animals

The domestic animals of this part of Arabia are goat, sheep, cattle – in small numbers except in Dhofar – chickens and of course dogs, including the graceful saluki, and cats. The country is more suitable generally for goats than for sheep. Omani camels are some of the finest, fastest and most graceful in Arabia, and much prized nowadays for racing rather than work. The donkeys of the Jebel Akhdar are sturdy and fleet of foot, with greater powers of endurance than the hardworking and patient donkeys of the plains and lowlands.

For many generations horses were exported from Oman to India on a considerable scale. Ibn Batuta, writing in the fourteenth century, mentions the export of thoroughbred horses from Dhofar, and Marco Polo, writing earlier, in the thirteenth century, refers to the export of fine Arabian horses – not only from Dhofar, but also from Qalhat.

Albuquerque in the sixteenth century comments on the export of horses from Qalhat, Muscat and Khor Fakkan, and horse and cattle breeding in the Sohar region. The trade statistics show that Oman was still exporting horses to India – many were required as mounts for the Army – in the first half of the nineteenth century, though some of these may have originated in Persia.

The Bani Battash tribe, who live in the Wadi Tayyin area inland from Quriyat, were amongst the most famous horse breeders. The Bani Jabir, the largest tribe in Oman – tracing their descent from the ancient Arab tribe of Dhubyan, famous in Arab poetry – were also renowned as horse breeders.

Omani tradition holds that the Ya'rubi Imam, Saif ibn Sultan, had no fewer than 90,000 horses in his regular army, quite apart from those owned by individuals, and even if one allows for some exaggeration, this is still an enormous number in a country where there are now so few. Other records refer to thousands of horses being used in various campaigns in Oman in past centuries.

Oman was undoubtedly in the past an important horse breeding and exporting country. This gives yet another indication that the area under cultivation in previous generations must have been considerably larger than that to which it had sunk by 1970, for feed, grazing and hay must have come largely from irrigated areas.

Horse breeding has frequently been an absorbing interest for Oman's rulers. Wellsted, who visited Oman in 1835, described Sayyid Said ibn Sultan's stud: "Several of the Imam's horses are of the noblest breed in Najd, some of his mares being valued at from 1500 to 2000 dollars; and one horse, the most perfect and beautiful creature I ever saw, was considered to be worth an equal sum."

Sultan Qaboos, himself a fine horseman, has led the revival of interest in Oman in the horse. He has created a notable stable and stud of beautiful horses, which merit more laudatory words even than those of Wellsted, and he has encouraged Omani riders to take part in equestrian events and pageants involving horsemen. In doing so, he has built on a very long Omani tradition. Others too have built up fine studs and an extremely active Oman Equestrian Society has been formed under Sayyid Shabib bin Taimur.

Marine Life

That great Leviathan, the whale, is found off the long coastline. Oman not only co-sponsored the world moratorium on commercial whaling but also played a leading part in establishing the Indian Ocean Whale Sanctuary and the Southern Ocean Sanctuary.

Dolphins gambol in their schools near the harbour in Muscat and often play round the bows of wooden ships. Sometimes too the great whales can be as frolicsome. Bertram Thomas describes how

> a playful whale helped beguile the moments – a ponderous dark green monster that came and lay alongside us like a submarine beside its parent ship, proud to prove itself not much smaller than the *Fath as Salam* [the local craft on which Thomas was travelling]. It seemed to me perilously friendly as it dived just under us, to rise but a few feet away and break surface with a snort, before sinking heavily again, with a little wash and multitude of bubbles to mark its going. Nor were our sailors unconcerned. With an eye on our dinghy, which lapped about astern of us, they kept up a frightening din by drumming empty kerosene tins. The wind freshened to deliver us, and by noon we came close hauled to Risut where I landed.

Oman waters have about twenty of the eighty or so species of the world's whales and dolphins, whose mysterious life and habits arouse universal wonder and whose Latin classification "*Cetaceans*" name derives from the Greek word for "sea-monster". The *Cetaceans* of Oman's waters are either toothed (*Odontoceti*) or baleen (*Mysticeti*), which filter their food by means of stiff plates like combs hanging from the top of their huge mouths and then use their tongue to propel it backwards. Oman's baleen Cetaceans belong to the family *Balaenopteridae* and are all large.

Of the toothed *Cetaceans* in Oman waters, the *Delphinidae* consist of the Indo-Pacific humpback, Risso's, bottlenose, pantropical spotted, spinner, and common dolphins and the killer and false killer whales (*Globicephalidae*). The sperm whale (*Physeteridae* family), the dwarf sperm whale (*Kogiidae* family) and Cuvier's beaked whale (*Ziphiidae*) are also found. Six species of baleen whales, mainly fish feeders, have been reported in Omani waters: the humpback, Bryde's, sei, minke, blue and fin whales. The sei, Bryde's and humpback whales may be 10m in length. The sei may exceed 14m, the maximum size of Bryde's. Sperm whales are of comparable size. The Oman Natural History Museum illustrates the story of Oman's whales very well with vivid exhibits.

The southern elephant seal (*Mirounga leonina*) and the dugong (*Dugong dugong*), which some believe gave rise to "sightings" of mermaids and mermen, appear to be occasional visitors to Oman waters.

Oman waters sometimes seem to boil with fish so full of them is the sea. These were formerly caught by the skilful Omani fishermen, who would go – with only a tin of water, a handful of dates, bait, hooks and line – as far as five miles out to sea in their long hollowed-out canoes propelled only by paddles. Single-handed they would catch an eight foot swordfish, kingfish, small sharks and sea perch. The sardines, which have played an important part in Oman's economy from earliest times, are divided into the Indian Oil Sardine (*Sardinella longiceps*) and the anchovy (*Stolephorus heterolobus*). The main fish in the Tunny group are the Yellow Fin Tuna (*Neothunnus*); the King Fish (*Scomberomorus*); the Little Tunny (*Gymnosarda alleterata*); the Marlin or Spear Fish; and the Indian Sail Fish (*Istiophorus*). Horse Mackerel (of the *Carangidae)* and *Trachurus* are also common. There are a large number of species of varying types of sharks, skates, rays and mantas of which mention may be made of the Mackerel Shark (*Garcharinus Isurus*), the Hammer-headed Shark (*G. Sphyrna*) and the Lesser Devil Ray (*G. Mobula*). Other important fish are the mullets (*Mugalidae*), the sea-bass or grouper, locally known as "*hamoor*", and the bream (*Lethrynus nebulosus*).

The author of *The Periplus of the Erythraean Sea* writing in the first century AD noted that Masirah Island produced considerable quantities of tortoise-shell of high quality for export and Masirah still has the largest nesting population in the world of Loggerhead Turtles (*Caretta caretta*) – estimated in 1979 at 30,000 in number. The Green Turtle (*Chelonis mydas inset, right*) also nests in large numbers on Masirah as well as on about 275 other beaches. Oman probably has the greatest number of nesting

The Green Turtle

The Natural History Museum at Al Khuwair, serves as a major centre of research and taxonomy, and as a centre of education for younger Omanis in their natural heritage. Its hall is dominated by a skeletal whale shark. from the neighbouring Arabian Sea.

green turtles of any Indian Ocean country. The other two species of turtle laying their eggs on the coast of Oman are the Hawksbills (*Eretmochelys imbricata)* and Olive Ridleys (*Lepidochelys olivacea*), which nest in much smaller numbers.

Oman is rich in corals from the long extinct forms found on the top of the Jebel Akhdar to the corals called stony, or Scleractinian – because of the limestone skeleton created – now growing in Omani seas. These corals derive from the *phyllum Coelenterata,* the other distantly connected members of which (including sea anemones, soft corals, jellyfish, black coral and hydrozoans, like the sting sea-fern) abound. The stony corals are of great beauty and the genera include vase, branching, fleshy, platy, knobblystar, smooth star, brain, and cup. The reefs, which are rich and magnificent in variety of colour, are the home of numerous fish and marine creatures, some with wonderful markings and hues. These include the dangerous crown of thorns and long spined sea urchin (*Diadema*), jellyfish, sea slugs, moray eels with vicious teeth, crabs, stonefish, sea-slugs, the beautiful lion fish, scorpion fish, fireworks fish, chicken fish, butterfly fish, butterfly cod, turkey fish, dragon fish, zebra fish, fire fish and feather fish.

In some years in early summer the sea is seething with jellyfish – blue Portuguese men-of-war and long "snakes" of purple jelly strung together. There are also molluscs of many kinds in abundance, cowries, volutes, cones, bivalves and clams; and at certain seasons the sea is stained with the orange of plankton which becomes phosphorescent at night. To complete the picture, the long sandy beach of the Batinah is alive with crabs emerging from their burrows and scurrying into the sea, with their protruding antennae, like visitors from another planet. Their cousins, hermit crabs, gather in huddles and exchange shells making a curious clacking noise as shells rub against each other.

Pearls

Oysters are found off the coast of Oman, but pearling has never been as important there as it was within the Gulf, where the waters are shallower and do not plunge swiftly to ocean depths. Nonetheless a certain amount of diving for pearls was done until the 1960s and Muscat has at various times been an important market both for pearls and mother-of-pearl.

4
The People

From time immemorial they have sailed the seas and tilled the land, mined its riches, terraced the high mountains and, with a complex pattern of falajes, *irrigated the earth.* Bedu *from the desert have traded with merchants of the cities, and those same merchants with the world. New horizons have opened. Modern industry has not only introduced many new opportunities and professions but supplied the wealth to foster a spectacular growth of hospitals, schools and colleges. The ancient strengths of Oman's people remain; and underpinning all lies the deep-rooted Islamic faith which has shaped and informs the brave new scene.*

Bahla – a past fortress-capital – is one of today's market towns of the country's historic interior. Haggling in the market places is not a common Omani practice, as elsewhere in the East: traders tend to hold to the prices they have quoted.

Origins

The Omanis are today manifestly a single people with a high degree of homogeneity. But they are spread over a large country the size of the United Kingdom and Ireland. In the days of camel, horse and donkey transport – before the advent of cars and aircraft – the differences in origin, culture, pursuits and even language were quite marked. The descriptions which follow picture the mode of life lived until the mid 1970s and illustrate the historical backgrounds and different roots from which the modern Omani has sprung. The changes since then have been enormous, in education and health in particular, and there has undoubtedly been some modification of custom. But a portrait of the past may help towards understanding modern Oman.

Let us therefore begin this section by tracing back, and then describing, those components of folk that comprise today's Omani nation – components which undoubtedly have enriched the whole yet whose contrasts in culture, custom, dialect and demeanour have inescapably progressively diminished since the mid 1970s, which we may take as our descriptive time-frame. The far-reaching changes since – exemplified by the coverage of education and health, which fall in this section – have both overlaid the old diversity, especially among the young, and sharply reinforced the national context of allegiances.

The people who reached such a high degree of civilisation in the fourth and third millennia BC may have been indigenous and the sprouting of civilisation in Oman may have been as rapid a phenomenon as it was in Iraq. Alternatively, there may have been immigration of people with a dominant culture. In the earliest days of human settlement, there may have been a curly-haired Vedda belt crossing the ancient world from Africa to Melanesia, occupying all the intermediate lands, including Arabia, Baluchistan and India. The middle parts of this belt later perhaps became transformed, giving rise to the Hamitic people of Africa and their cousins in the Indian subcontinent.

Thus the original inhabitants of the Arabian peninsula were perhaps Cushites, a Hamitic people who may have laid the foundations of the caravan roads and seafaring from the coastal ports. At an uncertain date – probably in late Pleistocene times – a Western Asian stock moved southwards into the Arabian peninsula and the lands linking Mesopotamia with the Punjab – Persia, Baluchistan and Afghanistan. At this time Arabia was a well-watered and fertile land such as to tempt a race of adventurous hunters. People with long-nosed Armenoid features then settled in northern Oman introducing brachycephalic features, and to some extent these features were also transmitted to the peoples of the south in Dhofar through migration and miscegenation. The peoples of the south nonetheless also retained something of their original features, which makes many of them akin in looks to the Somalis, Danakil, Hadendowa and Egyptians, their brachicephaly being unique.

> The nineteenth-century traveller, James Silk Buckingham, described Omanis as "the cleanest, neatest, best dressed and most gentlemanly of all the Arabs" who inspired a feeling of confidence, goodwill and respect. Though his comments referred to the people of Muscat in particular, many visitors to Oman would consider it true of the Omanis as a whole.

The Phoenicians

The origin of the Phoenicians, that great seafaring race of the Mediterranean, could possibly lie in Oman. The Greek historian, Herodotus of Halicarnassus, in the sixth century BC quotes the opinion of learned Persians that the Phoenicians emigrated from the Erythraean Sea to the Mediterranean, where they settled and from where they immediately started to make voyages. Disputes rage about what was meant by the Erythraean Sea of the ancients, which was named after Erythras, a King whose tomb is supposedly on the island of Hormuz on the north side of the entrance to the Gulf. However, the term Erythraean, or Red Sea, seemingly applied to the western part of the Indian Ocean together with the Persian Gulf and the Red Sea.

Similarity of the place names in the Levant on the one hand and in Oman and the Gulf on the other – for example Sur and Sha'm — and the physical similarity in situation and appearance between Sur in Oman and Sur (Tyre) in the Mediterranean have been thought by some to indicate a common Phoenician origin. The time scale could fit as well, for the Phoenicians first made a significant appearance in the Levant in the second millennium BC, a millennium on which there is relatively little archaeological evidence in Oman, suggesting that there might have been some collapse of civilisation in the area, leading to migrations. It is not entirely impossible, therefore, that shipwrights of Oman fathered those who built and sailed the "ships of Tarshish".

Traditional Oman

In past times the tribes and great families of Oman played significant roles in Oman's historical achievements at home and abroad – and not least in southern Iraq in the early formative days of Islam. Society is now much changed, though maintaining a balance between the various regions of Oman remains important. The main strands of internal Omani history from the period beginning two-and-a-half centuries ago centred round the Bani Hina and Bani Ghafir tribes. These gave their names to the two great Hinawi and Ghafiri factions which came to divide Oman and dominate its politics.

According to the Arab genealogists, the present inhabitants are descended from two main Arab stocks: the Yemeni or Qahtan tribes originating in south Arabia, and the Adnan or Nizar tribes who emigrated from north-west Arabia. The Hinawi faction traditionally represent the Yemeni tribes and the Ghafiri the Adnan, though centuries of feuding, and coalescence and splitting of alliances have increasingly blurred earlier distinctions. Nonetheless this factionalism, at times as bitter as between the Guelphs and Ghibellines in mediaeval Florence, affected not only the politics of inner Oman but also the southern region of Dhofar and the present United Arab Emirates.

The main groups in northern Oman may be divided into the *Hadhr* and the *Bedu* – the classical Arab division between town and desert dwelling people. Apart from the Bani Ghafir and Bani Hina, there are several important sedentary tribes in central Oman. Historically, the Bani Ruwaha, whose senior shaikhs are the Khalili family from which the Imam Muhammad ibn Abdulla al Khalili (1920-1954: 1338-1373 AH) came, lived in the Wadi Samail. The Bani Riyam controlled the Jebel Akhdar and the approaches to it from the south through Tanuf and Birkat al Moz; and the Abriyin of Hamra lived on the south side of the Jebel. Another significant group which dominated one of the strategic *wadis* of the central massif was the Bani Kharus who controlled the northern approach to the Jebel Akhdar and who also played an important part in east African history. The Maawil lived in the prosperous Wadi Maawil, and provided the Julanda kings of Oman before and immediately after the advent of Islam. The Hawasina controlled the Wadi Hawasina which leads through the mountains roughly from north to south and traditionally provided guards for the ruling family and many of the *Walis*. The other great gap through the mountains, the Wadi Jizzi, was inhabited by the Bani Kaab. The Sharqiyah area to the south of the Wadi Samail was the home of the Hirth who had not only played a dominant part in internal Oman politics but also in the colonisation and settlement of Oman's colonies in east Africa. The Awamir, who have a particular reputation for the making and maintenance of *falajes*, also lived in this area, though they also had sections in Buraimi and on the Batinah. South of the main Hirth area is the tract known as the Jaalan, with the settlements of Bilad Bani bu Hassan and Bilad Bani bu Ali, against whom British expeditions in aid of Said ibn Sultan were sent in 1820 and 1821. The Bani Khalid lived in a remote valley – one of the best watered in Oman – to

the north of Kamil and Sur in the Sharqiyah.

The tribes of the Dhahirah area to the east of the Hajar range north of the Jebel Akhdar itself included the Bani Kaab, who provided a number of eminent Omanis, with their tribal centre at Mahdha. Other sedentary tribes included the Bani Battash, who inhabited the area south of Muscat and were formerly famous for horse breeding, and the Bani Jabir, at times the paramount tribe in the country and latterly living mainly in the Wadi Samail and along the Batinah coast.

The desert tribes included the Duru who inhabited the area to the south and the east of Ibri, and the Naim, together with their sub-sections the Al bu Shamis and the Al bu Kharaiban, the only tribes in Oman who practised the Arabian sport of falconry.

To the south of the Sharqiyah there were other *Bedu*, the Wahiba, Harsusi and the Janaba tribes, the last of whom formerly owned towns on the desert fringe such as Adam, the home of the Al bu Said. The Harsusi, though probably not Mahra in origin, nonetheless spoke a dialect of Mahri.

In Dhofar, the main tribes were the Mahra, who lived both in the eastern and western part, the al Kathir, who inhabited the mountains and the plains to the north, and the Qaras, who lived in the central area. Several distinct languages are still spoken apart from Arabic: Mahri, Jibali and a Mahri dialect, Bathari.

In the extreme north of the country lived the Shihuh, among whom survives an Iranian dialect. These people may have produced a notable figure of ancient times mentioned in the Bible, Bildad the Shuhite, one of Job's Comforters.

Omanis were amongst the most important troops when al Muhallab led the Arab tribes in the conquest of Khorasan and Kerman. Later they provided the ruling dynasties in Siraf, Qais and Hormuz, the great trading *entrepôts* of the Gulf before the advent of the Europeans. There has in fact throughout history been so much coming and going between the northern and southern shores of the Gulf that Omani and Arab influence has traditionally been as much felt in southern Persia as Persian influence on the Arabian shore.

Coastal People

Muscat, Mutrah, Sohar, Sur and other coastal places underwent great changes in the quarter of a century after 1970. The greater part of the population became engaged in trade, government service or the service industries necessary for a modern trading nation. The ubiquitous motor car, truck and lorry replaced animal forms of transport. The lives of the people of the coast in the past were very different.

Mutrah changed from a small traditional place into a modern port capable, with good dock facilities and equipment, of handling large ships and every type of cargo. Mina al Fahal, a few miles away, became Oman's oil exporting port, set close to the refinery and other up-to-date installations. Muscat ceased to be a market town, as trade expanded greatly in Mutrah and Ruwi, and became the central heart of government around the Palace. Sohar grew in size and is today a pleasant modern seaside town with a long *corniche*. Sur too has developed a modern look, though traditional shipbuilding continued to be carried on there. Everywhere the fishermen on the Indian Ocean acquired modern boats and adopted more sophisticated fishing methods.

Omani youth responds readily to the policies of involving it in many national organisations and international, too, particularly Boy Scouts.

The pattern of navigation in the Indian Ocean was determined in the days of sail by the north-east, and south-west monsoons. Every December the north-east monsoon blows with remarkable steadiness until February. On this, Arab vessels sailed down to Zanzibar and the coast of east Africa with cargoes of dates, sailing back again with the south-westerly monsoon, which blows from April from September, with cargoes of ivory, beeswax, tortoiseshell – actually, of course, the shell of the turtle – and, until the trade was suppressed, slaves. Indeed Muscat was over a long period the chief port of Arabia for the reception, sale and onward transit of African slaves. Although the trade was infamous, once in Oman or Arabia slaves were treated remarkably well The Arab institution of slavery was never so harsh as that in the Americas and West Indies. Lt. Colonel John Johnson, for example, who visited Muscat in 1817, remarked, "The status of a slave

The Categorizing of the People

The Omani people were formerly divided into six main categories: first the inhabitants of Muscat, Mutrah, Sohar and Sur, and other coastal places where the people for generations lived by seafaring, trading and fishing; secondly the cultivators of the Batinah coast where agriculture depended largely on wells; thirdly the cultivators, the classical *Hadhr*, living in towns like Nizwa and Rostaq and settled villages of the Interior who depended on the *falaj* system of water conduits resembling the *qanats* of Persia; fourthly the *Bedu* of the plains to the south and west; fifthly the Shihuh, the mountain people of the Musandam peninsula, and sixthly the people of Dhofar, some of whom are Hamites and have much in common ethnically and linguistically with the people of south Arabia and parts of east Africa.

in the family of a Muhammadan very commonly resembles that of an adopted child, entitling the individual to some share in the property of his master at his decease and frequently before that event. The adopted slaves interest themselves strongly in the welfare of their masters and are ready even to lay down their lives in their defence; they are perfectly trustworthy and instances are not wanting in which they have been left sole heirs of the property which their care had helped to accumulate."

Nonetheless, the Sultans of Oman and of Zanzibar co-operated with the British in the gradual suppression of the slave trade. Indeed close friendship and association with the British made it inevitable that Oman would be affected by British attitudes. The slave trade greatly exercised reformists in Britain during the first half of the nineteenth century and their ardour and influence grew after Britain's own abolition of domestic slavery in 1833. By a strange coincidence, one of the leading lights in the reformist movement was General T. Perronet Thompson, a Member of Parliament, who, as a Captain in the Army and the first British Political Agent in Arabia between 1819 and 1827, was close to the Sultan, Sayyid Said bin Sultan, and led the British expedition against the Bani bu Ali in 1820.

The people of Muscat for many generations provided food, water and cargoes for visiting ships, though in the late nineteenth and early twentieth centuries this activity diminished as agriculture in Oman went into temporary decline. Indeed until very recently it would have been difficult to recognise descriptions of Muscat given by earlier travellers. Grattan Geary, the Editor of the *Times of India*, who visited Muscat in 1878, confirmed Albuquerque's impressions of the abundance of food in Muscat, remarking: "Dates are seen at every store; fruit and vegetables from the cultivated spots in the interior are abundant." This plentitude of produce suffered an eclipse for some decades but agriculture has since revitalised. Muscatis, however, including a number of Indian traders settled for many gener-

Eastwards along the coast from Muscat, a fisherman of Barka looks for a good price for his catch.

Along the 1,000 miles of coast, the boats have changed – and their form of power. But the skills of the fishermen and the lore of the sea remain an integral part of the life of the people. Most are still engaged in inshore fishing – but in the deeper ocean Oman is fast developing the scientifically controlled catching of fish as a significant industry, and fish processing plants are finding an export market.

ations, have grown rich on *entrepôt* trade as well as direct exports and imports, though *entrepôt* traffic is now not as important as it was in the eighteenth and early nineteenth centuries.

In their heyday, the ships of Muscat varied in size from 300 to 600 tons, the finest being the *baghalas* with high poops beautifully carved like galleons. These ships brought muslin and piece goods from Bengal; drugs and spices from the Far East; timber, rice and paper from Malabar; and European imports such as lead, iron and tin from Bombay. They were also involved in the rich coffee trade from Mocha on the Red Sea and Mauritius. From Zanzibar they brought gold dust, ostrich feathers, tamarind and ivory.

The market areas of Muscat and Mutrah were still in the 1970s a happy combination of traditional and modern. In the narrow streets of Mutrah market there are still people of every colour mingling with one another, Omanis with pale, grave, dignified faces, and beards, wearing traditional Omani dress; brown Indians and Pakistanis in their own distinctive white dress and caps, though many nowadays wear European clothes; people of darker colour denoting their African ancestry or origin. The women glide by in robes which may be black or in quite a wide range of colours. The men are there to shop, visit the barber or visit friends and chat. The women cluster round the cloth stalls with their rich display of gaily coloured materials looking for stuffs of their choice, for even the lady in black is likely to be wearing bright clothes underneath her dark *abaya* and veil. Women also flock round the silversmiths' and goldsmiths' shops looking for a piece which pleases, enquiring the price, fingering, inspecting and moving on to another shop to repeat the process. The atmosphere of the market is polite, and lengthy negotiation not customary. In fact, Muscat and Mutrah tend to be fixed price markets rather than the place for bargaining which so many oriental markets are – not that a bargain may not sometimes be struck!

There are few animals except for the occasional donkey in the wider streets, and near the vegetable market. Camels were never brought into Muscat and Mutrah and visitors with produce from the Interior or the Batinah seeking consumer goods in return left their mounts in the camel park outside the town. Now, however, the sight of a camel has become a rarity in the towns, so fast has been the onslaught of the internal combustion engine.

It has through many ages been customary amongst the merchants in the *entrepôts* of the Oman and the Gulf region to have an area of gardens to

and during the night fires, which they all carry, stabbed the darkness. The catch is not only sold for local consumption, but sharksfin and dried fish remain significant exports.

Batinah Cultivators

Along the shore of the Batinah coast there are rich plantations of dates, which continue almost uninterrupted for some 200 miles from Muscat to Khor Fakkan, where the rocky massif again breaks out into the

which they can resort in the summer months. Seeb has always fulfilled this need for the merchants of Muscat and Mutrah. No one can say when the custom started, but it may be significant that this was the practice in the Kingdom of Hormuz, which for so long was *suzerain* of the coast of Oman until the Portuguese came. It was remarked by Marco Polo who wrote: "The residents avoid living in the cities, for the heat in summer is so great that it would kill them. Hence they go out (to sleep) at their gardens in the country, where there are streams and plenty of water." Duarte Barbosa, the Portuguese who visited Hormuz in 1518 (924 AH) remarked: "The merchants of this isle and city are Persians and Arabia...These noblemen and principal merchants...have country houses on the mainland whither they go to divert themselves in summer." The residences in Seeb have grown more elaborate with time but the old custom is still continued.

If the trading importance of Muscat has fluctuated from time to time, the importance of fishing along the Batinah coast has never diminished. Fish has always been an important part of the people's diet, not only on the coast but also in the Interior, and the traditional pattern of internal trade involved the exchange of fish for the agricultural produce of the farmers living inland. The boats and techniques with the net used by local fishermen changed little through the ages, though from the early 1970s the long, graceful fishing canoes of hollowed-out tree trunks called *huris* were all fitted with modern outboard engines giving them greater range and indeed new types of boat were introduced. In 1975, it was still a familiar sight in Muscat to see scores of fishing boats scattered widely over the still sea,

sea. The people of this area are of mixed blood and over the centuries there has been a considerable influx from both India and Africa. Though there are traces of ancient canals on the Batinah plain, which have long since fallen into disuse, water is nowadays raised by mechanical pump. In the past it was done by a system whereby the bucket from the well was attached to a rope, which was drawn over a wooden pulley and pulled up by a bull, donkey or camel walking down a man-made incline.

The gardens here are lush and the varieties of date different from those grown inland. Certain fruits such as peaches and apricots which flourish in the mountains cannot be grown, but other varieties such as Indian almonds and figs do well. Between the cultivated area on the Batinah and the mountains there is a wide plain providing good grazing for camels, goats and donkeys. Bertram Thomas in *Alarms and Excursions in*

The Northern Coast

N
0 50 100 150
Kilometres

The Gulf
Kumzar
Khasab
Bukha
MUSANDAM
(Oman)
Lima
RAS AL KHAIMAH
Bayah
Dabba
Khor Fakkan
MADHA
(Oman)
DUBAI
Fujaira
Khatmat
al Milahah
Shinas
Liwa
Sohar
BATINAH
Saham
Dil al Buraik
Gulf of Oman
Khaburah
Suwaiq
Masna'ah
Barka
Seeb
Mutrah
MUSCAT
Uzaiba
Sidab
Ras al Khairan
Sifah
Qurayyat
Daghmar
Dibab
Fins
Tiwi
Qalhat
Ras al
Hadd
Sur
Hadd
Siwayh
SEE OPPOSITE

Map continues opposite

Pictured above is a reminder of Oman of the 1970s when catches were landed under the battlements of Fort Jalali; and between Sur and Muscat, carrying passengers and cargo, a packet boat plied nightly – nowadays superseded by a fast motorway bus.

Arabia has described the nature of the Batinah coast: "My journey with Sultan was to take us through this populous province: now along the golden beaches, past little Arab ports ever associated with Sinbad the Sailor, and little fishing villages whose men go forth to grope under the sea for precious pearls; now through the shady date-grove; and now along the hot dazzling plains beyond."

The People of the Interior

The heartland of Oman is the great central massif called the Jebel Akhdar or "Green Mountain" and each of its main towns has been the capital of Oman, before the present Al bu Said dynasty brought it to Muscat in the later eighteenth century. Ibadhism, on which the centuries old Omani Imamate was based and which is strangely confined to Oman and north-west Africa, has its deepest roots here.

The town and villages of the Interior

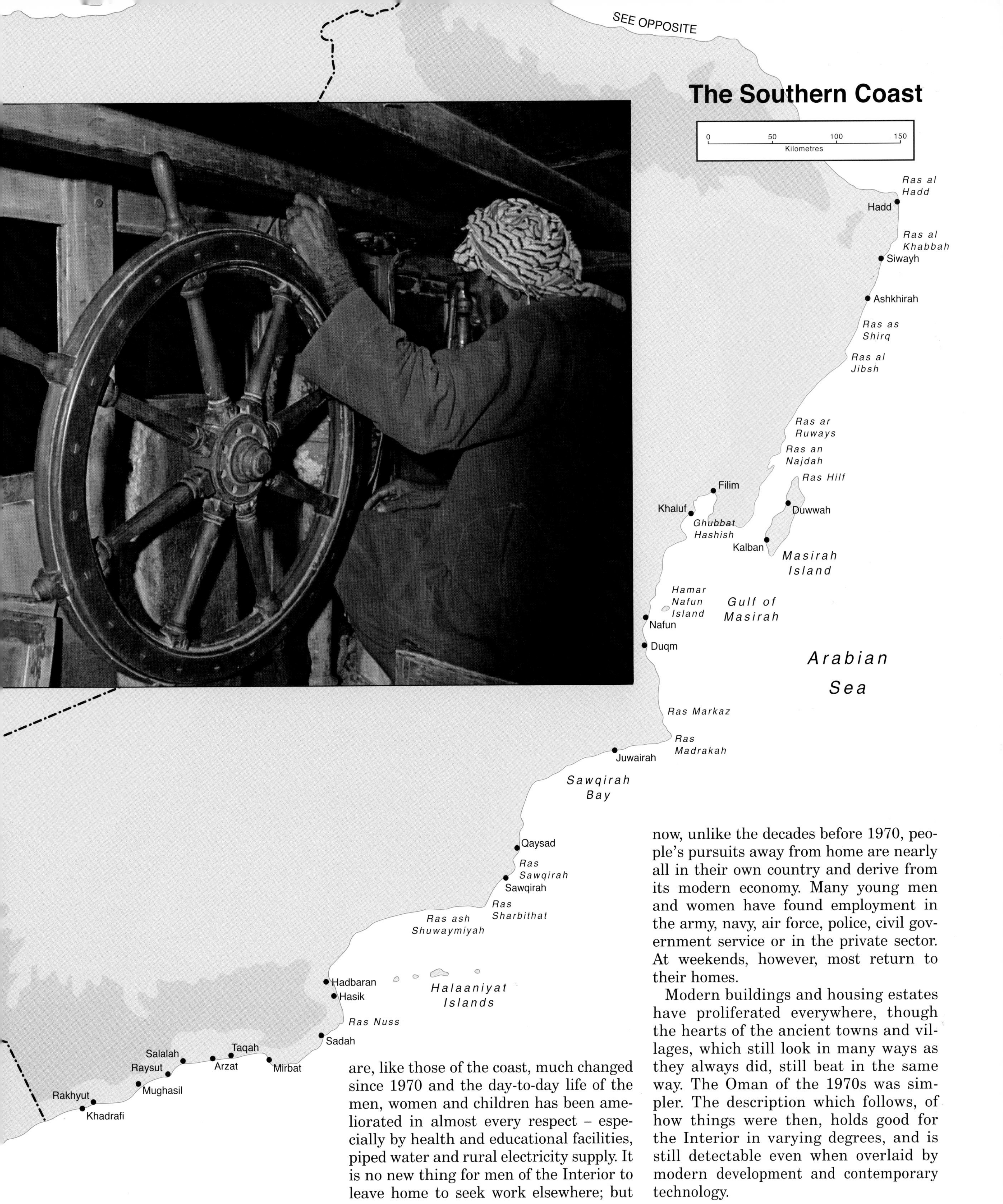

are, like those of the coast, much changed since 1970 and the day-to-day life of the men, women and children has been ameliorated in almost every respect – especially by health and educational facilities, piped water and rural electricity supply. It is no new thing for men of the Interior to leave home to seek work elsewhere; but now, unlike the decades before 1970, people's pursuits away from home are nearly all in their own country and derive from its modern economy. Many young men and women have found employment in the army, navy, air force, police, civil government service or in the private sector. At weekends, however, most return to their homes.

Modern buildings and housing estates have proliferated everywhere, though the hearts of the ancient towns and villages, which still look in many ways as they always did, still beat in the same way. The Oman of the 1970s was simpler. The description which follows, of how things were then, holds good for the Interior in varying degrees, and is still detectable even when overlaid by modern development and contemporary technology.

The Scene in the 1970s

In the markets of the Interior, the splendidly dignified Omani merchants sit outside their shops on stools or cross-legged on the floor, as their forebears always have. In the silversmiths' shops blowlamps glow and there is a confusion of purposeful activity on the floor of each square shop. *Khanjar*s, decorated guns and other ornaments hang from hooks and rails; the more recent articles are displayed in a small glass showcase.

The trade of the other shops is diverse. The seller of pots and pans offers both the work of the traditional coppersmith, and aluminium and enamel objects recently imported. The gunsmith with tools and equipment long defunct in Europe works busily on the old matchlocks and Martini Henrys. The spice shops display piles of cardamom, pepper, nutmeg, dried peas and other dried products, giving the market a distinctive smell. The fishmonger handles cuts of bloody fish brought from the coast, though nowadays a great deal fresher – if perhaps less tasty – than when it was brought by camel.

The *halwa* maker's shop has great pots to heat the glutinous and distinctive liquid which is so much a part of Omani life. Another shop may offer locally grown brown sugar and bags of rice, while coffee and dried vegetables are to be found in others. Woven trappings for camel, horse and donkey may be sold in some markets, together with saddlebags, rugs and other woollen articles for the tent or house. The fruit sellers display their oranges, limes, dates, bananas, and, in the season, apricots and peaches. The brilliant green alfalfa is always on sale close by for animal feed. In Nizwa an auction of animals is held under a great tree adjoining the market and the cattle, goats and sheep are driven round and round a ring of potential buyers, whilst the auctioneer calls the odds. Nearby is the area where the camels and donkeys are tethered whilst the owners visit the market; and all the while there are people coming and going on animals. (Car and lorry have been fast replacing more traditional means of transport.)

While his neighbours with open fields will have their tractors, this farmer of the Interior finds the ox-drawn plough indispensible among his palm trees.

Manufactures of this area include cloth, pottery, and *halwa*. The people of the Interior make their living from agriculture and their gardens of palms and fruit trees. The gardens are irrigated by tapping a water table and leading the water through channels to the land. (Huge areas are still cultivated in this manner, although observation of Oman from an aircraft immediately reveals that the area under cultivation was at one time much larger.) Oman was rightly once described as a land abounding in fields and groves with pastures and unfailing springs. The groves mainly consist of date palms, of which there are reputed to be more than one hundred varieties. Mangoes, pomegranates, peaches, apricots, grapes, citrus, lucerne, wheat and tobacco are also grown.

Each town of the Interior has its own individual character and yet the market area in each bears striking fundamental resemblance to the others. There is a characteristic Omani style of market akin to the Yemeni. In most places the market area is enclosed within walls which can be secured and guarded by night, and it is usually situated close to the fort, the local centre of defence and authority. The streets are narrow and the shops are in rows; they are square in design, giving immediately on to the street, and usually on a raised platform. At night the shop can be shut up completely – there is no glass front and thus each owner can secure his own with a simple lock. Some markets are completely covered and others have wide verandahs protruding from the shops themselves but construction varies from place to place. Frequently the shops are built of mud brick and faced with a rough mud mortar.

The flavour of the smaller Omani towns of the Interior is well captured by Ian Skeet. In his book *Muscat and Oman*, he describes how "Ghafat is in a crook of the mountains where Jebel Kaur sticks out almost at right angles from the main range, a monstrous landmark...the largest 'exotic' in the world, and the geologists love to wrangle over whether it appeared one primaeval day from the guts of the earth, or was tossed over from the sea. Ghafat is the capital of the Bani Hina; it is an extensive series of date gardens with full *falajes* flowing through them, and in the centre a collection of neat two and three storey mud houses emanating an air of strength and wealth."

He labels Hamra of the Abriyin, which is close to Ghafat on the south side of the Jebel, as the most attractive of all the towns in Oman: "There is a road encircling the gardens and beside it the *falaj*, and all the gardens at a slightly lower level – you walk down a couple of steps and then along well-ordered paths with neatly arranged gardens on either side, all very geometrical and systematised; walls, and lime trees spilling over them; sprays of dates like a skyful of fireworks; the bright green of the ubiquitous

As in the ancient Celtic west, the circle has long been known in Oman as man's natural social formation. In the market place (above) *men meet to share a* kebab, *pieces of lamb threaded on sharp skewers and grilled over an open fire. And* below, *although today they have given way to airconditioned modern buildings, the open-air "one tree" Qur'anic schools were a feature of the early drive to education.*

For women, opportunities increase, but the role of wife and mother and female companion prevails.

lucerne, the universal Omani animal fodder; the town centre with its tall elegant mud houses with wooden windows casting strong Italianate shadows, and a wide flight of steps leading from a sort of *piazza* to an upper level of the town. In the main *majlis* of the shaikh, which is a long narrow room (with texts from the *Qur'an* painted on walls and ceilings), the many windows open straight out on to a grove of lime trees, and what with the burble of water from a *falaj* beneath and the chirping of birds in the trees, you begin to lose grasp of desert realities; until you refocus on a room full of bearded Omanis clutching their rifles and their camel sticks, and your Umbrian dreams are dissipated. Behind Hamra the mountains slope almost from the roofs of the houses up at the peculiar tilted angle of the range towards its highest peak at about 10,000 feet."

In such communities as these the labour is divided between men, women and children. The male role includes participation in the business of the family and the community, attending the mosque, supervising the date plantations or working in them or in the fields, ploughing with a humped bull, keeping a shop, taking produce to market, visiting neighbouring places for trade or shopping, mustering with the other males if the Shaikh summons them, building houses, digging wells, making or repairing a *falaj*, shooting birds and game and practising shooting – for many are excellent shots – weaving and cloth making, grooming, riding and using the family donkey.

The small children, both boys and girls, (nowadays at school, at least by the age of six) might be herding goats, sheep and poultry, in which women have been traditional participants.The small boys stay with the mother and participate in activities on her side of the house until they are about eight, after which they gradually become more involved with the male activities.

Amongst the *Bedu* the division of labour may be somewhat different. For instance, the men often herd the camels and other animals and make the coffee, particularly when on the move. Indeed, even in the settled areas there are often goatherds for larger herds of goats and their cries and peculiar sounds as they communicate with the goats to keep them moving can be heard echoing strangely round the hills.'

Life in the Interior

A description of the Wadi Bani Khalid gives some impression of life in the Interior of Oman. Place names in Oman tell of great antiquity and it may be that, as suggested by Bertram Thomas in *Alarms and Excursions in Arabia*, the name of the *wadi* implies an ancient connection with the Chaldeans. It is one of the best watered valleys in Oman and at least in its upper reaches there is a constant stream emanating from an underground river. So strong is its flow that the saying among the local people is that it comes from Basra in Iraq! In its lower reaches it flows underground to Kamil, Wafi and other Jaalan settlements at Bilad Bani bu Hassan and Bilad Bani bu Ali.

How green this valley is. Mountains rise up above it bare, stark and magnificent in their brown and purple contour. In the *wadi* bed itself there are large pools and wide expanses of green water meadow with great clumps of oleander in pink flower, tall trees of various kinds – willows, acacia with yellow, mimosa-like flowers, and other thorny trees of Arabia as well as palms in the well-tended gardens.

The people have the attributes of mountain people the world over and during the *Id* holidays when they are in festive mood come down from the villages higher up the valley, men and women dressed in their holiday clothes, for the traditional *Id* dancing. Some come on foot and others on donkeys with bells jingling cheerfully. The men in brilliant white wear silver *khanjars* and belts with other silver ornamentation. They may still carry rifles – mainly old Martini Henrys – and on the head wear cashmere shawls of bright orange, red and purple, which show up strikingly against the tawny background of rock. The women and girls wear clothes of many bright colours edged with silver thread and embroidery, their heads covered by cloth in the manner almost universal in the East, but unveiled. The men are warm in

Wheat and maize are sometimes grown under the palms, which produce not only dates but fronds for housebuilding and making shasha *boats.*

their *Id* greetings – "Peace be upon you", "A blessed feast", "We are celebrating the feast", "May your feast be blessed" and so on, with the traditional "May you be in God's keeping" on departure. People can be heard playing drums for the dance and singing melodiously at the tops of their voices; this makes a wonderful harmony of mountain sounds, drums, human voices and bells all mingling. The ancient guns too have their role to play over the holiday in *feux de joie*.

Customs, Manners and Hospitality

Oman, no less than the rest of the world, has moved very fast in the last decades of the twentieth century. Social and material change has in varying degrees modified customs or the actual practice of them. Nevertheless the life and bearing of the modern Omani are based on traditions and practices going back far into Omani history, which prompts their examination.

Good manners and humanity are now, as they have ever been, a distinctive feature of Oman, drawing comments from many travellers throughout the ages. For example, Alexander Hamilton, the Scottish merchantman skipper trading with the East Indies, who sailed into Muscat in 1721 (the year before his death

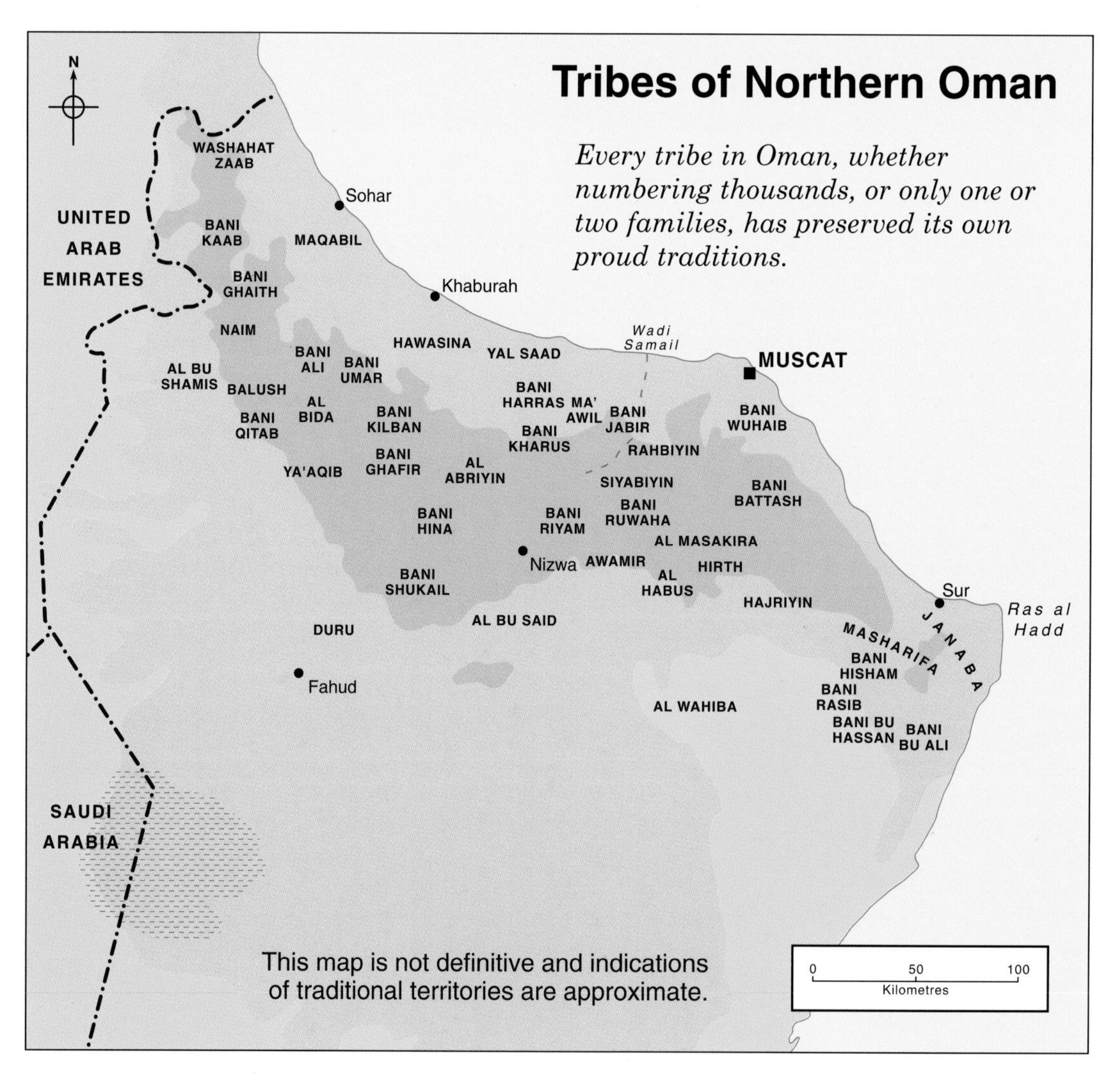

Tribes of Northern Oman

Every tribe in Oman, whether numbering thousands, or only one or two families, has preserved its own proud traditions.

From ancient times, women have done much of the labour in the fields. Here, as recently as the 1970s, they are seen harvesting the wheat crop.

at the age of 35), wrote: "The Muscati Arabs are remarkable for their humility and urbanity" and he recounts that he was walking one day in the streets when by chance he met the Governor of the city. "According to my duty," he says, "I went into the door of a shop to let him and his guards have the street, which are generally narrow, but he, observing by my complexion and garb that I was a stranger, made his guards go on one side and beckoned me to come forward and stood until I passed him." Hamilton goes on to contrast the treatment of prisoners of war taken by the Omanis and Portuguese in 1650. "The Portuguese use their captives with great severity, making them labour hard and inure them to the discipline of the whip. But the Arabs use their with very much humanity, only making them prisoners at large without putting them to hard labour and allow them as much diet money as their own soldiers receive."

These innate good manners among the Omanis still endure, in very changed circumstances. In the past they were clearly demonstrated by the natural ease, dignity and politeness of small boys in their fathers' *majlis*es or homes. Hospitality is one aspect. Any Omani would feel it incumbent on him to invite a stranger at least to take coffee with him. Hospitality is indeed a sacred duty and even the most impoverished *Bedu* must share his frugal meal with a stranger. Wilfrid Thesiger writing in *Arabian Sands* (1959) describes how, when passing some tents in the Omani desert, a man came running out shouting "'Stop! Stop!... Why do you pass my tent? Come, I will give you fat and meat.'... He took my camel's rein and led her towards the tents... The tents were very small, less than three yards long and four feet high, and were half-filled with saddles and other gear. An old woman, a younger woman and three children... watched us as we unloaded... They slaughtered a young camel behind the tents."

Another striking example of Omani hospitality was the conduct of an elderly man when a small body of troops arrived at his village to arrest him. He would not submit to arrest until he had served coffee to his captors, but, this done, he gave himself up willingly.

The traditional courtesies which Omanis exchange are deeply rooted in their Islamic traditions and nearly all the phrases used mention the Almighty, much as they have done and do in European tradition. Any phrase anticipating action in the future is prefaced by "If God wills". "Praise be to God" is similarly used in relation to all present conditions or past mercies.

It is usual, particularly away from the larger towns, to greet strangers. Frequently people hail one another over considerable distances of desert or mountain. Greetings are more demonstrative and often more dignified than in the West and courtesies are elaborate and repetitive. Indeed a degree of repetition is almost essential to ordinary politeness, and two people may spend a considerable time insisting gently – by using the word "*tafaddal*", be so good – that the other will precede him in taking coffee or beginning a meal, or walking through a door.

Food

The main items of diet are dates, rice, fish, meat, wheat cakes and fruits such as bananas, citrus and mangoes. The family usually start the day with dates and coffee and breakfast may consist of bread with sour milk or yoghurt *(laban)*, or possibly a vegetable stew. Wafer-thin bread made from wheat is eaten with butter and honey and sometimes eggs are put into the thicker round or flat bread. The main meal of the day, taken about noon, is rice with a fish, meat or chicken stew and the evening meal is usually light and similar to breakfast. Coffee, frequently flavoured with car-

damom, and dates are taken at any time of day, and *halwa*, the characteristic Omani sweetmeat – made traditionally in the very early morning of ghee, starch, brown sugar, cardamom and honey – may also be served to guests.

If a visitor calls on an Omani household, the men will be shown to the *majlis*, the preserve of the men, and the women taken to the *harim* quarters, the preserve of the women. The host will always offer *qahwa* or "coffee" – meaning anything from a cup or two of coffee to a comparatively large meal. This may include tea, fruit, fizzy drinks, wheat bread, a light meat dish, biscuits and *halwa*. A meal offered to a guest could well be much more elaborate with a *khuzi* – goat or sheep on rice – with side dishes of stews, meat and vegetable, and possibly mutton or goat.

It is a rare Omani who does not have the time to spare to welcome strangers, almost always with a cup of coffee and exchange of news.

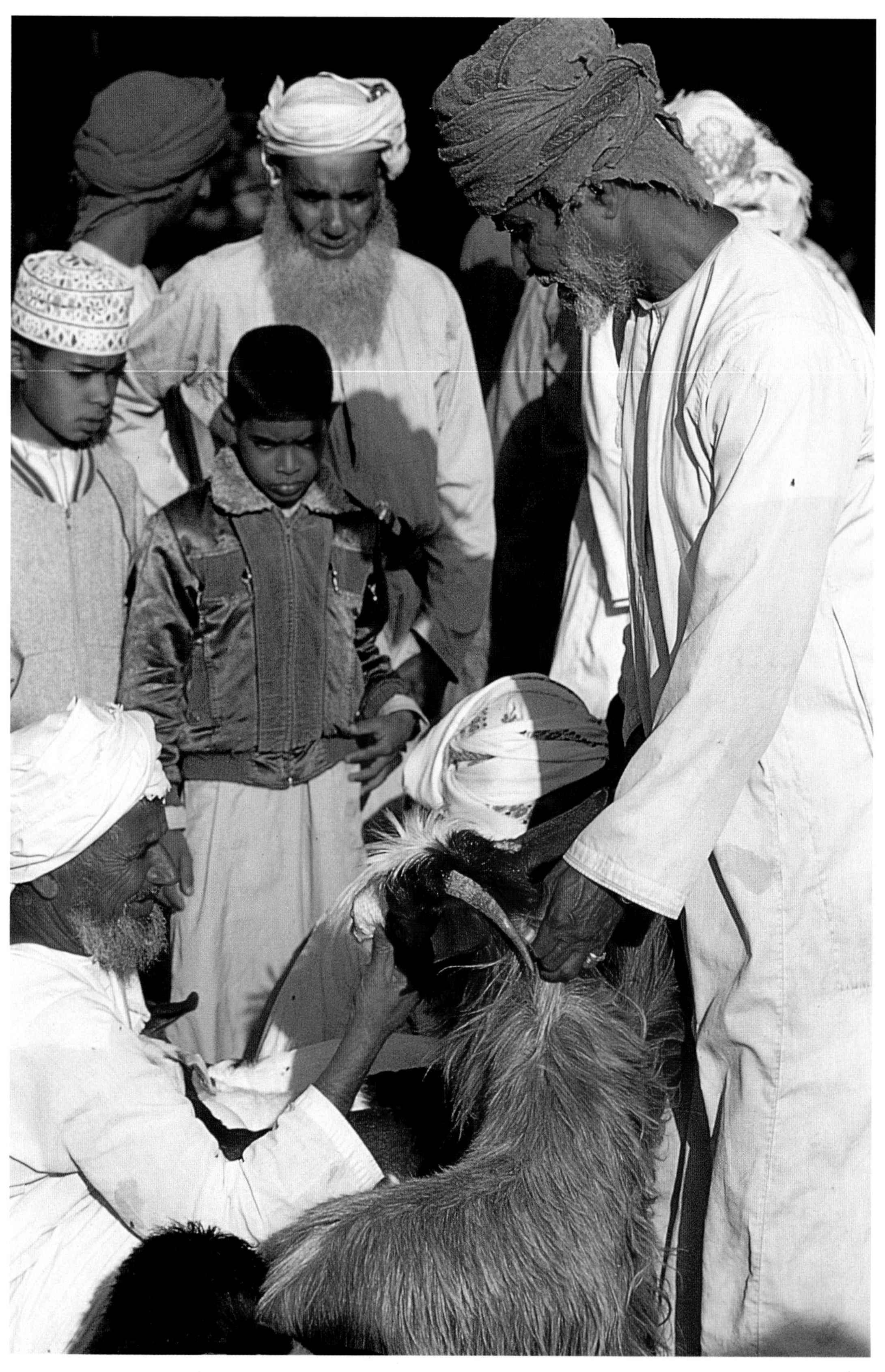

Careful scrutiny of the animal on offer will make the foundation of a good hard bargain in the goat market.

It is still usually *de rigueur* to drink about three cups of coffee before leaving and the host or his servant will go on filling the tiny cups until the cup is shaken – a sign that the guest has had sufficient. Although the custom is now dying, it used to be invariable for rose water to be sprinkled over a guest's hands and head, and for incense to be taken round in a smoking censer of silver or clay. This was the signal that the entertainment was over and the proverb runs, "After the incense, there should be no sitting on."

Dress

James Silk Buckingham, the celebrated journalist and traveller who visited Muscat in 1816, spoke with approbation of the simplicity of the people's dress and the "equality of the value between the dress of the wealthiest and the lowest classes of people".

The typical Omani man of the old school in the Interior has a long beard and wears a turban of dazzling white cloth, and a white robe or *dishdasha* with a distinctive little tie at the neck. Around his waist he wears a belt, very often of silver thread, to carry the *khanjar*, the typical curved Omani dagger, the sheath of which is frequently richly decorated in silver. He may well also carry a small silver container for *kohl* which men as well as women apply, and another silver tube-shaped container for tweezers – a sensible precaution in a land where thorns fallen from the trees are so prevalent! The usual undergarment is a *wazara* or *lunghi*, often brightly coloured, which is wrapped round the body and serves as the only daytime garment of people labouring in the hot sun.

Over his white robe the Omani man will often wear a *bisht*, a cloak which may be black, fawn or pale coffee-coloured or even off-white, edged with gold thread. Sandals of leather are worn on the feet. The men's headdress varies and, whereas the people of the Interior usually wear the turban of white cloth, the people of the coast wear an elaborately crotcheted cap most of the time. Some, however, both in the Interior and on the coast, wear turbans of cashmere wool of various qualities according to rank and means. The *Bedu* also often wear cashmere turbans of bright colours, orange, purple, yellow and green, which contrast brilliantly with the landscape.

The traditional Omani dress has been adopted for formal occasions both at home and abroad and Omani ambassadors in many capitals of the world have been helped to make their mark by their distinctive dress. Omani women's clothes vary somewhat from place to place. All the women, however, cover their heads with cloth in some manner. In the towns it was the custom, at least until recently, for the better off to wear a veil and a black *abaya* or cloak of fine material. There are areas, for instance in parts of the Batinah and Dhofar and amongst some *Bedu* tribes, where the women wear a mask, *birqa*, which sometimes takes quite an elaborate form and covers their noses, giving them a bird-like appearance. Some *Bedu* women wear a long black dress with a stiff black veil and only tiny slits for the eyes. In central Oman the women are frequently not veiled, but wherever in the country a mask or a veil is worn veiling begins at puberty. The coquettish effect of the veil is often enhanced by the women gathering the head-veil, *lahaf*, with the teeth and revealing one eye only.

Women's dress in Oman is generally far more colourful than anywhere else in eastern Arabia until Kurdistan is reached to the north. In fact, they are often dressed in a riot of colour. The usual pattern is a long straight dress with long sleeves,worn over trousers gathered tight around the ankles. The Batinah women also wear the *lahaf*, which trails behind them. Purples and blacks are popular colours there and the dress is made of the same material. The women in the Interior, in such places as Nizwa, Samail and Iski, wear similar clothes, thought the colours may be brighter than on the coast, with oranges, yellows and greens predominating. An additional outer garment, consisting of two large pieces of cotton sewn together, called a *laisu*, is worn in these regions.

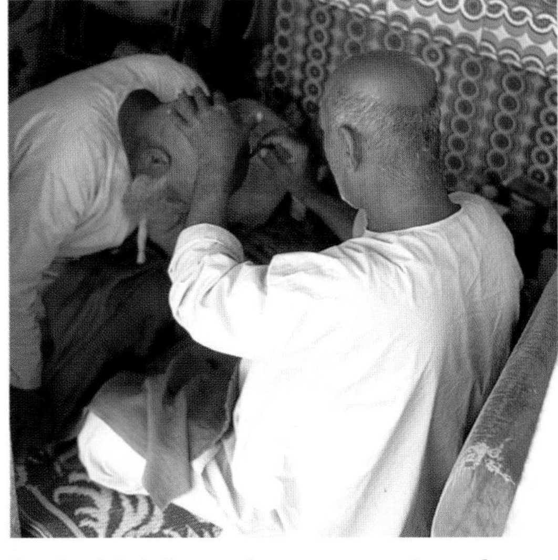

In the high heat of summer a close shave is the best haircut (above).
Headdress can indicate a man's origin or home area such as Sur (right).

In the Sharqiya and Sur areas a garment called a *shatha* is also worn – a shawl consisting of two pieces of cloth joined with lace.

Birth, Puberty and Death

Although even today there is more frequently greater joy when a male child is born, rather than a girl, there is not the shock and even anger which in the past has greeted the birth of a girl in other parts of the Arab world. (This attitude may possibly have its origin in the practice in parts of Arabia of infanticide of girl children before Islam – a practice of which the Prophet Muhammad deeply disapproved.) Nowadays, an increasing number of births take place in hospital but until recently the average Omani

child was brought into the world by a local midwife, usually an elderly woman. After birth the child would be anointed, dressed with *kohl*, ash, or a mixture of both. Salt was used for healing the woman and preventing infection, though it often produced unpleasant side effects.

Boys may be circumcised either at about fifteen days or at about six years. There are no puberty rites in the north, but there is usually a celebration to mark the occasion and there may be dancing. In the mountains of Dhofar, however, elaborate ceremonies may still attend male circumcision at the age of fifteen. Such ceremonies were graphically described by Bertram Thomas in *Arabia Deserta,* writing of the 1930s.

Large numbers of men and women assemble round a large open space. On a rock in the centre sits the boy of fifteen, a sword in hand. This sword, which has been blunted for the occasion, he throws into the air to catch it again in its descent, his palm clasp-

ing the naked blade. Before him sits the circumciser (usually a shaikh or man of good family), an old man; behind him stands an unveiled virgin, usually a cousin or a sister, also sword in hand. She raises and lowers her sword vertically, and at the bottom of the stroke strikes it quiveringly with the palm of her left hand. The stage is now set. The boy sits, his left hand outstretched palm upwards, in suppliant manner, waiting for the actual operation. This done, he has promptly to rise, bleeding, and walk round the assembly, raising and lowering his sword as if oblivious to the pain. The rite is terminated by songs and running, and the firing of rifles, the women opening their upper garments as a gesture of baring their breasts... Both male and female circumcision as practised in Dhofar bear resemblance to ancient Egyptian practices.

Hair fashions too may have an ancient sexual connotation, for Dhofari boys wore a central lock like the Egyptian Horus, with the hair shaved on either side. After the circumcision, the hair was permitted to grow normally.

When death comes, the body is washed carefully – washing is a very important part of the religious ritual both for the living and the dead. Certain spices, such as *riha*, which has a smell somewhat like lilac, and *kafour*, a dry white powder of great fragrance, are sprinkled over the body and between the fingers and toes. Orifices are blocked with cotton wool and the body is then swathed in a new piece of white muslin. The time between death and burial is very short, and burial takes place on the same day, unless death has occurred at night. Burials take place only during the day and the bier on which the body is laid is carried to the grave by close male members of the family.

After a man has died, his wife goes into mourning for a period of four months and ten days, and during this time she is not allowed to see another man; thus any doubt about paternity or succession is removed. During her period of mourning the woman stays indoors, seeing only the immediate members of her family. She

The shape and colour of traditional headdresses vary from region to region, person to person, season to season, and occasion to occasion – from that of the Dhofari herdsman, top left, *to the northern highland villager,* top right. Left to right; *an old soldier from Quriyat, a Rostaq elder, and a Wahibah tribesman.*

Each year those who live by the camel gather in Seeb to display the quality of their animals to an urban audience.

wears old clothes, not necessarily black ones, and does only her essential toilet, neither styling her hair nor painting her face, nor wearing jewellery. The night before a widow comes out of mourning she goes through a ritual bathing ceremony, and after this she is allowed to receive visitors.

Marriage

Marriage and the family lie at the heart of Islam; even though marriage is regarded in Sharia' law as a civil contract, the fact that it is legal and possible for a Muslim marriage to be terminated by the husband saying "I divorce you" three times to his wife has created an impression that divorce is easy and frequent in Islam. In practice, it is not particularly common, and many Omani marriages are essentially monogamous, although a man may legally have up to four wives at any one time. This, however, has usually been the prerogative of the rich and even then a man has a difficult task if he is to obey the Prophet Muhammad's injunction that all wives should be treated in every way equally. The sanctions of divorce are in themselves a deterrent, for the man who divorces his wife has to pay her alimony and there can be difficulties about custody of the children. Moreover, divorce is not to be taken lightly by Muslims and the oath on the divorce is the most binding of vows. For a divorce is regarded as an act of finality on which there can be no going back – at least without a devious legal process.

Though custom has been changing rapidly, it was common for a girl to be betrothed and married at the age of eleven or twelve. Such marriages were always arranged, and a man normally married his first cousin by his father's brother as his first wife. "Marrying a strange woman is like drinking water from an earthenware bottle; marriage with a cousin is like a drink from a dish – you are aware of what you drink." If the man and the girl came from the same vil-

lage they would normally have seen each other, but, if they came from separate villages they might well never have met until the arranged marriage took place.

In the case of marriage to a virgin girl, the arrangement is made between relatives of the two parties, though the girl herself has to give her consent to a proposal. A man may himself propose marriage to a widow or divorcee by raising the matter with a male relation of his intended wife. For the contraction of any valid marriage, bride price, *mahr*, has to be paid and the customary amount used to vary from area to area, being as high as 1,500 Omani Riyals in some places. However, one of the measures taken by Sultan Qaboos after his accession was to fix bride price universally at 300 Omani Riyals. *Mahr* is a bridal gift from the husband to the wife and becomes the property of the wife. She has full right to dispose of it exactly as she wishes and it remains hers even in the event of a divorce.

Mahr may take various forms. It may be in the form of a money payment, but more usually it comprises a series of gifts, including jewellery, clothes, and even a wedding bed or bed linen.However, part of it may also be in kind and such items – for instance materials and food – may be draped round the reception room at the wedding celebrations. There may be sacks of flour and rice, sugar, coffee beans, onions, dresses and fancy sandals. Often about half the bride price is paid in gold which it is easy for the bride to keep in the event of a divorce.

The formal arrangements for marriage are clear and well-recognised. The first stage, as we have seen, is the "asking". Then follows the commitment, *milha*, which stipulates the amount of *mahr* and the trousseau which the bridegroom and his family are to provide. It may also settle the date of the wedding. The legal completion of the ceremony comes with the signing of the marriage contract – or oral affirmation of it – in front of a religious judge (*Qadhi*). The *Qadhi* asks the bridegroom in the presence of witnesses if

*The orange head-cloth (*below*) is of home-spun cashmere, and chosen for its lightness.*

Feminine flair prompts the marriageable damsel from Sur to complement her golden skin with glowing russet.

he will take the girl and when the agreement of the girl's father, or other representative, has also been given, the civil contract is duly signed.

The legal ceremony over, there are usually wedding festivities, with separate parties for the men and for the women. The celebrations consist of eating and drinking – naturally with no alcohol – with dancing, and in some areas, singing. Sometimes there are a series of celebrations on different days. The girl is specially made up for the occasion, and in the Interior her hands, feet and face are painted with henna, which is used by men and women in all sorts of celebrations. In Oman, however, it is only used on the body and not to dye the hair. Some wear a yellow paste ground from the orange flowers of a small shrub called *shooran*, and a floral design is sometimes painted on the hands. For the first night a bride will often wear green clothes – green being a sign of fertility. The culmination of the marriage ceremony is when the newly-weds are escorted to their home, be it house or tent; this is the first occasion on which the two will ever have been on their own together, unless they knew each other as children before the age when small girls are veiled and put into *purdah*.

In the event of divorce a woman has to wait a certain period, *'idda*, before she may remarry. This provision of Islamic law is to ensure that there is no doubt about the paternity of any child which she may subsequently bear. The wife returns to her own family and usually takes with her any children under five. After this age, the father is entitled to, and usually does, take the children. The divorce rate is in fact much higher in the towns of the coast than in the Interior.

The Omani attitude towards woman is gentler than in many other parts of Arabia. The women are not so closely confined to the *harim*, are frequently not veiled and wear outer garments more colourful and indeed gorgeous than elsewhere. In Oman too, unlike most parts of Arabia, the male allows the woman to ride the donkey and walks himself. By the same token women, like their menfolk, have always been permitted to drive motor vehicles. This aspect of Oman was remarked on by the nineteenth-century British traveller William Gifford Palgrave, who noted that "in Oman...the harem is scarcely less open to visitors than the rest of the house; while in daily life the women of the family come freely forward, show themselves, and talk like reasonable beings, very different from the silent and muffled status...elsewhere."

The Changing Role of Women

The traditional role of the woman had its diurnal pattern, and today that pattern will still hold good in varying degrees, especially in the villages. A woman's day usually started at dawn, or even before. Her first duty was to heat water carried from the well or *falaj* on the previous day. Next she would make the *laban* (yoghurt), wash, and say her prayers before preparing coffee and waking her husband and children. After breakfast she and the children performed the chores of the household, which might include care of animals – camels, goats and hens – cleaning the house and preparing the midday meal. After the siesta in the heat of the afternoon, there followed a time for social intercourse – visiting friends and relations and partaking of coffee and dates. Soon after nightfall and the evening meal, the family would retire.

Sultan Qaboos believes that, within the Islamic tradition, an important role should be open to women in the modern world beyond that exclusively of family, if such be their opportunity and bent.

Women's steady educational emancipation, exemplified by the university students (lower picture),*has barely affected the traditional marriage celebrations.*

Many women play their traditional role, often ameliorated by greatly improved standards of living. Many others have taken advantage of new opportunities. In Sultan Qaboos University, a majority of the students are girls and the first Omani women doctors educated there have qualified and were already doing internships in the mid 1990s. Oman was the first country in the area to have policewomen. In the army, women have already attained the rank of colonel. In the Civil Service, there were already two under-secretaries in 1994, as well as Directors-General and Directors of departments. They have also entered the Majlis Ash'Shura, the country's representative assembly and women of course participate in elections to that body. Besides the field of medicine, women's role and abilities in education has long been recognised and careers in both these professions are popular with young women. Nursing in particular has in recent years become a sought after procession. Such "liberation", in the fashionable jargon, by which women have found and developed their talents, has evolved naturally, without ructions. It has occurred within their own deep-rooted culture and tradition and free from the stridency and self-consciousness of "women's liberation" in the west.

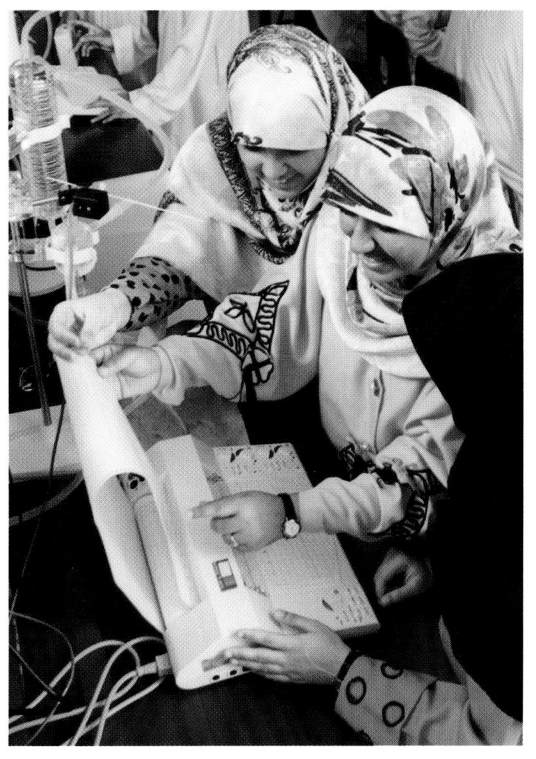

Local Authority

In all major centres the *Walis*, or Governors, are appointed by the central Government and the *Qadhis* or judges who perform the judicial function, remain key figures. This simple structure provided the bones of the administration for centuries and the *Walis* and *Qadhis* come from families which have traditionally given service to the state for generations. Such families have moved from post to post within the country, and sometimes in former days have been posted to Gwadur and other posts on the southern coast of Iran and the east coast of Africa. In some areas tribal shaikhs have always carried great influence, and government has traditionally been conducted partly directly through the *Walis* and partly indirectly through the most influential of these tribal shaikhs.

But a link between past and the present forms of government is the revival in the 1990s of the *barzah*. These are held once a month by the *Wali* in the restored forts, which were traditionally the seat of local government. The *Wali*, who is accompanied by the *Qadhi* of the

Shari'a Court of the *wilaya*, receives members of the public, deals with their cases and discusses affairs with the local shaikhs.

Ibn Batuta has left a description of how government was conducted in Oman when he visited Nizwa in the fourteenth century AD (eighth century AH). The inner part of Oman was then governed by the Bani Nabhan, who belonged to the Arik branch of the great south Arabian tribe of Azd. He writes: "Its Sultan is an Arab of the tribe of Azd bani al Ghawth and is called Abu Muhammad ibn Nabhan. Abu Muhammad is among them an appellation given to every Sultan who governs Oman, just like the appellation 'Atabek' among the kings of the Lurs. It is his custom to sit outside the gate of his residence in a place of audience there. He has no chamberlain nor vizier, and no one is hindered from appearing before him, whether stranger or any other. He receives a guest honourably, after the custom of the Arabs, assigns him hospitality, and makes gifts to him according to his standing."

opportunities for women are a striking reform.

This scene describes the way in which business has traditionally been done in Oman over the centuries. Until very recently, some *Walis* in the Interior held audiences outside the gates of their forts exactly as in Ibn Batuta's day.

In modern Oman, however, the *Wali*'s role has changed. He remains the representative of the Sultan and the central government in his *wilaya*, but he lives in an efficiently designed modern house and his office is up-to-date with telephones and modern equipment. In all the larger centres, too, are found other central government officials, such as directors of health and education and senior police officers, as well as officials of the fully structured municipalities. Local government has had to become more complex to fit the needs of modern statehood.

The mode of life of the people of the Sultanate has thus gradually changed with the spread of greatly improved educational and health facilities and the new found ease and speed of communications by road, air and telecommunications.

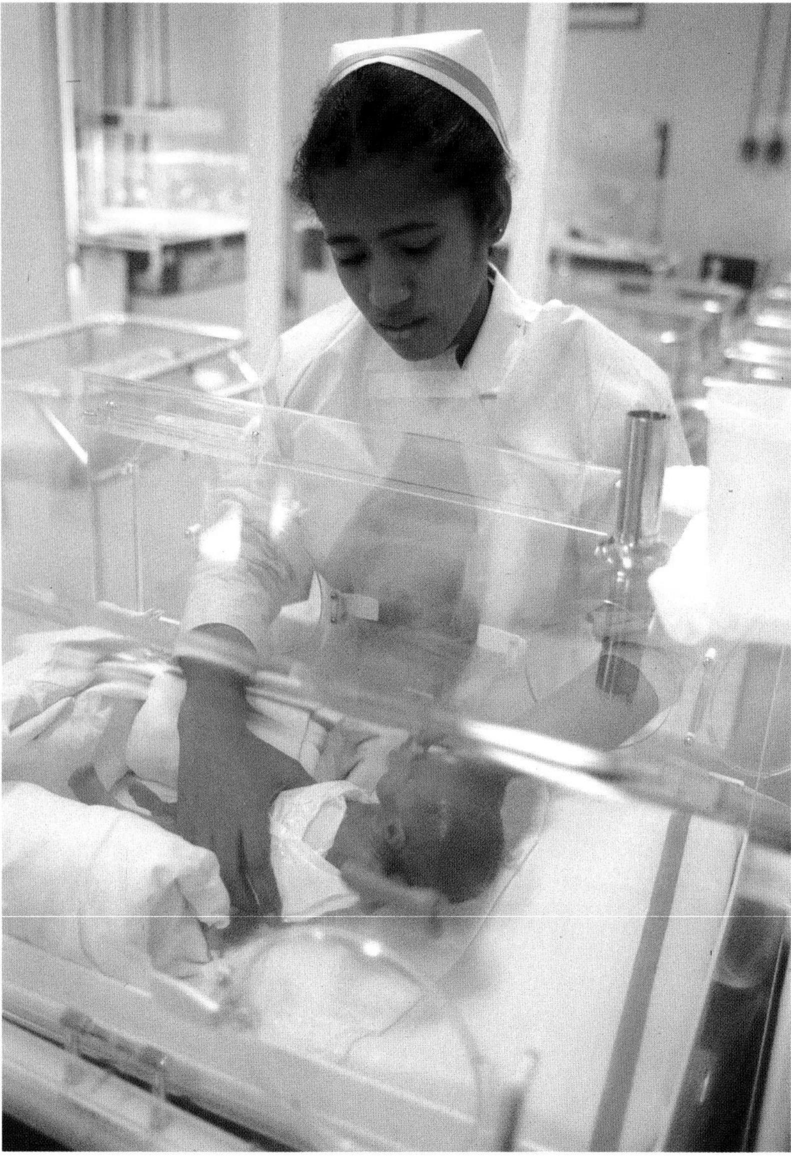

Women have filled a majority of posts in the expanding health service – like this maternity nurse at Khoula Hospital.

Education

The educational scene in Oman changed beyond measure after 1970. Until Sultan Qaboos's accession the country had only three schools with a modern curriculum – the Saidiya schools for boys in Muscat, Mutrah and Salalah, with 900 pupils in all. There were also traditional Qur'anic schools in many towns and villages, and groups of boys wearing dishdashas sitting under trees were a common sight, perhaps with a ring of small girls in brightly coloured dresses in an outer circle behind their brothers, being taught by rote by a single male teacher.

A small number of Omanis were able to receive an education in India, with the Sultan's consent, but many more found their own ways of starting, or continuing, their education in other countries – Bahrain, Iraq, Egypt or even Russia. With no opportunities for employment at home they remained abroad until after Qaboos' accession, when they were able to return, some to play leading roles in the new Oman.

The new Government responded immediately to the widespread hunger for education and opened many schools, initially in makeshift tents. There was a great dearth of qualified Omanis, so male and female teachers from Egypt and other Arab countries were hastily brought in. Girls' schools were opened for the first time and the enthusiasm of pupils of both sexes was so palpable that even 18 year-olds might join a primary class to begin to make themselves literate. The widespread opportunities for education at all levels in 2002 – including Sultan Qaboos University and other universities and vocational training centres – would have been utterly unimaginable in those early days.

A most striking feature of the reforms under Sultan Qaboos was the education and subsequent employment prospects for women. Not only were they offered the same opportunities as their brothers, but women were not required to leave their posts on becoming pregnant, nor if their husbands moved out of their district. Thus Omani women were able to start from a position achieved in other countries only after long campaigning. No longer confined to a purely domestic role, they have become involved at the highest level of government in many capacities.

Present State System

In 1999 a new Basic Education System was introduced to 'teach communication and learning skills, critical thinking, science and modern technology'. Arabic remains the medium of instruction, although English has become very much the second language. After secondary education, pupils can apply to Sultan Qaboos University or one of the other universities, colleges and institutes, including those specialising in vocational training. By 2002, no fewer than 33,772 students in high schools were specialising in science and 14,821 in the arts. In 2001 there were 1,008 state schools with over half a million pupils coming within the aegis of the Ministry of Education, which also has responsibility for children with special needs.

The process of increasing the numbers of Omanis to replace expatriate staff in the educational sector has developed at a determined pace. By 2002, 71 per cent of teachers and 96 per cent of school administrators were Omanis. Although teachers initially had to rely on text books from other countries, all text books have for many years been specially designed for the Omani education system.

Teacher Training

The first Teacher Training Institute for Omanis was inaugurated in 1977 with modest aims. By 1980, Teacher Training Colleges took graduates of the secondary schools on a one-year programme and by 1990 there were nine such colleges. In 1994, aims were set higher and two colleges were designated University Colleges and established in two of Oman's former capitals – one at Nizwa for male teachers and one at Rostaq for female teachers – and authorised to award BA degrees in teaching. In 1995 they, together with other male and female colleges of education, were placed under the control of the Ministry of Higher Education. In 2002, 8,896 students, male and female, enrolled at teacher training colleges and 6,049 obtained BA degrees. A particular problem developed regarding the number of female teachers leaving owing to maternity leave, and in 2002 programmes were launched to recruit 9,700 more – mostly women – to correct this imbalance.

Above: *Mathematics, languages, science and religious studies are all important areas of the syllabus.*

Other Schools

The Sultan's School, founded in the early 1970s, continues to provide an exceptionally broad education qualifying pupils to move easily into higher education in other countries such as the UK and US. Government policy has also actively encouraged the opening of private schools to help reduce the burden of government expenditure on education and by 2002-3 there were 134 such schools, supervised and monitored by the Ministry of Education.

Higher Education

The Sultan Qaboos University at Al-Khodh has become the lynch-pin of the tertiary education sector. Its foundation was heralded at His Majesty's Tenth Anniversary celebrations in 1980 and in 1986 the new university took its first 557 students. By 2002 the numbers had increased to 10,902, with the ratio of women to men being in nearly equal numbers. There are seven colleges: Engineering, Sciences, Arts and Social Sciences, Commerce and Economics, Medicine and Health Sciences, Education and Agriculture and Marine Science. Research is an important priority and the university collaborates with universities in other parts of the world – notably Britain, France, Germany and Japan. Highly qualified academic staff have also been drawn from other countries – particularly English-speaking ones. The university's specialised research facilities include Centres for Solar Cells Testing; Energy Research and Earthquake Detection. There are also Research Stations for

Water Desalination and Agricultural Research.

The College of Medicine and Health Sciences has gained a particularly high reputation, which qualifies graduates for internships in Britain and elsewhere without further examination. This reputation depends in part on the Sultan Qaboos University Hospital, opened in 1989, which has the advantage of sophisticated modern equipment and 500 beds. By 2001, 546 Omani doctors, male and female, graduated from the college.

The university is governed by a Council with a Vice-Chancellor at its executive and academic head. The academic year is divided into two semesters, one beginning in September and the other in February. Degree ceremonies are held in the charming open-air graduation theatre, resembling a small Greek theatre with Islamic features. To improve facilities yet further, the Sultan donated RO 5 million in the early 2000s for a multi-purpose auditorium for university activities, with a capacity of 6000 people.

For several years, Sultan Qaboos University was the only university in the country, but in the later 1990s it became policy to encourage the private sector to establish universities, colleges and institutes under the supervision of the Ministry of Higher Education. Some state assistance was given; in particular grants of land, exemption from taxes and duties, and subsidies. These institutions established links with recognised academic bodies, not only to maintain standards but also to enable them to award qualifications academically endorsed and recognised outside Oman. By 2002 there were already 12 such institutions: one university at Sohar; two university colleges – Sur and Waljat; the College of Administrative Sciences (Majan); the Modern College of Business and Science; Muscat College of Modern Sciences and Technology; the Caledonian College of Engineering; the National College of Science and Technology; Mazoon College of Administration and Applied Sciences; the Fire Safety Engineering College; Al Zahra College for Girls and Oman Medical College.

Sharia and Law College

The Sharia and Law College was set up in 1997 to train Omanis in judicial affairs over a four year BA course. The first batch graduated in 2000/2001 and 530 were enrolled for the following academic year.

A six-year course for younger pupils covers an extensive syllabus including Arabic, basic science and social studies. From the age of fourteen, children can choose between general education (including literary and scientific options), religious education, and vocational schooling in areas such as commerce, agriculture and teacher training. Schools are equipped with libraries, laboratories and workshops.

Sultan Qaboos University (below) *was opened in 1986.*

The college teaches Islamic Sharia Law and Civil Law to prepare the students for work in the Sharia and legal fields, such as criminal and commercial law.

Adult Literacy Provisions

Oman's sixth and seventh Five Year Plans aimed to teach 108,000 illiterates to read and write. By 2002 there were 346 literacy centres; some students even progressed from literacy programmes to gain university places and were specially honoured by the Government.

Vocational Training

With Oman's increasing population it has become inevitable that many skilled and semi-skilled jobs previously undertaken by expatriates – especially from the Indian sub-continent – should be performed by locals. The Sultan has personally and actively encouraged Omanis to think in this direction. The policy of Omanisation is designed to develop human resources and considerable effort has been devoted to training Omanis in the technical and vocational work skills required by the country's various economic sectors. The social affairs, labour and vocational training sectors – in close alliance with the educational and higher educational authorities – is responsible for effecting this through the twin vehicles of technical education and vocational training. By 2002 there were five Higher Technical Industrial Colleges offering, since 1999, the Omani National Diploma. They are widely distributed throughout Oman, at Muscat (which also offers a BA degree), Salalah, Nizwa, Musana'ah and Ibra, with a combined maximum intake of 1,500 students. The subjects offered are: commercial and business studies, information technology, engineering, building construction science and mechanical and electrical engineering.

The subjects available for vocational training include motor vehicle mechanical skills, carpentry, electricity, general mechanics and building construction and there are government vocational training centres at Seeb, Saham, Sur and Ibri. The private sector is also interested in training, and the Government has promoted the National Vocational Qualifications system, introduced in both public and private sectors, with certificates awarded by British institutions.

There are many examples of education tailored to the needs of the economy. In 2002 for example, the Oman Tourism and Hospitality Academy was opened, to give theoretical and practical training to young Omanis in tourism administration, hotel management and as tourist guides. The National Hospitality Institute meanwhile, runs short courses for those wishing to work in hotels and the hospitality industry. Another example of an educational establishment suited to current needs is the Administrative Science College in Darsait, a private sector venture set up by the Oman Chamber of Commerce and Industry (OCCI) in 1995 with a goal of 1,000 students. In 2001 the Sanad Fund was established by the Government to give practical help to young Omanis to set themselves up in business.

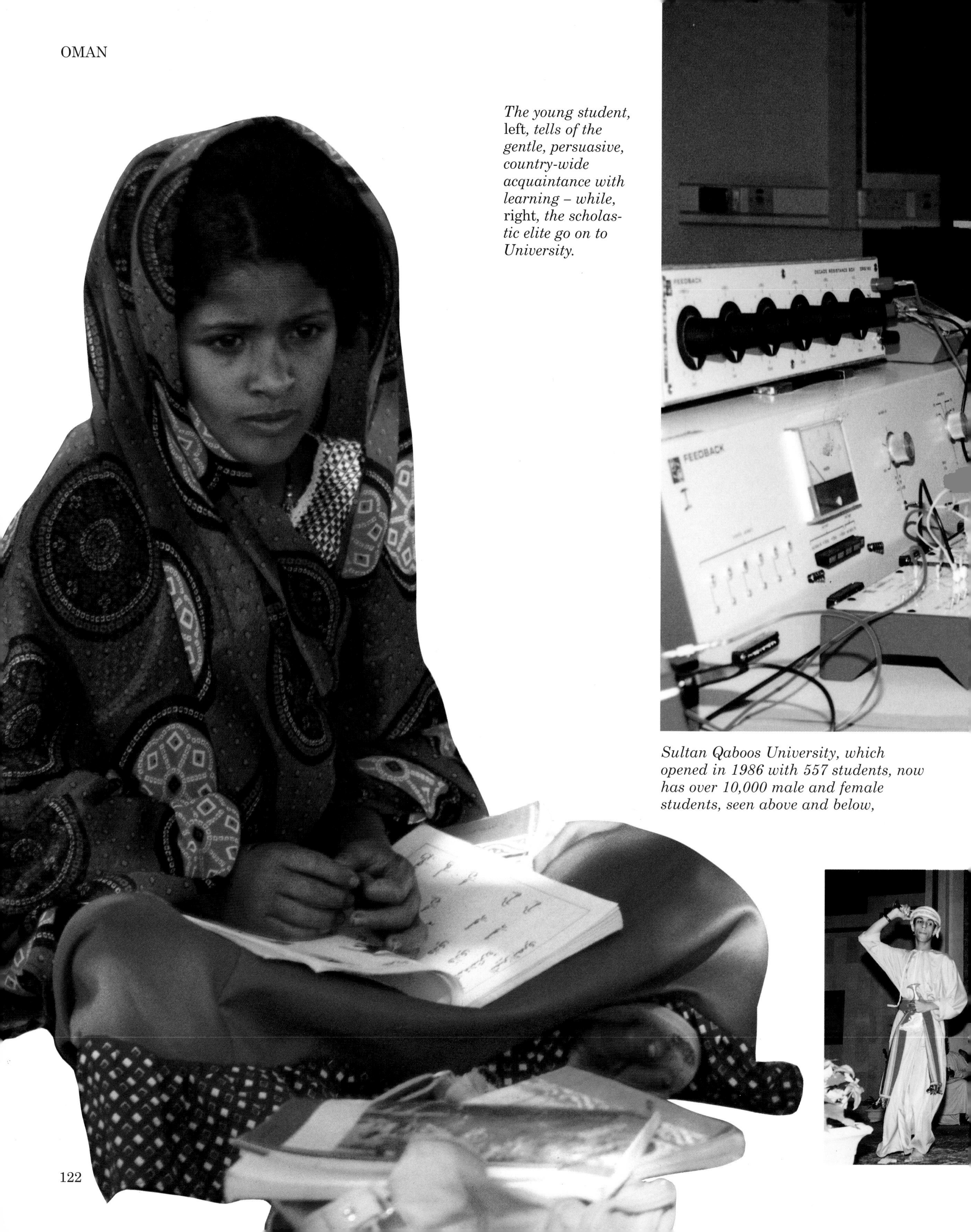

The young student, left, *tells of the gentle, persuasive, country-wide acquaintance with learning – while,* right, *the scholastic elite go on to University.*

Sultan Qaboos University, which opened in 1986 with 557 students, now has over 10,000 male and female students, seen above and below,

engaged in such varied degrees as science, drama, engineering, arts, agriculture, medicine and Islamic sciences.

Health

One of the most dramatic changes in Oman since 1970 has been the improvement in the general health of the Omani people. On Sultan Qaboos's accession there were only two hospitals in the country, neither of which was run by the Government – the American Mission Hospital and the small hospital run by the British Consulate. Today, an old man with a grey beard, carrying a camel stick in a hospital waiting room, may look the same traditional Omani as he was. However, while the common complaints, more often than not, used to be those associated with poverty and 'Third World' absence of development, by the mid-1990s it was the expectation of long life and healthcare of 'First World' quality that was demanding more of Oman's doctors. Today, less than five per cent of the population live more than an hour from a health centre, and the entire population is catered for by mobile medical teams.

In the early 1970s, Omanis were all-but resigned to widespread diseases such as the blinding eye infection trachoma. The achievements of a free national health service, nationwide health education and public hygiene campaigns have dramatically reduced such diseases, and have engendered a general sense of well-being in the average Omani.

The avowed aim of 'Health for All' requires preventative, curative and promotional measures. The Ministry of Health has overall responsibility, while regional directors-general manage individual governorates. In each *wilaya* too, there is a Mushrif responsible to the director-general. Most of the country's hospitals are administered by the Ministry of Health, but the healthcare sector is an important area in the development of privatisation. Several private hospitals are already in operation, while non-medical support services in government hospitals have long been run by private companies.

Oman's health system has won the acclaim of the World Health Organisation, which in 2000 ranked Oman eighth in the world for overall healthcare, and the country which had achieved most progress in improving health standards.

By 1995 every region in the country had a well-equipped referral hospital, providing specialist care covering such conditions as internal diseases, surgery, paediatrics, gynaecology, obstetrics, orthopaedics, eyes, ENT, skin diseases and oral health. There were also clinics for disease and tissue diagnosis, laboratories and radiology departments.

In 2001, over 10 million patients were treated at outpatient clinics, while Omani hospitals treated 226,000 in-patients and carried out 100,000 surgical operations. Omanisation has developed well in the health sector, with the overall level standing at 56 per cent. The first 48 Omani doctors, both men and women, graduated from the medical school of Sultan Qaboos University in 1994 and began their internships in Omani hospitals. The number of medical graduates has been steadily rising ever since. Internships at Omani hospitals are recognised as a qualifying base by the British Royal Colleges, and Omani medical students are now achieving world-class degrees and qualifications.

Agricultural students take a four-year course, with many specialisations. Here, date palm culture is under study.

Some hospitals specialise in particular fields. The Khoula Hospital for example, specialises in orthopaedics, burns, plastic surgery, gynaecology/obstetrics, and physiotherapy. Al Nahdha Hospital concentrates on ear, nose and throat problems, dermatology and dentistry. The Ibn Sina Hospital specialises in psychiatric and drug abuse problems, which is a relatively new phenomenon. There are also separate hospitals catering for the Armed Forces and the Royal Oman Police.

The rest of Oman is also well served by hospitals and clinics. In Dhofar, the main hospital is the Sultan Qaboos Hospital in Salalah. There are also several other small hospitals and over 20 health centres. There are ten hospitals in both the Sharqiyah and the Batinah regions, plus many health centres. Up in the remote Governorate of Musandam meanwhile, there are no fewer than three hospitals and three health centres.

The 630-bed Royal Hospital in Muscat provides a very high standard of care to patients, covering a wide range of specialisation. The department of internal medicine for example, covers gastroenteritis, neurology, nephrology, respiratory diseases, endocrinology, rheumatology and oncology. Apart from general surgery, the department of surgery covers urology, orthopaedics, paediatrics and cardio-thoracic and cardiovascular surgery. There is also first-class cover for obstetrics and gynaecology. The radiology and other support equipment is of the highest standard.

Emphasis is placed by the Ministry on prevention of disease, with a concentration on mothers and children, and the school health programmes. The Expanded Programme of Immunisation (EPI) has achieved 96 per cent coverage by inoculation of all infants under one year, against tuberculosis, diptheria, pertussis and tetanus, poliomyelitis, measles and viral hepatitis B. Infant mortality has dramatically decreased since the early 1970s – when it stood at more than 118 per 1000 live births – to just 17 per 1000 live births in 1999.

In 1994 the Ministry introduced two major programmes. Under the first, children between 15 months and six years were immunised against measles and rubella in the paediatric wards of out-patients departments at hospitals and health centres, while children between six and 18 were immunised at their schools. The school health programme introduced in 1993 has also resulted in primary school children across the country having comprehensive screening. Almost 99 per cent of all children in Oman are now being immunised against the main childhood killer diseases. UNICEF's report for 1997 listed Oman as a top achiever in reducing the deaths in children under the age of five.

The government's campaign against malaria intensified in 1992, with the

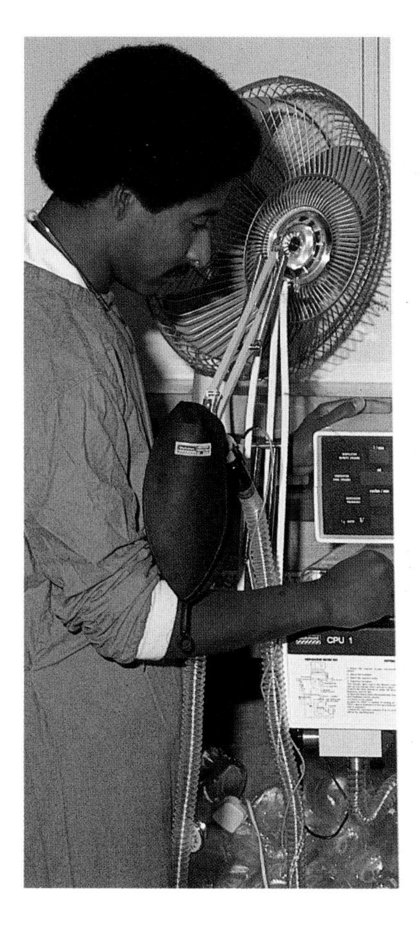

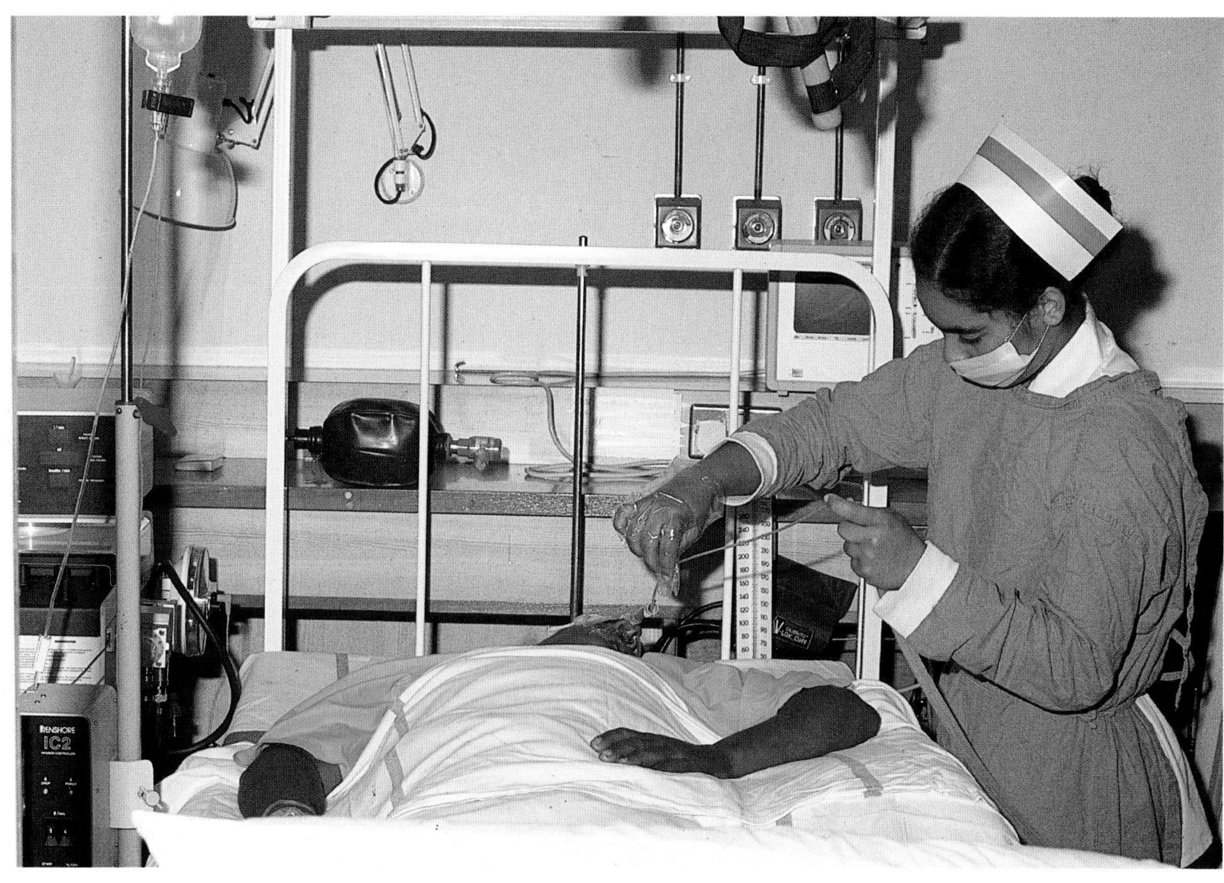

establishment of the Malaria Eradication Programme, which aims to eradicate the disease. The number of cases of malaria recorded in 1999 was only 696, compared with 1091 the year before, and the number is still decreasing.

The Ministry also has specific programmes for dealing with malnutrition, the control of a range of common diseases, oral and mental health and the prevention and control of accidents.

By the mid-1990s, an increasing number of Omanis were emerging in all medical spheres. The Faculty of Medicine at Sultan Qaboos University began in 1986, and is currently training close to 600 Omani doctors. The Ministry is responsible for 11 nursing training schools in, among other places, Nizwa, Salalah, Sohar, Sur, Tanam, Rostaq and Ibri. They have proved very popular with young girls of school-leaving age. These establishments are currently training over 1,200 Omani nurses. Since 1984, 2016 nurses have graduated, of whom 1,560 are women.

With the increased efforts to train and subsequently employ Omani nationals in place of expatriates, the proportion of nationals among medical staff has been increasing slowly but surely. At the end of December 1999, there were 297 Omani doctors and nearly 2000 nurses employed by the Ministry, representing 15 per cent and 31 per cent of the total manpower respectively.

With the high standard of training, the participation of the private sector and the many excellent government facilities throughout the country, Oman can take pride in the high standard of medical care provided for all the people.

The Royal Hospital at Ghubrah is a specialist hospital with 633 beds. It has over 2,000 specialist staff, 70 per cent of whom are female. The hospital has an accident and emergency department, and state-of-the-art equipment in paediatric, maternity, surgical, cardiac and radio-therapy departments. It is the hub of the country's medical services, which extend to the remotest regions of the country (below).

Dhofar

The people of the southern Governorate of Dhofar play a considerable part in the governance of Oman as a whole – as Ministers, civil servants, and members of the armed forces. Likewise their trading and commercial activities are integral to and significant in the national economy. Large numbers have houses in the capital as well as their original homes in the south.

Dhofar itself has changed beyond measure since the early 1970s, when the economy of the region was badly affected by war and the Jebel region was only accessible under cover of military operations. Now good roads cross not only the Salalah plain but the Jebel itself. Fine buildings, many of distinction, have grown up in and around Salalah, which has expanded significantly and covers a large area of the plain – where vegetables were grown in great quantities up to a few decades ago. The lives of the people on the Jebel has been markedly improved by well-built settlements with pleasing houses, mosques and schools and shopping facilities. Electricity has been brought to them and water is abundantly available both for the people and their animals. The herds have in fact grown to such an extent that overgrazing has become a problem. There is a good seaport at Raysut and a fine modern airport with frequent flights to Muscat and to international destinations.

Dhofar's isolation is ended, but it was not always so, as the following description of traditional Dhofar shows.

Some six hundred miles of desert separate the northern and the southern regions of Oman and consequently it is not surprising that the people in Dhofar differ from their northern compatriots. Throughout history, there have existed connections between the Dhofaris and some of the people of South Yemen, as excavations at Samhuram near Salalah show. The common industry was frankincense, of which Dhofar was the primary producer. However, there have also been deep-rooted tribal and governmental connections with northern Oman, and Dhofar's present unity with the north goes back far into the previous century. The tie is particularly close today since the present Sultan of Oman, Qaboos ibn Said, is half Dhofari.

The Dhofaris consist of people of the mountains and people of the plains. They are endowed with high intelligence. The mountain dwellers are divided into the Qara, who are traditionally the masters, the Shhero (sometimes transliterated as Shahra) who were formerly a serf class, and the Arabs of Al Kathir, whilst in the lower valleys the Mahra predominate. There are also minor divisions. All have by long custom looked to one of the coastal towns for their trade and supplies. The mountain people are intimately bound up with their animals, for which they have the same sort of affection as some of the African tribes. They pasture their sleek little cattle and their camels, goats and sheep on the grass which grows in great profusion following the monsoon, when for a while the stern bare valleys are turned into green rolling country. It is the mist and heavy rainfall that endows Dhofari country with its special character.

The Dhofaris probably did not exceed 25,000 or 30,000 in number overall in 1970. The 1993 census produced a figure of 175,000 for Dhofar as a whole, and today the population is closer to 178,000. Among the numerous tribes and sub-tribes, there are many languages spoken besides standard Arabic, including Mahri, Jibali (Shheri) and Bathari. Many, too, speak a dialect of Arabic. Some tribes are divided between mountain people and *Bedu* of the northern desert or the Najd plateau.

The frankincense tree, the *Boswellia sacra*, still thrives in parts of Dhofar. Apart from a revival of exploitation for a modern perfume factory in the capital, the gum is mainly used for local consumption, for the great trade in frankincense which flourished for so many centuries has virtually dried up.

In Salalah, the capital of Dhofar, there are considerable numbers of people whose original or ancestral home was in Africa and African influence is seen when on religious holidays they dance in the streets, the women wearing the brightest colours, to rhythms brought from the African shore.

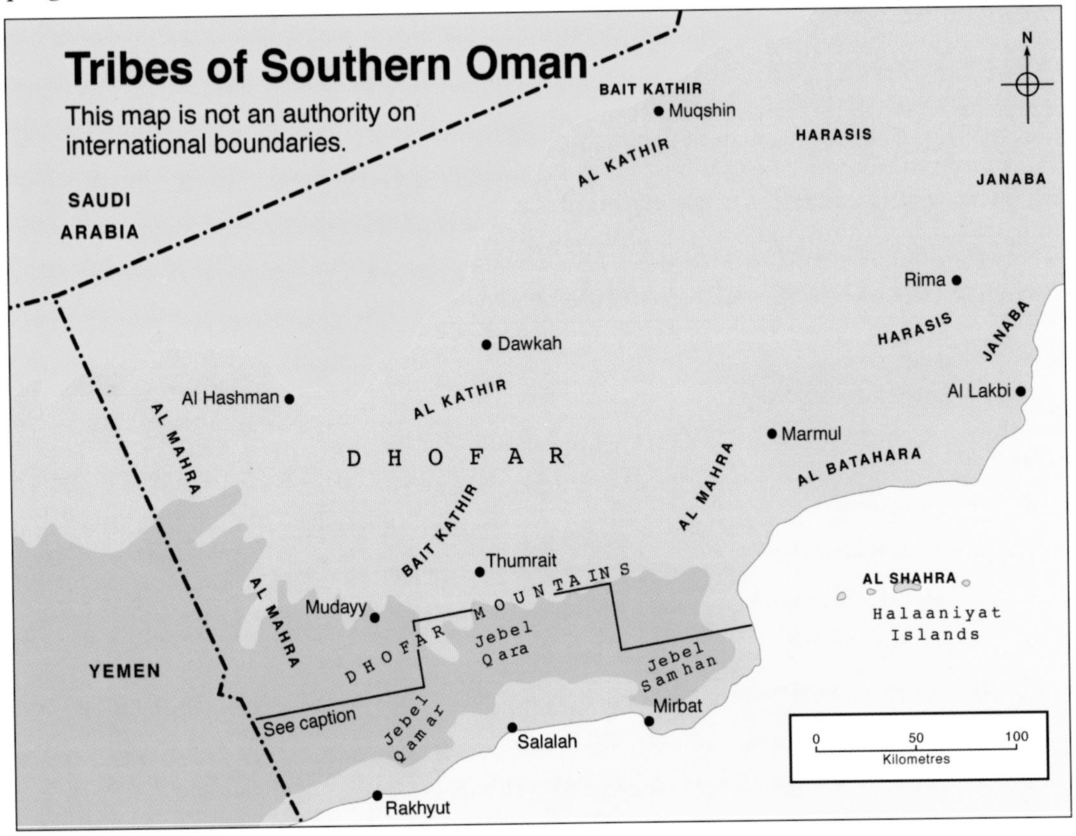

Tribes of the well-watered mountains of extreme south-east of Oman, some known as Al Qara, include Al Amri, Al Mashoni, Bait Kshob, Bait Tebok, Bait Said, Bait Hardan, Bait Akak, Al Awayid, Bait Qatn, Al Barami, Bait Jaboob, Bait Shimas, and tribal elements of Al Kathir, Al Mahra, Ahahra and Al Mashayikh. This map cannot attempt precision as to the territory of Al Kathir, Bait Kathir and Al Mahra of the northern deserts.

Musandam

The Musandam peninsula, with its lofty peaks and fjord-like inlets, was known to Sumerian navigators 5000 years ago as Kur-Maganna. Its geographic location made it a cultural island. The Shihuh are the people of the Musandam governorate, which until very recent times was all but totally isolated from the rest of the area – even from the main part of Oman. Lacking natural resources or commodities which might attract outsiders, Musandam remained *sui generis* until development started in the 1970s. This isolation has since then been greatly reduced by air transport, with regular internal flights, and by the roads linking the main towns – Khasab, Bukha, Lima and Baia – with Dibba and with Ras al Khaimah in the United Arab Emirates. As in other parts of Oman civil buildings, mosques, schools, hospitals and amenities of modern life like electricity and water – from desalination plant – as well as the motor car have changed centuries-old ways of life. This former life was hard.

Some people consider that the Shihuh are the remnant of the original population of the Arabian peninsula, who were driven into their mountain fastnesses, much as the ancient (Celtic) Britons were driven into Wales and Cornwall. They carry a small-headed axe on a long shaft of local wood, the *jerz*, which is their peculiar badge – as the *khanjar* is with the majority of Omanis. This also has practical uses as a stick in the mountain terrain, and in the past as a weapon of defence against the caracal lynx and the Arabian leopard, which, though few in number, inhabit the region.

The typical mountain dwelling, the *bait-al qufl,* is well suited to the seasonal migrations of most Shihuh, which causes them to leave it unattended for long periods. It is a low, virtually impregnable building with walls and roof of carefully selected local stone, though some roofs may be of wood and mud. Foundations a metre and a half or more below ground, and a low narrow entrance which can be shut by extremely strong wooden doors with bolts and locks of ingenious design, make it a unique type of house. It is safe to abandon during the summer months from June to September, when lack of water and the need to tend palm gardens and harvest dates drives the Shihuh from their ancestral mountain villages to the coastal areas. On the coast the dwellings are built of coral, rock, palm and imported wood and resemble those of other places in the general area.

In the winter the Shihuh return to the highlands to grow barley and wheat. Only a handful of people remain to tend the flocks and take them to grazing grounds and water holes hidden in remote areas of the mountains. Rainwater has always been collected in well-placed cisterns. Bukha hill fort, for instance, has a fine domed example. Water for travellers has traditionally been provided by the *kher*, a large earth-

In the weapons market of Salalah's suq, treasured symbols of personal defence are valued by the trader as much for their decorative and antique qualities as for armament, among a people at peace.

The all-purpose tool of this Shihuh of Musandum is the springy-handled axe. The Shihuh migrate from their mountain villages to seashore fishing settlements.

en-ware jar, left by pious individuals along a main track or among a group of houses.

There are two main groups of Shihuh; the Bani Shatair and the Bani Hadiya, whose influence seems to predominate in mountain areas. The Kumzaris are a distinct group within the Shihuh confederation. Though some live in Dibba, Khasab and elsewhere, their main centre in one of the northernmost bays of the peninsula is the small town of Kumzar itself, which nestles in a narrow cleft in the rocks with scarcely any flat ground around it.

Although the majority of the Shihuh speak their own form of Arabic, the Kumzaris have a distinct language, a compound of Arabic and Persian. Their culture too is distinct. Lacking land, they bury their dead under family houses in a manner similar to the custom in parts of Cairo. Cut off and dependent totally on the sea, they are fishermen, sailors and boat builders. They decorate their boats – *batils* – distinctively with cowrie shells, symbols of their former wealth. Even the small scale rearing of goats depends on the sea, for at certain seasons they take their goats across to graze on Jezirat al Ghanam, Goat Island.

Bedu

The day-to-day life of the *Bedu* has changed since 1970, particularly with their acquiring motor vans and cars – denied to them until then. Likewise increasing numbers of them have joined government service. But *Bedu* life is so important in Omani and general Arab consciousness that an account of their life before recent developments is necessary.

Oman's *Bedu* live in the deserts to the west and south of Muscat, some of them being true desert dwellers and others living on the fringe of the cultivated areas. Tribes such as the Duru have palm gardens which they care for in the summer months and there is a gradual tendency towards permanent settlement. Indeed a measure of settlement by *Bedu* has persisted since time immemorial. They may be "two house families" with a *Bedu* tent for most of the year and a house of mud or palm fronds for the summer. The *Bedu* tent may vary from something large and well equipped, though this is unusual, to a simple and primitive shelter. In either case, woven rugs of camel and goat hair are used, alternate red and black stripes being typical of western Oman, which when sold in the markets are known as *Ibri* or *Nizwa* rugs. The women weave the fabrics used for tent building, rugs, and the accoutrements of camels and horses. This area does not have the black tents of Najd but the cloth is usually hung over thorn trees to provide shade.

Wilfred Thesiger has drawn from Oman this description of the virtues of the desert life: "All that is best in the Arabs has come to them from the desert; their deep religious instinct, which has found expression in Islam; their sense of fellowship, which binds them as members of one faith; their pride of race; their generosity and sense of hospitality; their dignity and the regard which they have for the dignity of others as fellow human beings; their humour, their courage and patience, the language which they speak and their passionate love of poetry."

Omanis claim descent from the main stocks – the Qahtan tribes of south Arabia and the Nizar from the north. This pre-supposes a period of desert migration before their arrival in Oman, a fact which tends to confirm the age-long nature of the settling process. The *Bedu* own herds of goats and camels and sometimes range over great distances. Their life is changing as large numbers of *Bedu* are being employed in the oil companies and the ever-increasing contracting work. Even in the late 1970s, *Bedu* represented no more than three per cent of the population.

In *Arabian Sands*, Wilfred Thesiger gave a powerful description of the *Bedu* way of life:

> In the sharp cold of the winter morning we rode to the Saar camp, passing herds of fat milch camels, which the herdsboys had just driven out to pasture. Small, black, goat-hair tents were scattered about over the valley...and dark-clad women sat churning butter or moved about getting sticks or herding goats. The small children were seated in camel litters.
>
> ...We spent the following day at Ali's tent. This was only about twelve feet long, woven of black goat's hair and pitched like a wind-break under a small tree. Among these Bedu tribes there is no contrast between rich and poor, since everyone lives in a similar manner, dressing in the same way and eating the same sort of food.
>
> ...Most of them demanded only the bare necessities of life, enough food and drink to keep them alive, clothes to cover their nakedness, some form of shelter from the sun and wind, weapons, a few pots, rugs, water skins and their saddlery. It was a life which produced much that was noble, nothing that was gracious.

Among the Harasis of the central Jiddat it is a mark of social distinction and dependability of character to become one of the country's wildlife wardens, protecting endangered animals such as the Arabian Oryx.

The *Bedu* are garrulous and while away the long marching hours with chatter as they move over the barren terrain. Despite the great austerity of their life, they are merciless critics of anyone who lacks patience, good humour, generosity, courtesy, loyalty or courage. One of their greatest compliments is to tell someone that he "has not fallen short" of their ideal – which is a most exacting one – in matters of human behaviour. *Bedu* tribesmen are brought up from birth to endure the physical hardships of the desert, to drink the brackish water of the desert wells, to eat gritty unleavened bread, to

suffer the maddening driven sand and blinding glare in a land without shade or cloud, and to put up with extremes of cold and heat.

Thy are always awake and moving about as soon as it is light. When on the move they have little to cover them apart from the clothes they stand up in, however cold it may be, even if there is a frost on the ground. Early in the morning they rouse their camels from sleeping places and the strange, ungainly beasts rise to their feet, roaring and gurgling at being disturbed. The men shout to each other in harsh, far-carrying voices, and the hobbled camels shuffle past with their forelegs tied to prevent them from straying too far, their breath appearing substantial in the cold air. Someone gives the call to prayer. Amongst some *Bedu* tribes the men pray singly, but in others they pray together in line, facing towards Mecca. Every act connected with prayer has, as Thesiger described, to be performed exactly and in order: "He washed his face, hands and feet; sucked water into his nostrils, put wet fingers into his ears, and passed wet hands over the top of his head. [He] swept the ground before him, placed his rifle in front of him and then prayed towards Mecca. He stood upright, bent forward with his hands on his knees, knelt, and then bowed down till his forehead touched the ground. Several times, he performed these ritual movements, slowly and impressively, while he recited the formal prayer."

Bell-like sounds ring out as coffee is pounded in a brass mortar, the stroke varying and producing the semblance of a tune. If there is no hurry, bread is baked for breakfast – by the men if they are travelling alone; otherwise by the women when the family are all together in their encampments. Tea is drunk, sweet and black, and then coffee, bitter, black and very strong. Coffee drinking is a formal affair even in the middle of the desert when a few men are on the move together. The server stands to pour a few drops into the small round china cups which he then hands ceremoniously to the others with a little bow – and he will go on serving until the recipient shakes his cup to indicate that he does not want any more. Not more than three cups are usually taken.

The tents of the *Bedu* are often very temporary and flimsy affairs, and may be as small as three yards long and four feet high. They are not usually large like the tents in the northern part of Arabia. They will contain the saddles and other gear needed for their Spartan life. The family utensils may consist of a kettle and coffee pot, blackened with soot from the wood fires, sundry cooking pots of various sizes, a large round tray or two, and a few plates and cups. Such ephemeral dwellings leave but few traces, and H. St John Philby described "the characteristic odds and ends of old Badawin camps – horns of the Rim gazelle, cartridge cases, fragments of leather and the like", which he found on deserted Bedu sites.

Omanis ride a camel in a manner totally different from the style of north Arabia and most of the Arab world, where the rider sits on a heavy wooden saddle placed over the hump. Thesiger describes how his camel was saddled with the small Omani saddle:

> Sultan picked up my saddle, which was shaped like a small double wooden vice, fitted over palm-fibre pads and girthed it tightly over Umbriasha's withers, just in front of the hump. This wooden vice was

really the tree on which he now built the saddle. He next took a crescent-shaped fibre pad which rose in a peak at the back, and after fitting it round the back and sides of the camel's hump, attached it with a loop of string to this tree. He then put a blanket over the pad, and folded my rug over this, placed my saddle bags over the rug, and finally put a black sheepskin on top of the saddle bags. He had already looped a woollen cord under the camel's stomach so that it passed over the rear pad, and he now took one end of this cord past the tree and back along the other side of the saddle to the original loop. When he drew the cord tight it held everything firmly in place. He had now built a platform over the camel's hump and the fibre pad which was behind it. Sitting on this, the rider was much farther back on the camel than he would have been if riding on the northern saddle.

A Bedu who is going to mount a crouched camel stands behind her tail. He then leans forward and catches the wooden tree with his left hand as he places his left knee in the saddle. Immediately the camel feels his weight she starts to rise – for it is usually she-camels which are ridden in this part of Arabia – lifting her hindquarters off the ground, and he swings his right leg over the saddle. The camel then rises to her knees, and with another jerk, is on her feet. The *Bedu* either sit with a leg on either side of the hump and a little behind it, or kneel in the saddle, sitting on the upturned soles of their feet, in which case they are sitting entirely by balance. They prefer to ride kneeling, especially if they mean to gallop.

The nobility of *Bedu* life does not lie in material things, but is well epitomised in their greetings. As Philby says: "Very beautiful is the meeting of the Arabs in the desert, with their greetings of each other – very formal, very long-drawn-out and repetitive, for every member of each party exchanges the same friendly enquiries and assurances with each member of the other, until all have greeted all, and they part or proceed to any business that may be in hand. Peace be upon you! And on you be peace! How is your state, oh Salih? In peace; how are you oh Ali? In peace! May God give you health! May God improve your condition! How are you? In peace! And then follows the abrupt transition to business with: "What is your news?" This courteousness is characteristic of the *Bedu*.

For the Bedu (far left) *the relationship with the camel is intimate, even when, as above, they are also supported by their four-wheel drive vehicles.*

Islanders

The mode of life in other peripheral areas such as Masirah and the Halaaniyaat (Kuria Muria) Islands also differs from that in most of northern Oman. Masirah Island has most of the features of the Omani mainland – *jebel*, plain, coast, scrub and palm – in miniature. However, the people were not in recent decades – until the reign of Sultan Qaboos – permitted to erect buildings in any permanent material, a punishment for the massacre of the crew of the Merchantman *Baron Inverdale* in 1904.

Work at the British RAF Station from the 1940s to the 1970s brought people who had previously lived in palm-frond dwellings into a growing town on the edge of the camp; they built their houses out of oil drums. The improvement in standards of building have been very marked since the accession of Sultan Qaboos and the island has a life of its own with its Royal Oman Air Force facilities. These facilities, with Seeb's, played a critical role in the 1991 Gulf War.

The history of the Halaaniyaat Islands has been even stranger. These five small islands off the coast of Dhofar are called Halaaniya, Jibliya, Suda, Haskiya and Gharzaut. They were ceded to the British Crown by Sayyid Said ibn Sultan on 14th July 1854 without payment, although Lord Clarendon, the Foreign Secretary, did send Sayyid Said a snuff box in recognition of his generosity. A concession to extract guano from the islands was then given to Captain Ord, a British merchant captain. His company extracted 26,191 tons in 1857-58 (1274-76 AH) and 14,250 tons in 1858-59 (1275-76 AH), but their licence was terminated in 1861 when they fell down on royalty payments. Indeed the islands have been inhabited only by a small number of fishermen, who, latterly at least, have dwelt solely on Halaaniya.

British sovereignty was largely nominal and when the islands were visited by the Governor of Aden, Sir Richard Luce and Sir George Middleton, Resident in the Persian Gulf in 1960, the headman of the village asked them if they had a permit from the Sultan, The islands were returned to Oman in 1967 (1387 AH).

5 Habitat and Habitation

The great majority of Omanis are townsmen and villagers living where men have always dwelt. Styles vary - north and south, lowland and upland, merchant and peasant. Today among the coastal havens and city ports, the castle-dominated centres of the Interior, the settlements of the Batinah and upland compounds, a modern Oman has arisen of air-conditioned homes and public buildings, with their flowers and trees and fountains. Meanwhile, old buildings hold their own, and spectacular antiquity is devotedly preserved.

Muscat is unique, pivot of the extensive capital area, locked between steep hillsides and the sea at the head of a deep and beautiful bay. This panorama shows the Alam Palace, and the sixteenth century forts of Mirani (left) *and Jalali* (right). *The British Embassy was located in an historic house overlooking this bay until it was moved to Shatti al Qurm in 1994.*

The Omani of today lives in an environment very changed from that of 1970. The small twin towns of Muscat and Mutrah were then the political and commercial capitals of the country but their joint population probably did not exceed fifteen thousand. Today the Capital Area with its population of over 622,000 stretches from Quriyat to Seeb, a distance of 134 kilometres. The finest house in Muscat or Mutrah in the early 1970s probably did not reach the standards of amenity and even luxury of an average house today in Shati' al-Qurm or Medinat Qaboos. Likewise in Salalah, the capital of the Southern Region, the difference in amenity between the average house of 1970 and that of today is extraordinary. The introduction of many modern innovations, made possible by an expanding economy based on oil revenues, has affected many aspects of the modern Omani habitat.

From 1970 onwards the face of the country changed with startling rapidity as new buildings, businesses, industrial developments and new urban areas were constructed. The greatest transformation took place in the capital itself. Previously, Muscat and Mutrah, connected by a narrow coastal road of dramatic beauty, had both long retained their individual and traditional character. Soon, however, planners and public alike came to regard the capital area as the long, narrow coastal strip betwen Qurayyat and Seeb, where the new airport was built in 1973 in replacement of the one at Bait al Falaj, approached perilously between the mountains and soon to be swallowed up by Ruwi.

Muscat remained the centre of the political capital and was, therefore, the site of the impressive new palace new-built for the Sultan in 1972 on the waterfront between the sixteenth century forts of Mirani and Jalali. The best of the traditional houses were preserved and renovated and new gates and buildings, including the Diwan and the Ministry of Finance, were erected in the style of, or in harmony with, the well-proportioned buildings of the past. Thus Muscat itself retained a flavour of its traditional character after new construction had changed its physical aspect markedly.

The widespread change was symbolised by the sudden collapse of the ancient gate of Mutrah in 1972. Until then the great wooden gate within its lofty portal had been solemnly opened at dawn and closed after dusk, even though the road had been driven through the city wall a few yards away. Vibrations from the increasing traffic almost certainly caused the demise of this old landmark. Indeed the rapidly increasing volume of traffic was responsible for many of the changes to the country's appearance and way of life. In 1971 there were not more than ten saloon cars in the Sultanate, but some 275,000 vehicles were on the road by 1995, with the numbers ever increasing. As more roads were built, so development took place on an ever growing scale. In the Ruwi valley behind Mutrah for instance, areas were allocated in accordance with expertly produced plans for commercial and industrial premises, government development, hotels, housing and hospitals. Muscat, Mutrah, Ruwi and many other places have grown in consequence into elegant modern towns with beautiful tree plantings, gardens and roundabouts with lawns, flowers and Omani themes in stone and ceramic.

The broader natural harbour of Mutrah – a few miles along the coast from Muscat – made it for many years the country's natural commercial capital, as the façade of its elegant 19th century mercantile houses along the corniche suggest.

Grants of land were originally made through the Ministry of Lands, which not

only created a land registry and ensured that transactions were recorded on the register but also saw that the new construction conformed with zoning plans. The criteria for grants were first that an applicant should be a native of the area – although this was interpreted liberally; secondly that he should own no other residence, if applying for a residential plot; and thirdly that he should show sufficient means to be able to build in accordance with the building standards specified in the regulations – a provision which also applied to all applicants for commercial and industrial plots.

Planning and development have been continuous but during the second Five Year Plan several major projects were initiated including the Ruwi business district and the construction of "Information City", a telecommunications complex incorporating studios, transmitters, offices, radio stations and housing built at Qurm on the Batinah coast. The RO 41 million Sultan Qaboos sports complex at Baushar opened in 1985 in time for the celebrations of the fifteenth anniversary of Sultan Qaboos's accession. Covering 44 hectares of land, its main features are a stadium seating a capacity of 30,000 and a large sports hall with facilities for 23 games. Other large stadia have been opened, notably at Sohar and Nizwa, where celebrations of National Days were held with the Sultan himself presiding in 1992 and 1994 respectively. The Sultan Qaboos University at al Khodh built in 1986 is a magnificent complex of modern buildings in the traditional style set in fine parkland, a delightful feature of which is the open air degree-conferring theatre – a blend of classical Greek and oriental styles. The splendid 630-bed Royal Hospital – where the architecture, surrounding beauty of landscape and equipment are all notable – was opened at al Ghubra in 1987.

At the other end of the scale, a Social Housing Programme was instituted in 1973 for those on limited incomes, and 73 houses were built that year. There are now three Social Housing Programmes, each targeting different income groups. Between 1976 and 1990, the Government

The capital has spread mostly northwards along the coast from Muscat and Mutrah, and behind and sometimes across the line of hills that flanks the coast immediately west of Mutrah.

The popular suburb of Qurm is enhanced by fine architecture (left) *while the Al Alam Palace provides a dramatic backdrop for the performance of traditional Omani music* (below left).

provided 8,260 social housing units nationwide. Between 1996 and 2000, the programme provided 125,094 plots of land, and in 2001, over 8,000 plots were distributed. Housing loans distributed by the Oman Housing Bank, are an alternative source of finance for lower income families. In 2002, funding for 102 Omani families was approved.

The housing programmes in the north wre paralleled by those in the south, and at Salalah impressive development grew up along the modern road, leading to Raysut to the west and to Taqah to the east. Apart from the schools, hospitals and markets, the region's fine buildings were enhanced by the replication in the capital of Dhofar of the various Ministries of the central government in Muscat. On the *jebel* in Dhofar, complexes in particular areas grew from simple settlements with school, mosque, dispensary and water supply to well-built and architecturally pleasing towns with more sophisticated versions of these basic needs.

Special consideration too had to be given to the Musandam area. The Development Committee established there oversaw the construction of schools, clinics, ports, airstrips and housing, particularly at Bukha, Khasab and Bayah. An earth satellite station was installed to provide the area with modern communications, bringing the people of Musandam much closer to their fellow citizens in the main landmass of Oman.

Architecture and Construction

All this development and construction necessitated a very large architectural input. It is evident at fight that the aarchitecture of modern Oman, though

Most of Muscat lies within its ancient walls, within which a resident was not until 1970 permitted to move after nightfall without a lantern. Its main gate, above, *still follows the traditional style.*

varying considerably in style is remarkably homogeneous. This has been the result of Qaboos's very personal interest and influence. As in other spheres, there has been a conscious effort everywhere to preserve something of the shapes, features, colours and spirit of Oman's many historical buildings in the modern ones built since 1970 – from Palaces, Ministries, public buildings and private houses of varying degrees of pretension to the well-planned and harmonious low cost housing for the less well off. The residential areas and great town roads have been beautifully landscaped with trees and flowers and the resulting contrast between the lush irrigated areas and the bare deserts and mountains, which have always been among Oman's natural glories, is a striking feature of modern Oman.

The Ministries' area in the capital contains a number of distinguished buildings, from which it may be a little invidious to make selections. The Ministry of National Heritage and Culture, which also contains the fine National Natural History Museum, conjures up the feeling of Oman's great castles and forts. The Ministry of Foreign Affairs of beautiful white traditional design with crenellations revives the style of old houses in Muscat such as Bait Graiza and Bait Nadir and is suitably restrained in style for its diplomatic purposes.

The traditional mosques of Oman were always well proportioned and distinguished in their design with a simplicity and asceticism appropriate to the old Oman. Many new mosques have been built all over the country both by the government and private endowment. They

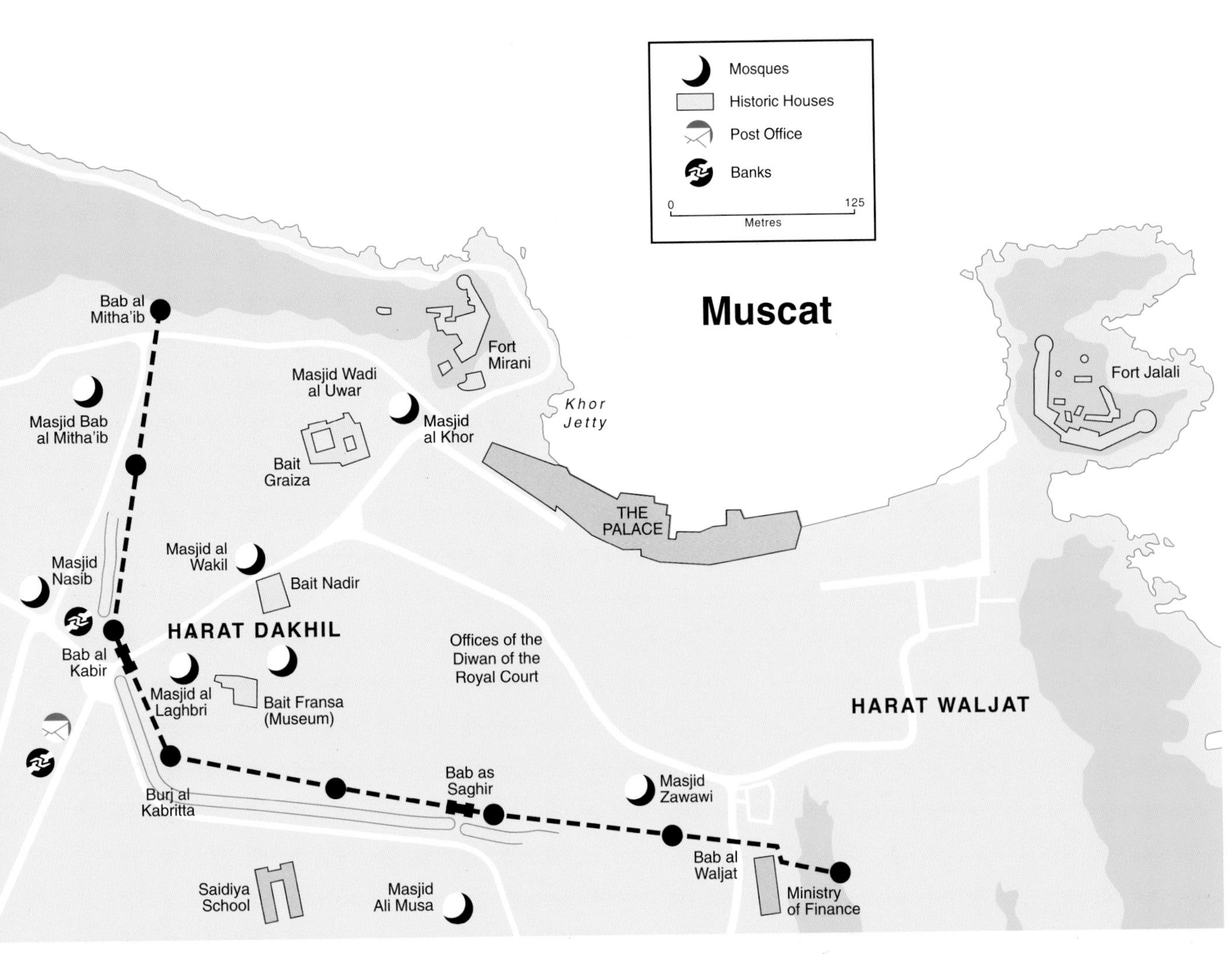

While some of the hidden ways of ancient Muscat (above) *have been overtaken by modernisation, the atmosphere and style of the ancient city have been preserved despite the modern administrative functions which prevail in the capital.* Left *and* right, *three of the gates in the city walls;* above right, *the white walls of Bait Graiza stand in contrast with the dark façade of Mirani fort.*

are larger and more ornately designed than the ancient mosques. But they reflect the importance of Islam to the Omani nation in the changed and more complex modern environment. Their decoration is frequently beautiful, and their minarets and domes are invariably magnificent. None more so perhaps, than the Sultan Qaboos Grand Mosque, which was opened in 2001. Its five magnificent minarets represent the Five Pillars of Islam (*see* pages 196-7 and 206-7).

A most distinguished and interesting modern example of the use of Islamic architectural motifs is the unique Al Bustan Palace Hotel. Seen from afar in its striking location, it stands like one of Oman's many forts, with its squared copper dome surmounted by a spike on a ball. Closer to, one sees it for what it is: a vast octagonal structure with harmonious outbuildings. Each of the eight façades represents eight cloister-like courses of verandas, one mounted upon the other, composed of Islamic pointed arches supported by slender columns of grey and black marble – reminiscent of the 13th century Salisbury Cathedral. Palm groves and green lawns surround, and through the delicate tracery of the palm fronds are seen the jagged surrounding hills with their infinite play of colours. The gardens are bright with flowering shrubs – red, yellow and purple bougainvilleas, lantanas, hibiscus, petunias, oleanders, and vinca.

The great atrium inside is the heart of the place. It takes the breath away at first sight with its sense of vast space and eight immense soaring Gothic arches – edged by gold rope-pattern frames and narrow mirrors – soaring to the upper wooden balconies. The supports between the arches are decorated with subtle, gently coloured tiles of blue, green, and apricot. All the decorative features are of striking Islamic geometric and floral designs right up to the dome – arches, tiles, friezes, decorative motifs in carved

wood and plaster and on the fine, pale wood doors. A splendid marble-based fountain plays in the middle. Altogether it is a monument in the tradition of the greatest Islamic architecture. The whole place is filled with the smell of the olibanum incense of Dhofar and the harmonious sound of gentle classical music – sometimes provided by a live pianist or harpist.

The Al Bustan Palace was built in 1985 in time for the celebrations of the fifteenth anniversary of Sultan Qaboos's accession, at which time Oman was also host to the meeting of the Heads of State of the Gulf Cooperation Council countries. It was specifically devised to accommodate all the Heads of State at one time in separate penthouse palaces of their own. The splendid complex thus includes not only lovely suites and bedrooms, decorated with Islamic tiles and motifs, but also great and small conference rooms, giving off corridors paved in marble, plus a fine theatre and beautiful concert hall with a magnificent organ. Thus dramatically Oman filled the gap, of which they were previously very conscious, in the availability of adequate accommodation for entertaining Heads of State and visitors at the highest level.

Water and Power

The provision of adequate water and power supplies were crucial to all these developments and owing to Oman's general aridity the problem was an acute one. In the early stages water could be supplied in most of the country from traditional sources or newly-installed pumps but more complex arrangements were necessary both in the capital area and in Salalah. Until the 1960s Muscat and Mutrah obtained water from local wells. From 1968, however, a new supply of water for the capital was piped from a large and previously untapped swell field at al Khod, where the Wadi Samail debouches on to the Batinah plain. By 1970 this supply was already proving inadequate. Water surveys were undertaken, new wells sunk and desalination plants constructed to supplement the older sources.

In Salalah the water supply came from bore-holes sunk on the plains, though in the past much of the supply had been brought down from the Wadi Arzat by the ancient falaj. This had been damaged during the Dhofar rebellion and reliance had to be placed on the new bore-holes. By 1982 new water systems were operating

Above, right *and* lower right opposite: *Bait Fransi, once the site of France's representative to Muscat, is one of the six finest 18th century houses in Muscat.*

effectively at Buraimi, Nizwa, Sohar and Sur. Water, for which the Public Authority for Water Resources (PAWR) has general responsibility, is of such paramount importance that close attention has been given to it in all the successive Five Year Plans from the start. Apart from fresh water for domestic supplies from desalination plants, all Oman's water resources derive from rain water, including water for the ancient *falaj* system on which so many towns in Oman depended, and from bore holes. The so-called fossil water, which lies underground at considerable depths and which may in future be used with care, also comes from Oman's rainfall during periods of the distant past when the climate was much wetter. Attention to the subject has been sharpened by the uncontrolled sinking of wells on the Batinah and Salalah plains, which has led to over-pumping with consequent saline invasion from the sea. The National Well Inventory Project was instituted in 1991 as an ongoing task to tackle this problem. More generally water resources investigations are also conducted in all regions of the Sultanate.

The provision of domestic water has developed greatly since the 1960s when even Muscat and Mutrah derived their supply from local wells. In 1968 the Water Department was established. In 1970 three Government wells were sunk at al Khodh and a pipeline constructed to Muscat and Mutrah. But the limitation of supplies from natural water resources for domestic purposes, as the capital and other towns expanded, led to the construction of the first desalination plant at al Ghubbrah outside Muscat in 1976 with a daily production of 6 million gallons. This was expanded to meet the needs of a growing population and a sophisticated infrastructure so that by 2002 Ghubrah, powered by natural gas, had a capacity of 42 million gallons a day.

Above: *characteristic of finer aristocratic and merchant houses, Bait Naiman at Barka has a room for prayer and for reading the Holy Qur'an.*

The great minaret of Mutrah's mosque shows Moghul influence, while the Mutrah façade below is classically Omani.

Interior Woodwork

Unlike most of the rest of Arabia, hardwood trees have in the past grown in parts of Oman. This source of wood, supplemented from India and Africa, has helped to keep alive in Oman a remarkable tradition of woodcarving and shipbuilding over hundreds of years.

Every window screen tests the designer's ingenuity.

The doorway screen (above) *declares the home-owner's taste.*

The rose inspires the woodcarver's handiwork (above).

Design is drawn from inventive geometry and sometimes Qur'anic verses.

Imaginative modern architecture and landscaping inspiration has made much of the capital area's aspect a source of delight to its inhabitants. Top left *the Ruwi Telecommunications Tower, also visible – illuminated at nightfall – to the right of the Ruwi panorama* above; *and* below, left, *ceremonial swords surmounting W. Kabir.*

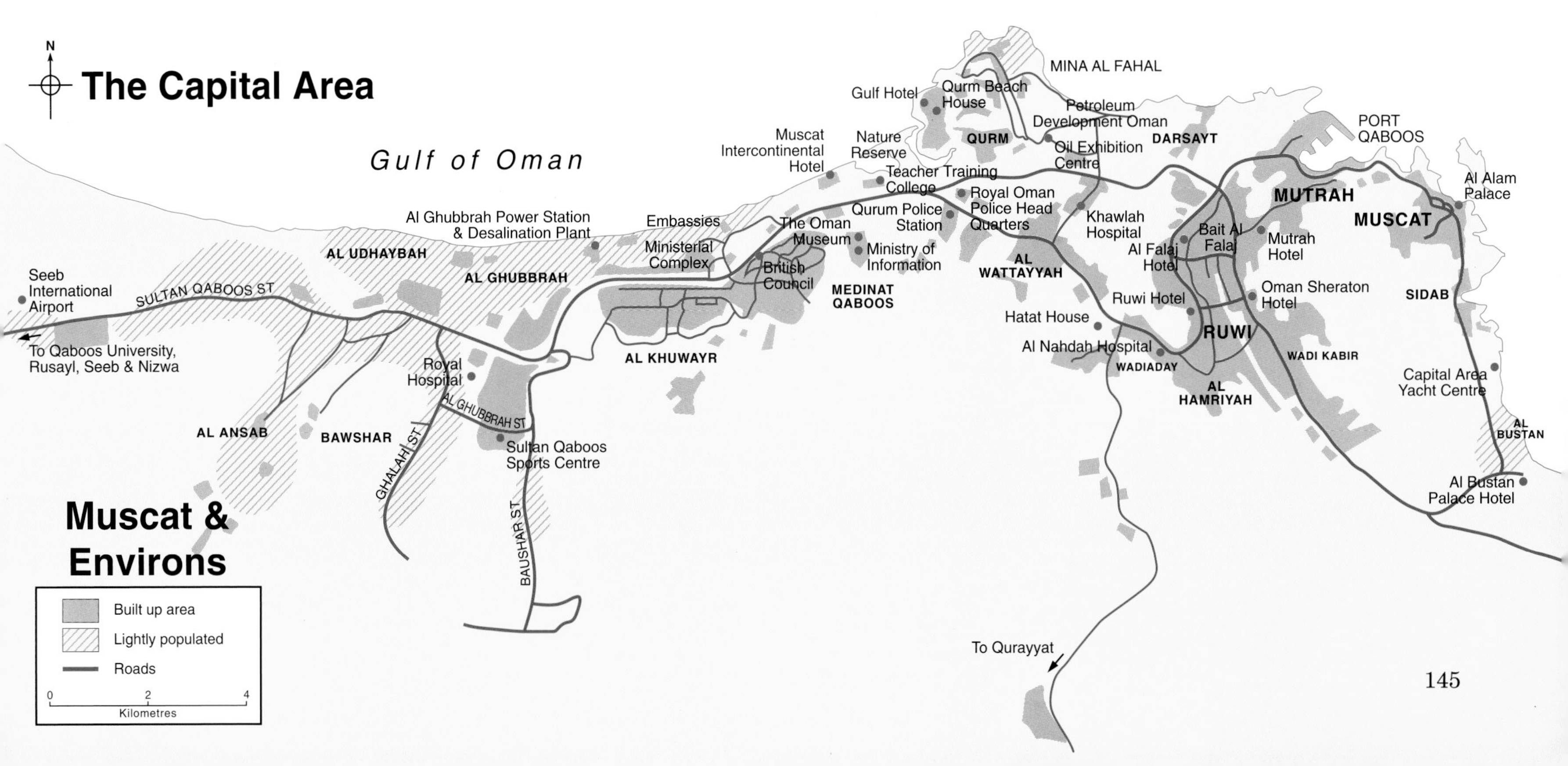

There is considerable reservoir capacity and, before distribution, the desalinated water is mixed with fresh water piped from Wadi Daiqah and Al Khodh. There are also more than 20 other desalination plants, mainly using the reverse osmosis process, in different parts of the country. These include Sur, Sohar, and Barka, where the power station and desalination plant was constructed by the private sector on the BOOT principle of 'Build, Own, Operate and Transfer'. Pipelines and house connections with fresh water reach an increasing number of users in ever remoter areas and the distribution system has been continually updated and improved. However, Oman is a country with a limited and variable rainfall, and continues to face a major challenge in providing for its future water needs, as demonstrated by its already great and increasing dependence on desalination.

Government ministries, like that of Foreign Affairs, above, *set impressive standards. An ibex model* (top) *surmounts a decorative waterfall.* Above right and opposite, *the world-famous Al Bustan Palace Hotel.*

Electricity

Early development in the field of electricity preceded Sultan Qaboos's accession; the Muscat Power Company was formed in 1967 to operate a small power station at Riyam between Muscat and Mutrah, generating 4.5 megawatts. In 1971 this was taken over by the Government and the amount of electricity generated grew rapidly. The first major new plant was the al Ghubbrah power station and desalination plant, with an initial capacity of 25.4 mw. This grew to 500 mw by 2000. The power station at Rusail, where the first industrial estate was created, had an initial capacity in 1984 of 250 mw, which was subsequently doubled. As late as 1978 there were no generating stations outside the capital area, except in Salalah and in oil industry areas. In the following year 22 were set up, initially diesel operated with an overall capacity of 27 mw, and later converted to gas turbine power and linked to the growing transmission interconnections. A new power station has recently been built at al-Kamil in the Sharqiyah region, with a capacity of 250 mw, linked to the Muscat supply.

By 2000 there were 31 power stations with an installed capacity of 1794 mw. Of this, 1280 mw was produced by gas turbines, 136 mw by steam turbines and 378 mw by diesel generators. With a national grid, supply kept pace with demand and the whole country – even the remotest areas such as the Halaaniyaat Islands – received an electricity supply. Increasingly, power stations came within the private sector, although transmission systems remained in Government hands. The Manah installation, commissioned in 1996, led the way. It was entirely financed by private capital and built on the BOOT principle by the United Power Company. The shares are held by a consortium of local and foreign companies; 40 per cent of the shares are publicly owned. Manah was the first privately owned power station not only in Oman, but in the whole of the Gulf.

The southern province of Dhofar has kept pace with the north. The trend towards the use of gas and privatisation was extended to this area too, and the whole of the Salalah power project was taken over in 1999 by the Dhofar Power

Corporation (DPC), with international investors having a 45 per cent stake, local companies 15 per cent and the rest open to public subscription.

Serious attention has been paid to expanding renewable energy projects for the future. Solar energy is used for domestic water heating, cathodic protection of pipelines, some water pumps, street lighting and telephones in remote areas.

Agriculture

Before the advent of oil, agriculture flourished on a large scale over many centuries, and was one of the Omani people's main occupations. In much of the north, cultivation depended on the *falaj* system – man-made water courses which tap into the water table and run along mountainsides to irrigate the terraced fields. On the Batinah coast in contrast, water was traditionally raised from wells by *shaduf*, a wooden structure of poles at the tip of which was a wooden wheel. Over this a long rope was pulled by a mule, bull or camel to draw up buckets attached to the other end of the rope. The size of most traditional Omani farms was up to two hectares. In Dhofar the pattern was rather different. The *khareef*, or annual monsoon, which affects that part of Arabia alone from May to September, both ensured good grazing for cattle and made the cultivation of subsistence level crops possible.

The areas under cultivation, which were considerably larger in previous centuries, increased after 1970 by 7.2 per cent per annum. Even so only 60,000 hectares of the potentially cultivable land of 100,000 hectares had been brought under cultivation by 1994, of which 37 per cent was date palm gardens for which Oman was traditionally famous. The other main crops in the north were wheat, lucerne, onions, limes, bananas, potatoes, peppers, aubergines and tobacco, while in the south coconut palms, bananas, papayas and other tropical fruit predominated.

In 1970 the Government envisaged a five point programme, the principles of which have continued to endure in subsequent plans. These were: the proper use and exploitation of water; introducing improved strains of crops and livestock; eliminating crop disease; assisting with the preservation and distribution of food, and harvesting the seas. All these aims required research, and a number of experimental farms, extension centres and research stations were established. By 2002 there were two major research centres, one for plant production and the other for plant protection. Special attention has been paid to date production, improvement of all crop varieties, modern irrigation systems, and to Oman's 3,200 bee-keepers.

By 2003, trials to improve *falaj* irrigation methods had resulted in the saving of an impressive 80 per cent of *falaj* water and a considerable extension of the land under cultivation. However, the protection of agricultural land has remained a special concern for the Government and, to prevent the loss of agricultural land, long flood protection barriers have been erected and anti-desertification measures taken. To help prevent an exodus from rural areas, education in rural matters

While Qurm, above, is largely residential, the landscaped Al Khuwair area is set aside for embassies and Government ministries, such as Housing (below left)*, and Agriculture and Fisheries* (below right). Opposite*, irrigated agriculture dominates the Batinah hinterland.*

and water conservation has been improved and agricultural credit facilitated by soft loans. The philosophy underlying agricultural policy has always been sustainable development. Oman was the first Arab country to set up a ministry exclusively concerned with the environment, and the Government's continued concern is publicly demonstrated by the celebration of Environment Day on 8 January every year.

The high quality of Omani dates is well known, and annual production from the seven million palms was estimated in 1995 at between 150,000 and 175,000 tonnes. About 40 per cent of the production was taken up by the owners and growers, 25 per cent by livestock, while 35 per cent was marketed. Recognising the importance of date production, the Government set up a cloning laboratory at Bahla in 1992 for the production of improved strains of dates and later pineapples and bananas. Two date packaging factories at Nizwa and Rostaq, taken over by the private sector in 1994, gave a boost to the export of dates in the early stages of Oman's modern development. Research on crop pests and measures to combat them were given high priority.

Agriculture and fishing remain a very significant element in Oman's social and economic life. By 2003 more than 100,000 Omanis – one third of them women – were employed in these pursuits and the sector accounted for over 35 per cent of non-oil exports, contributing RO 155 million in 1998 to GDP, for instance. Agriculture's continuing importance may be judged from estimates made in 2000, that 65 per cent of food and 69 per cent of animal feed consumed locally was produced in the country. By 2000, Oman was self-sufficient in dates and bananas and in vegetables in season, 53 per cent self-sufficient in milk, 46 per cent in beef, 44 per cent in eggs and 23 per cent in mutton.

Government subsidies have been used to transfer technology to the farmer and train him in modern methods. Initially, subsidies centred upon assistance to small-scale goat and poultry farms, plus the development of modern irrigation. Now however, the emphasis is on innovations and technology instead of direct subsidies, support is given to farmers through training and demonstrations of new agricultural equipment, irrigation systems and improved crop varieties.

Livestock

The Sultanate has always been the leading livestock producer in the region, with more than 950,000 goats, 317,000 sheep, 284,000 cattle and 120,000 camels in 2000. Over 70 per cent of cattle are reared in Dhofar, where they have been improved by artificial insemination and cross breeding with imported strains, including Sindhis, East Africans and Friesians. The construction of a slaughter-house in Salalah in the mid-1970s encouraged Dhofaris to sell their superfluous beasts, while milk and other dairy products were encouraged by a Dairy Project. A model sheep production unit was opened in 1994 and goat rearing has also been given priority.

Extensive veterinary services were provided from the early stages of Sultan Qaboos's reign, and country-wide vaccination against foot and mouth, rinderpest, pneumonia and other diseases helped the rapid growth of herds. A quarantine station in the Wadi Jizzi was opened in the mid-1990s, necessitated by increasing overland trade between Oman and her neighbours. Stock breeders were trained in Agricultural Development Centres and in 2002, under the National Livestock Immunisation Project, 1,414,037 animals were immunised and 741,870 were treated in veterinary clinics. In keeping with sustainable development in an area where resources are in delicate balance, a national strategy involving surveys, research, the introduction of higher yielding plants and new laws was launched in 2002 to manage and improve grazing lands, particularly in Dhofar, where overgrazing had become a problem.

In 1997, a fully-integrated poultry project was launched in Dhofar at a cost of RO12.8 million. The Modern Poultry Farm is one of the largest projects of its kind in the Gulf and the first to be established in Oman. It has a capacity for 94,000 hens to produce 55 million eggs annually. The plant includes storage for 11,000 tonnes of frozen poultry. About half the production from this project is intended for export. It is expected that this and other projects like the Barka Poultry Farm, will halve Oman's current annual imports of eggs and frozen chicken.

The monsoons of Dhofar provide pasturage and water for cattle – and camels (opposite). Above: *Inshore fishermen sell their catch at Mutrah – and all the coastal markets.*

Fisheries

More than 150 species of fish and crustaceans abound in Omani waters along the 1,700 kilometre coastline. Fishing has been an important part of the Omani people's life and economy since time immemorial – and certainly since the fifth millennium BC. The catch included shark, the fins of which were exported to the Far East; deep sea fish such as rock cod, snapper and cuttlefish; and surface feeding species such as sardines, tuna, anchovy and kingfish as well as lobster and other crustaceans. The shoals of sardines netted off the Batinah and Dhofar coasts were traditionally used as animal feed and fertiliser, both at home and for export.

During the period of the first Five Year

Plan, Omani fishermen were trained in modern methods and the introduction of ice plants enabled really fresh fish to reach the Interior for the first time. The flow of desertions from this traditional occupation was effectively stemmed by the Fishermen's Encouragement Fund established in 1978. Fishermen benefited from incentives such as soft loans and fibreglass boats to replace their canoe-like wooden *huris*, and engines were imported by the Government and made available at subsidised prices. Thanks to these measures, fishing continues to provide up to ten per cent of GDP.

Large-scale fishing enterprises were also introduced and expanded in the 1980s, particularly by the Oman Fisheries Company and the Korean Fishing Company. Fish were exported to GCC countries, the USA, Japan, Australia and Europe. A chain of fishing ports was established, including Masirah Island and the Halaaniyat Islands, to extend Oman's capability. A network of cold stores, ice plants, freezers, marine workshops, fish distribution centres and hygienic markets were also installed. The industry continues to flourish. Over 30 Omani companies export fish, 16 of them to EU countries.

Despite the abundance of fish in Omani waters in 1970, it was not long before over-fishing was identified as a serious crisis by the Marine Fisheries and Science Centre at Bustan. This institution was established in 1987 with the help of UNESCO and FAO to advise on fish stocks and on commercial fishing, in close collaboration with Sultan Qaboos University. Measures were taken to restrict the fishing of certain species, and to specify that the gauge of nets should be over 14 cm for deep sea fishing. Vision 2020 looks for an annual growth in the fishing industry of 5.6 per cent, but is also focusing on conservation and protective measures, in particular strictly limiting seasons for commercial deep sea fishing and for catching threatened species such as lobsters, abalone and kingfish. The Fisheries Quality Control Centre gives training to fishing companies in order to improve the management of the industry.

In the villages of the Hajar range, where life preserves its privacy, schoolchildren peep from their doorways – as here at al Bawdar: Opposite right; *a palm shades an entrance in Adam, in the Interior.*

The Traditional Habitat

The modern habitat has for the most part grown to be very different from that of earlier generations. Yet it has evolved from traditional ways of life. The following description of the Oman of 1970 will provide the perspective.

"The rich man in his castle, the poor man at his gate." These words might have been written to describe almost any Omani town or village in the past, for they were all dominated by a great turreted form – *qal'a* – the residence of the Sultan's Governor (*Wali*) or sometimes an important shaikh.

The fort was the traditional seat of authority, however impoverished the occupant may have been, and all the houses and market buildings paled into insignificance before its battlements and fortified walls, its massive gates, and gatehouses manned by *askars*, guards armed with rifles and bandoliers. Control of these fortresses, often strategically situated on great rocks, has always been the aim of anyone wishing to dominate the politics and government of Oman or of particular areas. Until recently, therefore, all the most important, such as Sohar, Rostaq, Nizwa and Muscat, witnessed the sort of Omani warfare which was common for many decades if not centuries, conducted with ancient muzzle-loading cannon, matchlocks, flintlocks, and Martini Henrys.

Towers and forts on the jagged hills around the areas of green cultivation – with vast areas of date palm gardens – typify the Omani landscape, defending the approaches to the towns and sometimes standing sentinel even over different parts of one place where tribes or groups have been in feud. However, the great forts in Muscat are Portuguese, both built by that same Philip of Spain who launched the great Armada against England after conquering Portugal in 1580 (988 AH). The western fort, Mirani, perhaps derives its name from the Portuguese *Almirante* (meaning "Admiral") and was completed in 1587 (996 AH). It was originally known by the Portuguese as Fort Captain, because it was the residence of their Commander.

The eastern fort built by Belchior Alvares was finished in 1588 (997 AH), and is now called Jalali, probably after one of its notably commanders, although it was originally known as San João.

Belchior Alvares' fort was not the first on the site of Mirani. In 1522 (929 AH) Dom Joao da Lisboa began a new fort, but his work was almost immediately destroyed by the Captain-General of the Turkish fleet, Admiral Piri Rais, who captured Muscat briefly in the same year. Muscat was again sacked by the Turks in 1582 (990 AH), and the Portuguese then directed their Viceroy in India to build up the two great forts and strengthen the defences.

In the early seventeenth century, the Portuguese extended the fortifications. In 1610 (1019 AH), a sea-level bastion was built at fort Mirani to prevent small boats running in close beneath the arc of fire of cannon emplacements in the fort itself, and an inscription commemorating this event reads in translation: "Experience, zeal and truth built for me the defence of the cross which defends me, on the order of the Very High and Powerful King Don Philip, third of his

name in the year 1610." In 1617 (1027 AH), Don Garcia da Silva, the Spanish Ambassador to Persia, visited Muscat, staying in the Augustinian Convent on the site of which Bait Graiza (a corruption of the Portuguese *igreja*, meaning church) was later built, and a detailed account of his programme in the town survives. Between 1623 (1033 AH), and 1626 (1036 AH), the wall of the city was rebuilt substantially in the same form as it stands today and the outlying watch towers, the fortifications of Muscat Island north of Jalali, and a new customs house date from this period. The original chapel in fort Mirani still survives, although its roof has been subsequently repaired and a massive column erected to support it. There is a cup for holy water in the wall with a Latin inscription: "*Ave Maria gratia sancta plena Dominus tecum.*"

Fort Mirani has never been taken by storm in its 350-odd years. When it fell to the Ya'rubi Imam Sultan ibn Saif in December 1649 (1059 AH), it was taken, according to Omani tradition, by a stratagem in which an Indian merchant of Muscat called Narutem played a key role. There was at the time an impasse between the Imam's troops and the defending Portuguese, but an affair of the heart brought matters to a head. Narutem had a very beautiful daughter whom the Portuguese commander Pereira wished to marry, but, despite the offer of a temptingly high bride price, Narutem refused his consent on religious grounds. He did not think it right for a Christian to marry a Hindu. Narutem was accountant to the Portuguese Treasury and contractor to the shops in Mirani and Jalali, and Pereira retaliated by threatening to deprive him of this profitable office. Narutem then asked Pereira for a year's grace to prepare wedding clothes and ornaments. At the same time, he advised that, if Muscat were to withstand a long siege, the foul water in the forts' cisterns should be replaced, the gunpowder removed and pounded and the old wheat discarded for new supplies. Pereira gave Narutem the year's grace and also authority to proceed with the replenishments he suggested.

Narutem then saw a way out of his dilemma and after depleting the fort supplies as instructed, but not replenishing them, he wrote to the Imam Sultan ibn

Saif recommending an attack on Muscat on the following Sunday, when, he said, the Portuguese would be drinking wine and playing musical instruments. The Imam took his advice and attacked successfully, thus paving the way for the final expulsion of the Portuguese.

Representatives of foreign powers have been resident in Muscat since the eighteenth century, towards the end of which a representative of the Great Moghul occupied a house known as the "Nabob's House". In the same period, a local resident acted as "Consul for the English", but it was not until 1800 (1215 AH) that a formal treaty with Britain provided that an "English gentleman of respectability should always reside at the port of Muscat." Since then there has been continuous British representation, although the succession of Britons in residence in Muscat was interrupted between 1810 and 1861 as the climate of Muscat was considered too unhealthy. Between 1800 and 1810 (1215 and 1225 AH) the first four representatives all died *en poste*. No permanent representative was again appointed until 1861. Since then there has always been a British Consul who was also known at various times as Political Agent or Political Resident, being an appointee of the British Government in India until 1958. Thereafter, appointments were made by the Foreign Office, and the first British Ambassador was accredited in 1971.

It was always the custom of the early representatives to live in local houses and even the greatly expanded British Consulate constructed in 1890 (1308 AH), was built in the Arab style with a central courtyard. This was a building deliberately designed to impress and was a far cry from the "miserable hovel" in which the first four representatives had lived. The British were the last to move out – in 1995 – from their Muscat diplomatic houses, to the new diplomatic area at al Khuweir.

The premises of the old British Embassy evoke many historical associations. A tombstone of a Portuguese soldier was to be seen in the courtyard. A gate on the east side, carved in authentic Omani style but decorated also with the British consular crown, was used for visits of ceremony between the British representatives and the Sultan, whose palace was situated beyond the customs area, on the other side of the Muscat Bay. The faces of the portraits which formerly hung on the staircase wall and have now been moved to the new Embassy bear testimony to the variety of the characters who have had the opportunity of observing, and playing a part in Omani history – such men as Sir Percy Cox, Colonel Jayakar, a surgeon and naturalist, who

*An exquisite mediaevalism – nowadays lovingly preserved – attaches to so many of Oman's towns with their cool, shadowed alleys and archways – like those of Bahla (*left*), and Nizwa (*below, centre *and* opposite, left*), Jabrin (*below right*) and Al Mudayrit (*opposite right*).*

gave his name to a unique species of goat, and Colonel Miles, whose book *The Countries and Tribes of the Persian Gulf* is still a classic. In the courtyard between the two main blocks of buildings rose an enormous flagpole, which stood until 1972 (1392 AH) when its superstructure became dangerous and it was dismantled. This was the flagpole which in the past was clasped by slaves claiming freedom.

Admiral Boyle Somerville has left an entertaining description of the vicious apes kept by Sir Percy Cox's wife in the courtyard of the Residency in the early 1900s. At the same time, in his Palace adjoining the British Consulate, Sultan Faisal ibn Turki, kept the King of Beasts, as Theodore Bent describes: "The palace is entered by a formidable-looking door, decorated with large spiked bosses of brass. This opens into a small court which contained the most imposing sight of the place, namely the lion in his cage."

The prosperity brought by sea trade up to the age of the steamship made Oman a country of gracious houses as well as of castles and towers. In Muscat itself there are still preserved six splendid houses built during the latter half of the eighteenth century and belonging to the Al bu Said family. The Bait Graiza ("House of the Church") is the largest and finest, and is named after the Augustinian Convent which formerly stood near the site. All these houses, which are of lofty appearance and well proportioned, have courtyards in the middle and the buildings which surround the square are surmounted by crenellations of a similar shape to those of Moghul architecture. The siting of the windows is absolutely harmonious, the doors and windows are finely carved, and simple stone stairways give access to the first floor.

In Ibra, in the Sharqiyah region, there was also an area of well-built houses of roughly the same date. A tunnel led from one house to the main fort of Ibra on the other side of the *wadi*. These substantial houses of stone were commissioned and lived in by very wealthy people in their heyday, which can be approximately dated by a beautiful carved doorway bearing the date 1192 – that is, corresponding to 1778 AD. The houses contained elaborate aches of Moghul design built perhaps by craftsmen from India or Persia. One house had a curious feature – a tower, round externally, but with a square room inside.

There was always a close connection between the Sharqiyah and the Omani settlements in east Africa, and wealth gained from the east African trade enabled merchants who had prospered to build these substantial houses – which perhaps explains why rough pictures of ships are so often depicted on old walls in Oman at great distances from the sea. Such large houses required plentiful labour to build and maintain and with the suppression of the slave trade they gradually decayed, reminders of a more prosperous past, though in the 1970s one still survived to house looms and carding gins for weaving loin cloths – *wazaras*.

The Omanis lived well in east Africa for many generations. The Portuguese arriving there under Vasco da Gama in 1498 (908 AH) were astonished at the prosperity of the Arab possessions. Vasco da Gama remarked that Malindi, near Mombasa, was a "Noble City" and the "King" received the Portuguese envoy in a palace strewn with carpets – oriental rugs at this date were so costly that they were used in Europe to cover tables rather than floors – and furnished with stools inlaid with ivory and gold.

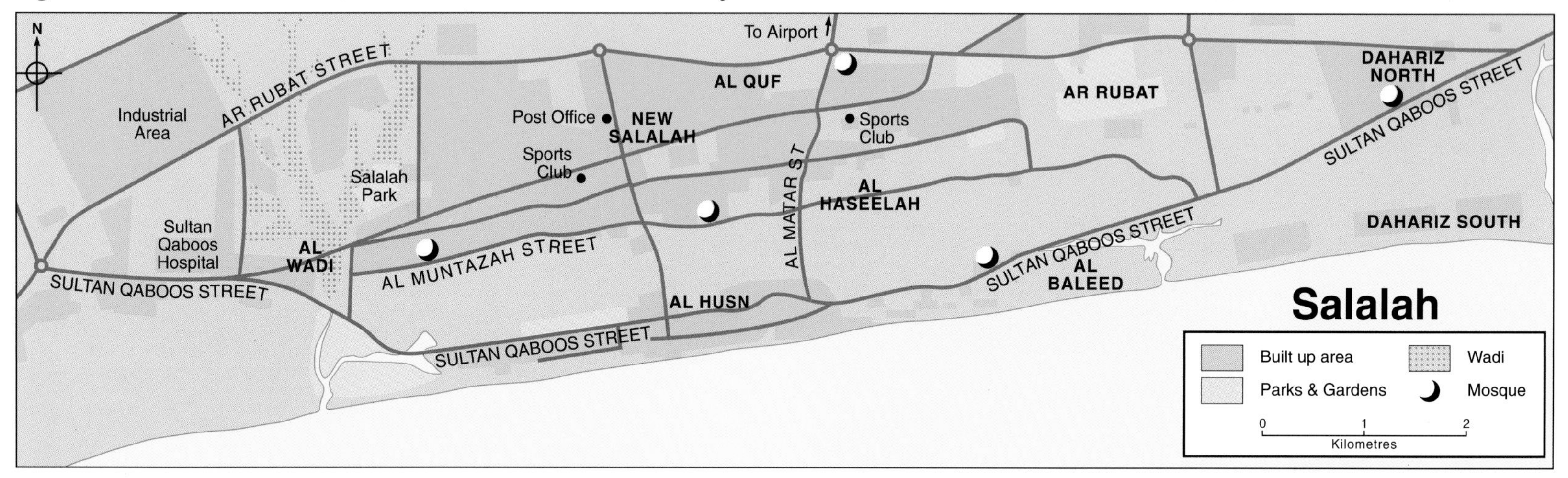

In the southern region of Dhofar the traditional homes of the people differed markedly from those of the north. In Salalah itself there were a number of square-set elegant houses of a design more distinctive of Dhofar itself and Hadhramaut than of the north. Built of mud brick covered in stucco, they were sometimes several storeys high and the arched windows were covered with wooden screens of the *mashribiya* type. Sometimes there were distinctive devices round the flat roofs. Some of these old homes have been preserved. In the coastal towns of Taqa and Marbat there were similar houses, and the forts occupied by the shaikhs and *Walis* were modified versions of these. The old palace of the Sultan on the sea shore in Salalah was originally built by Sultan Turki ibn Said but was added to subsequently by several Sultans until it took its grand and striking form under Sultan Qaboos.

The coastal plain of Dhofar has been important since time immemorial and the ruins of the town of Samhuram, a city which two thousand years ago depended for its prosperity on the incense trade, stands on the Khor Rori near Taqa. Other ruins associated with the incense trade are the larger fort at Shisur – which may be the remains of the "lost city of Ubar," – the fort in the Wadi Andhur and the fort and houses at Hanun on the desert road north from the *jebel*. All these old buildings are of stone, some of which is finely dressed.

Near Salalah itself – a garden city surrounded not only by groves of coconuts but also fields of lucerne and vegetables with clusters of paw-paws and other fruit trees – stands the ruined town of Balid, covering an extensive area. This mediaeval town was occupied until the sixteenth century and was visited by ibn Batuta and earlier by Marco Polo, who described it as a "beautiful, large and noble city". Ibn Batuta remarked : "The city of Dhofar lay in an isolated desert region." The Habudi ruler Ahmad ibn Abdulla had removed the town from inland to the coast in 1223 (620 AH) to protect it from attack. The new city, built on the ruins of an ancient Sabaean city which boasted a citadel of one hundred feet high, was named al Mansura. The *suq*, in which the majority of sellers were female slaves, was outside the city to the west in a pleasant area called al-Harja, but its smells did not please ibn Batuta on account of the fruit and fish presumably left to rot unsold.

The limestone cutter's craft is skilled: along a certain line, one blow suffices.

There are other ruins on the plain nearby at Robat and local tradition holds that this was once Eryot, the proud city of the Shhero (Shahra), who are by common consent locally the most ancient tribe of the area, being descended from Shaddad, son of Ad.

The coastline to the west of Salalah is magnificent, with great cliffs and little sandy beaches. When the sea is rough, the great waves break with cascades of white foam over the dark rocks and the headland of Raysut is especially dramatic. On this headland there is an old castle or fort of indeterminate date, attributed by some to the Portuguese, but probably dating from a much earlier period. It stands in marked contrast to the new part of Raysut commissioned shortly after Sultan Qaboos's accession.

On the mountains of Dhofar there were – and in places still are – many enclosures made of stone walls which, from the air, form an apparently unrelated series of circular and oval patterns. These were the walled areas inside which the people of the Qara mountains cultivated small fields of barley and maize protected from cattle, goats and camels. Sometimes

Dhofari Windows

Functional – but exquisite – trellis-work decorates this window.

A touch of African brilliance decorates some of the shutters of Dhofar's homes.

No window is precisely like another. Yet all are graceful.

enclosures of the same type, but smaller in size, are pens for the people's animals. The traditional houses were round in shape and sometimes of considerable size, perhaps fifteen feet or more in diameter. The roofs were thatched with the long grass which grows on the mountain during the rainy monsoon period. The house served as the focal point for each family and the sparsely furnished interior was made dim with smoke from the cooking fires which they kindled inside. Theirs was a hard life, revolving very much then – as even now in greatly improved conditions – round the small sleek cattle which thrive on the *jebel*, though they also keep goats and camels.

Bertram Thomas, who toured the area in 1930 (1349 AH), relates that it was the inviolable rule that one half of a man's cows should be slaughtered as a sacrifice after his death, in the manner of some of the ancient peoples. He also described well the setting of a settlement in the hills of Dhofar.

> we left the wadi by the pass of Sa'arin, to climb 500 feet into steep stony country. Then followed rolling yellow meadows where hay stood to a man's middle, and occasional clumps of giant trees crowned the hills or nestled in the hollows. Behind and below us in the distance, was the faint blue sea, and round us, undulating down country with the wooded cliffs above Nihaz occasionally edging the western skyline. Here at 1,500 feet the bird life so plentiful in the valleys below dwindled to a few sparrow-hawks and many large storks, but butterflies, grasshoppers and locusts were many and various.
>
> And now we looked down upon a pleasant vale that was our immediate destination, Al 'Ain, a Shahari settlement of Had bi Dhomari, where a spring comes bubbling out of the ground in the belly of a wooded trough. Two wild fig trees, as big and shady as good English walnuts, and bursting with apple-like fruit, made inviting bivouacs, and there I halted. A three hour's climb had made me thirsty, but it is impossible to obtain milk during the noonday, and the curds that were brought me arrived belatedly after I had dealt with the milk of a brimming fresh coconut.
>
> From over the brow of the hill appeared a party of Qara tribesmen of Sheikh Hasan, in extended order, singing their peculiar danadon chant of the mountains. Their fellow-tribesmen of Ain mustered to meet them, one drawing his sword to dance in honourable welcome.

Dhofari Doors

Doors in Dhofar, as in other parts of Oman, tend to give a house its personality and distinction. Dhofaris share with other Arabs a lively sense of privacy, and family life goes on within the walled confines of the home. Dhofari old doors are notable for their bright colouring, and carving is not such a feature as it is in northern Oman. The doors are fitted with large individual locks as protection, but this does not diminish the traditional hospitality offered when a visitor goes to a house in Dhofar.

Above and below: *the locksmith's art has developed along its own lines in Dhofar.*

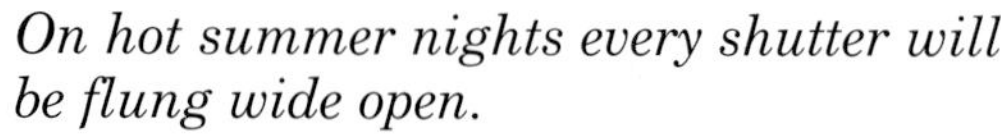

On hot summer nights every shutter will be flung wide open.

The ancient port of Sur, most easterly of Oman's havens on the Arabian Sea, was the natural landfall for vessels trading with Africa and India and the West. Today's booms *cluster in its harbour.*
Below*: crenellations decorate the exterior of one of Sur's many elegant merchant houses, while,* below right, *an eye gazing down upon the world beyond inspired the lintel's design.*

The Inland Forts

Many Omani forts are of great antiquity, and those at Bahla and Rostaq dating from the period before Islam were probably originally Persian in construction. Rostaq, the Arabised form of Persian word signifying an outlying or border district, probably traces its name to the Sassanid period when it came under the Persian capital at Dastajird or Sohar. The great fort at Sohar also pre-dates the Portuguese, who themselves carried out modifications and additions. Albuquerque found there in 1507 (916 AH) "a fortress of square shape, with six towers round it, having also over the gate two very large towers". The fort was so large that it then required more than a thousand men for its defence. It subsequently had a very turbulent history and most of the towers were rebuilt many times, only the north-western one retaining its original shape. It is now beautifully restored.

The great fort at Nizwa was built by Sultan ibn Saif (1649-1688: 1059-1079 AH), one of the great Imams of the Ya'ruba dynasty who finally drove the Portuguese out of Muscat. It took twelve years to build, and was reputedly financed from the spoils of the sack of Ras al Khaimah. Its enormous round tower has a diameter of approximately 120 feet and contains not only impressively strong fortifications but also dungeons and oubliettes.

The Ya'ruba dynasty is responsible for two other notable architectural achievements and the early Al bu Saids made some fine architectural additions to several forts and built some splendid large houses. The fort at Jabrin was commissioned by Bil'arub ibn Sultan in about 1670 (1081 AH) largely as a country home or retreat, though for a while it was regarded as the capital of Oman. Massive and impressively strong, it is also decorated with ornately carved doorways, painted ceilings of rare beauty and graceful arches in the Moghul style. The square windows are latticed and stone mullioned; and the fine plaster work included adornment of the entrance to the tomb where Bil'arub himself is buried and Qur'anic inscriptions. The Imam's private *majlis* at the top is a light, airy room, with a delicately painted ceiling and fine views over the plain towards the towering heights of the Jebel Akhdar. Learning flourished in Bil'arub's day and he founded a famous school in the shadow of the new "palace".

The fort at al Hazm, which stands on the approaches to Rostaq from the coast, in another great Ya'ruba monument. It was built in 1708 (1126 AH) and was for a while the capital of Oman when the Imam Sultan ibn Saif II moved from Rostaq. Its gun turrets, containing five huge Portuguese and Spanish cannon probably brought from Muscat in the nineteenth century in the time of the Imam Azzan ibn Qais (1868-1871: 1285-1288 AH), are magnificently decorated with fine plaster work, which is also a feature of the vaulted ceilings around the courtyard. A strong *falaj* stream, which also feeds the neighbouring plantation, flows through the fort, just as at Jabrin, and there is also a small school on the upper storey. The tall and splendidly carved entrance doors are oddly masked by subsequent mud construction and above them there is a slit in the ceiling and a water tank close by, so that if the attackers fired the wooden door the fire could be easily extinguished. There are also slits for pouring boiling honey – such was the custom – or oil on attackers, and the inevitable dungeons.

One of the forts built by the Al bu Said dynasty, in the eighteenth century, was at Bait al Falaj, which, as its name implies, was a house depending on a *falaj* water supply from the nearby mountains. When Oman formed its modern army, the fort there became its headquarters, and Bait al Falaj has consequently acquired a special fame in the army (now headquartered near Seeb at Muaskar al-Murtafa'a). In some way, therefore, Bait al Falaj corresponded to the Horse Guards at Whitehall – a military headquarters where old and new military traditions meet. All these great historic monuments have been well restored, and Bait al Falaj contains the Forces' Museum.

In the past it was only the most wealthy and influential section of the population who lived in fine houses. Along the whole of the Batinah coast and even in Muscat itself, the usual dwelling was made of palm fronds and called a *barasti*. They were sometimes quite complicated in design and, though normally a single room of varying size, they sometimes had two storeys. These light structures, which are kept together by cords of palm fibre, had obvious disadvantages in wet or cold weather, but for the greater part of the year, when it is hot or very hot, they provided shade and were cool, as the breeze could easily penetrate the walls. Many *barasti*s were rectangular in shape with a stout upright pole at either end and pitched roofs.

Omani men liked to have sitting-out places where they could chat with their neighbours, drink coffee, and offer hospi-

Sohar's fort remains to preside over Oman's once greatest port-city, seen in 1970 (below), *and restored* (right) Opposite, *a citizen of Qabil strolls homeward.*

tality to visitors, for offering hospitality was – and remains – as elsewhere in Arabia, simultaneously a sacred duty and pleasure. Traditional sitting-out places, which were usually mere palm-frond shelters against the sun, were open to the breezes and could be found by the sea, in the pleasant palm gardens of the Batinah or the Interior or even high in the Jebel Akhdar, with magnificent views over mountain and plain.

Many houses in former times were built of mud and some were very elegant, though some structures were a combination of stone and mud. In Nizwa, for example, there were narrow, winding streets of grey mud-built houses, where planning showed innate sophistication, and where winding streets were so aligned as to give shade to man and beast in the hot weather. The streets led out beyond the city's defensive walls and gatehouses to the gardens beyond, and there too were numerous well-proportioned houses among the groves, little country estates where the humped bull could be seen ploughing among the trees. Mud walls lined the paths which wind through the groves from one small settlement to another.

Bertram Thomas described a typical Omani house which he visited in the Interior in the 1920:

> Arab country houses are very much alike, being entirely without amenities or decoration . Glass windows are unknown, as is reasonable in so hot a climate, and interior decoration, where plain, unmade brick does not wholly forbid it, takes the form of a simple plaster stucco... The upper chamber was typical. Low, square-shuttered, iron-barred windows level with the floor surround the four sides, and each is carried up to a blind, pointed arch, a shelf flush with the upper window-sashing making a sort of alcove wherein gay coffee-cups, water-ewer, and incense-burner are the usual furnishings. The exposed rafters are black with smoke stain, for the chimney is unknown in tropical Oman, but the whole floor is covered with gay coloured carpets... Ornate wooden pegs punctuate the walls at man's height, and from them depends an armoury of rifles slung barrel downwards, common double-edged swords, cartridge belts, powder flasks and daggers..."

It is, however, a feature of many of the traditional houses of the Interior, even those built of mud brick, to have ceilings painted in bright colours and sometimes with illuminated texts from the Qu'ran.

Opposite, *modern life cheerfully proceeds beneath the walls of Nakhl's soaring ramparts. And,* above, *a Rostaq family promenades beneath their* Wali's *fort.*

Sometimes great and important structures too were built of mud, such as the old fort of the Shaikh of the Bani Riyam at Birkat al Moz, with its courtyards, doors and elegant rooms with painted ceilings. The great walls surrounding Bahla in a seven mile ring were also constructed of mud – parapets, steps, battlements and guard houses.

The old houses in the mountain villages in the Jebel Akhdar were rectangular in shape and, built on the rocky sloping hillside, resembled those of Kurdistan. Their flat roofs were turned yellow in autumn by the maize cobs put out to dry and ripen and the arches of stone stairways evoked a feeling of antiquity and timelessness. The animals were often kept downstairs whilst the family lived above, their reception rooms there.

Large villages like Shuraija, which earlier travellers such as Lieutenant Wellsted in the 1830s called Shirauzi, suggest a connection with Shiraz in the Persia. Vines and roses grow in both places. These villages are approached by mountain paths, made fit by the labour of man for sturdy and sure-footed mountain donkeys to traverse. In places, steps have been cut into the rock or constructed laboriously of stone against precarious rock faces. Shuraija itself, where, at this altitude, the deciduous tress such as the walnut turn to gold in autumn, is surrounded by steep terraces watered by a bubbling *falaj* stream.

In the mountains of northern Oman and Dhofar there are many caves to which people have traditionally resorted in time of trouble and where nomadic families and their animals still sometimes take shelter from the elements.

The *Falaj* System

The origins of the widespread and sophisticated water-system in Oman are very ancient. Omani legend attributes them to Sulaiman ibn Daud – Solomon the Son of David – who visited Oman on a magic carpet and caused his *djinns* to construct the 10,000 water channels in ten days. *Falajes* which never dry up, however dry the season may be – the majority of which are in the Dhahirah and Buraimi areas – are still called *Daudis*.

It is estimated that 90 per cent of the rain precipitation in Omani enters aquifers, which are tapped in three different but complementary ways – wells, and *falaje*s of two sorts (*ghayl* and *qanat*).

Falaj means a system for the distribution of water amongst those who have established rights to a source of supply. The word derives from a Semitic root of great antiquity which finds mention in the biblical book of Genesis, "And unto Eber were born two sons; the name of one was Peleg, for in his day was the earth divided."

The word *falaj* is commonly used to mean the whole of the irrigation channel system downstream of the water source. Thus it may mean a water channel which has tapped a flow in the upper gravels of a *wadi* (*ghayl*) and been constructed alongside or carved into the rocky walls of a wadi for several miles. Alternatively, it may mean a "man-made water mine in which the water stored in an aquifer is brought to the surface by means of a tunnelled conduit" in exactly the same way as the *qanat* in Persia. Sixty-five feet is the average depth of the mother well, though it may be as much as 200 feet. From the mother well – *Umm al Falaj* – until the tunnel debouches, there are shafts sunk at regular interval so some fifty to sixty feet, which are used both for the initial construction and for subsequent inspection. The tunnel may run between two to six miles underground.

A very large number of the *falaje*s of the *qanat* type were built in pre-Islamic times and those of al Jauf region, which was colonised and developed in Achaemenid times, date from some 2,500 years ago. The *falaj* called Daris in Nizwa may well date from this time. During another major period of construction in Sassanid times there was extensive development in eastern Oman based on Mazun – Sohar. With the coming of Islam and the expulsion of the Persians, the villages and cultivated areas were organised and regulated by the Ibadhi religious authorities (*Ulema*) and their legal rulings can be traced back to the very first Imamate in the ninth century AD (third century AH).

The walls of this chamber at Jabrin fort (above left) *are hung with an assortment of firearms, while the ladies' room at Nakhl fort* (above right)*, is adorned with a patchwork of colourful carpets.*

In central Oman, which has a relatively high population and reliable *falaje*s, land tenure is mainly freehold, held in smallish lots by tribesmen. Large-scale landholding by landlords has never been a feature of this region throughout history. However, in the northern part of the country which did not remain so firmly within the Ibadhi fold there was a different system of land organisation – a form of share-cropping. At the very root of village life is the need to preserve water rights. The distribution of water was and is, therefore, carefully controlled and recorded in *falaj* books and there may be no less than two hundred owners of permanent water rights in a single *falaj*, to say nothing of temporary rights.

Each community dependent on a single *falaj* in a settlement represents a self-sufficient hydrological society, whose members throughout history had to co-operate, despite deeply rooted difference and even tribal enmities which in the past caused separate fortified quarters with towers and battlements to be built in a single place. In Izki, for example, there were two adjoining quarters, called Yaman and Nizar – which represented the basic tribal difference in Oman like the divisions between Inawi and Ghafiri. The inhabitants of each quarter were historically opposed to one another but, as they were dependent on the same *falaj* system, were compelled to co-operate. Civil wars – particularly the disastrous wars of the ninth century AD (third century AH) – were responsible for destroying much of the country's *falaj* system and there is no doubt that large areas became lost to cultivation. The very art of *falaj* making was to a large extent lost, though the skill is preserved by the Awamir tribe, who also have a near-monopoly on repair work.

A reasonable-sized *falaj* of the *qanat* type might support about 1,000 people and produce a flow of about nine gallons per second to irrigate an area of some forty hectares of permanently cultivated land. A *falaj* with a really good flow might support larger settlements of up to 2,500, and if a number of *falaj*es was concentrated in one area they could thus sustain a population of about 8,000.

Virtually all the perennial water from a *falaj* was used for date palms, although citrus, bananas, pomegranates and mangoes were also irrigated. Lucerne – alfalfa – was planted in basins outside the palm groves, and grain and leguminous crops were grown from the winter surplus discharge of the *falaj*.

The high-ceilinged Wali*'s bedroom at Nakhl allows for cooling draught, and its alcoves for simple domestic utensils. Its economy of style and furniture recall similar chambers of late mediaeval Europe.*

The Falaj system

Falaj means a system for the distribution of water amongst those who have an established right to supply. It is commonly used to describe the irrigation channel system downstream of the point where the water originates. Thus it may mean a channel tapping a flow in the upper gravels of a *wadi* (*ghayl*) or a man-made mine in which the water is brought to the surface by an underground tunnel (*qanat*). Below right: *the course of a* falaj *is marked by a series of access holes used in tunnelling and for inspection.* Below left: *an outlet tapping the highland's water table yields its plentiful supplies to the irrigation channels* (bottom). *The* falaj *walls themselves often provide the simplest route from one community to the next.*

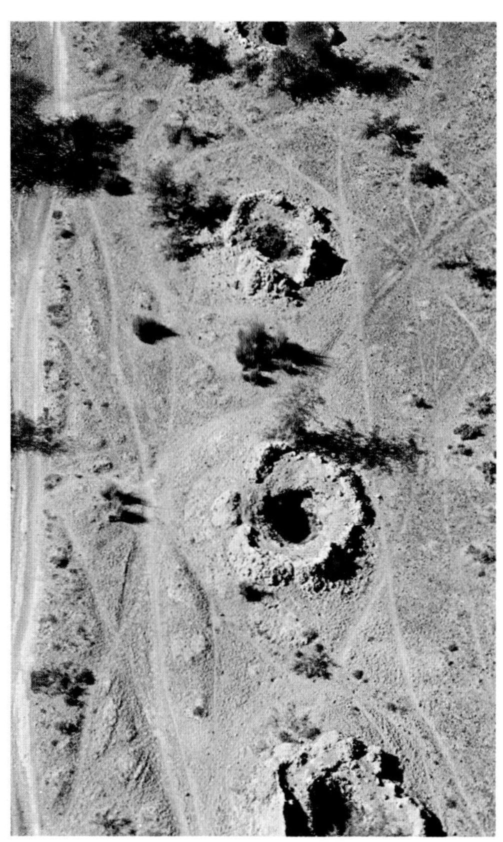

A strict system of priorities for the use of water always had to be followed. At the top of the *falaj* where it comes to the surface, there was an opening where drinking water could be drawn and all had free access to this. In the residential area, the water was also communal and the order of domestic usage was: drinking water, bathing facilities with the men's bath area upstream of the women's – each in little enclosures – and then the place where the dead are washed. Mosques often had their own direct access for ritual ablutions. After this the water was divided for irrigation and there were usually a number of bifurcations from the main channel. Underground channels had to be cleaned and channels kept in good repair by cementing, and upkeep of the main network of primary channels was the responsibility of the communal *falaj* organisation. Individual owners were responsible for channels in their gardens.

The principles of shareholding in the water are complicated. Distribution to the garden was, however, usually arranged in a set order and each plot of land had a prescribed period of time allocated to it. This was known as the cycle, and in many towns and villages there was a sundial in

Aqueducts are built to span depressions along the water's route to the villages.

the central place, by which the periods due to each garden were measured. Thus, though land, water rights and crops might be owned separately, land usually changed hands in practice with a set allocation of water based on a previously existing distribution system.

On small *falaj*es with only a few owners, arrangements for upkeep could easily be made on an *ad hoc* basis an in areas where there was a capitalist system, the landowner or a landlord would carry out maintenance and repairs. However, on *falaj*es with a large number of shareholders in central Oman, an agent was usually appointed for the administration of groups of primary shares so that reference to each of the owners did not have to be made very time money had to be spent. The group of primary shares – the *qa'ada* share – was registered as a trust, *wakf*, and administered by the agent, who sold shares in the available *falaj* water to people who required it but were without permanent shares. This could be done by auction. Those interested in buying a particular lot might hold out their camel sticks, touch the auctioneer and withdraw them as they retired from the bidding until the highest bidder was left.

The creation of a *qa'ada* share required the general agreement of the share-holders in the main *falaj*, but if there were objections these were heard by the *Qadhi*, the religious judge. The amount of water due to a particular plot was based on a time scale; the periods of time sold varied, but in much of central Oman and *athar* share was the equivalent of half an hour's watering. Prices also varied but they were computed in *qirsh* – the Maria Theresa dollar, which was formerly used as currency. The general rule was that a man draws his water for a fixed period from a fixed point, but in some places, for instance in Izki, he held a share above the point where the main channel first divided and in consequence drew his water where it suited him from the main network of *falaj* channels.

Agricultural work was largely done on a strictly traditional basis, and the *bidar* who had a key role carried out duties prescribed since before Islam. Historically always a free man, he received payment in kind for his labour, which included watering, cutting the ripe dates, fertilising the female flowers and tying up the date bunches. He did no weeding and was answerable in his task of distributing water within the village gardens to the supervisor of the irrigation channels of the *falaj* – the *aarif* – and not to individual owners. Weeding was done by another man called the *haris*.

Such then was the environment familiar to Omani's until the surge into modernity of the last decades of the twentieth century.

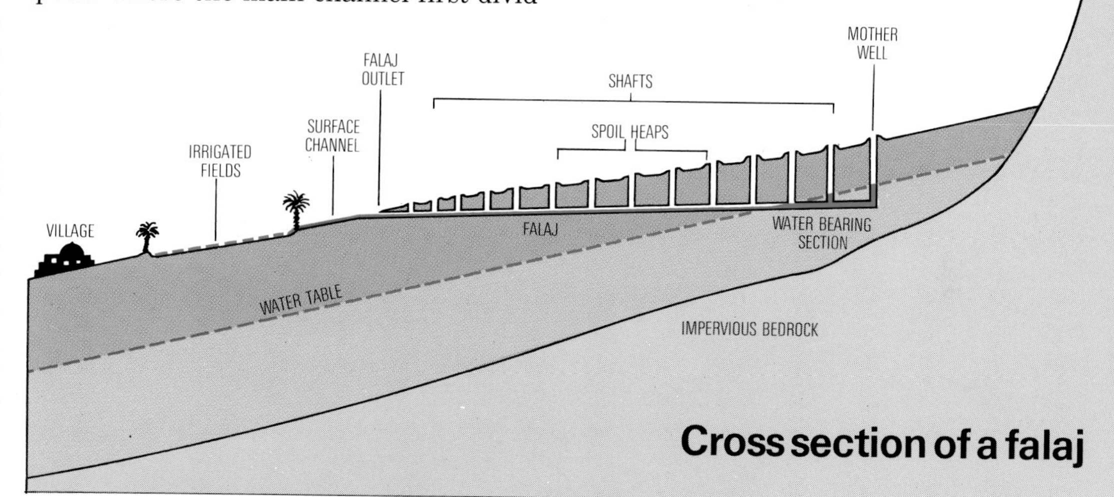

Cross section of a falaj

Care and upkeep of the falajes *are community responsibilities, and place on village life an obligation for friendly relations between neighbouring communties.*

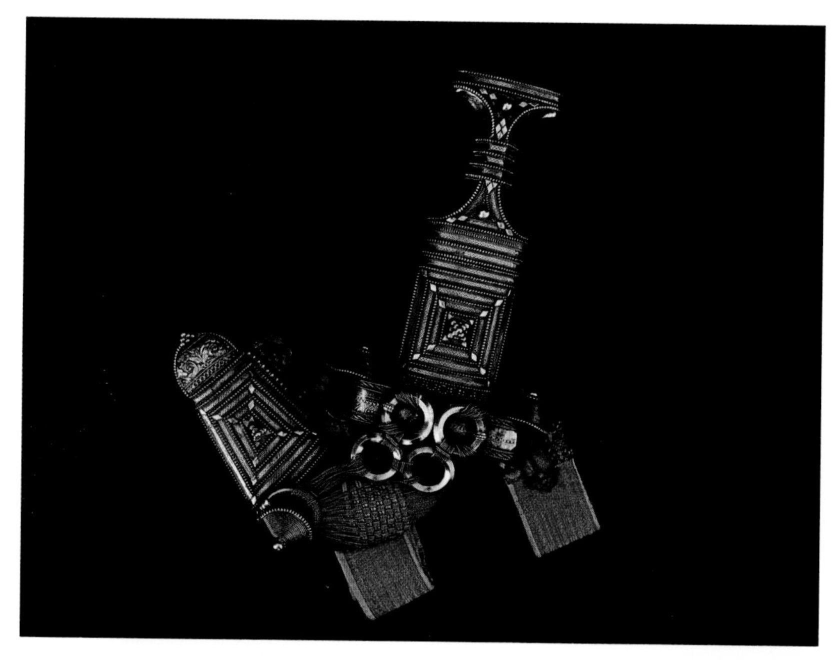

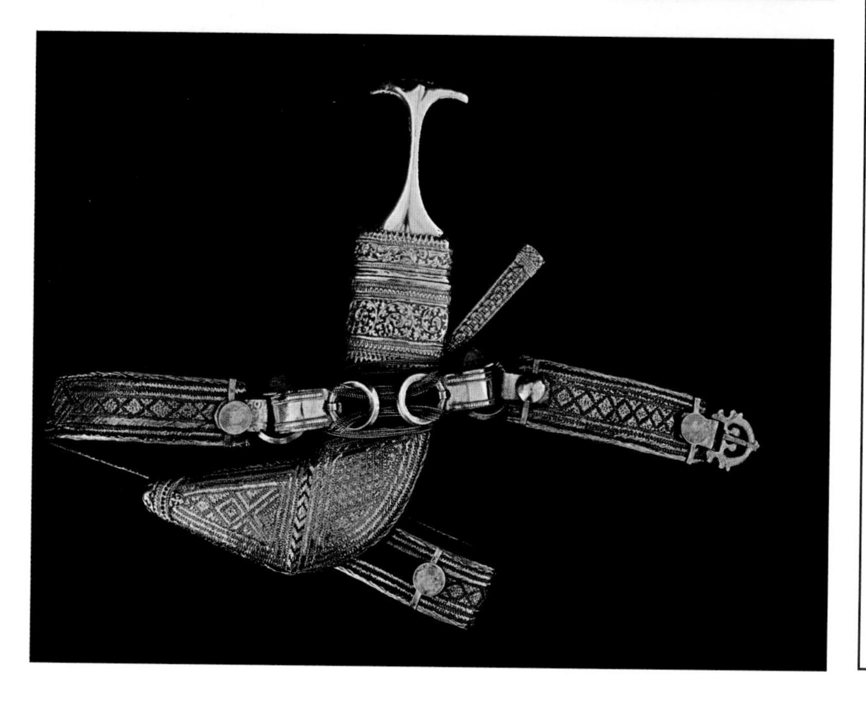

6 The Culture and its Roots

Omanis are instinctive designers. There is no single type of handiwork that they do not render in some way graceful and peculiarly their own. In wood, in silver, in gold, in plaster or clay, in cloth or dress, in beadwork or gold or silver thread, in housebuilding, shipbuilding, in tool-making, jewellery and weaponry, the story is the same: the sense of design prevails. Omanis have married hand and eye.

Far left: *The Omani ceremonial dagger, the* khanjar, *is sometimes provided with a hilt and scabbard of gold, when presented as a gift. Notice the five rings of the Sharqiyah* khanjar (top), *used for securing the belt. The fine* khanjar (centre) *is worn by the* Wali *of Sur. The delicately chased silverwork of the* khanjar (left) *is typical of the Nizwa area. The handle is made of horn and silver and, tucked in behind the sheath, is a sharp knife with a fine handle.*

OMANIS must be numbered among the innovators in the field of human culture. In the third millennium BC they were already building round structures of fine masonry. As one of the world's first recorded shipbuilding peoples, they later helped to pioneer the sea route to China and to develop the science of navigation. In the agricultural sphere they increased the efficiency of the *falaj* systems by the use of inverted siphons – a sophisticated way of leading water across a *wadi* bed below the surface. Their mining techniques were notable when, with bronze as the metal of civilisation, copper was the basis of Oman's economy.

Moving to historical times, we find a country fortunate in being able to preserve a continuous tradition of craftsmanship going back hundreds of years, though new methods have been introduced alongside the old. Traditional culture is still displayed in one way or another in the work of silversmiths, goldsmiths and coppersmiths; ship builders and carvers; potters, weavers and builders, and in human apparel. All Oman's traditional crafts live on, stimulated by the personal interest of the Sultan.

Mysticism surrounds the ancient art of metal smithing. Gold has been associated for thousands of years with the sun and silver with the moon. The silverwork of Oman exemplifies the variety and beauty of local craftsmanship. As in other Eastern countries, a considerable proportion of a family's wealth was, at least until recently, invested in the gold and silver jewellery worn by the women and silver objects used by men. Silver vessels and utensils such as coffee pots, incense burners and rose-water sprinklers used for formal entertainment, are also often of great beauty and value.

The curve of the Omani *khanjar*, the most distinctive badge of the Omani male, contrasts with daggers worn elsewhere in Arabia; its sheath has a near right-angle bend. The most exotic sheaths are made of gold and gold thread or a combination of gold and silver, but at the other end of the scale the simplest are of plain leather, though even these usually have some little decoration. *Khanjar*s are still generally worn on formal occasions and at feasts and holidays, and almost all Omani men boast one. The finely chased silver varies in design from place to place. The best handles are made of bone and silver and it is the mark of a good *khanjar* sheath to have seven silver rings, two to hold the belt and five through which strands of decorative thread are woven as ornamentation, The top handle of the most usual *khanjar* is flat. The Saidi type, worn only by members of the Ruling Family, has an ornate cross-shaped top. The design is attributed to the wife of Sayyid Said ibn Sultan in the early nineteenth century. She was a Princess of Shiraz who is also credited with introducing the distinctive many-coloured turban worn by the family.

*Khanjar*s are supported on belts of locally-made webbing, sometimes interwoven with silver thread, or on belts of leather covered by finely woven silver wire with handsome silver buckles. A knife with an ornate handle of silver thread may be stuck into a simple leather pouch behind the sheath. The handle and scabbards of Omani swords are also frequently ornamented with silver and silver thread in the same style as the *khanjar*s.

The firearms formerly carried by Omani men are usually decorated with beautifully executed silver rings round the barrel and stock; the amount and the quality of the ornament vary according to the owner's pocket. Crescent-shaped powder horns, a feature of the Sur and Sharqiyah areas, were often made of silver and sometimes also decorated with gold. Other silver objects used by men included small pipes for smoking a whiff of the locally grown tobacco, and toilet sets of tooth-pick and ear spoon.

The women and children in the past wore heavy weights of silver: necklaces, anklets and bracelets, earrings, head pieces and rings. Such adornment is rarer today, and confined to country districts or ceremonial occasions. A charm necklace with an oblong box delicately embossed or chased, called a *hirz*, containing verses from the Qur'an, was commonly worn on a silver chain as protection against the

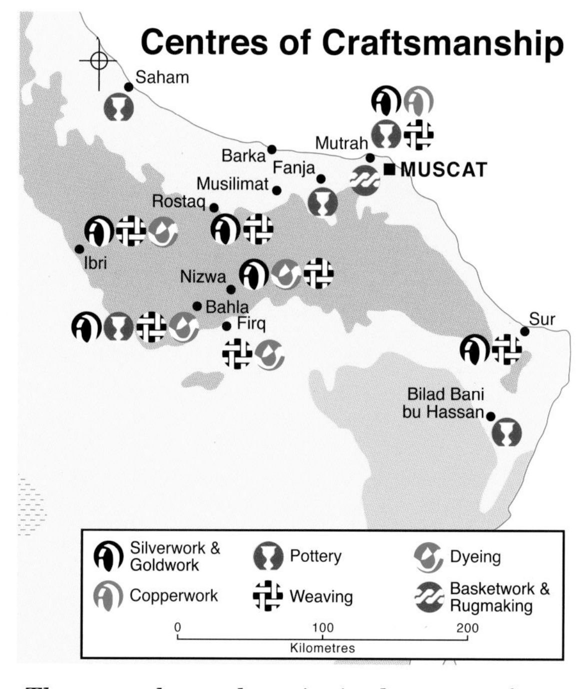

The map shows the principal centres of craft manufacture in the northern part of Oman.

Khanjars

Khanjars *in Oman are of various designs. But all are composed of many parts. Even a Minister in his office will wear his* khanjar *on formal occasions.*

Below: *Only the Al bu Said family uses the design of this Saidi* khanjar *hilt.*

This detail (below) *shows the trunk of a* khanjar *and its silver rings.*

The tip of the scabbard (below) *is said to be thus designed for balance .*

The most distinctive badge of the Omani man is the curved dagger called the *khanjar*, traditionally worn at the waist. The shape of the *khanjar* is always the same and is characterised by the curve of the blade and by the angle of the bend of the sheath. Sheaths may vary from simple covers of plain leather to ornate silver- or gold-decorated pieces of great beauty and delicacy.

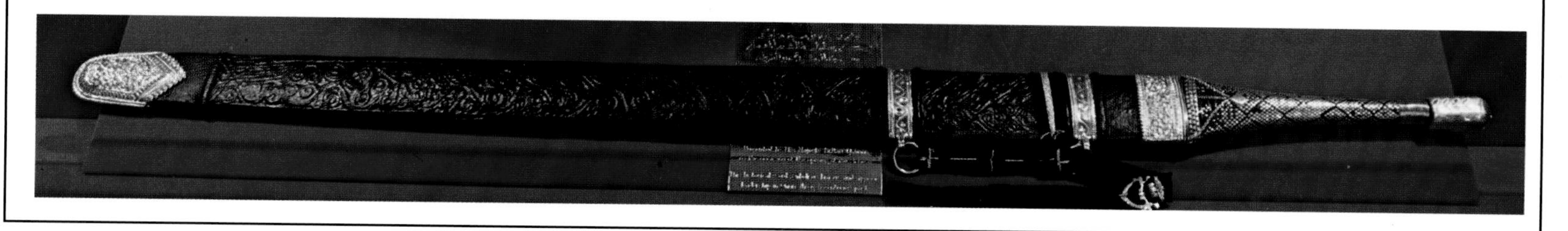

Jewellery

The silver pendants of such earrings are said to represent the hand of Fatima. The lower pair are from Dhofar.

Sometimes the heavy pendants are hung from decorative chains. The triangular sils *is worn in Dhofari headdresses.*

Most women wear anklets from their marriage onwards. They jingle as the girl walks.

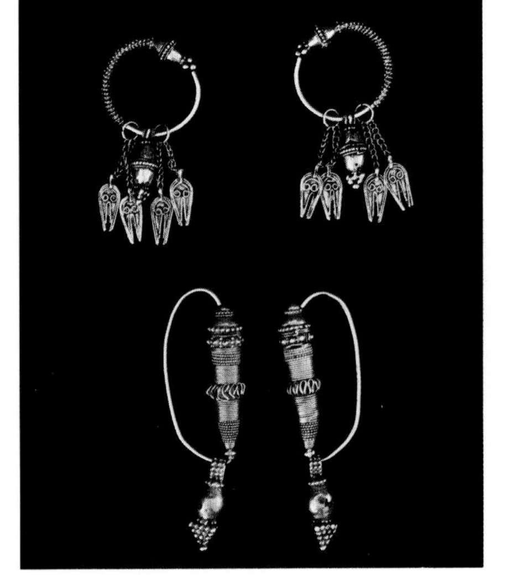

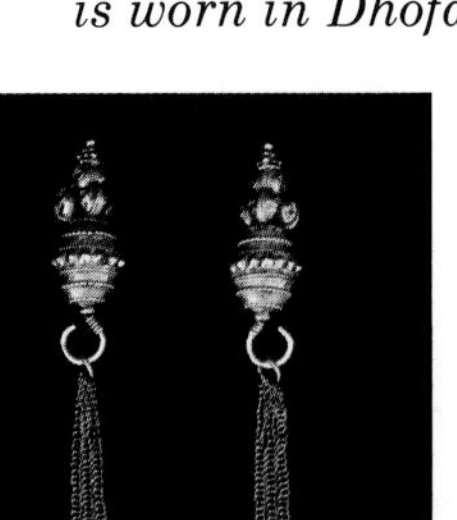

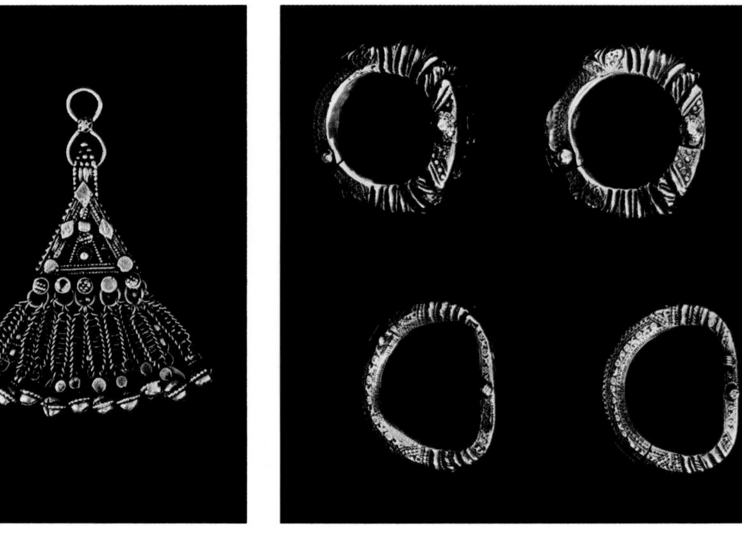

Bottom: *Anklets and bracelets from northern Oman which are hinged.*

Such a beautiful knife (below) *would be used for very practical purposes.*

Bottom: *The* manjad *necklace, from Dhofar, is worn over and under opposite shoulders.*

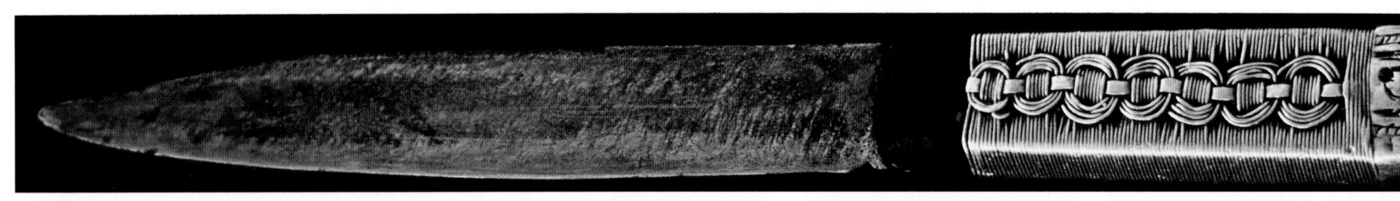

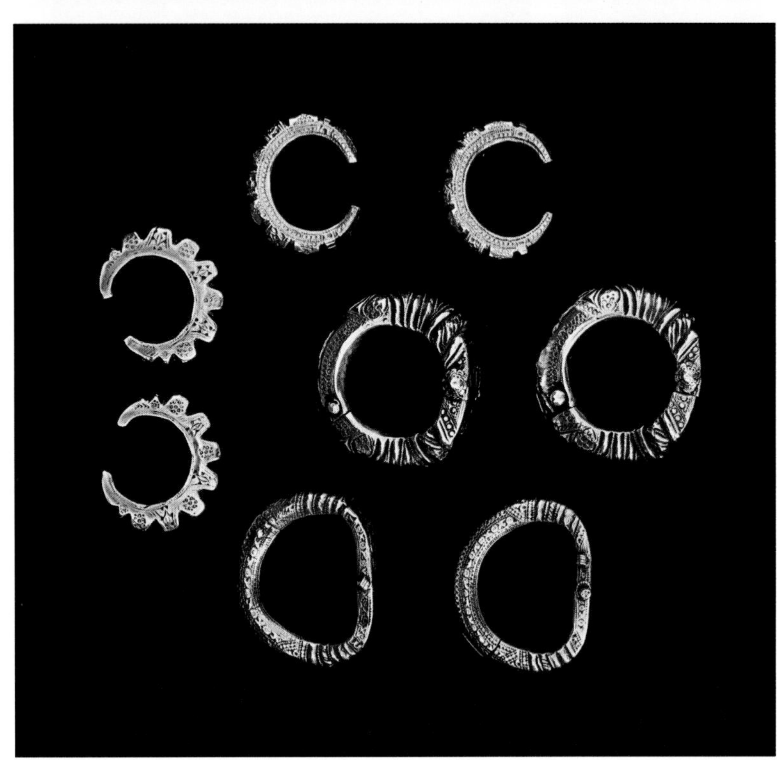

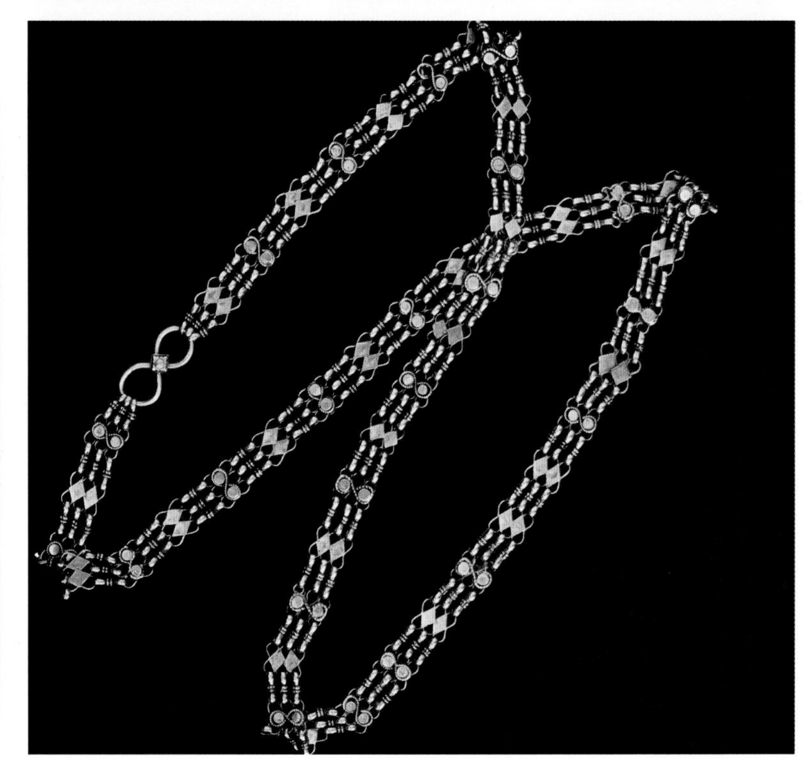

Left: *Thorn picks and tweezers are essential for men. The* hirz (above) *on its three-strand chain comes from Nizwa.*

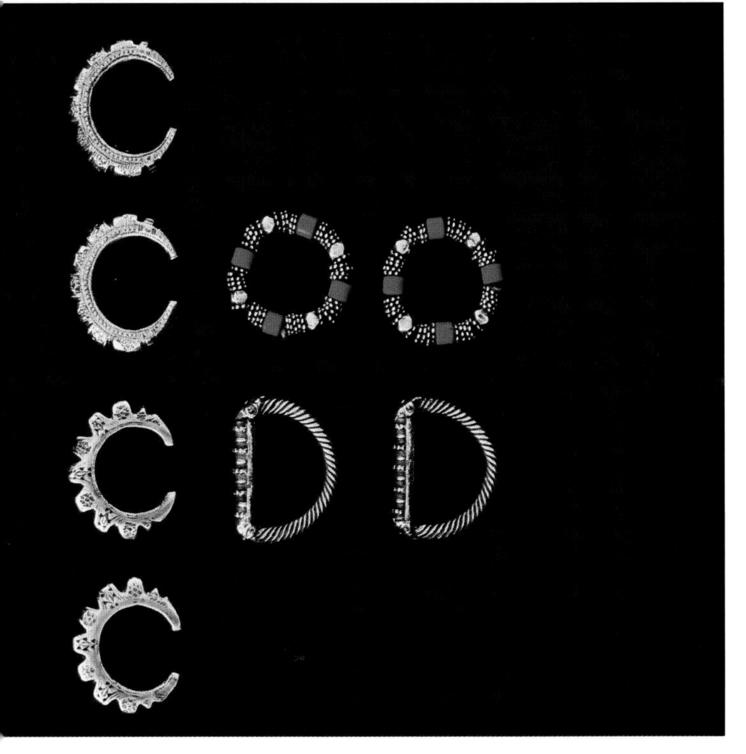

Left: *The bracelets on the left are from the north, while the others are from Dhofar.*
Above: *Inside the* hirz *is often a verse from the Qur'an*

The Omani woman, like so many of her counterparts in Eastern countries, tends to wear much of her wealth in the form of jewellery and gold and silver ornamentation. These objects are often of greaty beauty and represent the acme of the art of Omani silversmiths and goldsmiths. Nowadays jewellery is frequently of gold, but until relatively recently was more often of silver.
The main objects are rings, earrings, nose rings, headpieces, bracelets, armlets, anklets, necklaces, chains and amulets. Rings are worn on feet as well as hands and a complete set of hand rings consists of one for all five fingers of each hand. Each ring has a distinctive name.

Headpieces are of two main types. Those worn hanging down from the locks at the back of the head are usually of round or semi-circular design with small bell-like danglers and are sometimes mounted with stones. Another type worn hanging down on either side of the head give the impression of earrings and indeed may sometimes be worn alternatively as headpieces held in position by a silver chain or as actual earrings.

Coins or round pieces are used extensively. They are often worn in the centre of the forehead hanging down from the headpiece. Special wedding jewellery of gold is now made with small ornamental objects hanging down from a chain attached to the head scarf.

Anklets are usually of heavy silver. They open up so that they can easily be put on and are secured by a heavy silver pin. Bracelets and armlets differ in design from region to region, but both anklets and armlets often jingle attractively as the woman moves around.

Jewellery for the neck consists of ornate pieces on beautifully wrought chains or sometimes a number of silver pieces mounted on a thick cord. Such necklaces often include amulets, consisting of verses from the Qur'an inserted in an oblong silver box as protection, particularly against the Evil Eye. The beauty of gold and silver work is achieved by hammering, fusing and filigree techniques.

Traditional coppersmithing is carried on at Nizwa.

evil eye. Small silver shapes and tinkling bells which are attached to the *hirz* are an ancient device, used as long ago as the Achaemenid dynasty in Persia (*c.* 550-330 BC). Large silver medallions on chains, sometimes with inscriptions in Arabic, are common, while Maria Theresa dollars, mounted on barrel-shaped loops identical in design with those found in Iraq, Iran and in an Etruscan tomb, are frequently used on necklaces.

Silver bracelets, *banjari,* are often worn and many women's legs are heavy with thick silver anklets which jingle as they move – perhaps originally designed to monitor their movements as well as to sound attractive. Earrings are sometimes of enormous size and, while the women cover their heads with soft cloth, young girls are bareheaded but instead wear elaborate pieces of silver jewellery secured by wool thread in their plaited hair, often with jingling danglers. Large coins hanging over small girls' foreheads are a charming feature and women often wear paired rings on the fingers and thumbs of each hand and foot. Magic or talisman rings help to give a sense of security.

Dhofari jewellery differs in design and style from that of Northern Oman. The *manjad*, a heavy silver chain or elaborate linkage worn over one shoulder and under the other arm, is typical of the Southern Region which is also notable for the *sils*, a triangle of very finely

Metal Vessels

In such an incense burner (above), *sandalwood will usually be burnt.*

Vessels of copper, brass and silver are much used in household ceremonial in Oman as well as for ordinary domestic use. A formal meal of any sort will entail the use of several different sorts of vessel.

An Omani host will offer coffee to any caller and this is poured from a metal coffee pot into small round coffee cups. Traditionally coffee pots are made of copper or brass, or a combination of the two metals – or even of silver – and the usual shape in Oman is the waisted pot distinctive of Nizwa with a large beak and a round top ornamented with a spike or "coxcomb". At great tribal or family gatherings coffee is usually made in a coffee pot of enormous size, from which the usual sized pots are filled and the coffee served by servants.

The traditional Omani meal of mounded rice and meat, with garnishes of many kinds in separate bowls, is

Delicate silverwork distinguishes the beak of this coffee pot.

served on a large round brass tray. After a meal or after eating anything sticky, water to rinse the hands is offered in a beaked, round copper bowl, decorated with fine chased patterns.

After a formal meal it is usual, at least in wealthy households, to offer rose-water to the guests and this is sprinkled on the hands or over the head from a round silver bottle. The rose-water

Left: *Two typical Nizwa coffee pots flank a larger* Bedu *coffee pot, used at tribal gatherings. Decorations on sea chests were done by seamen on their long voyages.*

A rose-water sprinkler.

Smoke from the incense burner (above) *is wafted into the beard and under the armpits after formal meals.* Below: *Rose-water sprinklers give fragrance to a household.*

A brass pot for halwa.

A finely chased coffee pot.

Nizwa smiths combine brass and copper.

Floral designs are popular for the waists of coffee pots.

comes from the Jebel Akhdar where roses are specially grown. After the rose-water smoking incense may be served from a graceful silver vessel and carried round from guest to guest. Incense is the sign for departure as the Omani proverb shows: "After the incense, there is no sitting on."

Oman is rich in functional jewellery: tiny implements essential to daily use which are turned into miniature works of art. Such are the ear spoon and toothpick *(above),* and the little pick for piercing embroidered caps. The thorn pick *(below)* and its tweezers fit into a little silver sheath.

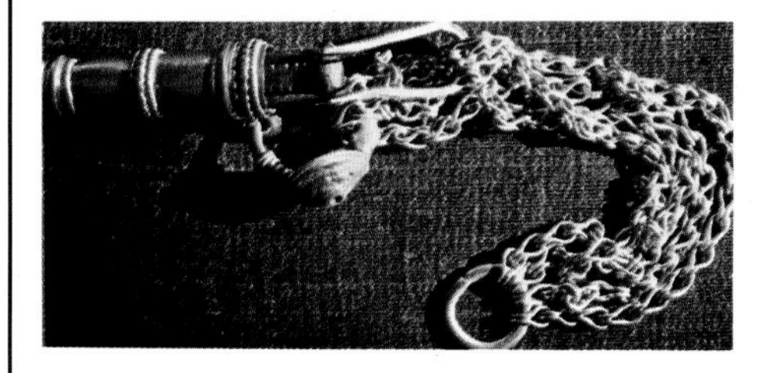

Firearms

The type of Omani matchlock seen on the right is known as the *gizail*. The match itself was of coconut or date fibre,bound with cotton thread. To fire the gun, black powder was measured and rammed down the barrel with a rod and wadding. The lead shot was poured in and rammed in tight with a further wad. Next, powder was poured into the powder pan, the cover was replaced, the match lit and firmly placed in the jaws of the cock. To fire, the powder pan cover was opened, and when the trigger was pressed, the match travelled forward in the cock, igniting the powder in the pan which in turn set off the powder in the barrel through the touch-hole.

Most traditional firearms are heavily decorated with silver. They are not made today, but fine examples are sought as collectors' pieces.

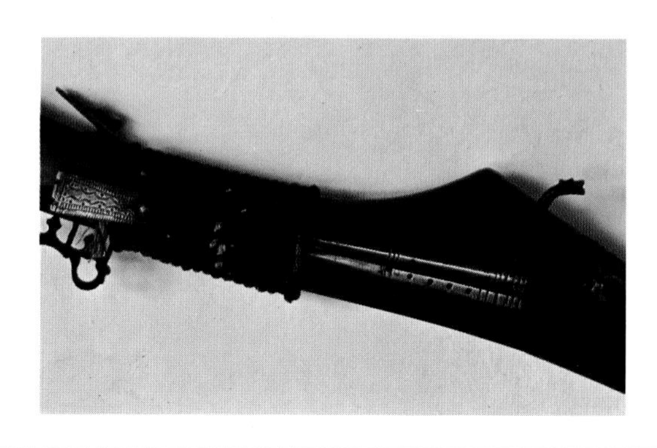

Such a decorative and jingling ornament is worn in the back of a plaited coil of hair.

decorated silver and little dangling chains with tinkling bells on the end, worn on the headscarf. Bahla, Rostaq, Nizwa, Ibri, Sur, Muscat and Mutrah all have a long tradition of silversmithing and each had its own distinctive designs. Nizwa's was *appliqué* geometric, Rostaq's a rose and stem pattern and Ibri's a lozenge shape.

The techniques still used resemble those in many other parts of the East. Sheet silver is heated and beaten into dies and then the two halves of the moulded shape are soldered together. Anklets and bracelets are sometimes made by forging pure silver, filling it with a mixture of hot pitch and resin, or wax, and when this has cooled, embellishing the surface by embossing. Chisels are used for this and for chasing, whilst round-edged punches are employed for decorative work involving no cutting. For engraving, a beaked anvil, flat and narrow pliers, a wooden filing block and a simple blow lamp and bellows are required. The silversmiths in Oman usually used melted down Maria Theresa dollars, which were until recently used as local currency, as the very high silver content engenders confidence in the customer that he or she is receiving value for money.

With increasing wealth, gold has tended to replace silver jewellery and goldsmiths flourish in Muscat, Mutrah and

A Mutrah silversmith works on a repoussé bracelet characteristic of Omani silverwork, whose designs bear affinity with those of great antiquity from Minos and Byzantium.

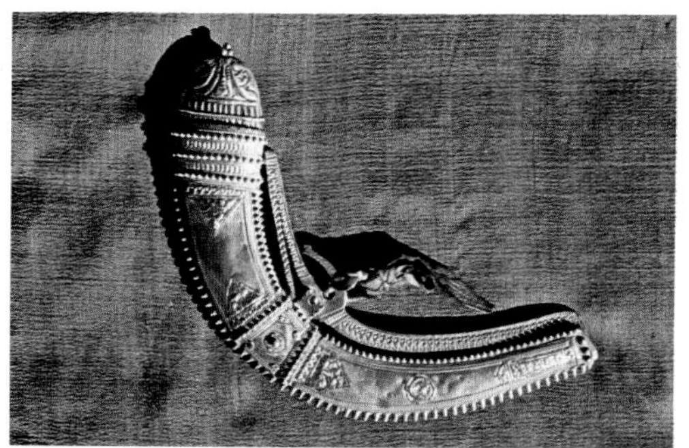

The powder horn from Sur (above) *lets out small quantities of powder by a spring catch.*
Below: *Bullet moulds and gunpowder scoops used to be essential.*

Delight in Ornamentation

Objects of common use are often charmingly wrought, like the floral box, the iron and brass lock and key, the Dhofari beaded bottle (made of horn and containing *kohl*), the Nizwa doorknob, and Bahla key, in these pictures.

other market centres. The techniques used are those used in other parts of Arabia, Iran and the Indian subcontinent and the small square jewellery shops savour of an age-old tradition. A favourite device on a piece of jewellery was the English gold sovereign. Weddings and festivals often give rise to commissions for special headpieces and gold rings for fingers, nose and ears, and bracelets, often following traditional silver designs. Salalah is noted for distinctive necklaces of gold beads interspersed with coral.

Household Utensils

Once again copper is mined in Oman. Today, copper and brass household utensils are made in Nizwa, Mutrah and one or two other places. The Nizwa coffee pot has a distinctive shape and is often made of copper and decorated with brass bands around the stem and on the spout and lid. A peculiar feature is a series of little diamond-shaped danglers hanging near the handle. It was common practice to insert small stones into the hollow of the lid supposedly as a precaution against poisoning; the clatter of the stones would betray the presence of a sinister hand if the lid were opened by some unauthorised person. Copper trays, incense burners and long-handled spoons are examples of the coppersmith's art.

Locally produced household utensils are relatively simple. They consist of coffee pots, pans for cooking – of copper or aluminium – kettles, bowls and round trays of various sizes, around which the traditional meal was, as it often now still is, eaten. Enormous coffee pots of copper or brass may still be used for tribal and large family gatherings, but the brew made in them is generally then transferred to smaller pots, or thermos flasks, before being served. It is customary to grind the coffee for each occasion.

Traditional chests decorated with brass nails are to this day found in many houses, particularly on the coast, though now often used merely for decoration. Formerly seamen would decorate the chests with brass ornamentation to while away the hours on their long voyages in sailing ships. Floors were often covered with matting made from palm fronds or reeds; and rugs, sometimes locally made and sometimes imported from Persia, Afghanistan or Pakistan, were brought out for special occasions. The compounds of houses on the coast, particularly Sur, were spread with clean pebbles.

Agricultural Tools

Spades are used to dig the gardens, and release or dam the water channels. The plough alone turns the soil – a wooden plough with an iron tip, small and light and traditionally drawn by a single bull or cow – though tractors have largely taken over. A long, slightly curved, toothed sickle, *minjal*, is used for cutting lucerne, alfalfa, and other fodder and also for pruning palm trees. A long chisel, *hib*, is employed to separate palm off-shoots from their parents. The date cultivators used the same sort of sling made of rope and leather, as in other date-growing areas in the Middle East and in the coconut groves of Africa for climbing trees.

Studded and coloured bandoliers are worn by Bedu *tribesmen.*

Below*: outside the kiln at one of the potteries at Bahla a row of pots await firing.* Right*: the slow kick wheel has been used since Sumerian times.*

Guns

For many generations guns have been weapon, ornament and source of interest to the Omani man. In fact, a gun had become until recently virtually an emblem of manhood. The most common and typical of these was the *gizail* or *abu futila*, which means the "father of the match" (the matchlock). They are still treasured. Many of these found their way into Oman through the Gulf from Ottoman Turkey in the eighteenth and nineteenth centuries, when the Ottomans traded such weapons with countries on the north-west frontier of India.

Many matchlocks were ornately decorated with strands of brass, silver or gold inlaid in grooves around the barrel. Some had attractive damascened patterns in gold or silver along the whole length of the barrel. Inlaying was a long operation. First the barrel was coated with an acid-resistant mixture of wax and resin. Next the design was either scratched in with a needle or painted into the coating with a stiff brush. Acid was then poured over the treated area to eat away the metal exposed, after which silver or gold was inlaid into the pattern of indentations either by hammering or with a dovetail cross-section. Each weapon was decorated differently – no two alike – and each was an individual piece of craftsmanship.

The *gizail* always had a very long barrel, as most muzzle-loading guns had, and some barrels were forged in lengths of about eighteen inches and welded together after the boring had been done; this was a long and complicated process involving the use of bamboo and iron borers. After the decoration had been completed the barrel was fitted to the wooden stock by a number of brass rings and a brass plate was finally placed underneath to protect the woodwork and house the ramrod.

Different methods of producing ball for the gizail were employed and moulds might produce one or two at a time or as many as a dozen. The match itself was made of coconut or date fibres with cotton thread. The ordinary powder flasks were usually of hard wood, often ornately carved, but some were made of silver and gold.

Firing was a lengthy process. First, black powder was measured and poured into the barrel, after which a wad was forced down with the ramrod. Next lead shot was put in and finally a further wad, all of which was rammed home. A small quantity of black powder was then poured into the powder pan, the cover of which was replaced, whereupon the match was lit and secured firmly in the jaws of the cock. When it was time to fire, the powder pan cover was opened, aim taken, and, when the trigger was pressed, the match travelled forward in the cock igniting the powder in the pan, which in turn ignited the powder in the barrel through the touch-hole.

Although the *gizail* was the commonest weapon, there were many other sorts of firearm carried by Omanis, such as the breech-loading Martini Henry, which was imported into the general area in large numbers at the end of the nineteenth century, and also the flintlock. These ancient weapons were the principal arms carried by the Omanis when they mustered at Sohar in 1952 to march on Buraimi after the oasis had been occupied by a Saudi force in that year. In the event, the march did not take place and the Buraimi dispute went to arbitration. It could well have been the last serious encounter at which to put this antique weaponry to the test .

Pottery

The earliest pottery found in Oman dates from the Jemdet Nasr period (early third millennium BC) and utilitarian pottery has been made there since man first needed pots. The pottery still made in the villages was until the 1970s used largely for practical purposes, consisting of items like porous water pots, cooking pots and cups. The standard of the finished product and methods used depended on the quality of the clay available and where clay was poor, methods tended to be primitive.

Bahla has long been a centre of pottery in Oman, with traditional craftmanship recently carried forward in the new modern pottery set up with a specialist Chinese input. Other centres of pottery

The pot's lip is finessed.

*Each pottery has its own skillled decorators (*left*). Below: the large pot requires considerable physical effort from the maker.*

are Bilad Bani bu Hassan, Hayyil, Musilimat, Mutrah, Saham and Salalah. In Bahla and Musilimat, where good quality clay is available, the craft was always relatively sophisticated and the potters highly skilled in their very ancient techniques, using a simple foot-operated slow wheel and firing the "green ware" in large mud-brick kilns, fuelled with brushwood. Potters in northern Oman are all men, but women also make pottery objects in Salalah, where true clay is not available. Nevertheless quaint and colourful incense burners, water bowls and other practical items are made there by hand without a wheel, as well as decorative pottery including highly individual representations of objects such as small boats, cars and aeroplanes.

Bahla is noted for its large jars used for storing dates. Incense burners, roof gutterings, water jars, water cups, *laban* or yoghurt jars, and *halwa* bowls are among the other items produced there. Containers for food are glazed inside. In centuries past, glass made in Sohar was probably used for such glazing. The glaze later produced was from locally ground substances of poorer material.

The basic materials for each product can be adapted according to the intended use of the finished article. For example, extra sand is added to the clay mix in order to make water jars more porous. A skilled potter can make up to fifty jars a day. The secrets of the craft are handed down from generation to generation usually within the same family and some potteries have been in one family for several centuries. A potter in Salalah informed a visiting expert that his business had been founded by forebears in the sixteenth century AD – a date which independent evidence has established as correct.

Music

Music was not encouraged under Ibadhi precept but the music of simple folk has a powerfully rhythmic African quality. It is associated with joyful occasions such as weddings and *Id* holidays. In some places on the coast in northern Oman and in Dhofar, there is regular dancing on Fridays.

To the strong beat of the drums the players of other instruments often move round and round in circles to encourage the dancers – both male and female. Melody may be provided by a type of trumpet made out of horn, a straight pipe, and a stringed instrument, a *rababa*, resembling those of east Africa. An entirely different sort of instrument is the curved horn, usually decorated with silver, used to summon the tribe.

Sailors on their long voyages used to sing songs and chants, and the Omanis have their own versions of sea shanties. In some of the remoter areas also singing is quite common amongst the *Bedu* tribes but not among the town-dwelling people of the Interior. Special chants are sung for special occasions and some tribes have distinctive airs for bringing camels to water, loading, or for trotting or walking them. There may be songs in praise of coffee, and, of course, love songs. The women sing in certain remote areas, but such conduct would be taken as very immodest in most places. In Salalah there are special songs for lute and drum which are sung on holiday and festive occasions, and in some places there are special chants used for exorcism (*zar*).

One form of dancing still carried on at *Ids* in Oman is the sword dance. These dances were originally in the nature of exercises for war and the participants engaged in mock fights, armed with sword, dagger and target shield – small,

round, embossed shields made of hippopotamus hide, wood, or sometimes of leather. Bertram Thomas in his book *Alarms and Excursions in Arabia* describes an Arab greeting in the Bani bu Ali country in the 1920s. The scene contains some of the elements still to be seen

Music and folk melody is rich and varied in Oman, and being carefully preserved. Dance and rhythm occurs in various forms, not least – with African influence – at the end of the fast, celebrated in the picture left, *in Dhofar.*
Below, *a potter's wife carries his wares to dry in the sun.*

at *Id* celebrations in various parts of the country.

Drums were beating, and the crowd swayed left and right to their rhythm; quivering sword blades flashed in the sun as sword dancers leapt hither and thither, and low chanting grew loud as we approached. Swinging round to form a corridor for us, the tribesmen, holding their rifle butts to their hips for the *feux de joie,* sent a hail of friendly bullets pinging over our heads. We went on to where the Amir stood, before the fort, on a carpet placed in the large open square, a favourable position for witnessing the horsemanship and camel-racing that now took place... A dozen horsemen galloped

past, now in this formation, now in that, curvetting and firing their rifles at the same time, or racing in pairs down the straight, one rider standing upright on his stirrupless saddle, gripping only with his toes, and maintaining a parlous equilibrium by placing an outstretched arm on the neck of his more comfortably seated fellow rider. Reforming, the party would move past in close formation at a jog trot, chanting heroic verse, an ancient *Badawin* custom deriving from the mighty Antar of antiquity. The leader gabbled his lines and at the end of each couplet, the rest of the party shouted in chorus 'Allahu Akbar'.

Dhofari Pottery

A comparable tradition persists in Dhofar, where the characteristic artefact is the incense burner – *top* and *right*. One pottery in Salalah has been in the same family for some 500 years; and a Dhofari exponent of the craft is seen at work in the big picture *overleaf*. Among the tribes of Dhofar a whole range of pots, each with its precise culinary or storage purpose, are made by the various tribes, of which a sample from those recorded by the ethnologist Miranda Morris are seen *below*.

The blue yarn is spun and wound on to racks to keep it tangle-free.

Great skill is needed to spin wool on the hand-held bobbin.

Weaving

Weaving was still carried on in many towns and villages, though most weavers were very old men. Carding and spinning are done on traditional implements made from palm-fronds, and the looms were of traditional design. The weaver sat in a kind of pit in front of his loom, the warp threads stretching some twenty or thirty feet in front of him. The cloth woven was mainly used for lengths of wazara or lunghi worn by men about the waist. Nowadays, the weaver's skill is preserved by the enthusiast. But the secrets of his techniques were being passed on for posterity by its ageing traditional practitioners.

Weaving was often done under the shade of trees. Originally, the whole process of growing cotton, spinning and weaving was done in Oman, but little cotton is now grown, and raw cotton or thread has to be imported.

This description bears eloquent testimony to traditional Omani horsemanship – an art and skill fostered and developed in Sultan Qaboos's reign. The words of the heroic chant as translated by Thomas demonstrate the warriors' pride:

We have filled every quarter with fear
till mankind grovels before us.
Chorus: God is great!
We have excelled the Pleiades
[*Thuraiyya*] in its zenith.
Chorus: God is great!
And whosoever approacheth us seeking trouble shall find us brave as lions.
Chorus: God is great!

Weaving and Dyeing

Traditional weaving was still carried on in most towns and villages until the 1970s, although weavers then tended to be old men. A younger generation of weavers is preserving the craft today. Originally the whole process of growing cotton, spinning and weaving was done in Oman but relatively little cotton was latterly grown and consequently raw cotton or cotton thread had to be imported. Carding and spinning were done on traditional implements made from palm fronds and the looms were of simple design. When working, the weaver sat in a kind of pit in front of his loom, the warp threads being stretched out over a distance of twenty or so feet in front of him. The cloth woven varied but was chiefly used for lengths of *wazara*, or *lunghi*, worn by the men round the waist. In Barka multicoloured cloth was woven for a greater variety of purposes.

Weaving was often done under the shade of trees and a distinctive cloak of black goat hair was woven in Bahla – a batwinged garment with an embroidered design at the back which gave it something of the air of an academic gown. The women amongst the *Bedu* tribes made various articles such as lengths of cloth for adorning tents, camel and donkey saddle bags, and rugs which could be used either for tent making or for covering the floor. In the Ibri area rugs of a distinctive red and black striped design are still produced. Goat and camel hair are the usual basic materials, but sheep's wool is also used particularly for making the *bisht*, the traditional form of cloak with gold edging worn by men over the white cotton *dishdasha*.

Dyeing was done for many generations

in a few places, including Firq near Nizwa, where indigo was the principal dye used. This indigo dye comes from the leaves of the indigo plant *neel*. When the Imam Said ibn Ahmad tried to make indigo dyeing a state monopoly in the eighteenth century, it caused him considerable unpopularity.

Boatbuilding

Boatbuilding is a very ancient craft. In the fifteenth century AD Ahmad ibn Majid, perhaps Oman's most famous seaman, attributed its origin to Noah whose ship, he remarked, was put together in the form of the five main stars of the Great Bear.

There is still boatbuilding at Sur and the trade continued until recently in Sohar and Mutrah. The trade is confined to a few families who have always plied it. On the shore at Sur in the mid 1990s there were usually three or four boats being built at any one time. However, the boats built are only about a tenth of the size of the great ships of some five hundred or more tons built earlier for sailing the oceans, though the traditional methods are still used.

The boat is built, after the keel is laid, within a framework of poles like scaffold-

Dyeing

A lifetime of dyeing indigo cloth shows in the old man's hands, above *and* right. Below, *a member of the Royal Oman Police celebrates his fellow-countrymen's delight in colour.*

Firq, near Nizwa, was long known for its indigo-dyed cloth. The deep-blue garments hang to dry beneath a castle wall.

ing. The wood is mainly teak from India, though the ribs and keels are natural grown timbers and the masts, a particularly expensive item, are Malabar teak trunks. The carpenters use the same tools as they have over many generations adzes, saws, chisels, hammers and bow drills. Modern boats are put together with iron nails, the old method of sewing the planks together having virtually died out except, until recently, for work on some parts of the ancient-shaped *badan*, a small craft propelled by oars. It is strange to reflect that when the Omanis made their greatest and longest voyages, the planks of their ships were only sewn together. It was a method which gave flexibility during storms, but at the same time led to a more rapid break-up in the event of shipwreck.

The traditional methods of Omani shipbuilders are described by Abu Said al Balkhi writing in the ninth century AD (third century AH) as follows: "There are people, at Oman, who cross over to the Islands that produce the coconut, carrying with them carpenter's and suchlike tools; and having felled as much wood as they want, they let it dry, then strip off the leaves, and with the bark of the tree they spin a yarn, wherewith they sew the planks together, and so build a hip. Of the same wood they cut and round away a mast: of the leaves they weave their sails, and the ark they make into cordage. Having thus completed their Vessel, they load her with coconuts, which they bring and sell at Oman."

The type of boat chiefly associated with Sur is the *baghala*, or its smaller version the *ghanja*, both of which had high poops and windows at the stern in the style of the old Portuguese galleon. Nowadays the craft are usually powered by motor, but until the 1960s they often moved under sail. The shipwrights' responsibility ended after building the hull and caulking the ship. Sailors who were taken on in advance sewed the sails, rigged the ship and floated her away from the dockyard. Alan Villiers, the marine historian, made a number of voyages on Arab craft in the 1930s and he describes one of the last really large *baghala*s built in Oman in his book *Sons of Sindbad*. It was called *Hope of Compassion* and was of about 200 tons with a capacity of 3,000 packages of dates. Even this was relatively small compared with earlier ships of 500 to 600 tons, which carried 400 men or more. By the 1930s, the *baghala* was becoming extinct, as *boom*s, with their distinctive long-nosed prow, were found more convenient by those plying the gulf and Indian Ocean trade. *Baghala*s were thought to be less seaworthy and their carved sterns, though stately and picturesque, were reckoned dangerous in a pounding sea. The *boom* is a versatile craft.

The *Hope of Compassion*, Villiers says, was:

beautiful from outside and beautiful on board with the picturesque romantic sweep of her ancient decks from the worn planks of the poop to the curved horn at the low bow. Her windowed stern was especially lovely. Its elliptical area of ancient teak was covered with intricate patterns of excellent carving and her curved bow swept up from the sea as gracefully as the breast of a swan. She was big for an Arab. Her oiled teak hull sat prettily in the water with a grace and strength and sweetness of line that sang of sea kindliness despite all Najdi's comments on the vulnerability of her stern... She was very old – more than half a century – and dated back to the slaving days. Like so many Arab vessels, every line of her flowed and blended perfectly into a harmonious and lovely whole, though she had been put together on the beach at Sur by carpenters...[without] even an elementary paper plan. She was built by the eye and she was built beautifully though she was but a heap of indifferent teak poorly fastened with weak iron and here and there an ill-butted plank had warped and all her fastenings wept with rust stains from every pitted head... Her quarter galleries were latticed delicately, like the narrow windows of a *harim* court: her five stern windows were protected by iron bars, and a teak shutter swung from the central window, richly carved in patterns of crescents and stars...

She was indeed a craft of an earlier age, though life on local craft in the Indian Ocean and Gulf may not have changed radically even by now despite the powerful engines which have replaced the great lateen sail. Villiers described the scene on board:

There was a carpenter working on his new dhow. There was a low forecastle head, heavy beams for belaying halliards and cables, a firebox over which a smoke-grimed cook crouched, wooden water tanks on either side, the great bole of the raking mainmast rising from the forward end of the long narow main hatch. There were, too, a number of ringbolts and a big capstan that looked as if it might have come from Nelson's *HMS Victory.* Wherever carving and embellishments could be added they had been and the poop was liberally decorated in this way. In the after part of the spacious great cabin there was seven feet of headroom and the whole break of the poop was carved with a delicate tracery of involved patterns into which texts from the *Qur'an* had been worked. The reclining

Boatbuilding

Oman has a great tradition of boatbuilding, and her sailors were probably navigating the oceans from the third millenium BC. The craft is still carried on in Sur, as it was until recently in Mutrah and Sohar. Traditional methods have not been abandoned and the trade is confined to a few families who have always plied it

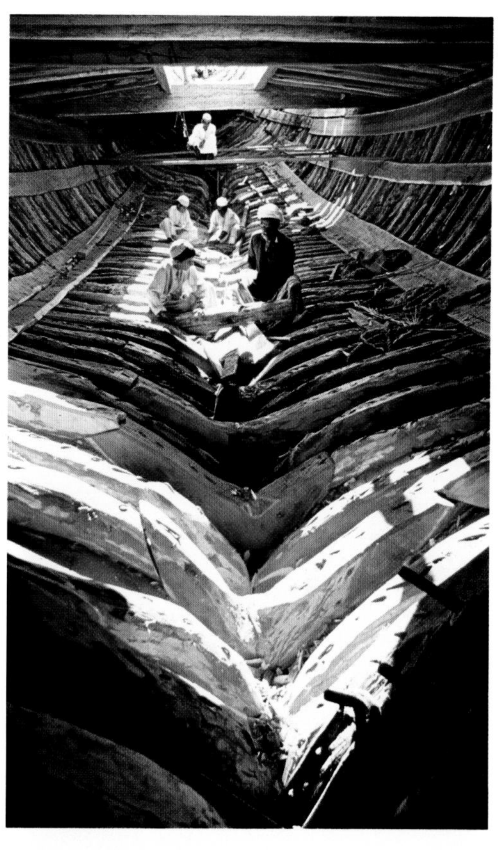

The ribs and keel are of natural grown timbers , usually teak from India. The boom (below) *flies the flag of Oman to mark its near-completion.*

The carpenters use the same tools as their forefathers.

The keel is constructed within a framework of wooden poles.

The adze is one of the oldest tools, and one of the most difficult to use

Far right: *Sultan Qaboos's dhow, styled and built in Oman by the country's own craftsmen, moves easily through the Arabian Sea under full sail.*

The bow drill, when skilfully handled, is the best tool for the job.

bench for the officers was an elaborately finished and well-joined piece of built-in furniture, protected by a carved teak railing. The poop had a small working capstan, rows of chests, a rising mizzen mast towering above, binnacle, wheel and helmsman's chair. When the *Hope of Compassion* sailed with a gentle breeze off the land, the sailors hove her short, raised the peak of the lateen main, broke out her hook and she turned on her lovely heel and went, a picture of grace and beauty as she turned her carved and galleried stern – a ship of romance, as the land wind filled her great sail. It took the sailors a long time to masthead the sail which fluttered out golden in the morning air. Her burnished hull slipped slowly through the blue water.

The daily life aboard a typical Arab craft was also described by Villiers.

Our days began long before dawn and the *muezzins* began their calls to prayer some time before I could detect the faintest tinge of greyness in the eatern sky... There are fairly well defined periods for the announcements of the five daily prayers – dawn with the first lighting of the sky; morning, a little after the sun has passed its meridian; third, or afternoon, when the sun has lost its glare and its redness is whitening and the shadows are long; fourth, or evening, immediately after sunset; fifth or night, any time between sunset and dawn, but usually, for the convenience of the ship, about two hours after sunset... Prayers, breakfast, cooking, eating, sleeping, catching fish, cleaning fish, looking at what went on aboard the other vessels... so the days passed.

By the messy smoky firebox, Jassi, looking sadder and blacker than ever, squatted on the tiny fore hatch and stirred the goat-pot with a piece of wood... Abdulla Najdi and his gang, regardless of all else, continued their packing of 'best' Basra dates... We had sixty large packages of these dates.

Beneath the poop of the new dhow a tiny girl lay sleeping, a fat little mite in a long print dress with a black hood, her chubby small hands and her chubbier small face liberally decorated with lines of black and henna. From her ears hung silver ornaments, about ten to each lobe, which jingled as she walked. There were two heavy silver bangles round her ankles... Some made coffee, in long spouted brass pots designed to extract the maximum heat from the minimum number of embers. Some drank coffee. The poorer the coffee the more elaborate the manner of serving it, some of the *beduin*

The boom (centre, below) *is recognised by its high, beaked prow and its sharp stern. The projection at the stern of the boat* (bottom)*, is the mariners' privy – less precarious than it seems!*

handing round the thimbles full...as if it were nectar from the gods, bowing and clicking the porcelain cups against the spout... Some answered the call of nature in the little pews along the ship's side... Old Yusuf Shirazi... was making medicine... Twisted pieces of weeds, odds and ends of leaves, dried and very ancient seeds, pieces of bark and lengths of something that looked like string – all these went in and Yusuf pounded and mixed them industri-

Careening

During many sea-voyages, the hull of a vessel inevitably becomes coated with barnacles, algae and debris. If allowed to accumulate it eventually slows the progress of the ship, and so it is necessary to careen the hull regularly. After scraping, the hull is treated with fish-oil to protect the wood.

Boats with sewn seams have been known since ancient times.

After careening and oiling, the smooth hull allows the boat to go faster.

The part-sewn badan *still survives.*

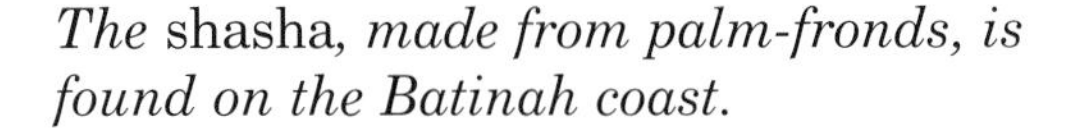

The shasha, *made from palm-fronds, is found on the Batinah coast.*

ously... I learned... that the 'medicine' was a concoction for increasing the flow of milk from the breasts of *beduin* matrons. Yusuf wanted milk to bathe his eyes...

Boats Found in Oman

There are many types of local craft other than the *baghala*. Those formerly common are listed below. All the smaller boats could be rowed with a paddle as well as having a sail, though the *huri* very seldom had any canvas. The word *dhow*, which is applied to all sorts of local craft by Europeans, is never used. It was originally used to refer to a now extinct form of craft found on the east African coast.

Whether sailing a wooden boat or a simple shasha, *the Omani seaman remains an example to the world with his great maritime inheritance.* Below, *the disappearing* shasha, *outpaced by technology, is preserved as a monument.*

Boat (general):	*khashab*
Boat (with enginge):	*launch*
Boat with upright prow stem and transom stern: (the word probably derives from the Portuguese *jalbuta* – cf Jolly Boat)	*jalbut*
Larger boat with beak, prow and sharp stern:	*boom*
Pearling boat:	*sambuk*
Small high-pooped boat (partly sewn together instead of nailed):	*badan*
Small fishing boat (similar in shape to *sambuk*):	*shu'iy*
Small dug-out or dinghy:	*huri*
Ferry:	*abra*
"Pram":	*shahuf*
Palm-frond boat: (found on Batinah Coast):	*shasha*

A warship used to be called *manwa*, a corruption of "Man o' War" – a lasting tribute to the former strength and influence of the British Navy, long familiar in Omani waters.

Wood Carving

Beautiful carved doorways are a distinctive feature of towns and villages in Oman. These carved doorways greatly enhance the typical Omani house, whether it is a fine stone dwelling, one merely built of mud, or a beautiful modern home built in the last twenty-five years. Some are great gates leading to palaces such as the gigant-ic and wonderfully carved doors in the fort at al Hazm. Other antique doors are more modest in size, but still ornately carved, perhaps opening into the houses of prosperous merchants. These often have little wicket gates like the bigger doors. Simpler doors to more humble traditional dwellings are also frequently well carved.

The tradition of carving doors extends to the Gulf, and similar doorways are also found in Zanzibar and the other former Arab colonies on the coast of east Africa. Designs are floral or geometric and very often, particularly on the larger doors, a date is also inscribed. In Sur, a distinctive tradition of carving which includes palm tree patterns is still carried on, though modern doors are distinctly less ornate than earlier ones. The wood comes either from east Africa or India and the tradition of carving seems to have eddied round the Ocean between the Indian subcontinent, Oman and east Africa. No doubt trading and maritime connections between these regions caused the spread of this form of culture and it is natural, in view of the common tradition, that houses as well as doorways in Zanzibar should resemble those in Muscat so closely.

Carving also finds expression amongst Omani boatbuilders. Various parts of Omani boats, particularly the poops, are still intricately carved. But in former times the scale was greater and the quality of the work high, for there was an immense amount of carving on the much larger ships which the Omanis used.

Literature and Scholarship

Oman has produced a large number of scholars throughout the ages, writing in Arabic from the earliest days of Islam on many subjects – Islamic studies and com-

Below: *a traditional Omani flower and leaf pattern;*(middle) *the carvings of Sur are distinctive;* (bottom) *ceilings, too, are decorated.*

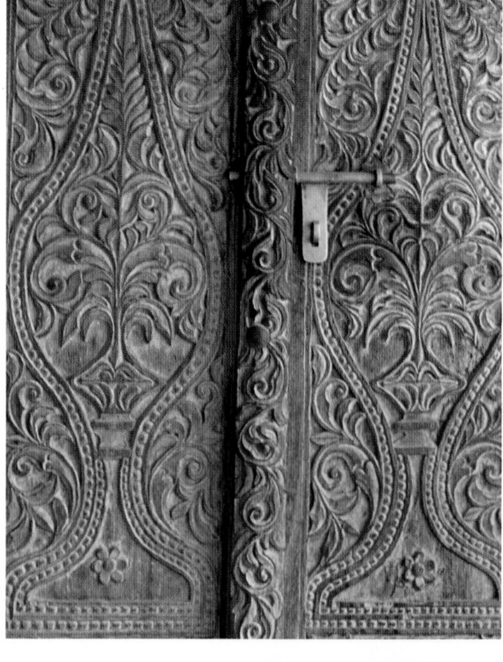

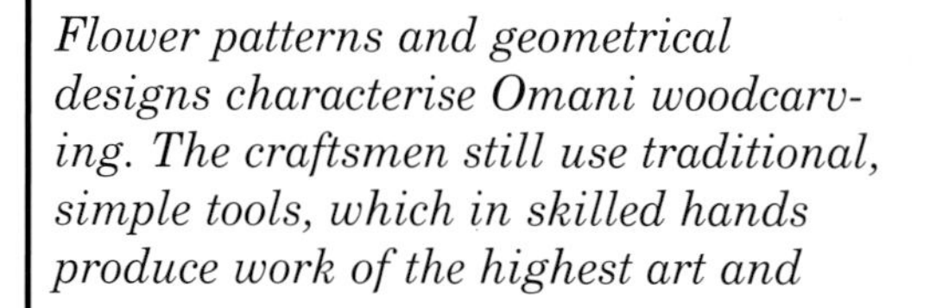

Flower patterns and geometrical designs characterise Omani woodcarving. The craftsmen still use traditional, simple tools, which in skilled hands produce work of the highest art and

Sur produces possibly the finest examples of the woodcarver's art, pictured on this page.

The Art of the Woodcarver

Art in Oman finds its highest expression, apart from in jewellery and silver objects, in woodcarving. Finely, and sometimes very ornately, carved doors are a feature of every Omani town and village, both in the Interior and on the coast. similar doors are also found in the areas of east Africa where Omani influence prevailed.

Traditional local craft were, and still are, decorated by designs carved on the stern and poop. The art has not died in Oman and carving is still done to decorate both doors and boats, particularly in Sur , where the method and style of craftsmanship has not changed for centuries. Doors frequently carry carved in-scriptions from the Qur'an with the date of the work. The designs on doors and lintels are invariably Islamic designs of geometrical or flower patterns, and the flower and leaf motif is a common one.

When Sur was famous for the great ocean-going ships built there, the sterns and poops were beautifully, extensively and cleverly carved. It is sad that virtually none of these great ships survive and their beauty can only be appreciated from old photographs and drawings. However, the ancient tools used by the carpenters and carvers – chisels, awls, adzes, hammers and bow drills – have survived and are still used by the shipwrights.

mentaries on the *Qur'an*, the Arabic language, law, genealogy, history, philosophy, and astronomy. Much admired works of calligraphy have also been produced and all the earlier copies of the *Qur'an* or other books were written in clear, even manuscript. Some contain illustrations and diagrams, though never of the human form. Many books have undoubtedly been destroyed in the past in civil and other wars. Owners of surviving books and manuscripts have been known to be hesitant to disclose them. Nevertheless, the Ministry of National Heritage and Culture has been building up its collections both of books and manuscripts for many years. Other important libraries remain in private hands. For instance the learned former Minister Sayyid Muhammad ibn Ahmad has a library of some nine thousand books, many of which are several hundred years old.

One of the earliest surviving manuscripts was written by Abu'l Mu'thir as-Salt ibn Khamis al-Bahlawi. It dates from the ninth century AD (second century AH) and is called *as-Siyar al-Umaniya* ("Omani Ways").

Another early work is *Ansab al Arab* ("Arab Genealogies") by Salma ibn Musaalim al-'Awtabi. This is a work of exceptional value not merely for its genealogy but for the detail which enables scholars to reconstruct the tribal pattern of the time. Awtabi's grandfather was the author of a notable work on *fiqh* (Islamic jurisprudence). Awtabi himself seems to have lived and written during the eleventh century AD (fifth century AH). The Awtabis were then important tribal leaders on the Batinah.

Commentators

Of the commentators on the *Qur'an*, two authors of massive works must be mentioned. First, Muhammad bin Ibrahim al Kindi was the author of *Biyan ash-Sharia* ("Commentary on the Sharia"); his exegesis runs to 72 volumes. Jamil bin Khamis as-Saadi, the author of *Qamoos ash-Sharia* ("The Dictionary of the Sharia") was even more prolific, with 90 volumes to his credit.

Among the commentators on the Arabic language, the most illustrious was Abu Bakr Muhammad ibn al-Hassan ibn Duraidh al Azdi ("ibn Duraidh"), who wrote *Gamma' al lugha* ("The Digest of Language). He lived in Basrah in Iraq, dying there in 933 AD (321 AH). He and his family, however, came from Oman and he wrote a number of poems on Omani themes. He and ibn Athir, who wrote the *Kamil*, are valuable sources on early Omani history.

Genealogy and History

Genealogy and history are often closely entwined in early works. Hisham ibn Muhammad al-Kalbi ("ibn Kalbi"), who established the formal structure of Arab genealogy under the Abbasids, remains another important source for early Omani history. The same applies to Nashwan ibn Said al-Himyari who wrote *Qasidat al-Himyariya* (Himyaritic Poems). Nashwan, however, has been accused of creating a genealogical fabrication – implying thet south Arabian unity had stemmed from Qahtan – for political ends during the Kalb/Qais rivalry of Umayyad times.

A later writer of importance was al-Qalhati, who probably wrote during the period of Qalhat's prosperity under the Hormuzis in the thirteenth to fifteenth centuries AD (sixth to the eighth centuries AH)

There are a number of more recent writers of significance. The work of Salil ibn Muhammad ibn Razaq was substantially translated into English by the Rev. G.P. Badger, appearing as the *History of the Imams and Sayyids of Oman*. Sirhan ibn Said who came from Izki and belonged to a settled group of the Tai, was the author of *Kashf al Ghummeh* ("Dispeller of Grief"). Both these nineteenth century authors are important sources for Ya'ruba history as well as being chroniclers both of the Al bu Said dynasty and the whole long history of Oman.

The most important historian subsequently was Nur ad-Deen as-Salimi who wrote *Tuhfat al-Ayan bi-sirat Ahl 'Uman* ("Description of Notables in the History of the People of Oman"). He died in 1914. His son Muhammad ibn Abdullah as-Salimi was in turn a significant historian and author of *Nahdat al-Ayan bi-hurriyat 'Uman* ("Renaissance of Notables in the Freedom of Oman"). His son, Shaikh Sulaiman ibn Muhammad as-Salimi, is a noted historian of our own day. Another writer of significance is Salim ibn Hamood as-Siyabi, who wrote *Is'af al-Ayan fi Ansab Ahl'Uman*, which may be loosely translated as "The Healing of Relationships among the People of Oman".

Scholars of our own time include Shaikh Saif ibn Hamoud ibn Hamid al-Batashi, among whose several books is *Ittihaf al-Ayan fi tarikh ba'd 'ulema' 'Uman* ("A Survey of Notables among the *Ulema* of History"), approximately comparable in content to Aubrey's *Brief Lives*. Another is Sayyid bin Hamoud bin Mohammed Al bu Saidi.

Among the finest of Oman's calligraphers was Abdullah ibn Bashir ibn Masoud al Hadhrami as-Sohari who completed his beautiful copy of the *Qur'an* in 1744 AD (1157 AH).

Language

Oman is unique in Arabia for the languages spoken by some of the inhabitants instead of, or in addition to, Arabic. The main instances are the Kumzar dialect, amongst the Shihuh, which is an Iranian dialect and the four languages of the Southern Region, which Bertram Thomas first identified as "Four Strange Tongues – the Hadara Group", but better named the Modern South Arabian languages since they are related to Old South Arabian languages such as Sabaean, Hadrami and Qatabanian.

These languages are Jibali or Shahri, Mahri, Harsusi and Batahiri, and the language of Socotra is also one of this group. The ancient South Arabian languages are associated with the culture which stretched from the Wadi Najran to the Wadi Hadhramaut, from roughly the ninth century BC to the sixth century AD. None of these languages is written by the speakers. They are Semitic, and bear resemblance to one another, though Mahri and Jibali are not mutually intelligible. There are two main groups: first the Jibali group, of which three major dialects have been identified, and a minor one used in the Halaaniyaat Islands. The name "Shahri" indicates the speech of a mountain people, since *Shher* means "mountain" in Jibali. It is probable that the "Shaharun" (Shahra), early inhabitants of the area, were overcome by the invading Qara or Mahra, who reduced them to a class of serfs and herdsmen. The old city of these people is reputed to have been on Khor Rori in Dhofar.

The second group is Mahri, Harsusi and Batahiri. Harsusi and Batahiri are Mahri dialects and a speaker of one of these languages can understand most of what speakers of the other two say. Mahri is probably the closest of these languages to the old South Arabian tongue, inscriptions in which have been found as far away as Delos in the Aegean and Ethiopia. Idrisi, writing in about 1100 AD (494 AH), states that the Mahri language is a survival of the ancient Himyaritic. Trilith monuments all over the area are inscribed with characters resembling ancient South Semitic characters, but there are also inscriptions in Dhofar in Old South Arabian.

The southern tribes and their languages are given in the caption to the foregoing map of the Tribes of Southern Oman. The name given to them by Bertram Thomas, *Ahl al-Hadara*, may be identifiable with the *Hadoram* of Genesis and the *Adramitae* of Pliny.

The Mahra are the most numerous group. They are split into an eastern and a western section, speaking closely related dialects of the Mahra tongue, though each section derives from a different ancestor. The eastern section are mainly nomadic and used to gather the frankincense during the harvest season whilst the western Mahra have long been largely settled and are coastal people.

The Qara, Shahra and Batahira are also settled tribes. The home of the former two is the Qara and Qamr mountains of Dhofar, whilst the latter live along the shores of the Halaaniyaat bay. Local tradition, supporting etymological evidence, holds that the Shahra were once the exclusive possessors of Dhofar whilst the Batahara possessed the steppes, but that the Qara overcame and absorbed the Shahra, taking their frankincense groves and herds, and that the Mahra drove the Bathara to the coast from the hinterland. The Qara also adopted the Shahra language (now known as Jibali). In just such a manner the Bait Kathir, who were also later comers, have learnt the original Shahri language, though their main language remains Arabic.

The Harasis tribe inhabit the area between Dhofar and northern Oman. They are associated with the Arab tribes of Awamir and Janaba. The small Afar tribe are also linked with them and speak their language. The Bil Haf share the steppe land with the Bait Kathir and Mahra and, though an independent tribe, speak Mahri. The Mashayikh speak Shahri. These Dhofari languages have features of pronunciation not known in modern Arabic. These include lateral fricatives, akin to the "*ll*" in the Welsh pronunciation of Llanelly, and (in Jibali) nasalised vowels, resembling French vowels as in *nom* and *matin*, and glottalised consonation in place of the Arabic emphatics. The lateralisation of "*dh*" and probably also the glottalised consonants (which were taken many centuries ago to Ethiopia) seem to be old Semitic usages lost in modern Arabic. Thus Oman demonstrates yet again the antiquity of its indigenous culture.

Archaic Cultural Evidence

It is perhaps strange that, despite the scale and undoubted antiquity of the frankincense trade, so few ancient settlements have been found. The precise site of fabled Ubar, has now however been identified by some with Shisur Ruins dating from between the first century BC and fourth century AD have however been found at various places in Dhofar – Hanun, Andhur and Khor Rori, now silted up but once the best harbour on the Dhofar coast. The incense city-port of Samhuram was built on Khor Rori with its Himyaritic fortress and a pre-Islamic temple dedicated to the south Arabian moon god, Sin. This contained an elaborate ablution system, two sacrificial altars, numerous bronze coins, and ancient frankincense. An inscription found there in 1952 reads: "*Shafsay and his mother Nadrat dedicated to their lord Sin, Him of [the temple of] Ilum, in [the city of] Samhuram for the protection of their persons and of their king.*" The name Samhuram has been approximately interpreted as "the Great Scheme".

Other inscriptions found at Samhuram refer to King Ilazz of Hadhramaut, mentioned by classical authors as Eleazus, King of the Incense Country and Shabwa. Samhuram was also referred to as the land of the Sachalites and was probably a colony Shabwa, 500 miles to the west near Aden. The Alexandrine geographer Ptolemy called it Abyssopolis, the "city of the abyss", on account of the huge waterfall above the city where the *Wadi* Darbat plunges precipitously. At that time world consumption of incense, above all in the Graeco-Roman empire, was particularly highand the trade was largely in the hands of the people of Hadhramaut. The head of a bull with a triangular leaf on its forehead has been found at Samhuram, together with *amphorae* from the Greek isles, demonstrating that the inhabitants had a taste for Greek wine and that lucrative trading contracts were well developed at the beginning of the Christian era.

Hanun, some thirty-six miles north of Salalah, with an excellent water supply of its own, was also apparently associated with Samhuram. An inscription in the Old South Arabian script, found there in 1962, mentioned Samhuram and the moon god Sin specifically and refers to the capital as Shabwa. It also calls Hanun Sa'nan, a name still used for it, and refers to Sa'kal or the country of the Sachalites. Hanun seems to have been a seasonal collecting station for frankincense. From there, it would have been taken either to Samhuram for shipment by sea, or overland to Shisur and thence by one of the camel caravan routes.

The style of a ruined fort or temple at Andhur, forty miles north of Marbat, suggests that it was contemporaneous with Samhuram. It lies in excellent frankincense country and was an important site on the old caravan routes to the Mediterranean and Gulf.

Rock Art

Rock art goes back to a time beyond calculation. Pictures and symbols are found particularly in the main *wadi*s such as Bani Kharus, Sahtan and Aday. Ancient grafitti tell of a wetter climate.

The pictorial effect is obtained by "pecking" at the limestone surface with a hard, pointed implement. Figures include horses, camels, ibex, oryx, dogs, goats, bulls, lions, leopards, foxes, snakes, scorpions, birds, and the now extinct Arabian ostrich and baboon.

The "stick" representations of people are stylised but others are more naturalistic. Sometimes bas relief or hollow relief is found as well as "pecking". Men, women and children are represented in a variety of ways. Some ride or stand on horses or bulls. Some carry rifles or swords and shields and others fight with bows and arrows. Some are represented fighting and others hunting, herding or moving in caravan.

One clearly ancient representation depicts a figure wearing a knee-length dress with a wasp waist, bird head, long-fingered hands and wrap-around snake. Its effect resembles a figure on a cylinder seal of the Akkadian period in the third millennium BC in Iraq. Words too are "pecked" out on rocks – mostly *Qu'ranic* texts but a short inscription in the Old South Arabian tongue has also been found in the Wadi Sahtan.

7
Faith and the Sacred

Islam came early to Oman, and has held the minds and hearts of the people ever since. The tolerance and straight-dealing for which Omanis are celebrated are outward reflections of an inner trust in God.

The Sultan Qaboos Grand Mosque stands resplendent against the sunset (left). *Its elegant arches and arcades create a sense of harmony and peace* (above).

OMAN was one of the earliest countries to accept the doctrine of the Prophet Muhammad. It was conquered not by the sword, as so many other countries were, but by the spirit. The Prophet, according to Omani tradition, said: "Blessed be the people of Ghubaira [an old name for Oman still used in Zanzibar] for they believed in me without seeing me."

The first Omani to embrace the new religion was Mazin ibn Ghadhuba of Samail, who was converted by the Prophet himself in Medina. However, it was Amr ibn al As, a prosperous merchant of Mecca of the Prophet's own tribe, the Quraish, and one of the first believers, who really won Oman over to Islam. Amr, who later conquered Egypt, came to Oman bearing a letter from Muhammad to Abd and Jaifar, the two brothers who then jointly ruled the Arab part of Oman The letter was similar in tone to that sent to other rulers such as the Emperor Heraclius in Byzantium, the Kings of Persia and Ethiopia and the Governors of Egypt and of Yemen.

It read:

> In the name of God the most gracious, the most merciful. From Muhammad the Messenger of God to Jaifar and Abd, the sons of al-Julanda. Peace be upon those who follow the true religion. After compliments I call on you to embrace Islam – accept it and you will be saved, for I am the Messenger of God to all humanity. I have come to warn the living that affliction will befall unbelievers. If you accept Islam, as I hope you will, all will be well but if you refuse to accept it, your Kingdom will vanish and my horses will trample your country and my religion will triumph over your Kingdom.

A council of the Azd tribe was then convened by Abd and Jaifar and they decided to embrace Islam. The main part of the Arab population followed the elders and apparently accepted conversion willingly. The Persians in the coastal towns did not, and were subsequently driven out of the country. Amr stayed in Oman until the death of the Prophet in 632 AD, after which he left for Mecca, taking Abd with him to visit the Prophet's successor, Abu Bakr.

In his speech of welcome to Abd, Abu Bakr referred to Oman embracing Islam voluntarily and to Amr's mission there "without army or weapon".

The five duties of Islam have been observed in Oman since the country's conversion. These are that the Believer must:

1. Say, with full acceptance: "There is no god but God and Muhammad is his Prophet."
2. Pray five times daily, facing Mecca, and say the Friday noonday prayers.
3. Give alms generously.
4. Keep the fast during the holy month of Ramadan, not eating or drinking between sunrise and sunset.
5 Make the pilgrimage – the Hajj – to Mecca and the holy places of Islam once in his life if he can.

In Oman itself the years following the first conversion were stormy and it must have taken some time for the whole country to become Muslim. Dhu't Taj Lakit, an Azdi who had previously tried to supplant the ruling Julanda princes, is reputed to have rebelled during the Caliphate of Abu Bakr (632-634 AD: 11-13 AH) claiming to be a prophet himself. Abd and Jaifar thereupon retired to the Jebel Akhdar where they were joined by Hudhaifa ibn Muhsin and two other generals, Ikrima ibn Abu Jahl and Arfaja al

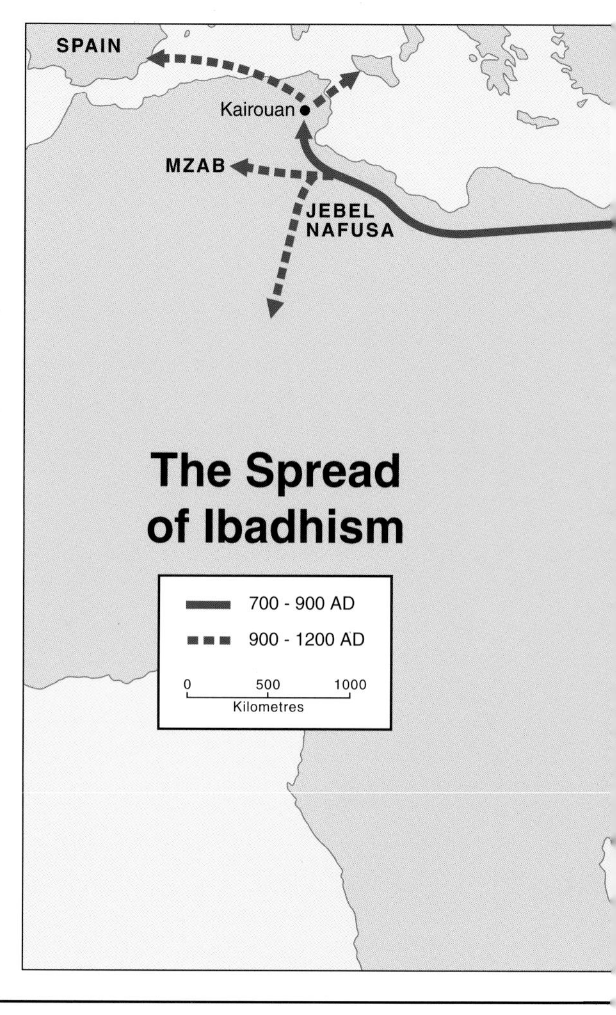

Nizwa's Early Mosques

Two mosques in Nizwa are reputed to date to these earliest days of Islam in Oman. The Shuadhna is believed to date to 623/4 AD (2 AH) and is remarkable for having apparently had a *mihrab* – traces of which remain – facing towards Jerusalem as the Prophet Muhammad first ordained. The later, still extant , *mihrab* faces towards

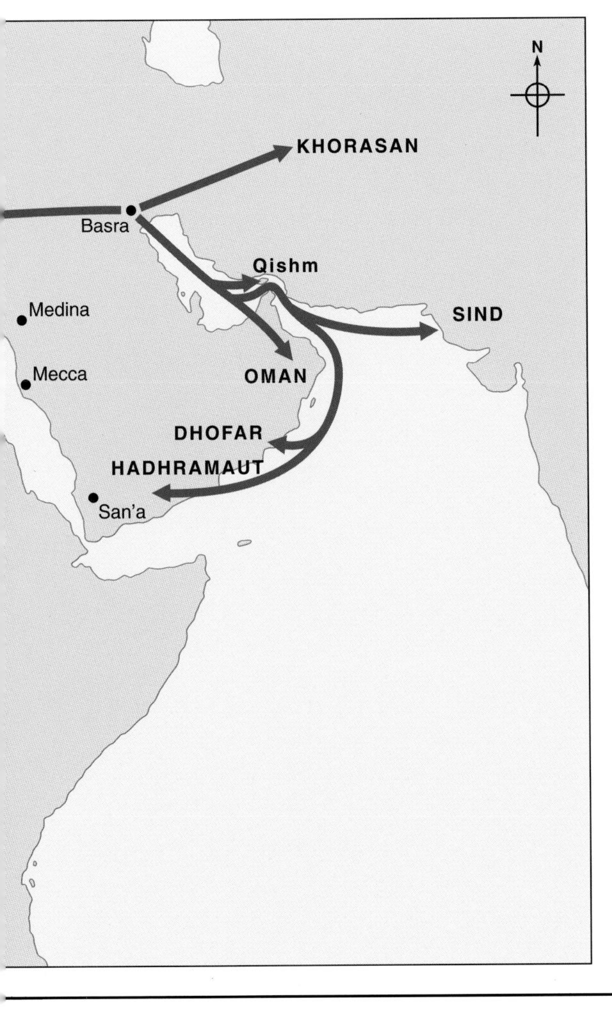

Bariqi, whom Abu Bakr had appointed to suppress the rebellion. A battle was fought at Dabba, where the rebel prophet had based himself, and ten thousand people were killed. Dabba itself, a wealthy town and the principal market of the area, was given over to the conquerors. This battle gave rise to the Omani phrase "the Day of Dabba", signifying the defeat of paganism by Islam.

However, Abdulla ibn Humaid as-Salimi refutes this story and gives another version of events. Hudhaifa's tax collectors had been sent to Dabba to collect the *sadaqa* tax and one of them demanded a fully-grown goat from a woman descendant of Malik ibn Fahm, the legendary leader of the first Azd settlers in Oman. A dispute and a fight developed after the cry "Oh Children of Malik" had been raised by the woman and her supporters. This cry was used before Islam as a tribal rallying call. It was misinterpreted by Hudhaifa's men as an act of defiance and apostasy. Consequently, the Caliph Abu Bakr realised that a mistake had been made a dn ordered the release of all the captives taken during and after the fracas.

Ibadhism

The Azd of Oman, after their early conversion, played a key part in the formative days of Islam when Basra in southern Iraq became an influential city and was the main base camp for Muslim conquests. It was here that the Ibadhi doctrine which predominates in Oman was evolved. As the Omani historian as-Salimi says: "The true religion has been compared to a bird; its egg was laid in Medina, it hatched in Basra and flew to Oman."

The Ibadhis derive their name from Abdulla ibn Ibadh who appeared on the scene in about 683 AD (64 AH), growing up in the Caliph Mu'awiya's reign and dying in Abdul Malik ibn Marwan's (685-705 AD: 66-87 AH). However, he and the early Ibadhis based their traditions on Abu Sha'atha Jabir ibn Zaid, an Azdi of the Yahmad clan, born at Firq near Nizwa. Sunnis and Ibadhis alike regard him as one of the most learned Muslims and of equal eminence with his friend the Mufti of Basra, Hassan al Basri. Abu Sha'atha was himself a *Tabi'* – a person in contact with the Prophet's Companions, the *Sahaba*, who transmitted doctrine direct-

Mecca, as the Prophet prescribed from Medina according to tradition in the second year of the Hijra. This mosque,with no minaret, is remarkable for being on the first storey, approached by a flight of steps rising from under and arch giving on to the street.

The other early mosque in Nizwa is the Si'al *(left)*, said to date from 629/630 AD (8 AH), which is notable for having a tower for its defence. Both this and the Shaudhna are constructed of mud and are rectangular in shape. The method of roof construction in both mosques is a very ancient one and found in the earliest civilisations of the region. The flat roof is supported by beams of palm wood standing on substantial round pillars connecting with each other by high pointed arches, which are covered with smooth and very old plaster. The beams are covered with palm matting covered in turn by mud. The carved *mihrab*s in both the Si'al and the Shuadhna mosques are of exquisite design, craftsmanship and great beauty. The Si'al mosque is also ornamented by a large frieze on the East side with large Kufic carved lettering glorifying Allah.The ancient city of Balid in Dhofar is also said to have had two *mihrabs*, respectively facing Jerusalem and Mecca.

ly from Aisha the Prophet's wife, ibn Abbas and others who had fought with the Prophet.

The Ibadhi ideal was to restore the pure Islamic state to what it had been during the time of the Prophet and the first Caliphs Abu Bakr and Omar. In their eyes it had become corrupted by Othman ibn Affan and the struggle between Ali and Mu'awiya for the succession. The Ibadhis believed that the Caliphate should not necessarily go to a member of the Prophet's family but that the best man available to lead the people at the time should be chosen. For a while they held a dialogue with the Caliph Abdul Malik, about the nature of the Islamic state; but this ended in disagreement and the persecution which eventually drove the adherents of the Ibadhi precept to seek refuge in their original homes – Oman in the case of the Azdis and Libya, Tunisia and Algeria in the case of the north Africans.

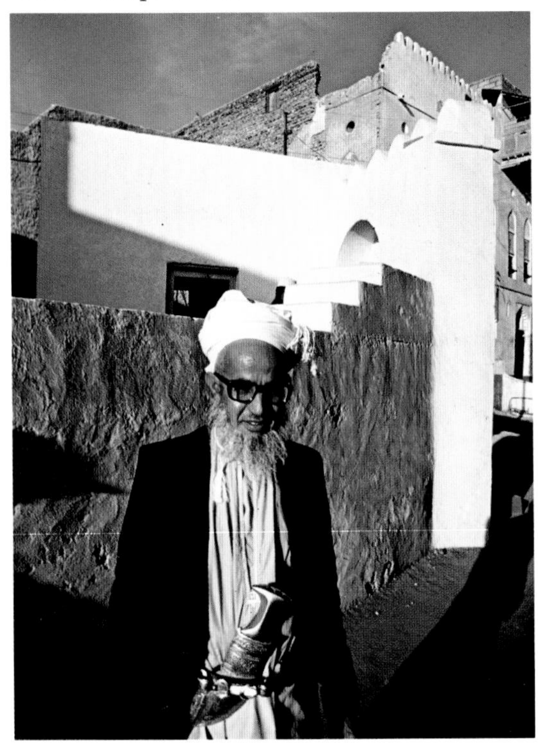

At this ancient Muscat mosque, the muezzin *ascends by steps on the outer wall.*

The Caliph Abdul Malik's failure to win over the less extreme opposition to the Umayyad in Iraq led his governor, al Hujjaj, to clamp down on the power and influence of the Azd. Abu Sha'atha then became the hidden leader of the Ibadhis during this difficult period known as *Kitman*, when the political circumstances dictated extreme caution. Later, Abu Sha'atha withdrew to Oman, where his traditions as well as those of other early Omani *Ulema* founded the corpus of the Ibadhi law.

The Ibadhis held fast to the tenets originally formulated in Basra and, unlike the Sunni and Shia, never reckoned that there must necessarily be a permanent or visible head of the Muslim state or *umma*. They constantly maintained that when a suitable man was available, he should be

The Zawawi mosque is at the heart of old Muscat.

elected by a prescribed pro-cess but otherwise the true Islamic state should rest in *Kitman* as in Abu Sha'atha's time in Basra. When such circumstances arose, they held that the community of true Muslims might have to conceal its actual beliefs.

The Ibadhis claim with justice that their school of thought, or *madhab*, had evolved a century or so before those of the four orthodox schools, the Hanbali, Hanafite, Malikite and Shafi'. Thus the Omani state has over the centuries been based on a very early and highly orthodox version of Islam – although Ibadhi beliefs have not prevented secular rule over the centuries by dynasties – and Shari'a law has been strictly followed in public and private matters. The isolation of the central part of the country has not infrequently centred round strict adherence to Ibadhism, which explains to some extent the dichotomy, so often apparent in Oman's history, between the Ibadhi Interior and the outward-looking Sunni and Shia seafarers of the coast.

Moderation and tolerance have always been essential elements in Ibadhism, even if, like most religions, it has had some fanatical phases.

This tradition of moderation dates back to the rise of Ibadhism in the later part of the seventh century AD (first century AH). Disputes then were as bitter and far-reaching as those between Martin Luther and Pope Leo X or between King Charles I of England and the "Westminster Assembly of Divines". The Ibadhis were, however, sufficiently realistic to recognise that expediency must sometimes temper the ideal and that the means adopted to establish the ideal Islamic state must be reasonable. They were known as "quietists", *qu'ad*, in their approach, yet as a result of perseverance succeeded in establishing individual communities both in Oman and North Africa, living in a state of *Zuhur*, that is, living openly in what they regarded as a properly constituted state.

From the eighth century, Imams exercising spiritual, political and military functions were appointed to rule in Oman. They were, however, strictly bound by the Shari'a and in general the Ibadhism of Oman has been characterised by puritanism without the intolerance which has marred other puritanical sects in all faiths.

The essential simplicity of the Ibadhi approach is reflected in the quiet dignity of old Omani mosques. They are beautifully proportioned but devoid of ornament apart from graceful stucco work around the *mihrab* niche and windows and from carving on the doors. The minaret is not characteristic of Oman except on the coast, and the call to prayer was until recently made from a rooftop, or from a small set of steps on the mosque wall, in the same manner as in the earliest days of Islam. The traveller, ibn Batuta, who visited Nizwa in the fourteenth century admired the "splendid clean mosques" which were centres of community life, where the inhabitants ate their meals, each person bringing what he had to contribute.

Ibn Batuta also describes how the Friday service was conducted by the Ibahdis of Nizwa, saying that they did not – perhaps because the Nabhani Maliks, who then ruled Oman, were not regarded as Imams – use the canonical Sunni form of Friday congregational prayer, but the everyday form of noonday prayer. After the "bowings" the Imam read some verses from the *Qur'an* and then delivered an address resembling the sermon, *Khutba*, during which he used the formula "God be pleased with him" in respect of the Caliphs Abu Bakr and Omar, but not of Othman and Ali.

The austerity of Ibadhism is reflected in the almost total absence of music in the Interior of Oman, except for dancing to the drums during the Id Holidays. Austerity is, however, sometimes relaxed in the mountain areas, where grapes are grown and wine made, for at times the people have been given a medicinal dispensation to drink alcohol on account of the extreme cold.

Other Muslims

The orthodoxy and paramountcy of Ibadhism in Oman has not prevented other forms of Islam from taking root. The tribes of the Dhahirah and of the area south of the Sharqiyah, as well as some on the Batinah coast, follow the Sunni precept, whilst the Bani bu Ali tribe in the Jaalan abandoned Ibadhism to become followers of the Wahhabi sect during the Wahhabi incursions from Saudi Arabia in the early nineteenth century. This puritan version of Islam, named after Muhammad ibn Abdul Wahhab, its eighteenth-century founder, spread considerably at this time, and fighting between Omanis and Wahhabis continued spasmodically as the century wore on without otherwise affecting Omani adherence to Ibadhism.

The Shia following is significant amongst the inhabitants of the coastal towns, particularly the merchant class. There are also Khojas or Lutis – Shia originating from Hyderabad in Sind – who have been established in Mutrah for several generations. The Khoja community lives for the most part in a separate walled precinct within the town of Mutrah, with its own mosque on the waterfront.

Below: *this mosque serves as the principal place of worship in Muscat where most residents are at work in Government service..*

The mosques of the coastal dwellers in the past were often more elaborately ornamented than those of the Ibadhis. Ibn Batuta has left a description of the mosque in Qalhat:

> The city of Qalhat...has one of the most beautiful mosques. Its walls are tiled with *qashani*, which is like *zalij*, and it occupies a lofty situation from which it commands a view of the sea and the anchorage. It was built by a saintly woman, Bibi Maryam, *bibi* meaning in their speech 'noble lady'.

Religious Toleration

Despite the extinction of early Christianity and later the behaviour of Portuguese Christians, who brought the cruelty of the Inquisition and a fanaticism derived from anti-Islamic warfare in the

Iberian peninsula, Omani religious tolerance extended to Christianity. Thus the treaty made between the Imam Nasir ibn Murshid and Philip Wylde in 1646 regulating trade between Oman and the East India Company at Sohar, provided specifically that the English should have licence to exercise their own religion. The same liberality has consistently applied to the Christian missions established since the end of the 19th century.

Lieutenant Wellsted, who visited Muscat in 1835, noted the general tolerance extended to all persuasions by Sayyid Said ibn Sultan, including the Bani Israel, and both he and James Silk Buckingham, who visited the country in 1816, observed that a number of Jews, who had fled the persecution of Daud Pasha in Baghdad, had been permitted to settle. In earlier centuries a considerable number of Jews had been settled all round the coasts of Arabia and there was a large Jewish population in Sohar in the tenth century AD (fourth century AH).

Beneath Dhofar's rolling uplands, the exquisite mosque at Taqah glows like a jewel in the evening light.

Pre-Islamic Religions and Superstitions

The pre-Islamic Himyaritic kingdom which extended eastwards across south Arabia to Oman followed Old Testament precepts and the Hebrew religion. This is established by Omani oral tradition. An inscription found at Husn Ghurab on the coast of south Arabia west of Mukalla illustrates early religious practice in a song attributed to early Arabian Adites: "Over us, presided Kings far removed from baseness and stern chastisers of reprobate and wicked men. They noted down for us, according to the doctrine of Heber, good judgements in a book to be kept; and we proclaimed our belief in miracles, in the resurrection, in the return into the nostrils of the breath of life."

The religion of the Sabaeans, who worshipped sun, moon and stars, also had a strong hold. A second century AD temple at Samhuram, the Himyaritic city situated near Taqah in Dhofar, was dedicated to the moon god, Sin. The triliths found in Dhofar as well as northern Oman may have been symbols of the south Arabian "Trinity" – sun god, moon god and Zahra, the Planet Venus.

There may have been animistic aspects to religion too, for some early tribes took their names from animals. There was, for example, the Dibba or lizard tribe and the Jaalan or water beetle tribe. Some worship of idols (*Sanam*) as well may have continued until comparatively recent times. A cave at Izki, which local people are afraid to enter, is said to contain an idol called Jurnan. Lieutenant Whitelock in the 1820s mentions the worship of idols which were smashed by the Wahhabis near Ras al Khaimah.

Much of the Old Testament is the common heritage of both Islam and Judaeo-Christianity. Long and complicated genealogies of the Semitic people are contained in the Book of Genesis, which also mentioned Mount Sephar, Dhofar and Obal after whom a place in Oman itself is named.

The tomb of Nabi Ayyoub – Job of the Bible – lies in Dhofar on the rolling hills to the north of Salalah. It is now a place of pilgrimage and a new mosque has been built beside the old mosque tomb, in which the seer's tomb stands. It is a reminder of the importance of this figure in the Islamic, Christian and Judaic traditions and accords with the description

Job's Tomb

Shared by Muslim Arabs, Jews and Christians alike is the patriarchal figure of Job, familiar to Islam as Ayyoub, who inhabited the hills of Dhofar among his flocks and dependents and underwent the grievous test placed upon him by the deity's wager with Satan. In this, of course, Job/Ayyoub was finally redeemed by his own unqualified acceptance of God's unfathomable authority. He was not helped – in the Judaeo-Christian tradition – by the so-called comfort of "Bildad the Shuhite" – conceivably of the Shihuh tribe of 3,000 years ago. The tomb is sited to the left of the picture above, and in close-up, left.

in the first chapter of the book of Job, one of the deepest and most moving in the Bible: "There was a man in the land of Uz, whose name was Job; and that man was perfect and upright, and one that feared God, and eschewed evil." One of his so-called comforters, Bildad the Shuhite, may well have come from the Shihuh.

Other Religious Manifestations
Miracles are attributed by the chroniclers to several Omani historical figures. The first Imam of the Ya'ruba dynasty, for example, was credited with several, the most noteworthy being that a basket of dates and rice provided enough to feed a hundred men for several days. He was also credited with curing a she-camel which had broken out in boils after eating food belonging to the *Bait al Mal*, and he may have had the gift of an aura, for it is related that a corner of the mosque at Rostaq where he was sitting appeared to be lit up as if by a lamp.

On the other hand belief in the *djinns* has not completely disappeared and there are still places to which people will not go for fear of them. In some *wadis* in Oman figures or rock features representing a devil have been pelted with stones since time out of mind. In recent times this has taken the form of shooting with a gun. Around Bahla, belief in a spectral witch who inhabits the Jebel Khumaila still persists and mothers give their children small quantities of mercury to guard them against her powers.

Belief in possession by an evil spirit called *zar* may survive amongst some sections of the population as has been remarked on by, among others, Wilfred Thesiger in *Arabian Sands*.

One night, near Mughshin, when sleeping on the open plain, I was awakened by a long-drawn howl. Again and again the uncanny sound quavered across the camp, sending shivers down my back. It came from a group of figures sitting twenty yards away. I called out: 'What is wrong?' and bin Kabina answered, 'Said is possessed by a *zar*.' I got up, walked round some camels, and joined them. By the light of the setting moon I could see the boy, one of the Bait Kathir, crouching over a small fire. His face and head were covered with a cloth, and he rocked himself to and fro as he howled. The others sat close to him, silent and intent. Suddenly they began to chant in two parts, while Said thrashed himself violently from side to side. More and more wildly he threw himself about, and once a corner of the cloth with which he covered his face fell into the embers and began to smoulder. Someone leant forward and put it out. Steadily the chanting rose and fell about the demented boy, who gradually became calmer. A man lit some incense in a bowl and held it under the boy's nose beneath the cloth. Suddenly he began to sing in a curious, strained, high-pitched voice. Line by line the others answered him. He stopped, grew violent again, and then calmed once more. A man leant forward and asked him questions and he answered, speaking like someone in his sleep. I could not understand the words, for they spoke Mahra. They gave him more incense and the spirit left him. A little later he lay down to sleep, but once again he was troubled. This time he sobbed bitterly and groaned as if in great pain. They gathered round him once more and chanted until he grew calm. Then he slept. In the morning he was all right.

Christianity

Some Omani Islamic scholars hold that the majority of the people in Oman before Islam were Christians and that Malik ibn Fahm himself was a Christian. Some also believe that the wars between the early Omanis and the Persians were religious in character just as the wars against the Persians in Mesopotamia were. Thus Zoroastrianism may have been practised at some stages in Oman. It appears that the Juland princes themselves did not profess Christianity. The second Caliph Omar appointed a Christian, Kaab ibn Sur al Laqiti, as *Qadhi* in Basra in 639 AD (18 AH).

The Christian population around the Indian Ocean held a strong tradition that Christ's Apostle St Thomas brought Christianity while visiting Oman and places in the Gulf *en route* to India where he suffered martyrdom.

Oman is also associated in oral tradition with the story of the Three Kings who were led by astrological signs to attend upon the infant Jesus at Bethlehem. The Indian Sibyl is reputed to have advised King Perimel of Ceylon to meet the two other Kings in Muscat on their journey westwards to Roman Palestine and Judaea. This is not inherently unlikely, for Dhofar is the source of frankincense, myrrh comes from south Arabia, and gold from Ceylon. King Perimel was buried in Coulan in a religious house consecrated – presumably at least three or four decades later – by the disciples of St Thomas.

Christianity in Oman centred round Mazun and Sohar, where there was a Nestorian bishop from at least as early as 424 AD when Bishop John was appointed. His representatives used to travel to church synods in Mesopotamia and Mazun is frequently mentioned in Nestorian records. This bishopric almost certainly fell within the area known as Bait Qatraya and probably came under the Metropolitan of Revi Ardashir, the Sassanid port on the coast of Pars. Nestorian missionary activity, in which the flourishing Nestorian community at Sohar was heavily involved, extended as far afield as Malaya by the seventh century AD. The last recorded bishop, Stephen, was alive in 676 AD but Nestorian Christianity had completely disappeared from Arabia by the ninth century AD.

Left, opposite, *rough-hewn stones mark the final resting places of past residents of Salalah.* Above, *in the hills of Dhofar, a simple mausoleum serves as an osiary for the last remains of the Binali family, near Mirbat.*

Portuguese Christians built this chapel at Fort Mirani during their occupation, overlooking Muscat.

Christianity was brought back to Arabia by the Portuguese who established two churches in Muscat, one of which was the See of the Vicar and the other the church in the convent of the Augustinian Friars. Both churches were dedicated to the Virgin Mary. Another small chapel, which still stands, was built in Fort Mirani, then known as Fort Capitan. These churches were still standing in the early eighteenth century when Alexander Hamilton visited them and commented: "A cathedral built by the Portuguese still retains some marks of its grandeur and is now converted into a place for the King" (the Sultan's palace on the waterfront). The earlier presence of the church is also commemorated in the name of the large and elegant house known as the Bait Graiza, a local corruption of the Portuguese word *"igreja"* meaning church, which still stands nearby.

Christianity again died out with the expulsion of the Portuguese from Oman in the middle of the seventeenth century and it was not until 1891 that Christianity returned once more to Oman with the arrival there of Bishop Thomas Valpy French, a former Bishop of Lahore – a remarkable man, described as "a Christian Fakir" and "the most distinguished of all Church Missionary Society missionaries". He ended his dedicated life in Muscat a few months after his arrival, and was buried in the Christian cemetery in the cove just west of walled Muscat. A poem in his memory by Archdeacon Moule, in Victorian vein, begins:

> Where Muscat fronts the Orient sun
> 'Twixt heaving sea and rocky steep
> His work of mercy scarce begun
> A saintly soul has fallen asleep.

The American Mission in Muscat was started at about the same time and its work continues. It operates mainly in the educational and medical spheres. Its dedicated staff include such notable figures as the Reverend S.M. Zwemer, the author of *Arabia, the Cradle of Islam* and several outstanding doctors like Dr Sharon Thoms and his son Dr Wells Thoms.

Christian worship in Muscat is now provided for at an ecumenical centre both beside Ruwi and similarly at Ghala, where there are separate Catholic, Protestant and Orthodox Churches which share a common hall.

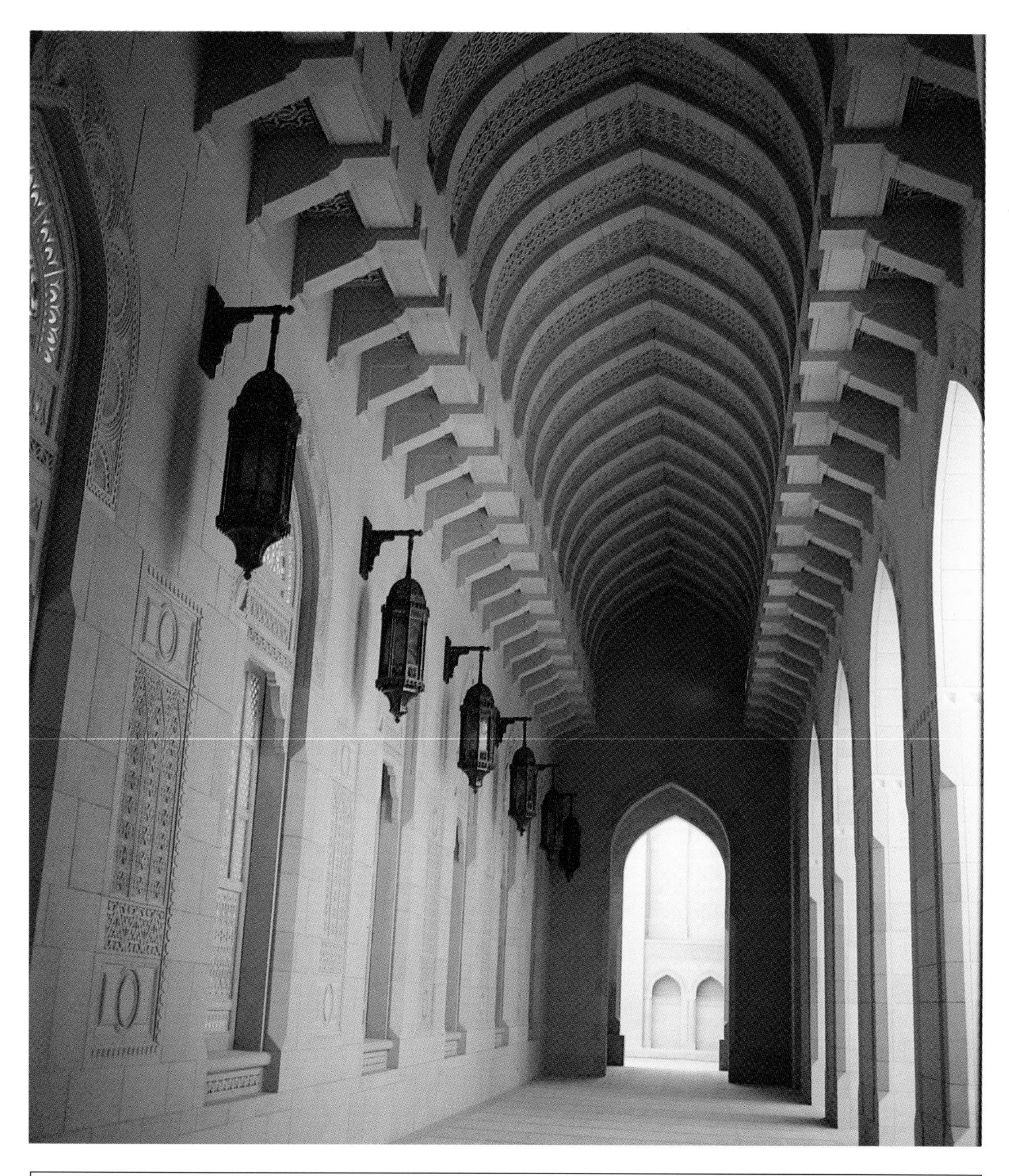

Sultan Qaboos Grand Mosque

The Sultan Qaboos Grand Mosque, in the *wilayat* of Bausher, was begun in 1995 and completed in 2001. It stands as a symbol of the nation's faith, and an embodiment of the declaration in the Basic Statute, that the religion of the state is Islam. It is a reminder too, that the harmony, peace and development which the Sultan and his Government has sought to promote, takes place under the guidance of God.

At around 40,000 square metres, the mosque is far larger than any other in the Sultanate, and it can hold up to 20,000 worshippers, including 750 women. The great carpet for the main prayer hall, with its 1,700 million knots, is the work of 600 weavers from Khurasan in Iran.

Following tradition, the mosque is endowed with a library designed to contain 20,000 books. It forms the genesis for the foundation of the adjoining Institute for Advanced Islamic Studies. In the beauty of concept and the craftsmanship of its execution, the mosque is a spur to human excellence in all its forms. Open to non-Muslims except at prayer time, with decorative elements inspired by all areas of the Islamic world, and without association with any of the schools or sections of Islam or any particular religious leader, the Grand Mosque stands as an embodiment of Islamic unity, peace and tolerance.

The Sultan Qaboos Grand Mosque is a tranquil, exceptionally elegant structure of vaults, minarets and shaded arcades (Left *and* far left). *Conceived as a place not only of prayer and worship, but also as an active centre of the Islamic religion, the mosque complex incorporates a library and conference hall, in addition to the main* musalla *and the women's* musalla.

Below *and* right: *a series of decorative niches display intricate mosaic and tilework designs from around the Islamic world.*

Below, *the full throated call to prayer-rings out across the ancient township of Sur, from the mosque's minaret. The* muezzins *of the mosques of any one locality may gently vie with one another in the reverential beauty of the sacred summons to the faithful. Some* muezzins *allow themselves the aid of an amplifier.*

Leading families contribute by the building of beautiful mosques as at Qurm, left*; Khuwair,* below *and* right.

Islam in Oman Today

In Islam there has historically been no basic distinction between the religious and the secular spheres. Nevertheless, the Ministry of Awqaf and Religious Affairs has specific responsibility for the role of Islam in Omani society. An important aspect of this remit is the building and administration of the country's mosques. Oman has many historic mosques, including some that date from the earliest days of Islam. Under the aegis of the Ministry, many more have been built, and a large number have been funded by private endowment. By 2002 there were more than 13,000 mosques in Oman, including the Sultan Qaboos Grand Mosque, which stands as a striking symbol of the nation's faith.

Among the Ministry's other duties are the overseeing and administration of *awqaf* or religious endowments and properties allocated for the maintenance of mosques. The Ministry also takes charge of the *Bait al Mal* (public treasury) properties and supervises the bequests of orphans in accordance with decisions made by the Sharia courts. On the judicial side, the Ministry has responsibility for the Sharia courts, which are presided over by a *qadhi*, whose role is to ensure justice for all who have suffered injury to person, property or rights. The system of lower and higher courts was prescribed by the Basic Statute of the State, issued in 1996.

A further function of the Ministry is the issuing of *fatwas*, or religious rulings and guidance. It also organises the revenues and expenditure of moneys collected from *zakat*, the tax that every Muslim pays in order to fulfil one of the five Pillars of Islam, on the basis of a tax on property amounting to between five and ten per cent of his or her income.

The Ministry's activities abroad include, most importantly, making preparations for the annual *Hajj* or pilgrimage. In this they co-ordinate closely with the Saudi Arabian authorities. It is also responsible for the training and appointment of Imams in the mosques and the supervision of the Qur'anic schools. By 2002, the state-run Qur'anic schools employed 322 teachers who taught some 10,500 students. There are also over 50 privately-run Qur'anic schools with 3,700 male and female students.

A number of different bodies have been set up to provide education in Islamic studies up to university level. At the 24th National Day celebrations in 1994, the Sultan announced that a new College of Jurisprudence and Law would be established in Muscat. The College's aims would be to unite, improve and enhance education in this field. At the same time

The seclusion and intimacy of worship is exemplified by the mosque in Dhofar, above. *The administration of the country's religious affairs is handled from the Ministerial complex in the capital area, pictured* below.

he announced the intention to have a Higher Institution in Nizwa to train members of the judiciary after obtaining their degrees in jurisprudence at university level.

The Sultan specifically reaffirmed his country's tradition of religious broad-mindedness and vision in his National Day Speech in 1994. Condemning fanaticism based on lack of correct knowledge among Muslim youth about their religion, which could lead to violence, discord and hatred, he gave a reminder that Islam rejects exaggeration and bigotry because it is the religion of liberality.

The Muslim Calendar

Oman with the rest of the Islamic world observes the main feasts and fasts of the Muslim calendar. The Muslim calendar, like the earlier Semitic and Arabian ones, is based on the movements of the moon, and the year comprises twelve lunar months. The Muslim calendar moves back approximately eleven days every year in relation to the solar year and thus every thirty-two and a half years it recovers its relative position.

In Oman the month does not begin until the moon has actually been sighted in Omani territory. This sighting, know as *ru'iya,* is of particular significance at the beginning of the month of Ramadan – the month of fasting from sunrise to sunset – and Shawwal, the following month, which begins with the celebration of the *Id al Fitr*. Two reliable eye witnesses have to satisfy the chief *Qadhi* that the new moon has been seen. He then notifies the Sultan who declares the advent of the new month.

The twelve months of the Muslim calendar are:

Muharram
Safar
Rabi'al awal
Rabi'al akhir
Jumada al ula
Jumada al ukhra
Rajab
Sha'ban
Ramadan
Shawwal
Dhu al qu'da
Dhu al hijja

The Muslim new year on the 1st of Muharram is celebrated as a holiday. Muslim years have, since the time of the Caliph Omar, been counted from the *hijra*, the emigration of the Prophet Muhammad to Medina in the year 622 AD, from which time he began his mission.

There are a number of holidays in the Muslim calendar. The birthday of the Prophet (Mulid an Nabi) – it is not certain whether his birth was in 570 or 580 AD – is celebrated on the 12th of Rabi' al awal. Another holiday is the night journey and Ascension *(Leilat as asra' wa al mi'raj)* celebrated on the 27th of Rajab. This commemorates the Prophet Muhammad's night journey and ascent into heaven, which is referred to in the *Qur'an,* The Prophet's ascension differs from Christ's in that it occurred during his lifetime, shortly after his call for a Prophet. He is reputed to have met Allah (God) face to face in the seventh Heaven and to have received instructions there about the obligatory prayers of Islam, which include the public prayers at *Id* festivals and the five daily prayers. He is also reputed to have travelled through all the other heavens accompanied by the Angel Gabriel.

The Id al Fitr, *following the breaking of the month-long fast of Ramadan, is celebrated whole-heartedly with music and dancing.*

The *Id al Fitr*, which follows Ramadan, denotes a breaking of the fast, and although it is strictly the lesser of the two major festivals, it is often celebrated more wholeheartedly as a result of the strain of fasting being relieved. It is referred to in some countries as *Id al Kiswa*, as it is the occasion for Muslims to wear new clothes. The *Id al Adha* means the feast of the sacrifice and it is celebrated on the 10th of Dhu al Hijja, sixty-nine or seventy days after the first day of the *Id al Fitr*. All Muslims are bound to make a sacrifice at the *Id al Adha.* At this time the pilgrimage to the holy places of Islam – the *Hajj* – reaches its climax. For it is then that those making the pilgrimage make their sacrifice of a sheep, camel, goat or ox at Thabir, the place in Saudi Arabia, where Abraham sacrificed the ram in place of his son Isaac.

At the two four-day *Ids* there is a great rejoicing, involving not only dancing, including elaborate sword dances, but also singing and much firing of guns. On the coast there is much more dancing and playing of musical instruments, in all of which the influence of Africa is envident.

The Shia minority also observes the 10th of Muharram as a day of mourning for the death of Hussain ibn Ali at the battle Kerbala in 680 AD (60AH), for they regard him as having had the right to the succession to the Caliphate, being the last surviving grandson of the Prophet Muhammad.

On the 10th day of Dhu al Hijja falls the Id al Adha, *sixty nine or seventy days after the* Id al Fitr. *All Muslims are bound to make a sacrifice at the* Id al Adha, *and the pilgrimages to the holy places of Islam (*Hajj*) reach their climax; it is the duty of the Muslim to make the* Hajj *once in his life if he can.*

The two Ids are occasions of rejoicing, including sword-dances and much firing of guns, pictured here in Salalah.

8 Economy, Commerce & Industry

Long before the age of oil, Oman dominated the Indian Ocean's commerce, and governed Zanzibar and Gwadur. Its oceanic trading enterprises reached eastwards to China, and westwards to America. Today, Oman is known throughout the world for the variety of its indigenous products, for its modern ports and for its oil and gas production.

Oman's newest port is Port Salalah, in the southern region of Dhofar. It has quickly become a focus of industrial energy. Built on the site of the ancient harbour of Raysut, it enjoys prime importance due to its location along world trade routes.

From earliest historical times, the economy of Oman has depended on exploitation of its natural resources and the country's favourable geographical position athwart major trade routes – by sea and land – between East and West. Oman has always been blessed with mineral resources, and copper was exported from at least the third millennium BC. The sea, trade, agriculture and some industry too have always been sources of wealth and livelihood.

Oil

Fluctuating oil prices have always posed a major challenge to formulating Oman's development plans, especially when they collapse as they did in 1986 and 1998. Economic policy is therefore focused on diversification into other areas such as industry, tourism and services. The Economic Coordination Council, constituted in 1999, is responsible for reducing Oman's dependence on oil and building up the strength of non-oil industries, including the contribution of the gas sector. However, the importance of the oil industry remains significant.

Modern Oman would not have taken its present shape without the discovery and exploitation of oil. Back in 1924-25, the Anglo-Persian Oil Company carried out a geological survey, but although Oman seemed promising, no oil was found and the company abandoned the concession. In 1937, Petroleum Development Oman Ltd (PDO) obtained concessions for the north and for Dhofar. The company was owned 23.75 per cent by British Petroleum; 23.75 per cent by Royal Dutch Shell; 23.75 per cent by Compagnie Francaise de Petrole (CFP); 23.75 per cent by Near East Development Corporation, and five per cent by C.S. Gulbenkian – later Partex. Exploration was interrupted by the Second World War, and in 1951, the Dhofar concession was surrendered. This allowed the Sultan to bring in other oil companies. In northern Oman, PDO explored and test-drilled their concession area between 1953 and 1960. Their work was hampered by differences between the Sultan and the Imam, Shaikh Ghalib bin Ali, who was attempting to claim independence for the Interior of Oman. Results were, at first, disheartening, and many wells were drilled and abandoned, leaving Shell and Partex (and later CFP) as the only participants. Faith and

Oil and gas comprise Oman's principal industry. The oil fields generally occur in desert areas of the interior. Drilling is seen right *and* opposite, top left. *Reserves are modest by Middle Eastern standards, but natural gas is more plentiful.*

All oil is pumped east or north to a high point in the mountains (above, right) *from where it flows to the refinery at Mina al Fahal* (below) – *whence much is shipped to Far East markets.*

perseverance were eventually rewarded in 1962, when oil was struck at Yibal on the edge of the Rub' al-Khali. This was the habitat of the Duru tribe, whose grazing and watering rights were preserved. Some of them were given jobs with the oil company, and other tribes in oil exploitation areas, such as the Harasis and Janaba, are similarly protected and employed.

Oman's oil is exported from single-buoy moorings at the Mina al Fahal terminal, where Royal Oman Police are seen maintaining security.

Exploitation and Further Discoveries

The Yibal well on its own was not enough, and PDO continued its exploration. In 1964 it announced plans for production jointly at Yibal, Natih and the newly-discovered Fahud. The Fahud well was only a few hundred metres from a dry well abandoned in 1956. A revised agreement was signed in March 1967 for the unexpired period of the 1937 concession, incorporating terms more favourable to the host country.

In Dhofar meanwhile, Cities Services had obtained a concession for the 30,000 square mile area in 1952, and in 1957 small quantities of oil were found at Marmul. By May 1960, a dozen wells had been drilled, with seismic work going on simultaneously. The results were disappointing however, and the participating companies abandoned hope.

Others persevered, and in 1969, PDO resumed the whole Dhofar concession under an agreement similar in terms to the revised 1967 agreement for northern Oman. They were given a deadline of six years in which to find oil in commercial quantities, and they did so, in 1974.

In the north, further production wells were discovered in the early 1970s at Ghaba, al Huwaisa, Saih Rawl, Habur and Lekhwair. In 1970, the Sultanate's share of actual or future profit was raised from 50 to 55 per cent, and in 1974 the Government's ownership increased from 50 to 60 per cent, with Shell retaining 34 per cent. A Joint Management Committee was set up. The Dhofar area was integrated into the main concession, and of this total, PDO relinquished 35,000 square miles. In 1980, PDO was incorporated as a limited company in Oman by Royal Decree, and the Joint Management Committee was replaced by a new board.

A new refinery was constructed at Mina al Fahal. It came into operation in 1982, with a capacity of 50,000 barrels per day (b/d), expanded to 80,000 b/d in 1987.

From then on, Oman's oil capacity and the facilities to support it were gradually expanded and adapted to meet current needs. Despite the price fluctuations, which have always complicated Oman's economic planning, a comparison of production figures in the late 1960s and early 1970s with those of the early twenty first century, demonstrate – irrespective of price variations – how Oman's remarkable progress has been made possible. Total production figures were 20.9 million barrels in 1967, rising to 106.25 million in 1971. In 2001, Oman produced around 349 million barrels of crude oil and condensates, of which 332 million barrels were exported – mainly to Japan, Korea and South-east Asia. Average production was 956,000 b/d, at a price of $23 per barrel.

New oil fields continue to be discovered on a modest scale, and foreign companies are invited to enter into exploration and production-sharing agreements. Although PDO remains by far the biggest producer, Occidental, Petrogas, Japex and Novus are also involved in production.

In the early days the country relied heavily on expatriate expertise and skills supplied by international oil companies

Sultan Qaboos opened the refinery at Mina al Fahal, and was shown around by petroleum specialists (above).

such as Shell. However, as increasing numbers of qualified Omanis became available, a target aiming for virtually complete Omanisation by 2007, was set. By 2000, the oil producing companies had achieved 87.3 per cent Omanisation while the exploration companies had achieved 50 per cent. From the start, PDO had an advanced training scheme and a large instructional centre. The process of Omanisation accelerated when graduates from Sultan Qaboos University became available to the oil industry.

In the late 1980s the Government set up the Oman Oil Company to undertake investment in foreign joint ventures and oil trading operations. Although some of its earlier projects were abandoned, the company remained involved with the Caspian pipeline consortium in Kazakhstan, in which it acquired a seven per cent share, and from 1998, with exploration of oil and gas in two off-shore blocks in the Kazakhstan sector of the Caspian under an agreement with Arco and Exxon.

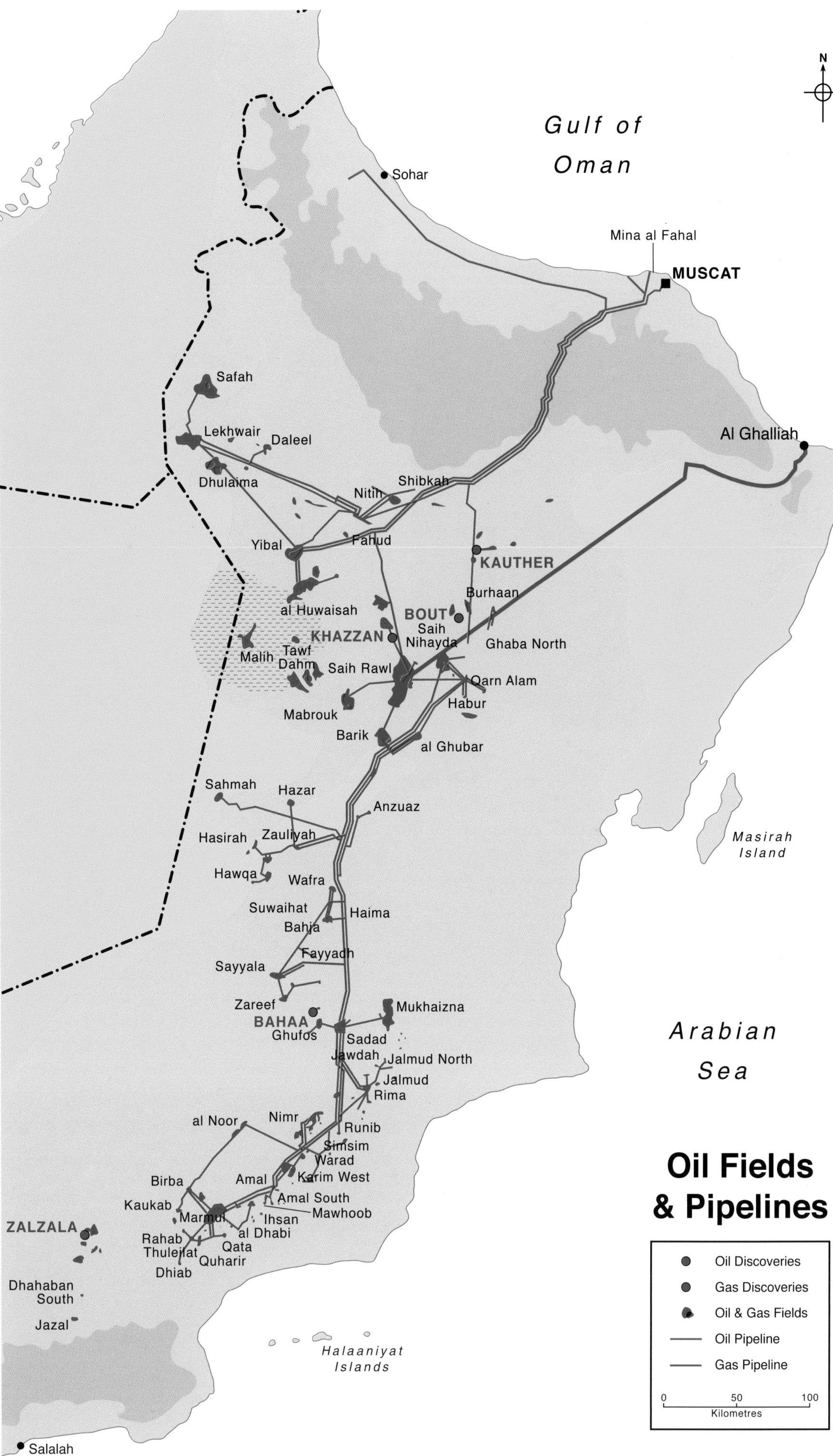

Left, *glimpsed through its gateway, Oman's Ministry of Petroleum and Minerals.* Above, *The LNG plant at Qalhat is one of the largest in the world, and the export of LNG is a key contributor to Oman's prosperity.* Opposite, *ore has become ingots.*

Gas

Natural gas on a large scale was discovered in 1991 at Wusta. The field there has estimated reserves of 22 trillion cubic feet, more than enough associated and non-associated gas for Oman's own developing industry. Total proven reserves in 2000 were estimated at 29 trillion cubic feet, of which over 25 trillion was non-associated gas. The export of Liquefied Natural Gas (LNG) has become one of the key means of diversification. In 2001, natural associated gas production was 270.7 million cubic feet with non-associated gas production 459.7 million cubic feet and known natural gas reserves, 24.4 trillion cubic feet. In the same year, 5.9 million tonnes of LNG were exported to South Korea, Japan, Spain, the United States and Belgium and 154,000 tonnes of condensates to the UAE and France.

The upstream and downstream operations were set up as separate operations with the upstream administered by PDO on behalf of the state and the downstream entrusted to the Oman LNG Company, a joint government/private venture; Government (51 per cent), Shell (30 per cent), KOLNG (5 per cent), Total (5.54 per cent), Mitsubishi (2.77 per cent), Mitsui (2.77 per cent), Partex (2 per cent), and ITOCHU (0.92 per cent). Its function is liquefaction, transportation, sales and export of the LNG. The $2 billion plant near Sur was the largest construction project undertaken in Oman, and one of the largest such plants in the world. The site of the modern plant is known as Qalhat on account of its closeness to the ancient city and seaport of that name, described by Ibn Battuta among others. The installation is designed to produce a nominal 6.6 million tonnes of LNG a year from two LNG process trains. In April 2000 the first shipment of 63,000 metric tonnes was made to Korea under a 25 year contract. Other agreements were made with Japan and France.

The gas operations involve a gas pipeline linking Yibal with al Ghubra power and desalination complex, while other internal buyers include power stations, industrial companies, the Ministry of Defence and the privately-owned power station and desalination plant at Barka. The 300 km Fahud-Sohar gas pipeline supplies natural gas to the large industrial estate adjoining the new port of Sohar, with its aluminium smelter, methanol plant and chemical fertiliser plant. Linkage between the gas fields and Dhofar was achieved by a 700 km pipeline between Seih-Rawl and Salalah, which was completed in 2002 and supplies industrial projects including the private power station and the Raysut cement factory.

Other Minerals

From the 1980s, copper was mined from the same deposits that were mined up to five millennia ago. In 1983 the Oman Mining Company reopened a mine at Lasail in the Wadi Jizzi near Sohar, where copper was extracted in 1000 BC. These deposits were depleted by 1994, and from then on the copper was imported for the smelter built earlier to refine and export through Port Sultan Qaboos. Copper deposits were also found at Rakkah and Hayl al Safil in the Wilayat of Yanqul, about 275 km from the smelter and also at Ghuzain near the Batinah coast. The Oman Chromite

Company, formed in 1991, produces around 25,000 tonnes per annum, and the ore is exported to China and Japan.

The mining sector has not so far been able to make a great contribution to the economy, despite small amounts of gold and silver from the copper oxide deposits near Yanqul and coal reserves of 122 million tonnes in the Sharqiyah area. Oman has large quantities of industrial rocks and minerals however, including silica sand – which is used by the Majan Glass Company – dolomite, limestone, and gypsum, all of which may have future uses.

The 2020 Vision

In June 1995 the Government held a 'Vision Conference: Oman 2020' in Muscat. Past economic performance was appraised, and plans were made for the next 25 years. The main aims were as follows: establishing economic and financial stability; reshaping the role of Government in the economy and stimulating private sector participation; diversifying the economic base and sources of national income; globalisation of the Omani economy, and developing human resources and improving the skills of the Omani workforce.

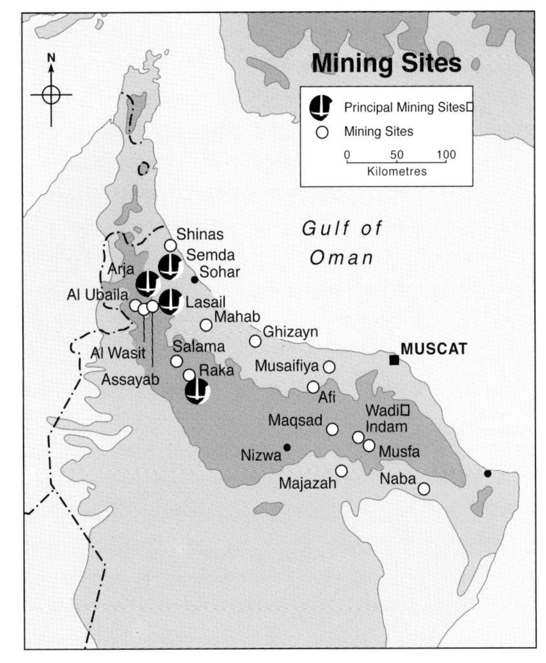

Privatisation should take two main forms: the privatisation of State concerns, and the encouragement of new private sector and foreign investment. Privatisation has already proved successful in several sectors: the airports sector; some power sectors, such as the privately-run power stations at Manah, Al Kamil and Barka and the privatisation of electricity in Salalah; telecommunications; and hospital supply services, and it will continue to grow in the coming years.

Part of 2020 was the establishment of a national committee in order to balance Oman's high population growth and provide a forum for the resolution of such questions as family growth, fertility, migration patterns and the changing role of women. The first national census, held in 1993, gave a total population of 2.018 million, of which 73 per cent were Omanis. The population is currently estimated at 2.324 million. Sustainable development and the environment are also factors which are being carefully considered, specifically in the light of the United Nations Development Programme (UNDP). Pollution avoidance is another area of concern, and Oman has already been praised by the United Nations Environmental Programme for its enviable record in conservation and pollution control.

The 2020 Vision aims to create a national economy based on private enterprise in a competitive environment without any monopolistic practices. In 1997 the first Oman International Economic Forum was held, followed by further meetings and attracting notable international speakers to promote Oman as a viable partner for foreign investment. The Businessmen's Council was set up in 1999, to liaise with Government on all matters of economic growth, and in October 2002 the Sultan announced the launch of the Sanad (support) Fund to help young Omanis set up their own businesses.

Water Resources

Oman lies in an arid and semi-arid part of the world. It is a place where water resources and the human population exist in a delicate balance. The discovery of new water sources and aquifers, geological surveys, exploratory wells and the installation of new recharge dams, all initiated by Vision 2020, have gone a long way towards easing the strain. The Ministry of Water Resources has tightened procedures in the granting of licences for new wells, and a Permanent Exhibition of Water Resources at the Ministry headquarters in Ruwi reminds the public of their duty to preserve water.

Industry

Until 1970 there was no modern industry in Oman, although handicrafts played an

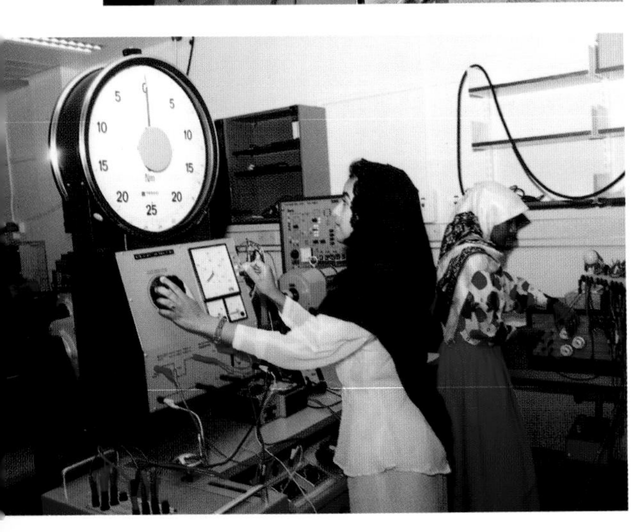

Rusail (top) *is the capital's manufacturing estate.* Centre, *a bottling plant.*

The service industries contribute more than half of the economic turnover of Oman. Hotels – with which Oman is well served (as by the Hyatt Regency, Muscat, left) *– and tourism are becoming significant contributors.*

important role in national life. Flour mills at Mutrah producing animal feed, together with cement factories at Rusail and Raysut, played an important part in the industrialisation of modern Oman from the 1970s. Among the earliest manufactured goods to be exported, under Government-sponsored projects, were food and beverages, furniture, textiles, paper products, chemicals and electrical and metal goods. By 1997 there were 812 manufacturing units in the country, both public and private.

Left, centre *and* below, *students at Sultan Qaboos University prepare for a role in industry, aware that Oman must diversify to maintain its high standards.*

The Omani people are expert at adapting their country's ancient resources to meet modern demand. In the early 1980s for example, Shaikh Abdullah Al Khalili invited the famous perfumer Guy Robert to produce a new scent combining Omani frankincense, myrrh and the rare Rock rose. The result was Amouage, which has become one of the most coveted perfumes in the world.

Since 1993, the Public Establishment for Industrial Estates (PEIE) has been responsible for the country's industrial estates. The operation is to be brought within the private sector. The major estates are: Rusail, Sohar, Raysut, Nizwa, Buraimi and Mazyounah near the border with Yemen, which has a Free Trade Zone. Manufacturing is a key part of the diversification policy, particularly: private sector export-oriented industries that use local raw materials; industries using gas as the main source of energy or feedstock; capital-, technology- or knowledge-intensive projects; projects employing Omanis on a wide scale, and precision engineering industries.

Investment Opportunities

Oman offers many advantages for the investor – a strategic location, political stability, good infrastructure, economic resources, convertibility of currency and a rate of inflation that has not risen above one per cent since 1992. Other added incentives include: no foreign exchange controls and no personal income tax; tax and import exemptions; duty-free access to the UAE; one-stop processing of investment proposals; protection of investment guaranteed by law; long-term use of land at favourable rates, and the possibility for some manufacturing projects, of 100 per cent foreign investment. The Oman Centre for Investment Promotion and Export Development (OCIPED), which began operations in 1997, is the one-stop-shop for foreign investors, while a new 68-hectare Knowledge and Information Technology Park (KOM) was established at Rusail in the early 2000s. Tourism projects include a multi-hotel complex at Bar Jissah near Muscat.

Banking

Banking in Oman began in 1948 with the opening of the British Bank of the Middle East (BBME) – a firm famous in its day, but subsequently taken over by HSBC. It remained the only bank in the country for 20 years, until the establishment of the Eastern Bank and Grindlays. Moves for

The grain silo, above, *at Mina Qaboos, and flour mill to its* left**,** *tell of one expanding industry, as does the Oman Mining Company's smelting works* below. *Cattle rearing* (left) *in Dhofar, fishing* (below left) *the length of the coast, are long-established contributors to the economy.*

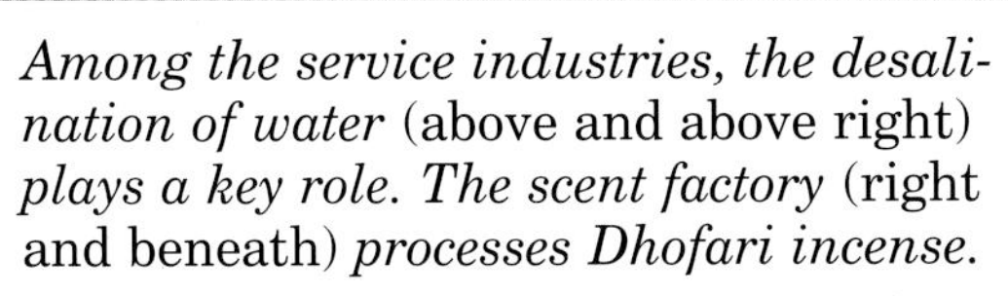

Among the service industries, the desalination of water (above and above right) *plays a key role. The scent factory* (right and beneath) *processes Dhofari incense.*

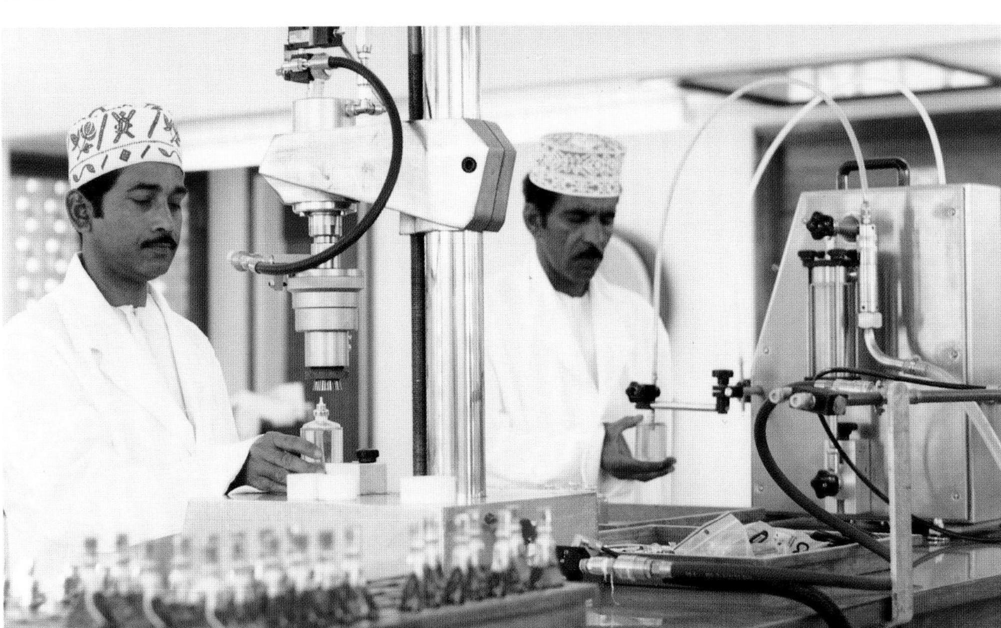

Oman to control its own banking sector began when the Oman Currency Board was established in 1972 and, with the authority of the Banking Law of 1974, the Central Bank of Oman (CBO) assumed full powers on 1 April 1975. Peter Mason of the BBME, played a personal role in creating Oman's new banking system. As the country's development progressed, the banking sector expanded until by the end of 2001 there were 15 commercial banks in the Sultanate – six national banks and nine branches of foreign banks – with a total of 324 branches, and three specialised banks operating a further 26 branches. Electronic banking is widely available to the public, with increasingly sophisticated ATMs and facilities for telephone and e-mail banking.

The CBO has encouraged mergers between national banks to improve their potential for offering services and has set a minimum capital ratio of 12 per cent, compared with the eight per cent set by the Bank of International Settlements. Share purchases from the Muscat Securities Market by commercial banks are closely monitored by the CBO and, to discourage any attempt at counterfeiting, Omani bank notes incorporate the latest security devices. The policy of Omanisation has resulted in the ratio of nationals employed in banking reaching 91 per cent in 2001, with 83.3 per cent in upper and middle management and 99.3 per cent in clerical positions.

Two specialised banks were set up by the Government in the 1970s. The first was the Oman Development Bank (ODB) – since 1997, a joint stock company established from the former Oman Development Bank and the Oman Agriculture and Fisheries Bank. The second was the Oman Housing Bank. Later the private sector Alliance Housing Bank came on the scene. More recently the Industrial Bank of Oman (IBO) was inaugurated in 1998 as a joint stock company with authorised capital of RO 40 million and issued share capital of RO 25 million. It was the first private sector industrial bank to be established in the Middle East and it had power to hold equity in industrial projects. In 1991 the Oman Development Bank (ODB) introduced an Export Guarantee and Finance Unit and this became the Export Credit Guarantee Agency (ECGA) in 1999.

Mutrah's Corniche, above *and* opposite below, *the Fanjah bridge* (below) *spanning the* wadi *on the way to Nizwa, and the clock tower circle at Salalah* (opposite) *are part of the network of highways and graded roads binding the entire country.* Opposite above, *Seeb's control tower is the hub of air transport.*

The Securities Market

The Muscat Securities Market (MSM) was established in 1988, and trading in shares began in 1989. It was established as one body comprising both the exchange and the regulatory authority, and in the early years, many fortunes were made and lost. In 1999, a separate regulatory body was set up – the Capital Market Authority (CMA) – charged with overseeing both the MSM and the separate Muscat Depository and Registration of Securities Company (MDRSC), which is responsible for the registration and transfer of ownership of securities and the safekeeping of ownership documents, linked by screen to the Salalah branch of the depository.

Electronic screen trading was introduced in 1998 and the MSM was linked with stock exchanges in Kuwait, Bahrain and Qatar, with the proviso that no share should be allowed to rise or fall by more than five per cent in any one trading session. Extensive disclosure requirements have been introduced, and listed companies are required to publish annual accounts conforming with International Accounting Standards. There are no exchange controls, however, and capital gains and dividends are not taxed.

Roads and Transport

In 1970, the only asphalted road in the country ran for a distance of about eight miles from Muscat, through Mutrah – where a khaki-uniformed policeman with a blue kepi on his head stood on a round platform directing traffic – to Bait al Falaj. There was also a graded road leading from the coast to Fahud in the Interior, constructed and maintained by PDO. Otherwise there were rough tracks over hard-going terrain, which only Land Rovers and Bedford trucks could negotiate. A

journey from Muscat to Nizwa took five hours.

Change, however, came rapidly. A good asphalt road between Mutrah and the new airport at Seeb, later extended to Sohar, was opened in 1973. A road from Sohar to Buraimi through the Wadi Jizzi soon followed, cutting the journey time from the capital to the other side of the al Hajar mountains from about 12 to around five hours.

From the 1980s, the remotest parts of the

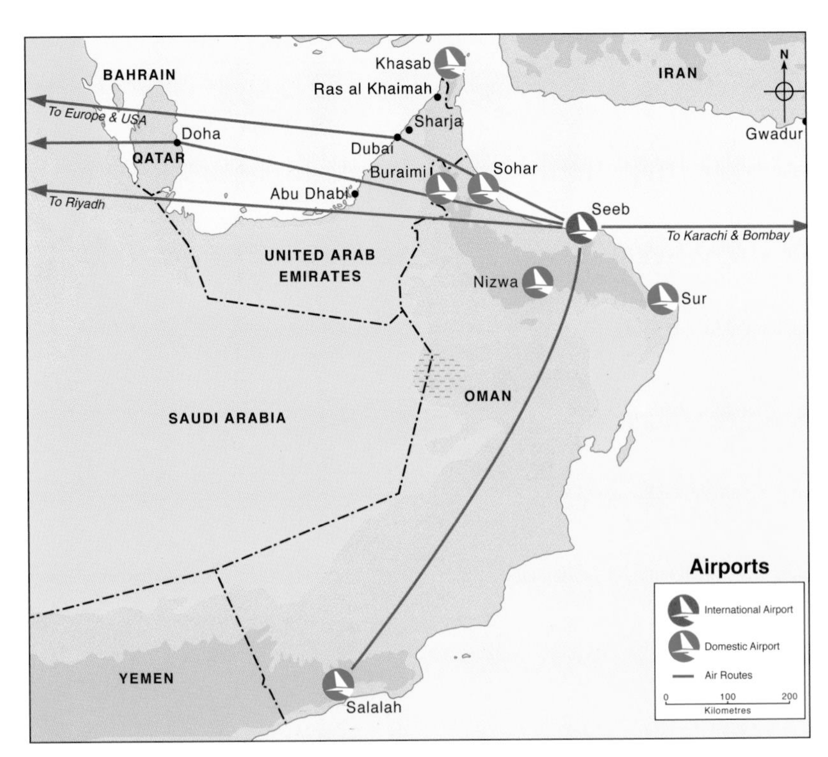

Salalah airport, above, *like the capital's Seeb, with its monument* (opposite) *to Oman's voyaging heritage, serves both international and domestic air traffic.*

country were made accessible to drivers when a network of roads were cut through the rugged and precipitous mountains of the Musandam and to the top of the Jebel Akhdar. In Dhofar, Sarfait – an outpost on the Yemen border – became accessible via an impressive road passing through magnificent coastal and mountain scenery. Further road building schemes followed throughout the 1990s, and the whole country quickly became linked by a network of fine roads. By 2000, more than 8,400 kilometres had been asphalted, much of which was dual carriageway, while a further 25,370 kilometres of road has been graded. The work included considerable bridge building over wadis, and flyovers in the capital area.

The needs of many more travellers and tourists were met with the inauguration of the state-owned bus service, Oman National Transport Company (ONTC). By 1986, the long and wearisome journey from Muscat to Salalah could be made in comfort on a Salalah Express coach. The company inaugurated a service to Dubai in 1989. In January 1997, a new service was introduced linking Ibri with Dubai via al-Buraimi, and in April 1999, the Company introduced a new express service between Muscat and Abu Dhabi. ONTC currently operates some 28 routes, covering over 20 million kilometres per year, with 19 long-distance departures daily to towns in the interior. ONTC acquired the franchise for public urban and suburban bus services, which are much used by workers and students. Although the Government has provided the lead, bus services are likely to fall within the private sector in future. It seems incredible now, that in 1970 there were only 840 registered vehicles in the whole country and about ten saloon cars. The number of vehicles has grown exponentially since then, bringing twenty-first century Oman firmly into the era of the traffic jam, despite its many excellent roads.

Air

In 1970 Oman had only one combined civil and military airport at Bait al Falaj, the approach to which through the mountains was somewhat daring. Some three years later, when the airport was moved to Seeb, the Chief Pilot of Gulf Aviation claimed that its demise had removed the last adventure in the civilian pilot's repertory in the Gulf area. At Salalah and on Masirah Island there were British RAF stations with good landing facilities, which were initially also used for occasional civil flights.

Construction of a new airport was an obvious priority. Seeb International Airport was ready for opening by the Sultan in December 1973. Since then it has been considerably extended and by 1998 main runways had been lengthened and passenger facilities in the terminal building much improved. In 2000 there were 2.7 million passenger arrivals, departures and transits and 38,184 flights handled.

In Dhofar, civilian aircraft used the military facilities in Salalah in the 1970s and 1980s. By the 1990s, however, the Salalah civil airport was completed, and in 1995 it became an international airport. By 2000 there were also other civil airports at Sur, Masirah, Khasab and Dibbah and in, 2001 management of Seeb and Salalah airports was privatised through a contract with the British Airports Authority (BAA).

Oman has 25 per cent of the equity of Gulf Air, together with the UAE, Qatar and Bahrain. From 1981 onwards, however, Oman has concentrated more on extending the range of its own airline, Oman Air. It began with domestic services but by 1994 the airline had Boeing 737s and a number of Omanis in its team of pilots. It continued to acquire more sophisticated aircraft, including Airbus 320s and A310s, and by 2002 its destinations included Abu Dhabi, Al Ain, Dubai, Jeddah and Kuwait in the Gulf region, as well as Chennai (Madras), Colombo, Dhaka, Gwadur, Karachi, Mumbai (Bombay), Peshawar and Thiruvananthapuram (Trivandrum).

Seaports

Modern seaports were also essential to the growth of Oman's economy. In 1970 all the shipments for the very first stages of the country's development were landed by lighter from ships in the Muscat Bay on the little quay in the small Customs area between the Sultan's former palace

and the then British Consulate building.

Very limited quantities of goods could be treated in this way, and the shipping companies charged a 10 per cent levy to cover the genuine risk of damage. Already a port for Mutrah had been planned; on Sultan Qaboos's accession more ambitious plans took shape. By 1974 Mina Qaboos was completed and able to handle two million tons of cargo annually. Later expanded and turned into a container port, it had ten deep-water berths for vessels of up to 10.4 m draught by 1995 and reclamation work at Shutaify Bay added to its area of operation. This then covered an area of 27,000 sq.m. with modern facilities, round-the-clock service, modern warehouses, engineering shops and deep-water wharfage.

Throughout history there have been a number of commercial ports along Oman's long coastline and in the late 1990s two major new ports in Sohar and Salalah, both famous harbours in former times, were added to the capacity of Port Sultan Qaboos at Mutrah. Of Sohar the Arab geographer Istakhri, writing in the tenth century A.D., wrote: 'It is not possible to find... in all the lands of Islam, a city more rich in fine buildings and foreign wares than Sohar.' The northern city's new port opened to shipping in 2003. The first phase of construction included dredging to a depth of 17 meters to accommodate the largest container ships in service, plus two liquid cargo berths, two bulk berths, two general cargo berths and a container berth. Sohar is fast becoming a flourishing centre of industry, with a gas supply from Oman's gas fields at Wusta in the interior, and a fertiliser factory, a methanol plant, Oman's second refinery and an aluminium smelter all being planned.

The small port at Raysut, 20 kilometers to the west of Salalah, was constructed in the early 1970s at the time of the Dhofar rebellion, for the import of military supplies. Raysut's favourable geographical position for seaborne traffic was once again recognised by the Government's decision to build a major container port there, thus reviving in modern times the ancient commercial sea routes.

The modern container port, formerly known as Raysut and now known as Port Salalah, immediately became an important element in Oman's economy. The plan for it was agreed in 1996 and the completion of the first phase was accomplished in 14 months, the port being run by a company with 20 per cent shares held by the government, 30 per cent by Maersk-Sealand, 19 per cent by Omani companies, 11 per cent by pension funds and the remaining 20 per cent of shares acquired by public subscription.

In the first full year of operation in 1999, no fewer than 584 ships called and 649,000 TEU [Twenty foot equivalent units] of cargo were handled. Salalah has become one of the largest and most sophisticated container terminals in the world, with 11 berths for freight, one with a 650-metre jetty and a harbour depth of 16 metres – sufficient to accommodate the largest ships in the world – and another jetty for oil. Each berth, with an area of 50 hectares, was equipped with five cranes including two of the world's largest cranes – super post Panamax.

On 24th May 2000 the ceremonial off loading of the largest container ship in the industry – the one million TEU Susan Maersk – took place. The 'Salalah crane', the largest in the shipping industry with a boom capable of reaching 22 containers across the vessel, was employed to unload it.

Salalah has a distinct advantage over its competitors, not only because it is sheltered from the seasonal monsoon, but also because it is close to the direct shipping lanes between Europe and the Far East. In addition, it has a Free Trade Zone, with first-class facilities and services including industrial buildings, offices, a resort and golf club. The transshipment operations here include the unloading of cargo into smaller ships for local distribution in the Gulf area.

There are also dhow ports at Khasab and Bukha in Musandam, and smaller harbours at Sohar, Sur and Khaburah.

Post and Telecommunications

Oman's first post office opened in Muscat in 1856, but there were no subsequent postal developments for over a century. Until 1947, Indian postage stamps were used, but following India's independence, the British General Post Office was given responsibility for postal agencies in Oman and the Gulf area. Overprinted British stamps were used until 1966, when the Sultanate took over postal services and started issuing its own stamps. In 1970, there was still only one post office in the country, but a system of numbered post boxes was introduced. By 2002, there were 95 post offices and 435 postal agencies using the latest computer technology. These regional post offices issue and renew commercial registrations. Six new stamps are issued each year, illustrating Oman's progress in many fields.

Although the post is envisaged as retaining an important role, Oman's communications strategy for the twenty-first century has a new focus. In the light of the world-wide communications revolution, Oman's priority has shifted towards the development of its already sophisticated telecommunications network. This is one of the prime candidates for privatisation, and the Government-owned General Telecommunications Organisation (GTO), established in 1980, has been converted into an Omani closed stock holding company, named the Oman Telecommunications Company, or OMANTEL. Fifty one per cent of the shares are to be owned by Government, 40 per cent by a 'Strategic Partner' and the remaining nine per cent by the private sector and pension funds. Oman was the first country in the region to privatise all its terminal equipment sales and the installation and maintenance of equipment.

While Mutrah's Mina (port) Qaboos remains the country's major entrepôt – above *and* opposite – *Port Salalah,* left, *serves Salalah and all of Dhofar, and boasts two of the world's largest cranes.*

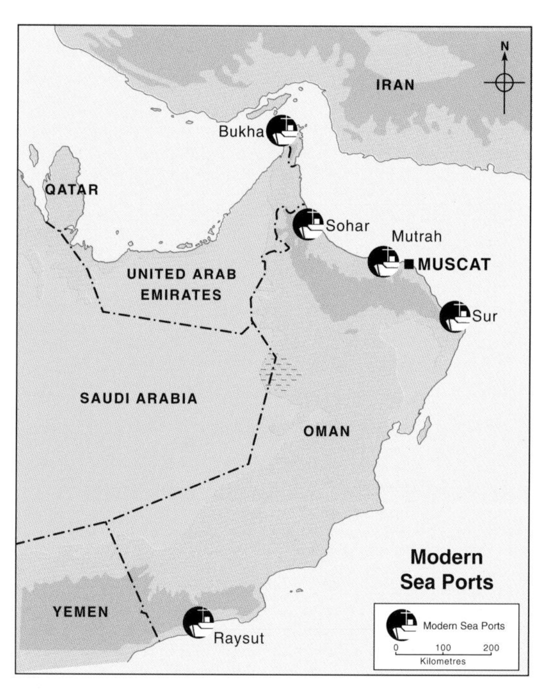

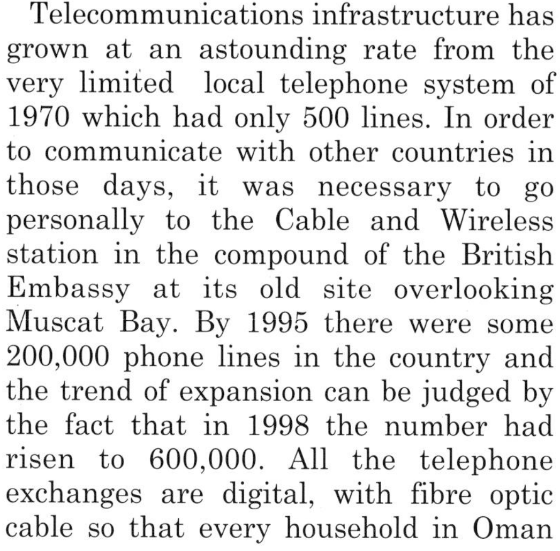

Telecommunications infrastructure has grown at an astounding rate from the very limited local telephone system of 1970 which had only 500 lines. In order to communicate with other countries in those days, it was necessary to go personally to the Cable and Wireless station in the compound of the British Embassy at its old site overlooking Muscat Bay. By 1995 there were some 200,000 phone lines in the country and the trend of expansion can be judged by the fact that in 1998 the number had risen to 600,000. All the telephone exchanges are digital, with fibre optic cable so that every household in Oman can have a telephone and enjoy related telecommunications services. Projects such as satellite and terrestrial transmission links are co-ordinated with other states of the AGCC, and Oman plays an important role in international bodies such as the International Telecommunications Union (ITU).

Oman was among the first country in the Arab world to complete its ARABSAT earth station in 1985, and in 2002 it was converted to the Intermediate Data Rate (IDR). Together with INTELSAT, this enables OMANTEL to receive and transmit television programmes to almost any country in the world. The Internet, which has revolutionised the lives of so many throughout the world, became available in Oman in 1996, with OMANTEL as sole access provider.

Mobile phones were first introduced into Oman in 1985. By 1996, GSM (Global System for Mobile communications) became available, and by 2000 there were 124,281 subscribers. In 2002, OMANTEL launched its 'Thuraya' mobile phone service which connects directly to satellite and gives world coverage. Coin-operated payphone services, which became available from 1980, have largely been supplanted by card and pager services.

Future developments will be affected by

The Ministry of Social Affairs, Labour and Vocational Training is responsible for guiding the school-leavers and graduates of Oman into the world of work.

Oman's membership of the World Trade Organisation, which it joined in 2000. Under the Sixth Five-Year Plan, OMANTEL aims to introduce Asynchronous Transfer Mode (ATM), a cell relay communications system which can carry voice, data and video information concurrently.

Media

In 1998 Oman Radio started broadcasting to the country from new, high-tech studios. A wide variety of programmes were aired around the clock in Arabic, and for a substantial part of the day there were also broadcasts in other languages, including several programmes in English. By 2003, Oman Radio could be received throughout the whole Arab region and was being listened to in countries as far afield as the Indian sub-continent, Africa and Europe.

The development of television in Oman has proved to be a rapid process. In November 1974, colour transmissions began to be made from Muscat. Only a few people owned individual television sets in those days, and crowds would regularly gather to watch their favourite programmes in front of the public television displays, one of which was placed prominently at the port end of the corniche at Mutrah.

Transmissions from a television studio in Salalah meanwhile, were reaching the whole of the Dhofar Governorate by 1975. By 1995 there were no fewer than 12 television transmitters – five in the Muscat area, three in Salalah and one each at Nizwa, Sur, Saham and Buraimi. By 1998 Oman Television was broadcasting around the clock, using satellite technology in order to facilitate domestic coverage of the whole country. Oman was in fact one of the first countries in the Gulf region to use such technology. By 2002, land-based transmission was also coming into wide use, and transmissions were reaching many parts of the world via Arabsat, the Egyptian Nilesat, European Hot Bird 4 satellite systems and the Internet.

With a devoted audience, television has developed rapidly since the first colour transmission went out in 1974. The service covers virtually the entire country, with an Omani news service, documentary features, and a vigorous drama department, from whose programmes a selection of stills appear here. Radio has evolved likewise, paying special regard to the country's cultural tradition, not least in folk music.

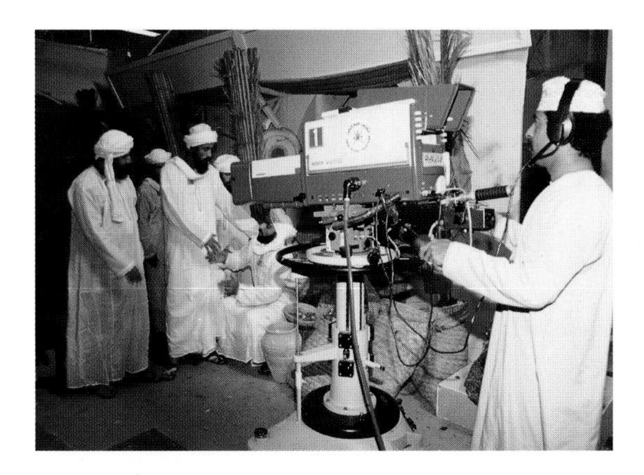

Oman quickly made up for its rather late start in the media field by producing its own distinguished radio and television programmes, a number of which have gone on to win international prizes and awards, including a gold award for *The Miraculous Nature of the Holy Qur'an* at the Seventh Gulf Radio and Television Festival in the Kingdom of Bahrain in 2001, and a gold award for the film *Disaster* at the International Traffic Safety Film Festival in Tunis in 2001. A few years earlier *The Sindbad Voyage* had taken the Toulon Sixth International Prize for the best maritime exploration film. Omani documentary films, covering such occasions as the annual National Day celebrations and the Sultan's 'Meet the People' tours, are invariably beautifully produced and very popular.

In 1970 there were no newspapers in the country at all. The desire to promote national unity however, as well as the need to increase awareness of Oman abroad, led to the establishment of a number of publications. The whole process began in 1970, when the Ministry of Information issued a free daily news circular immediately after Sultan Qaboos's accession. At the time, this was considered a revolutionary innovation. The *Official Gazette* also began to be issued at around the same time, for the publication of legislation, governmental notices and other official information.

The Omani press has been granted specific freedom of expression by the Basic Statute of the State, and by 2002, there were 36 newspapers and magazines being published in the Sultanate. There are three daily papers published in Arabic: *Oman*, *Al Watan* and *Al Shabiba* and two more published in English: the *Oman Daily Observer* and the *Times of Oman*.

The magazines cater for many different target groups, including women's interests, the commercial sector and financial markets, and the environment among others. The country's official news agency, the Oman News Agency (ONA), falls within the wider remit of the Oman Establishment for Press, News, Publication and Advertising, an organisation which plays a key role in disseminating information about Oman to news agencies and the media around the world.

Commerce

With all these dramatic changes of fortune and economic environment, much

of Oman's commerce continues to be carried on in traditional ways in towns all over the country. The heart of the bustling and colourful market in Mutrah, with its narrow crowded streets, gives much the same impression today as it did in 1970.

Omani merchants have a long tradition of trading, and have adapted quickly to the modern world. Trade has grown rapidly, and the retail sector has seen the construction of many complexes and showrooms in most of the cities and towns.

By the late 1990s, shopping centres, or malls, were also becoming a common sight, and by 2000 there were no fewer than nine in the country. The largest such mall is the Sultan Centre in Muscat. It was set up by a prominent Kuwaiti establishment at a cost of RO 6 million, and is a good example of the way in which foreign capital investment is increasingly being attracted into the country.

The volume of imports has of course, grown vastly since 1970, and the range of goods has been augmented by the same products that consumers demand all over the world – not least domestic and electrical goods.

Trade and investment is supported by the Oman Chamber of Commerce and Industry (OCCI) from its headquarters in Ruwi as well as from its regional branches in Salalah, Nizwa, Sur, Sohar, Ibra, Ibri, Buraimi and Khasab. The Chamber has been granted, *inter alia*, the power to legalise documents, invoices, agency and labour contracts and other certificates required for trading.

The resourcefulness and versatility of Omani merchants has always been a vital factor in the country's economy. The country's modern commerce is essentially built on a tradition that dates back – with some interruptions – over five thousand years.

So let us now review Oman's past patterns of trade.

The Early *Entrepôt* Trade

The exotic has played an important part in Oman's trade, and the gifts of the East – gold, myrrh and frinkincense – have all featured, as well as monkeys, mynah birds, ivory, slaves, coffee, cloves and spices. The *entrepôt* trade throughout history was one of the main planks in the Omani economy, but shipbuilding,

Throughout the country the local suqs *– some al fresco, like that at Sohar,* left, *or covered like the one at Mutrah,* above *– flourish as they have for centuries. Salalah,* below left, *has its own frankincense* suq, *while other merchants display precious artefacts created by Oman's silver and goldsmiths.*

shipowning and privateering, agriculture and horse breeding, copper mining, and latterly oil have all contributed in large and varying measures.

In the fourth and third millennia BC Oman – Magan – was already renowned as a seafaring and mercantile nation. Magan's trade centred largely on copper, and Sumerian inscriptions list the goods sent in return for this most sought after of metals – barley, garments of high and medium quality, skins, wool, sesame oil and "merchandise for buying copper".

The recorded exports of Magan, apart from copper, were wood, diorite – both used, for example, in building the temple of Nin-Gir-Su by Gudea of Lagash in about 2200 BC – ivory, precious stones, red ochre (perhaps brought from the islands of Abu Musa or Henjam), "Magan onions", and bamboo. Other Magan exports were multicoloured beads, wooden curiosities and Magan chairs and tables. Could the stools inlaid with ivory and gold, which astonished Vasco da Gama when he was entertained by the Arabs of Malindi in 1498, have been latter day versions of these? Whether the wood for this furniture came from Magan itself or from Malabar to Oman, like the teak exported in subsequent generations, remains obscure. But some of Magan's trade with Mesopotamia was certainly founded on imports from Maluhha (at this period, almost certainly the Indus Valley area), for example, gold, wood, ebony, ivory and monkeys. Magan may also have exported goats on the hoof, for the country was famous for these and its goddess was called Nindulla, "Queen of the Flocks".

Omani copper in former times was pro-

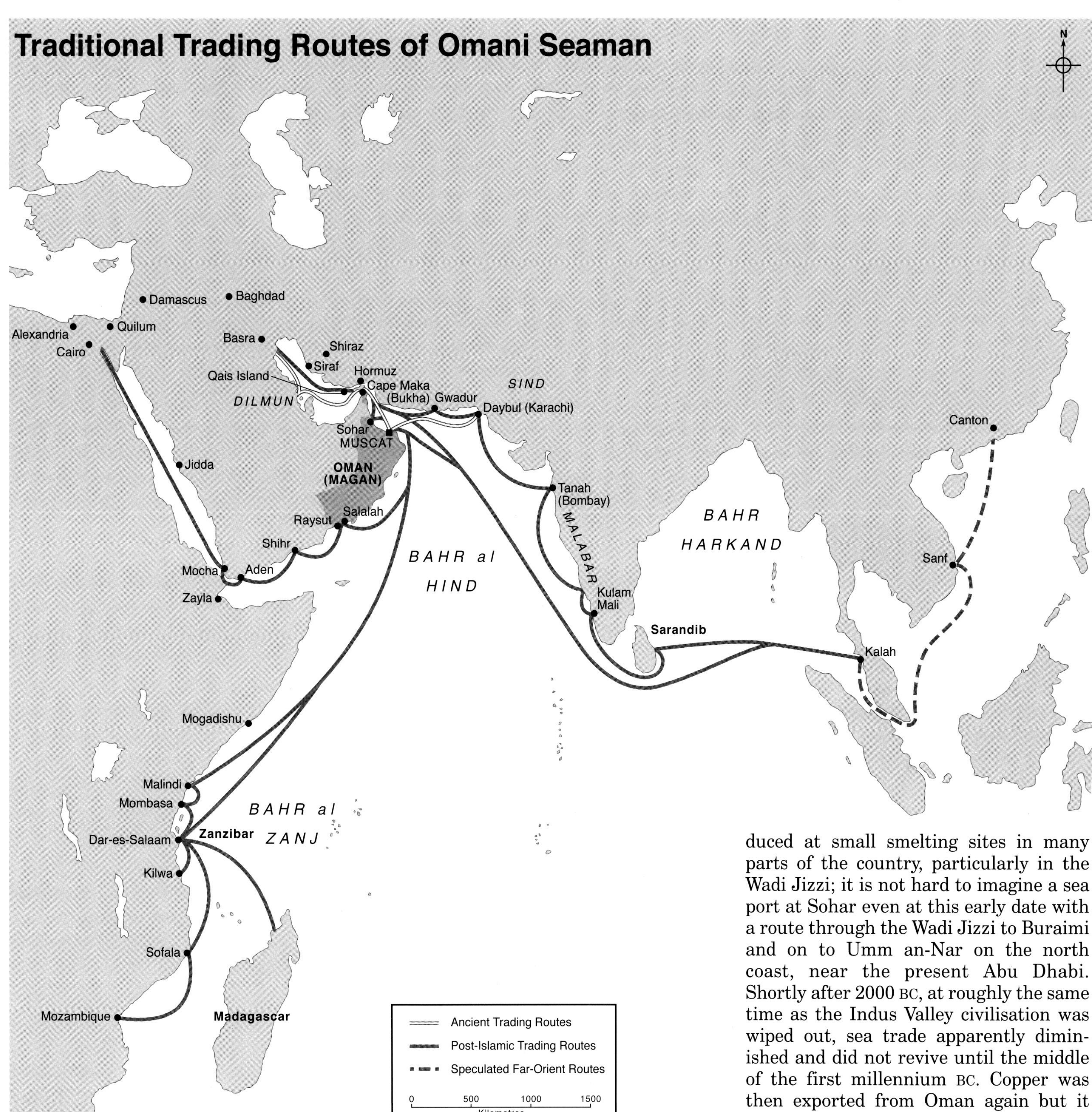

In the tenth century AD Sohar's commanding position near the Straits of Hormuz brought prosperity to the adventurous seamen of Oman. Through Sohar and Muscat passed the exotic products of the Far East and Africa to Persia and Arabia, in versatile vessels such as the sewn boom, like that seen under full sail opposite.

duced at small smelting sites in many parts of the country, particularly in the Wadi Jizzi; it is not hard to imagine a sea port at Sohar even at this early date with a route through the Wadi Jizzi to Buraimi and on to Umm an-Nar on the north coast, near the present Abu Dhabi. Shortly after 2000 BC, at roughly the same time as the Indus Valley civilisation was wiped out, sea trade apparently diminished and did not revive until the middle of the first millennium BC. Copper was then exported from Oman again but it was not until Sassanid and early Islamic times that it was mined on a vast commercial scale. The scale of the operation during this epoch is indicated by slag heaps of 100,000 tons at Lasail in the Wadi Jizzi. The widespread workings were used for some centuries subsequently and copper smelting was certainly important in Sohar's heyday in the tenth century. Supplies were indeed so plentiful then that broken pots were mended with copper rather than iron staples.

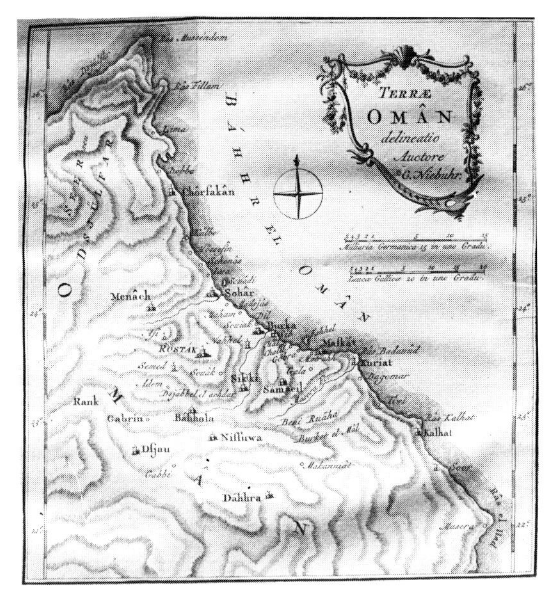

Carsten Niebuhr made this map of Oman in the eighteenth century.

Sohar

During the tenth century AD, the fourth century of Islam, Sohar was richer in fine buildings and foreign merchandise than any other port in the Islamic world. Ibn Hauqal claimed that "its traders and commerce cannot be enumerated" and al-Muqadassi called it the "hallway to China, the storehouse of the East and Iraq, and the stay of the Yemen". It was the greatest sea port of Islam and yet its fame is relatively unsung. Ibn Hauqal himself said that the rest of Islam hardly knew it existed.

Sohar's importance was attributable to several factors. First, it is conveniently situated on the eastern coast of Oman, looking outwards towards the coasts of Africa and India and the Far East. Secondly, its hinterland is and always was very fertile. Thirdly, its situation at the end of the Wadi Jizzi gives it easy access through the mountains to Buraimi and to the northern coast of the present UAE.

In the tenth century, and probably subsequently when the Omani coast was under the suzerainty of Hormuz, the goods passing through Sohar and Muscat were very varied. Omani seamen brought aloes, wood, bamboo, camphor, sandalwood, ivory, tin and spices of all kinds from Kalah, an important trading city on the coast of Malaya, which became the neutral meeting place between Arab and Chinese merchants after the foreign community in Canton had been massacred in 878 AD (265 AH). Earlier Omani and Gulf merchants had taken their ships to China itself to trade and Chinese ships had come to Oman and the Gulf. There was a vast trade in chinaware. Other imports from China included musk, silk and jewels. The exports to the Far East included costly fabrics of linen, cotton and wool – perhaps from Persia – rugs, metalwork, iron or bullion and possibly dates. From Africa, Omani seamen brought ivory, tortoiseshell – though some of this may have come from Masirah, a resort of several of the world's known species of turtle – leopard skins, ambergris and slaves.

The Omanis of Sohar in its heyday were building on a well established foundation. The spread of Islam in the seventh century led to the Arabs occupying all the coasts of the Gulf and reuniting the great economic area of western Asia. This was first united politically under the Persian Achaemenids, split by the successor of Alexander the Great and reunified under the Sassanids. The Gulf and Red Sea were no longer rival routes to the markets of Rome or Byzantium, but parallel routes to the nearer lands of the Caliphate. In fact, the Muslim countries of the Middle East dominated and controlled the lucrative trade between the Far East and the West until the arrival of the Portuguese in the Indian Ocean in the sixteenth century, lying across this great belt like a "Moslem Colossus".

Omani mariners of the tenth century were remarkable for their skill, courage and endurance. The planks of their ships were only sewn together with yarn spun from the bark of the coconut palm and yet they sailed as far as China to the east and Madagascar to the south. The beginnings of this renaissance for Omani shipping was – strangely – attributable to the Persian Sassanid dynasty. Sohar, which was called Mazun during the Sassanid period, already boasted notable seafarers in the third century AD and Ardashir, the founder of the Sassanid dynasty, moved some sailors of the Azd tribe from there to Shihr, thus perhaps establishing the long seafaring tradition of the Hadhramaut. There is little evidence about the size of the ships used during this period but a clear distinction was drawn by the Arab geographers between the great seagoing ships, which carried as many as 400 men, and those used for coastal traffic in Gulf waters. In the years before Islam, Nestorian Christians amongst the inhabitants of Sohar were active in trade with India and beyond, and their missionary activities – after the establishment of the Nestorian bishopric in about 424 AD – extended even as far as Malaya.

Lucrative sea trade between the Gulf and China was made possible by the simultaneous existence of great empires at each end. The whole Muslim world from Spain to Sind was united under the Umayyad Caliphs from 660 to 749 AD (40 to 132 AH) and, with the exception of Spain and North Africa, for over a century, 750 to 870 AD (133 to 257 AH), under the Abbasids in Baghdad. The

Forts like that at Qurayyat helped to defend the trading ports.

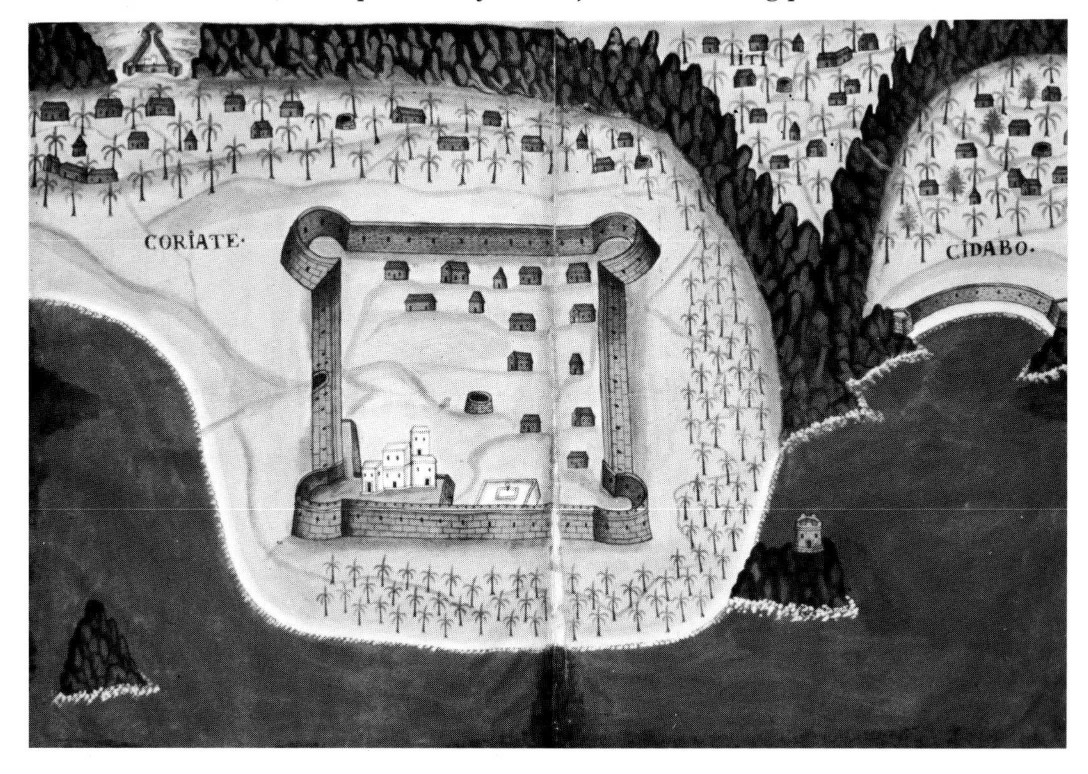

Ta'ng dynasty ruled over a united empire in China from 618 to 907 AD (-4 to 295 AH). Thus conditions at either end of this long trade route were relatively stable and the Omanis profited. By the middle of the eighth century AD an Omani called Abu Ubaida Abdalla ibn al Qasim made the first recorded voyage to China, taking about two years to cover the distance of some 4,350 miles. It is no coincidence that *Kitab Aja'ib al Hind (The Book of the Wonders of India)*, the forerunner of the Sindbad stories, was produced during Sohar's heyday.

It was in commemoration of this that the *boom* – meticulously constructed to resemble *booms* of the period – in which Tim Severin and his crew made their historic voyage from Muscat to Canton in 1980 was named *Sohar.*

Al-Muqaddasi described the port of Sohar in detail. The anchorage was about a *farsang* – four miles – in length and breadth and was always busy with ships. Near the shore was a great mosque with a high minaret and a magnificent many-coloured *mihrab* on a spot where, according to tradition, the Prophet's camel had knelt. It is hard now to reconstruct this Sohar in the mind's eye, but it is possible that the two creeks were open to the sea and that there was a mole built out into the sea. The town, which consisted mainly of red brick buildings, was then four times as large as it was in 1970. There were 12,000 houses; each sea captain lived in a separate dwelling. The agricultural land was also about four times as large as it was at the beginning of Sultan Qaboos's reign and covered thirty-eight square miles, producing dates, bananas, figs, grapes, subtropical fruit and citrus varieties from India. The old kilns still survive on the northern edge of the town and tradition ascribes this brick industry to the Jewish community, whose strength at this period is attested by the large number of Jewish graves. Copper smelting, glass manufacture and shipbuilding were amongst the most important industries. Sohar's prosperity was, however, largely built on the entrepôt trade and it was this which caused Istakhri to write: "It is not possible to find on the shore of the Persian Sea nor in all the land of Islam a city more rich in fine buildings and foreign wares than Sohar."

Later *Entrepôt* Trade

After the devastating sack of Sohar of 971 AD 360 AH) by a Persian force despatched from Fars by the Buyid dynasty in Baghdad, Oman never had an *entrepôt* port so magificent. However, Sohar, which rose again, Qalhat, Qurayyat, Muscat, and Khor Fakkan were all prosperous during the period of Hormuzi supremacy on the coast, from the thirteenth to the sixteenth centuries, as Marco Polo and ibn Batuta noted. Albuquerque himself commented on their prosperity when he reduced them to Portuguese sovereignty and Oman became part of the pattern of the Portuguese trading network. During the same period Balid in Dhofar was also flourishing under its own Sultan.

Before the advent of the Portuguese, Omani sailors, who were to be found all over the Indian Ocean, had evolved a sophisticated system of navigation. Navigational theory, and indeed the whole gamut of seamanship, are the subject of a nautical book by Ahmad ibn Majid, the most famous navigator of his day, called *Kitab al-Fawa'id fi usul al-bahr wa'l-qawa'id (The Book of Benefits on the Principles of Seamanship).*

Ahmad, who may have piloted Vasco da Gama from Malindi to Calicut in 1498 AD (904 AH), was born in Julfar but his home town was almost certainly Muscat. At least, he described Muscat in glowing terms as "the most well-known port in the world" and went on: "Muscat is a port the like of which cannot be found in the whole world. There can be found business and good things which cannot be found elsewhere. There is a rock at the head of the port which the traveller to and from any place sees, whether he aims for India and Sind or Hormuz or Makran or the West, and North West by West of it is a high red island called Al Fahal and these are landmarks sufficient for even the ignorant man when he comes across them night or day. Muscat is the port of Oman where year by year the ships load up with men, fruit and horses, and they sell in it cloth, vegetable oils and new slaves and grain and all ships aim for it. It is a cape between two different routes safe in every wind and possess fresh water and a hospitable and sociable people who love strangers."

Ahmad's father and grandfather were also well known navigators and his work is based on their writings and experience as well as those of the "three lions" of the sea, Laith ibn Kahlan, Muhammad ibn Shadhan and Sahl ibn Abban, all of whom were also famous for voyages of exploration. Ahmad's navigational and intellectual successor, Sidi Celebi, the Ottoman sailor who took command of Sultan Sulaiman's fleet after Piri Rais had left it in Basra, the Captain General of the Turkish Navy, carried the Indian Ocean version of the art a step further forward.

The pilots of the Indian Ocean relied on compass bearings and on taking the altitude of the stars, whereas the early Mediterranean method depended on the compass and on measuring the distance travelled through the sea. As ibn Majid and other captains in the Indian Ocean calculated latitudes by reference to stellar altitudes and there is no evidence that they ever "shot" the sun, their measurements must always have been taken by night. However, during the day they relied on *isharat*, the physical signs such as tides and discoloured water to which they attached great importance, to help their navigation and keep them on course.

After the Portuguese seaborne empire was established in the sixteenth century, Portugal held a chain of forts, including those of the Omani coast, stretching from Hormuz to Sofala (in today's Mozambique) in the west and to the Moluccas and Macao on the edge of the Pacific. Pepper came from Malabar and Indonesia; gold, silks and porcelain from China; gold from Sumatra and south-east Africa; horses from Persia and Arabia and cotton textiles from Gujerat (Cambay) and Coromandel. The various items of merchandise which originated in Asia either passed through the local *entrepôts* or were shipped round the Cape of Good Hope to Lisbon. The kernel of this trade was the export of pepper from the East to Portugal and of silver bullion to Goa.

The pattern of trade, during the later reign of the Imam Ahmad ibn Said, is illustrative of the type of commerce which prevailed in the area for long periods. The carriage of coffee from Mocha in Yemen to Basra, in which the mariners of Sur played an important part, was a notable feature at this stage. In 1765 about fifty vessels formed the annual "coffee fleet" which sailed every year from Muscat to Basra, Oman's principal trade at this juncture being with Turkish Iraq. By 1775 Muscat had become the principal *entrepôt* for trade between the Gulf, India and the Red Sea and by the

The historic 1840 voyage of Oman's tall ship Sultana *to the United States (then 15,000 miles via the Cape) to consolidate the good relations established by the 1833 Treaty of Amity and Commerce, was approximately reenacted 146 years later by the handsome 468-tonne sailing barque (*left*), the Sultan's Naval Vessel* Shahab Oman

last decade of the eighteenth century about five-eighths of the total trade of the Gulf and half the produce of Yemen passed through Muscat. Sayyid Sultan ibn Ahmad then claimed the exclusive right to protect navigation and tried – though without ultimate success – to make a preliminary visit to Muscat obligatory on all vessels proceeding up the gulf. This stratagem had made other great *entrepôts* in the area – Hormuz, Qais and Siraf – prosperous in their own heydays.

Oman's own exports during the latter half of the eighteenth century were gums – perhaps frankincense from Dhofar; ostrich feathers – presumably from the now extinct Arabian ostrich, though it is possible that they came from east Africa; hides, skins, honey, beeswax and live cattle and sheep. Re-exports from Persia were copper, drugs, rosewater, dried fruits, raw silks, raw cotton, sulphur and rock-salt. From Iraq came dates, copper, gall-nuts, tobacco, gum, catgut, pen reeds and horses. Imports from abroad for Omani home consumption included Indian piece goods, pepper, ginger, rice, tobacco, coffee, sugar, English cloth, cutlery and toys.

In Sultan's time in the last years of the eighteenth century, Muscat alone had fifteen ships of 400 to 700 tons, along with three brigs; and Sur was the headquarters of a fleet of a hundred seagoing vessels trading directly with Bengal, Batavia and Malabar, whilst smaller ships traded with the Gulf, east Africa and Abyssinia. In fact, Suris and Omanis from the Shariqiyah area played a considerable part in the opening up of east Africa. From the 1930s, Europe was developing steamboats, railways, telegraph systems and other engineering skills. Nevertheless, about five-eighths of Gulf trade still touched at Muscat in the 1840s and as late as 1854 Muscat-owned ships carried about half of the trade. Thus Muscat remained important as an *entrepôt* well into the nineteenth century and its *entrepôt* trade was estimated to be worth £1.8m in the 1830s. By the 1870s, however, the situation had changed, the competition from steam ships had become too intense, and Muscat's trade dwindled to £425,000 in 1874-75.

Trade in the western Indian Ocean began to interest the Americans in the 1820s and the first American vessel, the *Laurel* from Salem, called at Zanzibar in

July 1825, a time when Sayyid Said bin Sultan was becoming increasingly preoccupied with his east African possessions. This preoccupation was heightened by the action, subsequently disavowed, of Captain William Owen in provisionally declaring a British protectorate over Mombasa at the request of the Mazrui shaikhs – the dominant Omani group there who had renounced Omani suzerainty on Said's accession.

Oman gave the 74-gun Imaum *(third from left) to England's King William IV.*

Edmund Roberts of Salem, New Hampshire, placed American trade with Said on a sound and formal basis. After obtaining letters of credence addressed to Said from his kinsman, Senator Levi Woodbury, Secretary of the Navy, Roberts took a small naval squadron to conclude treaties with Siam, Cochin China, Japan and the powers of Arabia on the Red Sea as well as Said.

Roberts travelled on the United States sloop-of-war *Peacock* and arrived in Muscat in September 1833. A Treaty of Amity and Commerce was signed on 21st September which stipulated *inter alia* that American traders would only pay 5 per cent import duty in the Sultan's dominions. Unfortunately there were discrepancies between the English and Arabic texts, which later gave rise to misunderstanding, but at the time Roberts carried away not only the signed treaty but also a friendly letter from Said to President Jackson expressing his determination that the treaty should be faithfully observed "as long as the world endures"; this echoed the provision in the 1800 treaty with Britain that the friendship of two states should "remain unshaken till the end of time, and till the sun and moon have finished their revolving career". The treaty was ratified in 1834, and thereafter American commerce with the Sultanate rested on a most-favoured-nation basis.

Trade between Americans and Oman grew, particularly after the appointments as Consul of Richard Waters in Zanzibar in 1837 and Henry Marshall in Muscat in 1838 – though the latter appointment was short-lived. Cotton sheeting, crockery, muskets, gunpowder, ships' stores, clocks, shoes and spices were brought from America, and return cargoes consisted of gum copal, copra, cloves and ivory.

Said, who was personally one of the largest importers, decided, on the advice of Edgar Botsford of New York, to add a new dimension to relations by sending one of his own vessels to the United States and purchasing munitions – for he still aimed to drive the Portuguese from Mozambique. The *Sultana*, named after his first consort, the Sultana Azza bint Saif who came from his own family, was designated for the voyage to New York, and Said tried to persuade Richard Waters to go too, as he had no Omani navigator to pilot the ship across the Atlantic, all his crews being experienced in the Indian Ocean only. Waters did not take up Said's invitation and William Sleeman, a Britisher who had previously commanded the Omani frigate *Prince Regent* and who was a good navigator, was instructed to sail the vessel as sailing master, leaving early in February 1840. Unfortunately, he had an addiction to the bottle.

Ahmad ibn Na'man, Oman's first trade envoy to America, in 1840.

The great Sayyid Said ibn Sultan (above) *despatched Ahmad bin Na'man to America.* Below, left, *Zanzibar in the mid-19th century, shown in a contemporary print, was ruled by Oman and rivalled the motherland's wealth. Dutch East Indiamen traded with Zanzibar* (below).

Said's confidential private secretary, Hajji Ahmad ibn Na'man, was chosen to represent him in the United States and he too sailed on the *Sultana* via St Helena. It was he who stole the limelight in New York, for – perhaps on account of Sleeman's bad conduct – he announced that he was in command and that his name rather than Sleeman's should appear on official port documents. Ahmad was small and slightly corpulent, his complexion tawny, and his eyes black and piercing. He wore a gaily-coloured turban on his head, a bright cashmere shawl around his waist, and a splendidly embroidered *qaftan* trimmed with gold over his long white undergarment.

He was the first Omani envoy to the United States and he made a great impression. His upbringing was as cosmopolitan as that of many Omanis. Of the Bani Kaab tribe on his father's side, with a Persian mother, he had been born in Basra. Having joined Said's service in 1820 he travelled to China, Cairo and Europe on his behalf, and also made the pilgrimage to Mecca.

Amongst the passengers on the *Sultana* were two young Englishwomen – Mrs Robert Norsworthy, wife of an English trader in Muscat and Zanzibar and her maid Charlotte Thompson. They were closely guarded in their cabin to ensure privacy, a security precaution which gave rise to rumours in the United States that Said had sent "two or three Circassian slaves of outstanding beauty" as a gift to the President!

Ahmad and the crew were fêted in New York and he was entertained by the Mayor of Brooklyn as well as Commodore Renshaw of the Navy Yard, who had been instructed by the Secretary of the Navy to pay him every attention. Ahmad carried no letters to the President, however, and so no arrangements were made for him to meet President van Buren. Nevertheless, gifts between Said and the President were exchanged. Said had sent two fine Najd stud horses, jewels, attar of roses, rose-water and a beautiful gold-mounted sword. The return gifts included a fine pleasure barge, beautifully fitted out, and four five-chamber rotary repeating pistols and two eight-chamber repeating rifles made by Colts. There were also items for Said's own use, such as candles, gold thread, perfumes, vases, musical boxes, mirrors, rifles, paper, glass and plates.

The *Sultana*'s cargo grossed $26,257. It consisted of 1,300 bags of dates, 21 bales of Persian carpets, 100 bales of Mocha coffee, 108 prime ivory tusks, 81 cases of gum copal, 135 bags of cloves and 1,000 dry hides. The whole cargo was sold on Said's account and the return cargo comprised 125 bales of grey sheeting called "Mericani", 24 bolts of scarlet cloth, 13 cases of red, white and blue beads, 20 dozen prints, 300 muskets, gunpowder and china plates.

On the return journey the *Sultana* ran into bad weather, but under an American master, Captain Sandwith Drinker, who replaced Sleeman, the ship was brought safely back to Zanzibar ten months after it had set out. Thus Ahmad ibn Na'man accomplished his unique journey, the first Arab diplomatic mission to the United States.

The years 1862 to 1872 in fact brought about the destruction of the formerly flourishing *entrepôt* system. The introduction of European steamers immediately affected the Omanis who did not have the capital or the knowledge to acquire the new invention for their own use. Though Gulf trade expanded considerably during this time, the Omanis did not benefit. On the contrary, the trade formerly carried in large Omani ships was increasingly carried by steamers calling at ports in the Gulf, bringing prosperity to them and taking it away from Muscat.

It was in the period of Sultan Turki (1871-88) that steam supplanted sail and Oman's entrepôt trade and victualling income fell drastically.

The large Omani ships which had carried trade over the oceans began to disappear and by the late nineteenth century the largest ships built in Oman were of 100 to 200 tons, whilst even smaller craft of only some ten tons were in greater demand.

The pattern of trade also changed. Whereas there was a great variety of items, including luxuries, to be had in Muscat as long as it remained an *entrepôt*, the trade was confined largely to staples and necessities in the last quarter of the nineteenth century. The decline was marked by a drop in the population; Muscat was estimated to have 55,000 inhabitants in the 1850s and Mutrah somewhere between 8,000 and 20,000 inhabitants. By the 1960s, Muscat's population had dropped to a mere 5,000 or 6,000. Mutrah was only a little larger and the trend was not reversed until the change of regime in 1970, when prosperity returned to the area.

Limes

Small round green limes have been one of the agricultural products of Oman, particularly the Batinah, for many generations, and as an export they have been second only to dates. The drying and packing of limes has always been an important supplement to the income of people in the coastal towns. The dried limes were, and are, mainly exported to the Gulf area and large quantities of them found their way to southern Iraq, from where they were distributed throughout the country. In Iraq they are still known as *Lumi Basra* and are made into a drink like tea called *shai hamudh* – sour tea – which is usually taken with sugar. By the early 1970s limes were the most important export apart from oil, and contributed a considerable amount to Oman's income; in 1971 they were worth RO333,300.

Dates

The date palm flourishes in all parts of Oman, except Dhofar, even at a height of 2,000 feet. The plantations on the Batinah were in the past sometimes seven miles deep along the coast and the number of palms in the Wadi Samail was estimated at 600,000 at the turn of the century. The best dates in Oman are known as *mibsali, fard* and *khalas,* and dates have throughout history been one of the country's main exports. In the late nineteenth century date exports increased in absolute value until they became Oman's single most valuable export, and by 1880 AD (1298 AH) they were exported in increasing quantities to India and the United States, the *fard* being preferred by American importers. Sales of wet dates were increased by the railways in India, which took them from Karachi to the populous Punjab, and other varieties were shipped dry for distillation into spirit. In an average year in

Opposite: *dates are staple exports.*

the 1890s the value of Omani date exports reached some 750,000 Maria Theresa dollars. However, by the middle of the twentieth century, the trade had greatly declined and in 1973 date exports were only worth RO118,000.

An industry revived. From Samhuram, below, Dhofari incense went to Rome. Today it goes to Muscat.

At the funeral of Poppaea, the Emperor Nero burnt more incense from Dhofar than a whole year's production.

The best quality incense is Najdi, *from north of the Dhofar hills. The tree seldom grows taller than 9 feet. Its oliganum globules ooze from skilfully made incisions and are collected in March and April before the monsoon rains.*

Frankincense

Dhofar's fame and prosperity, which emerges from the mists of antiquity, arose from the trade in frankincense, of which truly vast quantities were used in the ancient world. The famous visit of the Queen of Sheba – the Sabaean Kingdom – to King Solomon in the middle of the tenth century BC was probably to secure an agreement on frankincense and myrrh advantageous to both parties. Herodotus, in the sixth century BC, records that about two and a half tons of it were burnt annually in the temple of Bel at Babylon alone and it was used in the temples of Egypt and Mesopotamia from the earliest historical times. Frankincense, together with myrrh and gold, was brought as a gift to the infant Jesus, and the Roman Emperor Nero burnt more than the average annual production of Arabia at the funeral of Poppaea.

Frankincense is the exudation of olibanum from the incense tree, *Boswellia*, caused by deliberate incisions which lead to the formation of globules of gum resin. These are then collected by tribesmen who have marked the trees earlier. The trees, which are rarely more than eight or nine feet high, are incised when they are three or four years old and the globules are collected in March, April and May before the monsoon. "The mount of myrrh and the hill of frankincense" mentioned in the biblical *Song of Solomon* may well refer to Dhofar. For, though myrrh grows extensively throughout south Arabia, Somalia and Africa, frankincense trees are confined to Dhofar and certain other parts of south Arabia and Somalia. The best area for frankincense is the home of the Bait Kathir tribe in the Najd or steppe area to the north of

the Dhofar hills, which the Book of *Genesis* refers to as Mount Sephar. *Nadji* is the highest quality of frankincense. *Shazri*, which is collected in the Qara mountains, is the next in quality and *Sha'abi*, collected on the coastal plain, is the poorest.

In antiquity incense was exported by sea, but much of it was carried by camel caravans to the markets in the north. There were three main routes, which led across the Wadis Mitan and Fasad.

One route went across the Empty Quarter, the Rub' al-Khali, in a north-westerly direction; a second route, which according to Pliny was acomplishedin sixty-five stages, skirted the sands and went to Hadhramaut to join the major land route which began at the city of Shabwa, from which it went to Timna', Marib, Ma'in, Yathrib (now Medina), Madain Salah, Petra, Dedan and Gaza.

A third route, taking forty days by camel, joined the route leading from Had-hramaut across the middle of the Arabian peninsula to the Chaldean city of Gerrha on the Arabian shore of the Persian Gulf opposite Bahrain, albeit still unlocated.

By the late third century BC Gerrha had become the principal commercial centre in the Gulf and it seems to have remained so for several centuries, for Pliny (23-79 AD) describes its walls as being five miles in circumference.

Other Exports

A small quantity of tobacco has long been grown along the Batinah and in a few other places in Oman. Some of it has been consumed locally, some exported, mainly to the UAE. The trade was worth RO34,800 in 1973. In the past, Oman provided considerable quantities of vegetables and fruit for visiting ships and exports, particularly to the UAE. No statistical record was kept. With the change of regime in 1970 a new impetus was given to agriculture, and fruit and vegetable exports were worth RO160,000 in 1973. A trade in dried, salted and wet fish such as sardines has flourished on a small scale for generations.

Chronology

BC

c.12000 Stone Age civilisation in northern Oman and Shisur in Dhofar
c.3000 Earliest pottery – Jemdet Nasr period
c.2350 Magan ships trading with Sargon of Agade in Sumer
c.2275 Magan conquered by Naram-Sin of Agade
c.2025 Shipwrights mentioned in Sumerian tablets
c.2025 Magan trading with Ibbi-Sin of Ur
c.2000 Rise of Dilmun
c.1400-1300 Connections between Oman and Luristan in Iraq
c.800-700 Invasion from South Arabia by Ya'rub, whose brother Oman may have been appointed Governor
c.700 Trading with Gulf and Babylon resumed
c.563 Oman conquered by Cyrus the Great of Persia
Falaj system developed

AD

c.50 Oman mentioned by Roman author Pliny
c.200 Azd migration into Oman led by Malik ibn Fahm
c.230 Ardashir I, founder of Persian Sassanid dynasty, regained firm control of Oman
c.520 Khosrau I of Persia dominated Oman in rivalry with Axumites of Ethiopia for control of Arabia
c.5th to 7th centuries Christian bishopric at Sohar
630 Amr ibn al As arrived in Oman with letter from Prophet Muhammad
Conversion of Oman to Islam
c.690 Apogee of Azd (of Oman) power in Basra
c.720 Fall of Azd from power and return to Oman
8th century Sulaiman and Said, joint rulers of Oman, went to the "land of Zanj" (east Africa) when Caliphate troops occupied Oman
751 Election of first "rightful Imam" of the Ibadhis, Juland ibn Mas'ud
893 Oman overrun by Caliphate troops led by Muhammad ibn Nur, and civil wars
8th century Omani voyages to China
c.929 Carmathian conquest of Oman
c.950 Sohar the greatest sea port of Islam
71 Sohar devastated by the Buyids
1064 Oman invaded by the Seljuks
c.1153-1435 Oman without Imams and ruled by the Maliks of the Nabhar
c.1100-1300 Omani dynasty ruling Qais, then the centre of Gulf trade
1250 Hormuzi suzerainty estblished over Omani coast
1435 Imamate restored
1497 Omani pilot, Ahmed ibn Majid, navigated Vasco da Gama from Malindi in east Africa to Calicut in India
1507 Albuquerque brought Oman under Portuguese domination
1550 Muscat attacked by Piri Rais, Captain-General of the Turkish fleet
1581 Muscat again attacked by Turks under Ali Beg
1587-88 Forts Mirani and Jalali completed in Muscat by Portuguese
1624 Nasir ibn Murtshid, first Imam the Ya'ruba dynasty, elected
1646 Treaty of Commerce between the Imam and Philip Wylde of the English East India Company
c.1650 Imam Sultan ibn Saif recovered Muscat from Portuguese
1659 Treaty between the Imam and Colonel Rainsford of the East India Company about English trading in Muscat
c.1660-70 Imam Sultan ibn Saif built fort Nizwa
1670 Dutch East India Company rented office in Muscat
mid-17th century Oman controlled much of east African coast
1694-98 Omanis attacked Portuguese in Bombay and east Africa
c.1675 Imam Bil'arub built fort at Jabrin
1708 Imam Sultan ibn Saif II built fort at al Hazm
1718-47 Omani civil war
1748 Ahmad ibn Said elected first Imam of Al bu Said dynasty. Persians involved in civil war expelled from Oman
1756-1804 Ottoman Sultan paid *kharaj* as friendly gesture to Imams through *Wali* of Basra
1760 Treaty between Imam and Mogul Emperor
Establishment of Mogul mission in Muscat in "Nawab's House"
1775 Death of Imam Said at Rostaq
1794 Sayyid Sultan obtained Hormuz, Qishm, Henjam, Bandar Abbas, Chahbar, and Gwadur; all of these except Gwadur reverted to Persia in mid-19th century
1798 *Qalnamneh* negotiated between British Government in Bombay and Sayyid Sultan by Murza Mahdi Ali Khan
1799 Napoleon addressed letter to Sayyid Sultan ibn Ahmad as Imam
1800 Captain (later General Sir John) Malcolm signed treaty between Oman and Britain
Wahhabis captured Buraimi and began series of incursions into Oman lasting until 1860s
1804-56 Reign of Sayyid Said ibn Sultan
1807 Treaty of Amity and Commerce between France and Oman (short-lived)
1809 Sayyid Said joined with British in attack on Ras al Khaima and British and Omani troops attacked Wahhabis established at Shinas
1819 Sayyid Said joined with British in further attack on Ras al Khaima against Qawasim pirates
1820 Eclipse of Qasimi power and treaties signed with Trucial States
1820-21 Omani/British expeditions against Bani bu Ali
1829 Sayyid Said took Mombasa from Omani Mazari and, making Zanzibar his second capital, concentrated on east African Empire
1833 Treaty of Amity and Commerce signed with US
1840 Mission of Ahmad ibn Na'man to US, sent by Sayyid Said
1856 Sultanates of Oman and Zanzibar divided – confirmed by Canning award of 1862
1856-66 Reign of Sayyid Thuwaini ibn Said in Oman
1862 British and French agreed mutually to respect independence of Oman and Zanzibar
1868-871 Reign of Imam Azzan ibn Qais
1869 Fort at al Hazm taken from Ya'ruba family by Azzan and Ibrahim ibn Qais
1871-88 Reign of Sayyid Turki ibn Said
1877 Commercial declaration between Holland and Muscat
1879 Dhofar re-occupied by Sayyid Turki's troops after 50-year interlude
1888-1913 Reign of Sayyid Faisal ibn Turki
1895 Muscat occupied by dissidents led by Shaikh Salih ibn Ali of Sharqiya Hirth

1901 Muscat telegraphic cable installed (earlier cable via Suez, Aden and Muscat to Karachi had failed in mid-19th century)
1913-32 Reign of Sayyid Taimur ibn Faisal
!913 Salim ibn Rashid al Kharusi elected Imam
1920 Agreement at Seeb between Sultan Taimur and tribes of the Interior
Muhammed ibn Abdulla al Khalili elected Imam
1932-70 Reign of Sayyid Said ibn Taimur
1952 Saudis occupied Buraimi
1954-59 Rebellion of Imam Ghalib ibn Ali
1955 Buraimi re-occupied by Omanis
1958 Gwadur ceded to Pakistan by purchase
1960 "Question of Oman" first debated at UN
1965-75 Rebellion in Dhofar
1967 Oil first produced in commercial quantities
1970 Accession of HM Sultan Qaboos ibn Said
1971 Oman admitted to United Nations and Arab League; end of the "Question of Oman" at UN
Diplomatic relations established with Britain, India and Pakistan, and later with US, Iran, Egypt, Saudi Arabia, France and other countries
1972 Death of Sayyid Said ibn Taimur
1973 Seeb International airport opened
1974 Oman Chamber of Commerce and Industry established
Port Qaboos opened
1975 End of rebellion in Dhofar
1976 Start of the first Five Year Plan
1979 Oman Mining Company began production; Public Authority for Water Resources established
1979 White Oryx Project launched in the Jiddat al Harasis
1980 Gulf Cooperation Council and State Consultative Council founded; start of second Five Year Plan
1981 Rima oilfields and Mina al Fahal terminal refinery opened
1984 Oman Technical and Industrial College opened
1985 Sixth Sumit Conference of GCC Heads of State, and 15th National Day celebrations; diplomatic relations opened with the Soviet Union
1986 Nimr oil fields opened for its first academic year; voyage of the Shabab Oman to New York
1987 Royal Hospital at al Ghubrah opened; Said bin Sultan Naval Base in Wudam opened
1989 Muscat Stock Exchange opened; biggest gas find for 22 years at Saih Nihayda; tenth summit conference of the GCC Heads of State held in Muscat
1990-1 First Gulf War, for the liberation of Kuwait
1991 Majlis Ash' Shura inaugurated
1994 Sultan Qaboos University graduates its first batch (48) of Omani doctors
1995 Sultan Qaboos's Jubilee celebrated
1996 Basic Statute promulgated; beginning of privatisation
2001 Sultan Qaboos Grand Mosque opened
2003 Second Gulf War in Iraq

Rulers of Oman

Reign begun (if known) AH	AD	*Imams*	*Capital (if known)*
135	751	Julanda ibn Mas'ud	–
–	–	Muhammad ibn Affam	Nizwa
185	801	Warith ibn Kaab	Nizwa
192	807	Ghassan ibn Abdulla	Nizwa
208	824	Abdul Malik ibn Hamad	–
226	840	al-Muhanna ibn Jaifar	Nizwa
237	851	as-Salt ibn Malik	–
273	886	Rashid ibn an-Nadhr	–
277	890	Azzan ibn Tamim	Nizwa
284	897	Muhammad ibn al-Hassan	–
285	898	Azzan ibn al-Hizr	–
286	899	Abdulla ibn Muhammad	–
287	900	as-Salt ibn al Qasim	–
287	900	Hassan ibn Said	–
292	904	al-Hawari ibn Matraf	–
300	912	Omar ibn Muhammad	–
–	–	Muhammad ibn Yazid	–
–	–	Mullah al Bahari	Nizwa
?328	939	Said ibn Abdulla	–
–	–	Rashid ibn Walid	Nizwa
400	1009	al-Khalil ibn Shadzan	–
?445	1053	Rashid ibn Said	–
445	1053	Hafs ibn Rashid	–
446	1054	Rashid ibn Ali	–
?549	1154	ibn Jabir Musa	Nizwa
		Maliks of the Nabhan Period	
809	1406	Malik ibn Ali	–
549	1154	al-Fallah ibn al Muhsin	Muqniyat
		Arar ibn Fallah	Muqniyat
		Mudhaffar ibn Sulaiman	–
809	1406	Makhzum ibn al Fallah	Bahla
		Imams	
839	1435	Abu 'l Hassan	–
855	1451	Omar ibn al Khattab	–
896	1490	Omar as-Sharif	–

Reign begun (if known) AH	AD	*Imams*	*Capital (if known)*
–	–	Ahmad ibn Muhammad	Bahla
906	1500	Muhammad ibn Ismail	Izki
936	1529	Barakat ibn Muhammad	Nizwa
967	1560	Abdulla ibn Muhammad	Bahla
		The Ya'ruba Dynasty	
1034	1624	Nasir ibn Murshid	Rostaq
1059	1649	Sultan ibn Saif [I]	Rostaq
1079	1688	Bil'arub ibn Sultan	Jabrin
?1123	1711	Saif ibn Sultan [I]	Rostaq
1123	1711	Sultan ibn Saif [II]	al Hazm
1131	1718	Saif ibn Sultan [II]	–
1131	1718	Muhanna ibn Sultan	Rostaq
1134	1721	Ya'rub ibn Bil'arub	Nizwa
1135	1722	Saif ibn Sultan [II] (restored)	Rostaq
1137	1724	Muhammad ibn Nasir	Jabrin
1140	1728	Saif ibn Sultan (II) (restored)	Rostaq
1151	1738	Sultan ibn Murshid	Rostaq
		The Al bu Said Dynasty Elected Imams	
1154	1741	Ahmad ibn Said	Rostaq
1188	1775	Said ibn Ahmad	Rostaq
		Sayyids and Sultans	
1193	1779	Hamad ibn Said (Regent)	Muscat
1206	1792	Sultan ibn Ahmad	Muscat
1219	1804	Said ibn Sultan	Muscat & Zanzibar
1273	1856	Thuwaini ibn Said	Muscat
1283	1866	Salim ibn Thuwaini	Muscat
1285	1868	Azzan ibn Qais	Muscat
1287	1870	Turki ibn Said	Muscat
1306	1888	Faisal ibn Turki	Muscat
1332	1913	Taimur ibn Faisal	Muscat
1351	1932	Said ibn Taimur	Muscat
1390	1970	Qaboos ibn Said	Muscat

Glossary

A	*aarif*	supervisor of *falaj* irrigation
	abaya	cloak worn by Arab women
	abra	ferry
	abu futila	matchlock gun
	arad	salt-bush
	ashgar	sodom-apple
	askar	guard
	Awqaf (*sing. Waqf*)	religious or administrative trusts, e.g. of falajes
B	*badan*	small boat traditionally made with sewn planks
	baghala	large ship with carved poop
	bani	tribal prefix meaning "the sons of "
	banjari	silver bracelet
	barasti	house of palm wood and frond construction
	Bawarij	Indian pirates of ninth century AD
	Bibi	noble lady
	bidar	villagers responsible for certain communal tasks
	birqa	mask worn by some Omani women
	bisht	cloak worn over dishdasha (q.v.)
C	*Caliph*	successor of the Prophet Muhammad and thus head of the Islamic world
D	*Daudi*	named after Sulaiman ibn Daud (Solomon, son of David)
	dhabi	gazelle
	dibba	lizard; tribe name
	dishdasha	white robe worn by men
	Diwan	the Sultan's Court administration office
	djinn	spirit
F	*falaj*	channelled water distribution system
	fard	kind of date
G	*ghanja*	small *baghala* (q.v.)
	ghayl	method of irrigation from a wadi source
	gizail	matchlock gun
H	*Hajj*	pilgrimage to Mecca and the other holy places
	halwa	sweetmeat of starch, sugar, ghee, almonds, etc
	harim	women's quarters in private house
	haris	man in village community in charge of weeding
	hib	long chisel used in cultivation of palm trees
	hijra	the migration of the Prophet to Medina in 622 AD
	hirz	charm necklance often of oblong shape
	huri	canoe made from hollowed out tree trunk
I	*Ibadhism*	the form of Islam widely followed in Oman, based on the doctrine of Abdulla ibn Ibadh
	Id	Muslim festival holiday
	'Idda	period during which a divorced woman or a widow may not contract a new marriage
	Imam	spiritual and secular leader of the people who at times held a position akin to kingship; also a leader in prayer
J	*jaalan*	water beetle; name of tribe
	jalbut	boat with upright stem and transom stern
	jebel	mountain
	jihad	holy war
K	*kafour*	kind of spiced powder used in burials
	khalas	type of date
	khanjar	curved dagger worn by Omani men
	kharaj	tax imposed on non-Muslims
	khashab	boat (general word)
	khuzi	meat on top of a pile of rice
	Kitman	in Ibadhi doctrine, a period when true beliefs have to be concealed for political reasons
	khol	eye shadow
L	*laban*	yoghurt
	lahaf	headscarf worn by some Omani women
	laisu	outer garment worn by some Omani women
	lakh	100,000 Indian rupees
	lunghi	loin cloth
M	*madhab*	school of thought or doctrine of a sect
	mahr	price paid to prospective bride by bridegroom
	majlis	room where men receive their visitors
	manjad	heavy silver chain worn in Dhofar
	manwa	warship (deriv. from man o' war (English))
	mashribiya	wooden window screen (c.f. Egyptian style)
	mibsali	type of date
	mihrab	niche in mosque, where an Imam stands to lead prayers, facing towards Mecca
	milha	marriage commitment
	minjal	toothed sickle
	muezzin	the summoner to prayer
	Mutawwa	fervent follower if Ibadhism
N	*najdi*	of the Najd; incense of the best quality
	neel	the indigo plant
P	*pice*	Indian coin
	purdah	seclusion in which Muslim women are kept
Q	*qa'ada*	primary shares in *falaj* ownership
	Qadhi	judge of Islamic law
	qaftan	outer garment
	qahwa	coffee
	qanat	underground water channel as in Iran
	qaulnameh	form of treaty
	qashani	tile decoration
	qirsh	Maria Theresa dollar
	qu'ad	"quietists", according to Ibadhi school
R	*rababa*	stringed musical instrument
	ras	cape, head
	rheem	gazelle
	riha	kind of spice used for burials
	ru'iya	sighting of the new moon
S	*sadaqa* (*pl. sadaqat*)	tax; voluntary alms used for religious purposes
	Sahaba	the Prophet Muhammad's companions
	sambuk	boat used for pearling
	sha'abi	lowest quality frankincense
	shaduf	mecahnism for raising water by means of bucket
	shahuf	"pram" boat
	shaihamudh	tea-like drink made from limes
	shaikh	tribal leader
	shasha	boat made from palm-fronds
	shatha	shawl made from two pieces of cloth
	shazri	middle quality frankincense
	shher	moutain (in Jibali)
	Shia	major division of Islam, whose adherents believe that only the first four Caliphs were legitimate and that the Caliphate succession should have gone to the sons of Ali ibn Abu Talib, the Prophet's cousin and son-in-law
	shu'iy	small fishing boat
	sils	silver decoration worn with headscarf
	Sunni	orthodox Muslim
	suq	market place
	surra	small tree
T	*Tabi'*	person in contact with the Prophet's companions
	tahr	mountain goat, *Hemitragus Jayakari*
	Tuman	currency formerly used in Oman and Iran
U	*Ulema*	body of learned men in Islam
	umma	the Muslim state
W	*wa*'al	mountain goat (used for both *tahr* and ibex)
	wadi	dry river valley
	Wahhabism	the form of Islam taught to Muhammad ibn Abdel Wahhab of Saudi Arabia
	Wali	local governor of an area
	wazara	Omani name for the *lunghi* (q.v.)
	Wazir	minister
	wilaya (*pl. wilayat*)	governorate
Z	*zalij*	faience, ornamental tile
	zar	evil spirit
	Zuhur	state of living openly as Muslims

Bibliography

Abdul Amir, Amin *British Interests in the Persian Gulf* E.J. Brill, Leiden, 1967
Abdul Nayem, Dr. Muhammed *The Sultanate of Oman (c. 1,000,000 BC to 100 BC)* Hyderabad Publishers 1996
Aitchison, Charles *A Collection of Treaties… Relating to India and Neighbouring Countries* Calcutta, 1932
Akehurst, General John *We Won a War: Campaign in Oman 1965-75* Michael Russell, 1982
Albuquerque, Alfonso de *Commentaries* Hakluyt Society, 1964, reprinted 1970
Allama, Syed Sulaiman Nadvi *The Arab Navigation* Lahore, 1966
Allfree, Philip S. *Warlords of Oman* Hale, 1967
Al-Maamiry, Ajmed Hamoud *Whither Oman?* Lancers Publishers, New Delhi, 1981
Al-Rashid, Z.M. *Sau'di Relations with Eastern Arabia and Oman (1810-1870)* Luzac &Co. Ltd., 1981
Al-Rawas, Isam *Oman in Early Islamic History* Ithaca Press, 2000
Al-Yusef, Mohamed bin Musa *Oil and the Transformation of Oman 1970-95* Stacey International, 1995
Al-Zubair, Mohammad *This is Oman, 1985* Stacey International, 1985
Annals of Oman, Sirhan ibn Sa'id ibn Sirhan (1723) translated and brought up to 1883, with a 'Note on the Tribes of Oman' by S.B. Miles and 'The Ibadhiyah of Oman' by E.C. Ross Oleander Press, 1985
Baldwin, Robert and Salm, Rodney *Whales and Dolphins along the Coast of Oman* Muscat, 1994
Barth, Fredrik *Sohar – Culture and Society in an Omani Town* Johns Hopkins University Press, 1983
Belgrave, Sir Charles *The Pirate Coast* Bell, 1966
Bell, Gertrude *The Arab War* London, 1940
Bell, Sir Gawain *An Imperial Twilight* Lester Crook Academic, 1989
Bent, Theodore *Southern Arabia* Smith Eldon, 1900
Bertram, G.C.L. *The Fisheries of Muscat and Oman* H.M.S.O. for the Sultanate of Oman, 1948
Bibby, Geoffrey *Looking for Dilmun* Stacey International, 1996
Bidwell, Robin *Arabian Gulf Intelligence – Being Selections from the Records of the Bombay Government, 1856* Oleander Press, 1985
Birdlife Conservation Series No. 2 *Important Bird Areas in the Middle East* Birdlife International 1994, Cambridge
Bosch, Donald *The Seashells of Oman* Longman, 1982
Boustead, Hugh *The Wind of Morning* Chatto & Windus, 1971
Buckingham, James *Silk Travels in Assyria, Media and Persia* Henry Colburn, 1829
Burckhardt, J.L. *Notes on the Bedouins and Wahabys* London, 1830
Burrows, Sir Bernard *Footsteps in the Sand* Michael Russell, 1990
Busch, Briton Cooper *Britain and the Persian Gulf 1894-1914* University of California Press, 1967
Capper, James *Observations on the Passage to India* London, 1785
Carter, J.R.L. *Tribes in Oman* Peninsular Publishing, 1982
Clements, F.A. *Oman: The Reborn Land* Longman, 1980
Corderio, Luciano 'Maskat' in *Geographical Journal*, Vol XI, No. 2, February 1898
Coriat, Percy *Soldier in Oman* printed privately by Amalgamated Authors
Costa, Paolo M. *Musandam* Immel Publishing, 1991
Coupland, Reginald *East Africa and its Invaders* Oxford, 1938
Cox, Sir Percy 'Some Excursions in Oman' in *Geographical Journal*, Vol LXIII, No. 3, September 1925
Darlow, Michael and Fawkes, Richard *The Last Corner of Arabia* Quartet, 1976
Dickson, H.R.P. *Kuwait and her Neighbours* Allen & Unwin, 1956
Disputes between the Rulers of Muscat & Zanzibar Proceedings of Government Commission, Education Society Press, Bycula, 1861
Eccles, G.J. 'The Sultanate of Muscat and Oman' in *Journal of the Central Asian Society,* Vol. XIV, 1927
Eickelman, C. *Women and Community in Oman* New York University Press, 1984
Eilts, Hermann F. *Ahmad bin Na'aman's Mission to the US in 1840: The Voyage of Al-Sultanah to New York City* Petroleum Development (Oman) Ltd. Originally published by Essex Institute, Salem, Mass., 1962
Fenelon, K.G. *The United Arab Emirates* Longman, 1973 (first published as *The Trucial States: A Statistical Survey* Khayats, 1967)
Fiennes, Sir Ranulph *Where Soldiers Fear to Tread* Hodder & Stoughton, 1975
Fiennes, Sir Ranulph *Atlantis of the Sands* Bloomsbury, 1992
Firouz, Kajare *Le Sultanat d'Oman* Paris, 1914
Fouda, Moustafa M. and Hermosa, Gregorio V. *A Checklist of Oman Fish* Sultan Qaboos University, 1993
Fraser, James B. *Journey into Khorasan* London, 1825
Freeman-Grenville, G.F.P. *The Muslim and Christian Calendars* Oxford University Press, 1963
Gallagher, Michael and Woodcock, Martin W. *The Birds of Oman* Quartet Books, 1980
De Gaury, Gerald 'A Note on Masirah Island' in *Geographical Journal*, Vol. CXXIII, No. 4, December 1957
Geary, Grattan *Through Asiatic Turkey* London, 1878
Gerachty, Tony *Who Dares Wins* Arms and Armour 1980
Germain, Adrien 'Quelques Mots sur l'Oman et le Sultan de Maskate' in *Bulletin de la Ste. Géographique*, October 1968
Goldsmid, Sir Frederic John *Telegraph and Travel* Macmillan, 1874
Gratz, Liesl *The Omanis Sentinels of the Gulf* Longman, 1982
Graham, G.S. *Great Britain and the Indian Ocean* Oxford, 1967
Graves, Philip *The Life of Sir Percy Cox* Hutchinson, 1941
The Gulf: Implications of British Withdrawal Washington DC Center for Strategic and International Studies, 1969
Green, Frances and Keech, Richard *The Coral Seas of Oman* MEED, 1986
Groom Nigel St. John *Frankincense and Myrrh,* London, 1981
Gwynne-James, David *Letters from Oman,* Blackwater Books, 2001
Hamilton, Alexander *A New Account of the East Indies (1688-1723)* Edinburgh, 1727 and Argonaut Press, 1930
Handbook of Arabia Intelligence Division, War Staff Admiralty, London, 2 vols, 1916-17
Hawley, Sir Donald *Courtesies in Arabia, Oman and the Gulf* Stacey International, 1998
- *Desert Wind and Tropic Storm* Michael Russell 2000
- *The Trucial States* Allen & Unwin, 1970
Hawley, Ruth *Silver, the Traditional Art of Oman* Stacey International 2000
- *The British Embassy in Muscat, A Short History 1974*
Hay, Sir Rupert *The Persian Gulf States* Washington Middle East Institute, 1959
Henderson, Edward *This Strange Eventful History* Quartet, 1988
Herbert, Thomas *Some Yeares Travels in Divers Part of Asia and Afrique* London, 1638
Huges Clarke, Michael *Oman's Geological Heritage* Petroleum Development Oman with Stacey International, 1991
Heude, William *A Voyage up the Persian Gulf* London, 1819
Historical and Other Information Connected with the Province of Oman, Muskat, Bahrein and Other Places in the Persian Gulf. No XXIV of *Selections from the Records of the Bombay Government* Bombay, 1856
Hitti, Philip *History of the Arabs* Macmillan, 1970
Hogarth, D.G. *The Penetration of Arabia* Alson Rivers, 1905
Holden, David *Farewell to Arabia* Faber, 1966
Hopwood, Derek (ed.) *The Arabian Peninsula* Allen & Unwin, 1972
Hourani, George *Arab Seafaring* Khayats, 1963
Hulton, Jessop *The Journal* Preston, 1844
Husain M. Al Barharna *The Legal Status of the Arabian Gulf States* Manchester, 1968
Ibn Battuta *Travels* Hakluyt Society, Vol 2, 1962
Jayakar, A.S.G. 'The Shahee Dialect of Arabic' in *Journal of the Bombay Branch of the Royal Asiatic Society,* No. LVIII, Vol. XX
- *Omani Proverbs* Oleander Press, 1986
- 'The Omani Dialect of Arabic' in *Journal of the Royal Asiatic Society of Great Britain and Ireland,* Vol XXI (new series) Part II, July 1889 and Part

IV, October 1889
Jeapes, A.S. *SAS: Operation Oman* William Kimber, 1980
Journal of Oman Studies Vols 1-11, 1975-2001
Journal of Oman Studies Special Report No. 1: The Scientific Results of the Oman Flora and Fauna Survey 1975 Ministry of Information and Culture, 1977
Journal of Oman Studies Special Report No. 2: The Scientific Results of the Oman Flora and Fauna Survey 1977 (Dhofar) Diwan of H.M. for Protocol, Sultanate of Oman
Journal of Oman Studies Special Report No. 3: The Scientific Results of the Royal Geographical Society's Oman Wahiba Sands Project 1985-1987 Office of the Adviser for Conservation of the Environment
Kelly, J.B. *Sultanate and Imamate in Oman* Chatham House Memorandum, December 1959
- *Britain and the Persian Gulf 1795-1880* Clarendon Press, 1968
- *Eastern Arabian Frontiers* Faber, 1964
Keppel, George *Personal Narrative of a Journey from India to England* London, 1827
Kumar, Ravinder *India and the Persian Gulf Region* Asia Publishing House, 1965
Landen, Robert G. *Oman Since 1856* Princeton University Press, 1967
Larsen, Torben and Kiki *Butterflies of Oman* Bartholomew, 1980
Lees, G.M. 'The Geology and Tectonics of Oman and Parts of South Eastern Arabia' in *Geographical Journal*, Vol. LXXXIV, No. 4, 1982
Lorimer *Gazeteer*, 4 vols 1908-1915
Low, Charles Rathbone *History of the Indian Navy (1616-1863)* London, 1877
Luce, Margaret *From Aden to the Gulf* Michael Russell 1987
Mandaville, James P. *Wildflowers of Northern Oman* Illustrations by Dorothy Bovey Bartholomew, 1978
Mansur Shaik *History of Seyd Said, Sultan of Muscat* London, 1819
Marlowe, John *The Persian Gulf in the Twentieth Century* Cresset Press, 1962
Maurizi, V. *History of Seyd Said, 1819* Oleander Press, 1984
McLeod Innes, N. *Minister in Oman* Oleander Press, 1987
Memorials of the UK and Saudi Arabia submitted to the Arbitration Tribunal in Geneva on the Buraimi Dispute 1955
Miles, S.B. 'On the Road between Sohar and El-Bereymi' in *Journal of the Asiatic Society of Bengal,* Vol, XLVI, Part 1, 1877
- *The Countries & Tribes of the Persian Gulf* Second edition, Cass, 1966
Miller, Anthony G. and Morris, Miranda *Plants of Dhofar; Traditional, Economic and Medicinal Uses* Office of the Adviser for Conservation of the Environment, Muscat, 1988
Monroe, Elizabeth *Britain's Moment in the Middle East 1914-1956* Chatto & Windus, 1963
Morris, James *Sultan in Oman* Faber, 1957
Morris, Miranda and Shelton, Pauline *Oman Adorned* Apex Publishing 1997
Moyse-Bartlett, M. *The Pirates of Trucial Oman* Macdonald, 1966
Nicholls, C.S. *The Swahili Coast: Politics, Diplomacy and Trade on the East African Littoral 1798-1856* Allen & Unwin, 1971
Niebuhr, Carsten *Description of Arabia 1774* Various editions
Omar, Umberto *Il Sultanato di Oman* Rome, 1912
Osborne, Christine *The Gulf States and Oman* Croom Helm, 1977
O'Shea, Raymond *The Sand Kings of Oman; Being the Experiences of an RAF Officer in the Little-Known Regions of Trucial Oman, Arabia* Methuen, 1947
Ovington, John *Voyages* Paris, 1725
Owen, R. *Away to Eden* Collins, 1959
- *The Golden Bubble* Collins, 1957
Owen, W.F.W. *Narrative of Voyages to Explore the Shores of Africa, Arabia and Madagascar* London, 1833
Palgrave, William Giffard *Narrative of a Year's Journey Through Central and Eastern Arabia 1862-63* 2 vols. Macmillan, 1868
Peck, M.C. *The United Arab Emirates* Croom Helm 1986
Peterson, John E. *Oman in the Twentieth Century: Political Foundations of an Emerging State* Croom Helm, 1978
Petroleum Development Oman Ltd. *A Short History of Oman from the Earliest Times* Muscat, 1972
Peyton, W.E. *Old Oman* Stacey International 1983
Philby, H.St.J. B. *Arabia of the Wahhabis* London, 1928
Phillips, Wendell *Unknown Oman* Longman, 1966
- *Oman: A History* Longman, 1967
Pilgrim, G.T. 'The Geology of the Persian Gulf and the Adjoining Portions of Persia and Arabia' in *Geological Survey of India,* 1908
Polo, Marco *Travels* Various editions
Potts, D.T. *Ancient Magan* Trident Press 2000
Rice, Michael *The Archaeology of the Arabian Gulf* Routledge, 1994
Risso, P. *Oman and Muscat: An Early Modern History* Croom Helm, 1986
Roberts, Edmund *Embassy to the Eastern Ports of Cochin, China, Siam and Muscat in the US Sloop of War 'Peacock'* New York, 1837
Ross, E.C. *Annals of Oman* Baptist Mission Press, Calcutta, 1874
Ruete, Emily *Memoirs of an Arabian Princess* New York 1907
Ruschenberger, W.S. *Narrative of a Voyage... including An Embassy to the Sultan of Muscat and the King of Siam* London, 1838
Said Ruete, Rudolph *Said bin Sultan* Alexander Ouseley, 1929
St. Albans, Suzanne, Duchess of *Where Time Stood Still: A Portrait of Oman* Quartet, 1980
Salil ibn Razik *History of the Imams and Sayyids of Oman from AD 661-1856* (trans. and ed. by G.P. Badger) Hakluyt Society, 1871
Salm, R., Jensen, R.A.C., and Papastravrou, V.A., *Marine Fauna of Oman: Cetaceans, Turtles, Seabirds and Shallow Water Corals* World Conservation Union 1993
Saunders, D. *The Journal of the Sufferings ...* Salem, Mass., 1794
Searle, Pauline *Dawn Over Oman* Allen & Unwin, 1979
Severin, Tim *Sinbad Voyage* Hutchinson, 1982
Shepherd, Anthony *Arabian Adventure* Collins, 1961
Skeet, Ian *Muscat and Oman* Faber, 1974
- *Oman: Politics and Development* Macmillan, 1992
Skinner, Ray *Christians in Oman* The Tower Press 2000
Smiley, David *Arabian Assignment* Leo Cooper, 1975
Somerville, Vice-Admiral Boyle *The Chart-Makers* Blackwood, 1928
Stiffe, Arthur W. 'Ancient Trading Centres of the Persian Gulf' in *Geographical Journal,* Vol X, No. 6, December 1897
Thesiger, Wilfred *Arabian Sands* Longman, 1959, reprinted by Penguin, 1964
Thomas, Bertram 'Among some Unknown Tribes of South Arabia' in *Journal of the Royal Anthropological Institute,* Vol. LIX, 1929
- 'Arab Rule under the Al Bu Said Dynasty of Oman 1741-1937' Raleigh Lecture on History, *British Academy,* Vol. XXIV, 1938
- *Arabia Felix,* Cape, 1932
- 'A Journey into Rub' Al Khali' in *Geographical Journal,* Vol. LXXVII, No. 1, January 1931
Tibbetts, G.R. *Arab Navigation in the Indian Ocean Before the Coming of the Portuguese* Luzac, 1971
Townsend, John *Oman: The Making of a Modern State* Croom Helm, 1977
UN Economic Commission for Western Asia *Food Security in Gulf States: Oman* Beirut, 1979
Villiers, Alan *Sons of Sindbad* Hodder & Stoughton, 1940
Ward, Philip *Travels in Oman, a Compendium of Exploration and Travel in the Sultanate of Oman* Oleander Press, 1986
Weisgerber, G. *Mehrals Kupper in Oman* Der Anschnitt, 1981
Wellsted, J.R. *Travels in Arabia* 2 vols. John Murray, 1838
- *Travels to the City of the Caliphs, along the Shores of the Persian Gulf and the Mediterranean* 2 vols. London, 1840
Wheatley, Paul *The Golden Khersonese* University of Malaya Press, 1961
Whelan, John (ed.) *Oman – A MEED Practical Guide,* 1981
Whitelock, H.H. *An Account of Arabs who Inhabited the Coast Between Ras Al Khaimah and Abu Thabee in the Gulf of Persia* Tr. Bombay Geographical Society, 1835
Wikan, Unni *Behind the Veil in Arabia* Johns Hopkins University Press, 1982
Wilkinson, J.C. *The Organisation of the Falaj Irrigation System in Oman* University of Oxford School of Geography, 1974
- 'A Sketch of the Historical Geography of the Trucial Oman down to the Beginning of the Sixteenth Century' in *Geographical Journal,* Vol. CXXX, No. 3, September 1964
- *Water and Tribal Settlements in Southeast Arabia: A Study of the Aflaj of Oman* Clarendon Press, 1977
- *The Imamate Tradition of Oman* Cambridge University Press, 1987
Williamson, Andrew *Sohar and Omani Seafaring in the Indian Ocean* Muscat, 1973
Wilson, Sir Arnold T. *The Persian Gulf* Clarendon Press, 1928
Wingate, Reginald *Not in the Limelight* Hutchinson, 1959
Zwemer, Rev. S.M. 'Three Journeys in Northern Oman' in *Geographical Journal,* Vol XIX, 1902
- *Arabia, the Cradle of Islam* London and

Index

Note: Where proper names are preceded by the article *al,* they are listed under the name itself. The same procedure is adopted in respect of *ibn*, *de* and *d'*. The choice of the forms *ibn* or *bin* in this work has been governed by familiarity of usage. Numbers in italics refer to pages on which relevant illustrations fall, sometimes together with textual references.